The Baffled Christian's Handbook

by
Jon Christian Ryter

1st Edition

Published by R. James Bender Publishing,
P.O. Box 23456, San Jose, California 95153

Printed in the United States of America

ISBN No. 0-912138-65-3

A special acknowledgement from the author to Gregory Douglas and Kevin Anderson for their expert diligence in proofing this book, and for the editorial contributions each made to the text of *The Baffled Christian's Handbook.*

TABLE OF CONTENTS

VI. The Church Age

VII. The Endtime

VIII. The Millennium

This work is dedicated
to Anne and Anjie, who surrendered
much of the time that rightly belonged to them
during the writing of *The Baffled Christians Handbook;*
and to VeAnne, who, before her marriage
shared those moments when her father was either
behind a typewriter or on a computer, compiling
the data which is presented here for your edification.

INTRODUCTION

As an avid reader who loves to browse through bookstores, I occasion ally find a book whose title catches my eye, and moves me to pick it up and explore the brief synopsis inside the dust jacket. If I am intrigued by the highlights detailed inside the cover, I will casually flip through a few pages on my way to the flap tucked between the final page and the back cover of the book—to "check out" the credentials of the author. I am a very critical reader, you see, because I know how easy the mind can be influenced with bad doctrine or faulty research. If I am not impressed with the author's scholastic or theological credentials or career achievements, I carefully place the book back on the shelf and continue browsing.

It was not until the Holy Spirit revealed to me it is the substance of the material within the covers, and not an impressive resume on the back flap, that determines the worthiness of any book. The Holy Spirit found it necessary to remind me, again, that God had already ordained the works He "would work through me" the night I fell on my face and accepted Jesus Christ as my Lord and Savior. It was then that I decided to sit down and complete this work—an effort actually started in 1985. I have been reminded that of all the "authors" of the Bible, only one was a scholar—Luke, the physician. Granted, one, David, was a king; and one, Moses, was the adopted grandson of an Egyptian pharaoh. Most were an odd assortment of uneducated fishermen, craftsmen, tentmakers, tax collectors and laborers—all called upon by the Holy Spirit to record God's words, His wisdom, and in many cases, His warnings to His people, the nation of Israel; and later, to His adopted children in the Gentile nations of the world.

I have likewise been reminded by the Holy Spirit of the manner in which I came to the Lord some seventeen years ago, and of the miracles which permeated my salvation experience. Because the spiritual phenomenon I experienced is directly linked to my credentials as a Christian writer and an eschatalogical expositor of the Word of God, it is important to relate those occurrences so you may judge the validity of my credentials—and the accuracy of these expositions—for yourself. I also feel it is necessary to state, most emphatically, I am not an end-time prophet of God. I have not been provided with any special vision or apocalyptic foreknowledge; nor have I been divinely inspired or ordained to lead the masses to Jesus Christ. I am, to the best of my knowledge, one small candle in a vast cathedral of light. It may very well be that my singular purpose is to provide a single ray of understanding to only one person—perhaps you.

Like many, I am a Christian who has found the Christian walk is not a blissful stroll. It has been a walk fraught with countless heart-wrenching pitfalls: hardship, death and personal misfortune. And, considering the adversarial nature of the spiritual contest which is unfolding on the global stage as the world prepares for the final conflict between Christ and Satan, as well as the potential toll in human souls, it is not in the least surprising that the Christian is under attack—not only from demonic forces engaged in that spiritual warfare for those souls, but from humanistic forces who envision the creation of a secular, Godless utopia here on Earth as well.

We have recently embarked on a new course in America. It is called the path of political correctness—a suave public relations phrase used by proponents of humanistic endeavors and secular rights to desensitize immorality and perversion. To be truly politically correct is to ignore, in most instances, that which God both abhors and condemns. For the past thirty years the moral fiber of our society has been unraveling. Unfortunately, because each thread of that fiber was so thin, many Americans either failed to notice, or felt each singular concession to apostasy was so insignificant that fighting was not worth the benefits which would be derived from the effort.

One woman, Madeline Murray O'Hare, decided her rights as an atheist superseded the combined rights of a Christian nation, and filed what became a landmark case, *Murray vs. Baltimore Board of Education*, in which the United States Supreme Court rewrote the First Amendment of the Constitution in 1965 by creating a "separation of church and state" clause which did not, nor does exist within that document. However, the apathy of America in 1965 allowed the creation of a legal precedent upon which all First Amendment Church & State cases are now argued—with the free practice of religion being consistently struck down. Today, contrary to historic reality, political correctness suggests our founding fathers were all atheists or agnostics who were determined to create a nation in which religious rights were narrowly construed to prevent free expression of worship.

Since January 22, 1973, when the United States Supreme Court issued its ruling in *Roe v. Wade/Doe v. Bolton,* we have been part of a world community which sanctions the murder of our unborn children because the feminist believes the human life within her body is an extrinsic extension of her body, and that she has a Constitutionally protected right to determine whether or not that life is allowed to live outside the womb. It is now politically correct to have an abortion. It is a stain on the very fabric of society to fight the abortionist. It is, in fact, now a violation of federal law to even peacefully interfere with the commerce of baby killing. It is politically correct to use the term *pro-choice*; but, it is an enigma to use the term *pro-abortion,* because the term implies an option to elect murder.

Yet, it is not politically correct to refer to those opposing abortion as *pro-life.* They are usually referred to by the liberal press as either *anti-abortion rights extremists* or *anti-choice.* Anti-choice is a preferred term because the phrase suggests those being described want to usurp a woman's Constitutionally protected right of choice by arbitrarily forcing womanhood to blindly accept their ultra-right wing philosophical view of right and wrong—the fact that the liberal view currently expounds attempts to do precisely the same thing, notwithstanding.

The identification of the HIV virus, and its related epidemic has drawn the homosexual from the closet as homosexual and lesbian activist alliances were forged to press for Congressional action and funding to find a cure for AIDS—and to secure a Congressional stamp of approval on their lifestyle. A major public relations effort was launched over a decade ago to alter America's perception of this deviant Sodom and Gomorrah lifestyle; an effort, which has been largely successful thanks to *political correctness.* Although most Americans abhor homosexuality and lesbianism as much as they ever did, it is no longer politically correct to view this form of apostasy as perversion—it is now a government sanctioned, acceptable alternate lifestyle. Gay Rights groups now have their own political lobbyists, and spend millions of dollars to influence both state and federal legislation favorable to the proliferation of their perverted lifestyle.

Forty years of liberalism in Congress has furthered their objectives beyond the wildest dreams and expectations of the homosexual/lesbian communities. On November 6, 1995, the voters in the state of Maine were asked to cast their ballots for or against a referendum which would have prevented state lawmakers from enacting legislation which granted special rights to the homosexual/lesbian community, or treating those who practiced homosexuality as a recognized minority entitled to inclusive protection under existing federal anti-discrimination laws, in particular, the Civil Rights Act of 1964. The two state-level grassroots organizations promoting the referendum were labeled as homophobic—even by the politically correct governor of the state, who contributed $1,000 of his own money to the Gay Rights activists who spent over one million dollars to defeat the referendum—which lost by a very narrow margin.

Public opinion polls show the professing Christian is still a *majority* in America. Unfortunately, we are far too often a *silent* majority, bowing to each whim and will of political correctness. If you recall, when Christ stood before Pontius Pilate, the governor of Judea found Him to be innocent of all of the charges brought by the chief priests, Annas and Caiphias, and the Sanhedrin—who both feared and envied the Messiah. Because tradition dictated that one condemned prisoner be pardoned at Passover, Pilate asked the crowd which man should be released—Christ, or the Zealot insurrectionist and murderer, Barabbas. The Zealots within the crowd, instigated by the Sanhedrin, screamed for the release of Barabbas. Because their voices were the loudest, Barabbas was released. Those among the crowd who knew Christ to be at the very least a righteous Rabbi, were silent.

Although prophetically predestined, Christ was crucified in part because the silent majority of His day remained silent. Since His crucifixion was preordained, we know He would have been crucified even if that silent majority had demanded His pardon. However, that multitude, who less than five days earlier met Christ's entourage on the road to Jerusalem shouting Hosanna to the Son of David, did not know His crucifixion was imminent. It was not politically correct, even in those days, to resist the will of the Sanhedrin.

How much difference is there between that multitude and the Christian today? We are outspoken within our own congregations; and equally vocal in our assemblies with others of like faith or conviction. But, we are strangely silent in confrontational situations which pit us against a liberal establishment that appears determined to create a humanistic utopia devoid of family or family values.

My purpose in this struggle is not that of conservative activist. It is your voice that needs to be heard. My role, as clearly as it has been defined, is that of a teacher. My job is to help the Christian better understand the Scriptures, and either particular verses, events or prophecies which baffle them. To that end, I dedicate this effort.

My salvation experience occurred exactly fifteen years after a bizarre, freak accident took the life of my eldest sister. Frances was killed shortly after leaving St. Mary's Catholic Church in Sault Ste. Marie, Michigan on Easter Sunday, 1963. As we later learned, the fire engine which struck the car in which she was riding was responding to a false alarm which was called in, we later learned, from somewhere down the street from my parent's modest two-story home in that small upper peninsula community. Frances, a devout Catholic, was twenty-six years old when she passed from this life, leaving behind three small children who could not understand why their mother would no longer be there to prepare their meals and tuck them in their beds at night.

I couldn't understand it, either.

Being a more or less lukewarm Catholic at best, I did not attend mass that day. Easter, like Christmas, was in my mind one of the two days of the year when all of the hypocrites, backsliders and lukewarm Catholics would fill the pews of the church, all decked out in their spring finery. Since such a contemplation was more than I could bear, I declined Frances' cordial invitation to join her, and slept in that morning. I was drinking my morning coffee shortly before noon when the telephone rang. It was my brother, informing me that Frances had been in a car accident.

I hurried to the hospital, and was allowed to speak with Frances for only a few minutes before a nurse chased my two brothers and me from her room, advising us we could return that afternoon during regular visiting hours. Frances' injuries were not thought by the attending physician to be serious, and as I remember, she was not hooked up to any of the life support paraphernalia one might expect to see on a patient who had just been involved in a serious auto accident—one in which she was thrown from the car on impact, her body striking, first, a telephone pole, and then a pedestrian walking down the street. I found the fact that the hospital did not feel it was necessary to electronically monitor her vital signs comforting. Because of that fact, our conversation with Frances was cautiously optimistic, with no thoughts given to saying good-bye. As it turned out, I never got the chance to speak those words within her hearing. By the time I returned home some fifteen minutes later I learned Frances had passed on less than five minutes after my brothers and I left her bedside. According to the autopsy which was performed the following day, she died from an undetected ruptured spleen.

On the way to the hospital that afternoon, I had prayed fervently to God for His protection of my sister. Death was not a stranger in our family. I lost my mother from diabetes when I was four years old, watching, but not understanding, her death. A year before, I lost my paternal grandfather and, only a few months earlier, my paternal grandmother.

In Christianity, Easter is the season of life. While we are acutely conscious of the crucifixion of Jesus Christ at this time of the year, it is His resurrection we celebrate. While His death atoned for our sins, it was His resurrection which assures the Christian of eternal life. It was a fact not lost on me that day as I wondered why my God had forsaken me.

My faith in those days was a shallow, undiscerning faith. God was an omnipresence whose name I had known from childhood; but, I did not know Him—and was, in fact, not even aware that it was possible for man to enjoy a personal relationship with Him. God was the stern taskmaster who watched over the affairs of man from on high and who only selectively became involved in the lives of His creation. Because I was not grounded in the Word, my faith was easily shattered. On Easter Sunday, 1963, my faith in the God I did not know, and suddenly doubted, died. It would not be resurrected for fifteen years.

During that fifteen year period, I, like Saul of Tarsus, persecuted the believer whenever the opportunity presented itself. While I did not literally stone the Christians I encountered, I used what I viewed as inconsistencies in the Bible to create doubt in their minds as to the validity of the Word of God. I had a few pet questions I threw at the believer who attempted to witness to me; questions which invariably stonewalled them.

Questions like: *"If Adam and Eve only had three sons (Abel, Cain and Seth), and they were the first humans on earth, who did Cain marry when he was exiled to the land of Nod?"* Or, *"If Christ was in the grave for three days and three nights, how did He rise on the third day?"* Or, *"If there is a Hell, where is it?"* Or, *"If the world was really created in six literal 24-hour days; and , since Bible exegetes claim the creation occurred 6,000 years ago, how do you explain all of the fossils which scientists claim are millions of years old?"*

The *coup de grâce* came one evening when my wife, Anne, and I were enjoying an evening out at a local bowling alley. On the lane next to us was a Catholic priest. We initiated a conversation with him—a dialogue which ultimately drifted to the subject of the "Good Book" and whether or not the Bible contained the irrefutable word of God or if it, like Greek mythology, was merely a hodgepodge of fables created in the minds of ignorant men to explain their existence. Again, my standard questions were offered to establish the fact that obvious inconsistencies existed in the Bible. The priest finally conceded that, as far as the Old Testament was concerned, it was his personal belief that it did, indeed, contain fables—adding quickly that fact did not otherwise detract from the validity of the New Testament.

However, his defense of the New Testament was too little, too late. My wife was suddenly added to my list of conquests to agnosticism—although in her case I suspect it was more a case of doubt than disbelief.

Our life during the next decade was probably as full as any Godless life could be. I was relatively successful in business. We lived in a nice home in a nice neighborhood. And, we possessed most of the human comforts man designed for use in an ever-increasing secular world. What more could a man want?

I loved my job. I was earning enough money that Anne did not have to work outside of the home. In my mind we were the perfect suburban family. Had I bothered to ask her, Anne would have undoubtedly disagreed with my assessment of our lives. At the time, we had one daughter, VeAnne, who was ten years of age. She was beginning to discover interests of her own which did not include her mother. And, needless to say, I was far too busy to involve Anne in my interests as well.

Whenever she managed to get my attention, which was, regrettably, not often, Anne expressed her desire to have another child. My stock answer was that I did not want to bring another life into a very troubled world that was, in my opinion, hellbent on self destruction. I, like many Americans at the time, was convinced by the end of the century, the United States would be involved in a thermonuclear war with the Soviet Union, and that mankind as we know it would very likely be destroyed.

Had I been more attentive, I would have noticed subtle changes in Anne's personality which indicated she was suffering from deep depression. I was too involved in my quest for success, and chose not to notice these changes. Nor did I pay attention to the fact that Anne could no longer sleep, and would sit up throughout most of the night watching television. Selfishly, her nocturnal habits only meant I could stretch out more in our bed. I had no idea that, while VeAnne and I slept, she contemplated suicide each night.

In February, 1978, something happened that changed our lives forever.

While channel surfing one evening, Anne chanced upon a Christian network, and because the topic being discussed was depression, she began to listen to the program. Before the night was over, she accepted Christ as her Savior, and turned her life over to Him. The program she was watching was the *PTL Club.* The hosts of the program were none other than Jim and Tammy Bakker. There is no doubt in my mind today that Jim and Tammy Bakker saved Anne's life—and contributed to my salvation, my daughter's salvation, and the salvation of Anne's mother as well.

While America—largely through the persecution of the Bakkers by the liberal *Charlotte (NC) Observer*—had been extremely critical of the Bakker's ministry, Jim and Tammy still held a special place in our hearts. I do not, however, intend to use even one page of this book as a bully pulpit to defend the Bakkers because the misappropriation of millions upon millions of dollars of ministry funds is indefensible, and would require far more pages than this book will contain to defend.

Bakker's crimes, with respect to the misappropriation or misapplication of ministry funds, while perpetuated against his fellow man, was actually committed against God. For that reason, Bakker is ultimately answerable to Him. There is no doubt that Bakker grossly oversold his timeshares at *Heritage USA;* or, that he was not a good steward of God's money—or, even that he committed adultery, or engaged in perverse sexual activities. Bakker openly confessed to those things. As contributors to that ministry as well as visitors to *Heritage USA,* my wife and I have long since forgiven them and feel, once asked of the Lord, God forgave them as well. God brought a corrupt ministry down, and in accordance with Scripture with respect to the last days, He will complete a thorough housecleaning of the church as we reach the end of this age.

The changes which occurred in Anne were as dramatic as they were immediate. The following day she found an Assemblies of God church and with VeAnne, began attending. Prior to that night, Anne—being an Italian—was very easy to provoke into an argument. In fact, arguments permeated from her very being. Simple conversations about inconsequential things could erupt into arguments which lasted for days. Usually, by the end of the argument, neither of us could remember what instigated it.

Suddenly, I could no longer provoke her—and, after enjoying a few days of serenity, I actually tried! Anne was the epitome of piety. Instead of saying, "Thank you, Lord," and enjoying this sudden aura of peaceful bliss, I was troubled by it. What strange powers did this mythical God—the God I denied—have? I waited for what I imagined was a temporary phase in her life, like PMS, to pass, but strangely and thankfully, it did not.

I have always prided myself on being a logical human being, but what I was witnessing defied all logic. A quiet, submissive Italian woman? Such a creature does not exist on planet Earth! God must be real—or, was it simply a trick, devised by so-called church people to get me into their congregation so I would begin tithing?

Anne tried, several times, to get me to go to church with her "...just to see what you think..." she would tell me. Her efforts fell on deaf ears. I even refused to attend the service in which Anne, VeAnne and her mother, three generations, were baptized together.

At the same time Anne, at the suggestion of a couple of prayer warriors in her church very subtly began removing all of my typical bathroom reading fare: *Newsweek, People Magazine,* and even my *TV Guide*, and began substituting Christian magazines, books and literature in their place. I never suspected the conspiracy. And, since I usually forgot to bring any new reading materials with me when I visited the porcelain library, I began reading the planted literature. Anne felt if she could feed me enough information, I would at least re-examine my position, and dig for the truth—if only to prove her position was wrong. I began reading. The more I read, the more confused I became. This caused me to read even more, to search for an answer my conscious, logical mind was willing to accept.

In approbation to Anne, and something every woman or man who is attempting to witness to a spouse should know, she did not beat me over the head with religion, nor did she constantly talk about what Christ was doing in her life. Her actions and demeanor testified to the influence Christ was making in her life so convincingly that words were not necessary. I was totally and absolutely confused.

Spring came early to Charleston, West Virginia in 1978. In early March only a few remnants of the previous winter remained and the crocuses were already struggling to break free from the cold wet earth, eager to announce to the world that spring had indeed arrived. With that spring came another Easter.

In a moment of spring fever weakness, I agreed to attend church with Anne on Easter Sunday. She couldn't have been more pleased if I had told her I had just been promoted to president of the company I worked for, and my income had quadrupled.

As Easter drew closer, I began to wonder how I was going to get out of my promise without either hurting Anne or creating an argument. I was getting too used to our peaceful coexistence. A few days before the holiday, the lymph gland under my left arm began to swell. My justification was being created! Praise God!

By Good Friday I would have gladly exchanged that lymph gland for a front row pew in any church in the country. The pain was so intense I called my office and told them I would not be at work. And while I refused to go to the emergency room at the hospital, I did agree to let Anne try to find a physician who would see me in his office, ignorantly believing the doctor would simply write out a prescription for medication which would miraculously shrink the gland to normal—an hour or so after the Easter service had concluded.

We quickly learned that Christian doctors don't work on Good Friday. Anne did, however, manage to find a Jewish physician who agreed to fit me in later that afternoon. He prescribed a strong antibiotic to kill the infection. However, he made two things abundantly clear. First, the antibiotic would not reduce the size of the gland; and, second, the gland needed to be excised, and a biopsy of the tissue checked for cancer. With the "C" word firmly etched in my mind, he scheduled an appointment for Thursday of the following week, during which time I was to meet him at the hospital where the procedure would be performed.

By Easter Sunday morning, the antibiotic was doing its job. The pain was far less intense, and much of the redness under my arm had dissipated. Although I felt a little guilty, I played the game to the hilt, pampering my arm as though I was enduring excruciating pain. Anne was very sympathetic and understanding—particularly after I agreed to go to church with her soon. Soon, I knew, would be in her dreams!

My joy at Easter, like that of most non-Christians, atheists and agnostics was in coloring and hiding Easter eggs for my daughter to find in the morning, and sitting down to a nice baked ham dinner in the afternoon. Attending church, or worshipping a mythical Savior who died for my sins, was simply an intrusion into those events, and was something for which I had no time. And, thanks to a swollen lymph gland, my plans would not have to be altered. That is not to say I was any more or less confused about the existence of a Supreme Being or the Savior, Jesus Christ, whose death and resurrection was acknowledged on that day. I simply granted myself a reprieve from the contemplation of deity.

Because they were already running late (something which invariably happens when two females are forced to share the same bathroom), Anne suggested they wait until after church to conduct our annual Easter egg hunt. Sensing my disappointment, Anne finally relented and VeAnne began the routine of pretending the brightly colored eggs, which were all partially in view, were completely invisible to the eye. In a matter of minutes, my daughter had found all of them except one I had hidden earlier that morning in the hollow leg of a parson's table, which itself was unobtrusively out of view in the corner of the living room.

Using a large stuffed rabbit as a bribe, I encouraged VeAnne to keep looking for the last egg. After several minutes it remained securely hidden. Anne glanced at the clock, and ended the egg hunt with, "If we don't get dressed now, we're going to be late for church. She can look for the last egg when we get home."

Then, as most men do, I made the mistake of underestimating my wife. "I'll tell you what," I replied baitingly, not wanting the fun to end, "if either of you can find the last egg, I'll go to church with you."

"What about your arm?" Anne asked.

"I'll survive," I replied, pleased that my clever ploy had worked so easily.

"Well, if you're sure you feel up to going..." her voice trailed off as she walked directly to the parson's table as though she knew all along where the egg was, quickly retrieving it. As she matter-of-factly dropped it into my hand, she added, "You'd better hurry up and get ready. I got your clothes ready last evening—just in case."

Over the years, I've asked her several times how she knew the last egg was there. To this day she insists she didn't know. An easy explanation would be that she watched me conceal it there, but I know she didn't—she was sleeping when I hid them. Was it a miracle? I don't think so. A little Holy Spirit guidance, perhaps, but a long way from a miracle.

However, because I could not logically explain it, the incident rattled me. I had finished dressing long before Anne and VeAnne were done, but that again is not surprising, since the act of getting dressed is never a simple task for a woman. As I stood in the kitchen sipping coffee, I contemplated again what had just happened, paralleling it with several other events which had transpired over the past couple of months, and while I wasn't ready to admit it vocally, I suddenly knew in my heart that God was, indeed, very real.

However, being something of a Doubting Thomas with respect to spiritual matters, I needed more proof than just something I couldn't explain, so I asked God for a supernatural sign to prove He was who He was. In point of fact, I asked for three—all of which I fully expected to see before noon that day. As a very conservative former Catholic whose wife was attending a Pentecostal church, the signs I sought should be obvious even to a novice Christian.

I asked God for proof that the gift of tongues was a genuine, active gift for the 20th century. I asked to feel the Holy Spirit (since that was all Anne spoke about). And, finally, I asked that He heal the lymph gland under my left arm. I did not feel that was too much to ask of an omniscient God, even if asked by an unrepentant skeptic such as myself. The question concerning the gift of tongues was asked not because it was a gift I either sought or wanted; nor did I ever ask for that particular gift. Quite frankly, what little I had previously witnessed with respect to the phenomenon Christians call *tongues* clearly suggested it was something which did not fit my particular personality, and was the only real turnoff to visiting Anne's church that morning.

Rather, I asked for that particular sign because I remembered, a few years earlier, attending a Pentecostal service with Anne and her niece, who was a member of such a denomination. It was not a pleasant experience. I thought the church was completely out of order, and that the congregation consisted of crazy religious fanatics who had all been prematurely released from a mental institution. The contemplation of hooting, screaming, and rolling around on the floor was not my idea of worship. Worship, in my mind, was epitomized by the ceremonial solemnity of the Latin mass, where a man could communicate silently with his God without a flailing arm striking him in the head, or someone in the pew behind him drenching him with holy spittle as they babbled incoherently. I was, therefore, understandably skeptical when we entered Anne's church that morning. My eyes darted around the small, unobtrusive sanctuary for a side exit. Because there was none, I insisted we sit close to the door through which we entered—just in case.

The pastor of Glad Tidings Assemblies of God Church in Hurricane, West Virginia, was an elderly gentleman named Roy Mallory. Brother Mallory, who was in his late seventies, has since passed on—a monumental loss to those of us on Earth who cherished him, but a tremendous gain to Christ's heavenly army of saints. The service opened, I imagined, pretty much the way any Protestant church service would open, with the reading of announcements. So far, so good. No holy rollers yet. As unobtrusively as I could without attracting Anne's attention (since I somehow knew she would be watching me from the corner of her eye throughout the entire service, afraid I would embarrass her at any moment by bolting from the pew and darting from the sanctuary), I surveyed the congregation which had assembled to hear the Easter message.

I was so intent on my investigation of those faces around me that I was not listening to the pastor until I heard these words: "The Lord has revealed to me that someone in this congregation asked Him, just this morning, to be healed of an affliction. He wants that person to know if he will step out in faith at the conclusion of this service, he will be healed." My pulse quickened a beat; but logic stepped in. I quickly decided that what I had heard was a standard church line, since, I logically concluded, everyone wants to be healed of something, whether that something was the common cold or a boil on the back of their neck.

However, he did get my attention and, from that moment on I was more attentive to the pulpit. I was determined to be open-minded, but I was likewise determined not to be duped! I was, as I said, the original Doubting Thomas!

Have you ever asked anyone what they liked most about a particular church service, and have them respond: "Well, the Holy Spirit really touched me during the reading of the church announcements..."? Such was the case with me. As he was reading from a list of upcoming church social events, Mallory suddenly raised his head, and his arms towards heaven. He was piously quiet for a moment—it was almost as though the Lord was speaking to him. Then he began praying in tongues.

Well, I thought, here it comes—I'm going to be hit in the back of the head with some religious idiot's flailing arms! I glanced at Anne from the corner of my eye, only to discover she was watching me. I was partially distracted when suddenly I heard, from the pastor's own mouth, some words in this strange language he was uttering—words which I knew and understood—words in perfect Latin. To be even more precise, the words he was uttering were from the Catholic Mass! While I did not know it at the time, Mallory, for all of his saintliness, was a devout anti-papist, believing all practicing Roman Catholics were doomed to hell. The words he spoke registered in disbelief. "No," I remember thinking, "I didn't hear that!" Even before the thought was formed in my mind, Mallory repeated the phrase. It was the altar boy's response to the priest before the offering of the Eucharist.

Suddenly, the first message took on a new significance. That's two, I remember thinking. About halfway through the service God honored my third request: He allowed me to feel the presence of the Holy Spirit. At the time I did not realize this was an impossible request for a sinner to make of God, since the Holy Spirit cannot act within an unclean vessel. However, because I didn't request an indwelling experience (and in fact, didn't know such a thing existed), God was able to sufficiently prove Himself to me.

I felt a warm whisper of a breeze which floated ever so gently down from the ceiling like a fine, sheer gauze that I first attributed to the overhead fans—except, when I looked up, I discovered the fans were not operative that morning. The warmth caressed my face and ever so slowly the breeze encircled me, bathing me in a serenity I have never before, or since, experienced. Even a logical mind such as mine would have to admit what I experienced was supernatural. The entire experience lasted perhaps fifteen minutes. I did not want it to end.

At the conclusion of the church service there was the promised altar call. I knew my healing was at hand—all I had to do was step out in faith and walk down the aisle to the altar to receive it. However, even with the Holy Spirit experience vividly stamped in my mind, I stood my ground, and watched as a procession of believers filed past me in search of my healing. I was, as I said, the original Doubting Thomas.

Over the past decade I have put out the fleece more times than probably any ten Christians, and God has always honored my lack of faith with proof that He is there, and that He is who He is.

I was excited as we drove home that morning. Anne did not seem to notice at first. Perhaps it was because she had been so apprehensive that I would do something to embarrass her to such a degree that she would not have felt comfortable returning to Glad Tidings in the future. Hesitantly, she asked me what I thought of the service.

I replied, I believe, that I thought it was "interesting." Then I dropped my bombshell.

"I asked God for three signs this morning," I began, "to prove—"

Before I could finish, she interrupted me. "You can't do that," she insisted defensively. "You're a sinner! You have to be saved before God will listen to your prayers!"

"That's the whole point," I replied, "He did!"

"He did? What do you mean, He did?"

Even Christians underestimate the benevolent compassion of God.

I explained my strange request, and the even stranger occurrences which served as confirmation that God does, indeed, exist.

"That healing call was for you," she said, as the full realization of what I was telling her blossomed in her mind. "You should have gone up—God would have healed you!"

Hindsight being what it is, I wholeheartedly agreed with her assessment.

I wasn't worried because I knew that God would shrink the lymph gland under my arm. I decided to go back to church with her again that evening; and, I also decided, at that moment, that I would not have to keep my Thursday appointment with the doctor at the hospital's outpatient center. Although I had not yet accepted Christ as my Savior, I mentally accepted His healing of my body!

It was an interesting morning. I now knew God was very real; yet, I still had mental reservations about walking down the aisle in a church filled to overflowing with people I did not know, and committing my life to Christ. Perhaps it was my conservative Catholic upbringing. The Catholic was required to do nothing more than be sprinkled in a private baptism ceremony, and then quietly slip into a pew where he or she could quietly worship his or her Maker. Quiet. Uneventful. I liked quiet. And, more than anything else, I definitely liked uneventful!

Anne assured me that the evening service would be much more dynamic and more to my intellectual liking, since the assistant pastor, a fiery preacher named Terry Kirk, would be in the pulpit. Mallory, she concluded, was fairly dry—and only the old people like his preaching. All of the young people, she confided, loved Kirk.

For the first time in my life I was honestly excited at the contemplation of going to church; and waited impatiently for the day to pass so I could return to Glad Tidings that evening. Somehow, although I had not asked for additional signs, I knew God would personally intervene in my life again that night. What He would do I did not know but I looked forward to it with enthusiastic anticipation.

True to Anne's word, Kirk was a dynamic preacher. It would have been apparent to any observer that the congregation was truly moved by the words Kirk spoke from the pulpit that evening. Even I could see it. Unfortunately, I could not feel it.

While God had allowed me to externally feel the presence of the Holy Spirit that morning, I now had the sense that I was encased in an invisible tomb of clear plastic, through which I could see everything, yet feel nothing. Again, there was no doubt in my skeptical mind that the experience was supernatural. Although I had privately decided that if there was an altar call, I would walk to the front of the church and accept the promised healing of my body, there was no altar call that evening—something Anne admitted later had not occurred before. Every service she attended ended with an altar call.

As the congregation funneled out of the church at the conclusion of the service, I was deeply troubled. There was too much I did not know—and now I suddenly felt an urgent need to know it! I needed desperately to understand this strange God who had suddenly become so important in my life. And although I still had no intention of accepting Christ as my personal Lord and Savior, I took the opportunity when Anne introduced me to Kirk, to invite him over to the house the following evening to speak with me about Jesus Christ.

Not realizing there was any special significance which could be construed from inviting a minister to one's house, I was surprised when one of Anne's friends was at the house when I returned from work on Monday evening. She was there to lend moral support to Anne, I was told later, just in case I did not fall to my knees, confess my sins and accept Christ as my Savior; or, to rejoice with Anne in the event I did. Again, my purpose in inviting Kirk had nothing to do with being led to Christ. Instead it had everything to do with learning more about Christianity—and, in particular, to understand the experience I had the day before. I was still very much puzzled and, admittedly, equally intrigued. I wanted to hear a logical explanation for what had happened, and even more specifically, why it happened.

While salvation is usually an emotional experience for most Christians, I could not, nor would not, allow myself to be motivated emotionally, since emotional decisions are based exclusively on feelings and are not necessarily grounded in reality. In other words, I didn't want to be sold an emotional bill of goods. I needed very much to understand the reality of the person, Christ, and those facts which clearly and indisputably established that He is the Son of God. As I have said repeatedly, I was the original Doubting Thomas.

Kirk had his hands full—something he quickly learned when he arrived shortly thereafter. We discussed creation verses evolution for some four hours. In conversations with Kirk over the next few months, he confided that he was pretty much out of his element in that discussion, particularly when words like *Australopithecus Erectus,* which he'd never heard before, were introduced into the conversation. It proved to be good training for him, however, because it tutored him on witnessing to educated atheists and agnostics in the future. I even gave him some literature to study before he ran into either; in particular, a book written by a scholarly paleontological Jesuit priest, Teilhard de Chardin, who plaintively argued that although it was an established scientific fact that man was a product of evolution, God created the anthropoid from which he evolved. The distinction between man and ape, according to the learned scholar, was the human soul—added by God at the precise moment that ape became man!

As the hour of eleven was rapidly approaching, Kirk, as I learned a few minutes later, decided I was not ready to take such a leap of faith, and had made a mental decision to quit for the night, promising himself to return on another day and complete the effort. However, our timing is not always God's timing. In God's timetable this was my night my one opportunity to come to Him. He had proven Himself sufficiently to me, and it was now my turn to prove myself to Him! In that instant—I believe, that exact, precise moment—the thought of leaving entered Kirk's mind, God spoke to me in an audible, human voice which I heard through my ears, rather than as a thought in my mind.

God said: *"If you don't come to me tonight, you will never have the chance again!"*

The voice which reverberated through my ears was not the gentle, coaxing voice of a patronizing Father—it was the harsh, intolerant voice of a Master whose patience had worn thin with a disobedient servant. In that instant I fell on my face on the carpet in my living room and accepted Jesus Christ as my Lord and Savior. God then said, *"My son, I have waited for you a long time. I have great works to work through you."*

I am acutely aware that few Christians experience what I experienced that Easter in 1978, and most would be content to go through life having heard the audible voice of God, and possessing nothing else. Most Christians have a sufficient level of faith that such a phenomenon is not necessary to either set them on the right track or keep them focused on their Christian role throughout their lives. They are the fortunate ones. Unfortunately, I was the prodigal son who strayed from the path of light and stumbled aimlessly in darkness for fifteen years. I was now a work in progress. My job as the Advertising Director of a discount store chain was suddenly secondary to learning the Word of God. My appetite for God's Word was unquenchable.

On my way home from work on Thursday of Easter week, the lymph gland under my left arm began to itch, reminding me that this was the day I was supposed to meet the doctor at the outpatient center to have it excised. I hadn't thought much about the infected gland since Easter because the pain had completely vanished. By the time I arrived home that evening the gland was driving me absolutely crazy, as any unreachable itch will. I took off my suit jacket and tossed it across the back of a chair as I strolled into the kitchen where Anne was cooking dinner.

Those were memorably good moments in our life. When I arrived home from work I would usually sit down at the kitchen table and, as I watched her prepare our meal, we would discuss whatever had happened that day. For the past couple of days our conversations centered on what new things I had discovered in the Bible, which I read during my lunch break. As I walked into the kitchen that evening I was rubbing the lymph gland through my shirt. Anne immediately noticed what I was doing and frowned.

"Is it still hurting?" she asked. "Maybe you should have kept that appointment with the doctor this afternoon."

I shook my head. "No, it just itches."

The rubbing, however, was having absolutely no effect. If I had had a wire brush at that moment, I would have used it! I unbuttoned my shirt and slipped my hand inside to gently scratch the skin around the gland. It was then that it happened. Apparently a very strange look must have crossed my face at that moment, because Anne said, "What's wrong?"

I removed my hand from inside my shirt. In my hand was a mass of grey, smelly flesh. Under my left arm was a small hole from which it came. The Jewish physician was right. He said the gland would have to come out on Thursday. It did. It was excised by the great Jewish master physician, Jesus Christ. I had now fully realized all three of my requests.

My commission as a Holy Spirit ordained teacher of the Word happened the following week. It took me over five years to understand the significance of the event I am about to describe since I have never encountered any other Christians who have openly admitted to such an experience. At the time I knew it was performed by the hand of God, and I was humbly blessed by the occurrence. I accepted it, was puzzled by it, and searched in vain for the answer to this phenomenon. It was not until the Holy Spirit supplied the answer that I knew.

It was Tuesday evening. I had now been a Christian eight days. Anne was preparing dinner, and because I did not have an opportunity to read the Bible during my lunch period that day, I was sitting in the living room reading the third chapter of 1 Timothy. Something on the opposite page caught my eye. As my glance shifted to it, I noticed an extremely bright light had haloed verse twelve in the fourth chapter. Imagine, if you will, that you are watching television on Sunday morning (although you and I both know you are in church). The tele-evangelist is reciting scripture, and the appropriate page of scripture is displayed on the screen. On that page the particular quoted scripture is highlighted. You now have an image of what I saw only the page from which I was reading was in my hand, not on a television screen.

I blinked my eyes, believing at first that I was merely seeing spots. The halo remained. I moved the Bible, feeling perhaps (since I do not specifically remember the logic for my actions), the floor lamp over my right shoulder was the culprit. The halo, however, remained on verse twelve. I shook the Bible, closed the Bible, opened the Bible, and shook it again. The light remained on verse twelve.

At that point I knew I was either hallucinating or something very supernatural was happening. As a brand new Christian I honestly did not know what to think. However, as a very logical human being, I knew I was seeing something which defied every rule of logic which had previously governed my life. I called Anne from the kitchen and extending the open Bible. I said, "Look at these pages and tell me what you see."

Anne gave me one of those *"Is this a trick question?"* looks.

"What do you mean, what do I see?" she queried, "I see the Bible..."

"No, what do you see on the pages?" I sputtered in frustration.

"I don't see anything. What do you see?"

"You don't see the light?" I asked incredulously.

"What light?" she asked. Fortunately, she didn't sound like she thought I was crazy.

I described the halo which highlighted 1 Timothy 4:12.

"I think," she said matter-of-factly, her voice rich in womanly common sense, "God is telling you to read that verse." A man tries to understand why the light is there; his wife instinctively knows it's there for a purpose. Read. Don't question it, read it!

I read verse twelve:

"Let no man despise thy youth, but be thou an example of the believers, in word, in conduct, in love, in spirit, in faith, in purity..." (1 Tim. 4:12 KJV)

When I concluded the last word, the halo moved from verse twelve to verse nine.

"This is a faithful saying and is worthy of all acceptance..." (1 Tim. 4:9 KJV)

Again, the halo moved. Now it highlighted verse fourteen.

"Neglect not the gift that is in thee, which was given thee in prophecy, with the laying on of the hands of the presbytery..." (1 Tim. 4:14 KJV)

After reading this verse, the halo moved again. This time it appeared on the number four which designated the chapter. But instead of a constant light, as it appeared on the individual scriptures, it now blinked like a warning beacon. As this spiritual phenomenon unfolded, I described what was happening to Anne, who could not see what my eyes beheld.

"God is telling you to read the entire chapter," Anne theorized.

Of course, by this time I had also figured that out as well.

The substance I was to extract from these scriptures, my commission from the Holy Spirit, is found in this chapter, starting with verse nine:

"This is a trustworthy saying that deserves full acceptance (and for this we labor and strive), that we have put our hope in the living God, who is the Savior of all men, and especially of those who believe. Command and teach these things..." (Emphasis added.) "...*Don't let anyone look down on you because you are young, but set an example for the believers in speech, in life, in love, in faith and in purity. Until I come, devote yourself to the*

public reading of Scripture, to preaching and teaching. Do not neglect your gift, which was given to you through a prophetic message when the body of elders laid their hands on you. Be diligent in these matters; give yourself wholly to them, so that everyone may see your progress. Watch your life and doctrine closely. Persevere in them, because if you do, you will save both yourself and your hearers." (1 Tim. 4:9-15; NIV)

For the past ten years I regretfully ignored that commission. The secular world of which I had become all too much a part is fraught with humanistic pitfalls which distract from, and ultimately defame and destroy the spiritual dignity of man as he searches for plurality of purpose with other lost souls: fortune, fame and fifteen minutes of peaceful solitude once that success is achieved. Yet, the prospects of worldly wealth and success are so alluring that it is difficult at times to keep a correct and balanced perspective on the need to consistently nourish our souls as we nurture our bodies.

The nutrients our souls require are found only within the Word of God. By this I do not mean the superficial sampling most Christians receive as they endeavor to speed read the Bible once a year. This concept is akin to deciding you need a more healthy diet, and supplementing your diet with vitamins, only to decide that since you were now taking vitamins, there is no longer any reason to eat solid food. To glean the nutrients which abound in the Bible it is necessary to do more than skim through a certain number of the passages before bed each evening, or devote one or two hours each day to listening to someone's denominational teaching tapes. It is necessary to read prayerfully, seeking spiritual enlightenment from the Scriptures, which is something that comes only from the Holy Spirit and not from holy men of God who proclaim the gospel through religious infomercials loosely disguised as church services through which the mass sale of Bible teaching tapes are promoted.

To fully understand the Holy Scriptures, you must both comprehend and appreciate the world in which the Scriptures were written, as well as the nature and customs of the Semitic people from which the analogous similitudes which abound in the Bible are based. To appreciate the fullness of the New Testament covenant, the student of the Word must understand the context of the law established in the Old Testament. Many of the theological questions I was asked during the five year period I wrote the syndicated column *Answers From The Bible* might not have been asked if the readers of that column had been grounded in the traditions of the Semitic people, or paralleled their New Testament reading with constant concordance references to the Old Testament. Questions like: "If Jesus Christ was in the grave for three days and three nights, how did He rise on the third day?"

What would you, as a witnessing Christian, say to an atheist or an agnostic if that specific question was raised? Would you find a convert to Christianity, or would you walk away from a soul on it's way to hell?

FOREWORD:

THE HISTORY OF THE BIBLE

Contrary to the humanistic view regarding the divine authenticity of the Holy Scriptures which is increasingly promulgated by a rapidly expanding worldwide secular brotherhood, the Bible is not a simple collection of cunningly devised fables (2 Pe. 1:16) or meaningless ancient diaries which have no practical value to the vast, global society which has emerged during the latter half of this century. The Bible is the infallible, divinely inspired Word of God:

> *"...and is profitable for teaching, for reproof, for correction, for training the righteous; that the man of God may be adequate, equipped for every good work."*
> (2 Tim. 3:16-17; NASB)

The Word of God is as timely and necessary today as it was during the era when it was originally penned. Perhaps it is even more imperative today since we, as a society, reek of the stench of Sodom and Gomorrah, and because we appear unwilling, or unable, to return this nation to the Christian value system it will require to survive.

The divine inspiration *(theopneustos)* of the Word is frequently affirmed in both the Old (Ex. 4:15; 2 Sam. 23:2-3; Isa. 29:13; 59:21; Jer. 1:9) and the New Testaments (Mt. 5:18; Ac. 1:16, 4:24-25, 28:25; 1 Cor. 2:13; 2 Tim. 3:16; Heb. 1:1, 3:7; 2 Pe. 1:16, 21; Rev. 1:1, 1:10-19). The phrase "thus saith the Lord" (or its equivalent) is used in the Bible some 400 times, confirming over and over exactly whose word is being spoken. As we study it is important to remember that while the Holy Scriptures were penned by men, the words themselves are God-breathed through the auspices of the Holy Spirit, and (in the original text) are without error. The best proof which may be offered by anyone to support the infallibility and inspiration of the Bible is found in the fulfillment of prophecy.

> *"Time and again I told you what was going to happen in the future. My words were scarcely spoken when suddenly I did just what I said. I knew how hard and obstinate you are. Your necks are unbending as iron; you are as hardhearted as brass. That is why I told you ahead of time what I was going to do, so that you*

could never say, 'My idol did it; my carved image commanded it to happen!' You have heard My predictions and seen them fulfilled, but you refuse to agree it is so. Now I tell you new things I haven't mentioned before; secrets you haven't heard. Then you can't say, "We knew that all the time!'" (Isa. 48:3-7; LB)

Man has attempted countless times over the centuries to disprove the Bible. Man has never succeeded. To minimize the value of the prophetic content of the Bible, man has offered the writings of secular prophets like Nostradamus to suggest that there is neither anything divine nor supernatural in prophecy.

The prophetic content of Nostradamus' writings are vague and could be equally applied to countless events throughout history. The prophetic content of the Bible is specific and applies only to the event, or events, described. Some prophecies in the Bible have dual fulfillment views: one immediate, one future; particularly those with endtime similitudes. One such similitude is Daniel's prophecy concerning Antichrist, which was partially fulfilled during the seven year reign of Antiochus IV Epiphanes, the Selucid who sacked the city of Jerusalem three and one half years after establishing a covenant with the Jews, and sacrificed a pig on the altar in the Temple. It was this event that led to the Maccabbean revolt which overthrew the Selucids and briefly restored a Davidic monarchy to the nation of Israel.

Before mankind can become truly egocentric it must destroy the concept of God. If God does not exist, men logically become the supreme beings of this world. When morality is torn from its biblical moorings and placed in the hands of each individual, materialism and chaos logically follow. As long as the Bible presents factual evidence of the existence of God, men remain subservient, and therefore answerable, to God for their actions on earth. As long as God exists, eternal life—and eternal damnation—exist; and rewards and judgments will follow man's exodus from this life into his eternal state.

For this reason, the Bible is important to you. Through its passages, you can better understand your God and His purpose for your life.

Prior to the invention of the printing press all Bibles were penned by hand. For that reason very few copies of the Word of God were ever seen outside the church. Around 1445 Johann Gutenberg (1400-1468) invented the process by which multiple copies of the same document could be printed with the use of blocks of separately cast reverse-image type pieces organized into pages of text upon which ink was applied. Pages were then singularly applied, and enough pressure was applied that the negative type image became a positive impression on the paper.

Without the necessary funds to pursue the commercial prospects of his invention, Gutenberg approached money lender Johann Fust for financing. Quick to see the potential value of Gutenberg's invention, and desiring to control the company they would form, Fust negotiated his son-in-law, Peter Schoeffer into the deal, making his employment into this revolutionary industry a condition of the loan. A partnership was formed between Gutenberg, Fust and Schoeffer in

1450, and the new company began operation in Mainz, Germany.

Gutenberg's technique enjoyed modest success, but not enough to repay the Fust loan. Since there was little demand for multiple copies of any documents in the fifteenth century, their services were difficult to market with any degree of profitability. Pressured by Fust for payment on his loan, Gutenberg accepted a commission from the Catholic Church to print the *Latin Vulgate.*

While Gutenberg is generally credited with printing the *Gutenberg Bible,* it is likely he was not even associated with his company when the work was actually performed. Realizing the promised commission from the Catholic Church would provide the liquidity Gutenberg needed to meet his financial obligations, Fust quickly filed a lawsuit against his junior partner for non-payment of debt, and took over the company in 1455. The completed *Gutenberg Bible* was actually the work of Gutenberg's former partner, Peter Schoeffer.

A perfectly preserved copy of the *Gutenberg Bible* was discovered among the affects of Cardinal Jules Mazarin (1602-1661) sometime during 1790, and that copy became known as the *Mazarin Bible.*

The traditional *King James Version* of the Bible, as we know it, contains 773,692 words that are divided into 31,173 verses, and which appear in 1,189 chapters. The data is compiled in sixty-six books which were penned by forty-four different writers over a period of fifteen centuries.

Cardinal Stephen Langton (1155-1228 A.D.), the Archbishop of Canterbury, divided the Bible into chapters in 1207. In 1448 R. Nathan divided the Old Testament into verses. This was followed in 1551 by the division of the New Testament into verses by Robert Stephanus. The first Bible to use the chapter and verse format was the *Geneva Bible* which was printed in 1560.

Around 250 B.C. Ptolemy Philadelphus (308-246 B.C.) commissioned the translation of the Hebrew scriptures into Greek, which was the universal language of the world during that period. Jewish scholars were brought to Alexandria, Egypt to complete the translation. Because seventy scholars were assigned to the project, the completed work was called *The Septuagint.* Initially, only the Pentateuch was transcribed. Several years passed before the balance of the Hebrew Scriptures were translated and became part of the vast library found in Alexandria, which had been the intellectual capital of the known world. In 130 B.C., the Apocrypha was added to the Hebrew scriptures.

Sophronius Eusebius Hieronymus (347-420 A.D.), who would later be canonized as St. Jerome by the Roman Catholic Church, translated the Scriptures into Latin. Augustine, fearful that the plethora of inadequate Biblical translations which were starting to appear would utterly corrupt the Word of God, was instrumental in the commissioning of Jerome to translate the Greek text into the language of Rome. Jerome retired from Rome to Bethlehem sometime around 396 A.D. and began his translation. His work became the Latin Vulgate.

Surprisingly, as the influence of the Roman Catholic Church grew throughout Europe, the Bible fell into general disuse. Church leaders believed the Scriptures were too complex for use by the laity because, in the estimation of the scholars assigned to interpret the meaning of God's message—who themselves could not understand much of its content—that common man had neither the spiritual insight nor the intelligence to understand God's word. Additionally, this allowed singular interpretation in a singular church, with a singular point of view which completely curtailed theological debate. Dogmas, decrees, doctrines and papal bulls replaced the Bible as the Word of God, and the Light was effectively snuffed out for almost four hundred years. During this period the Roman Catholic Church secured an almost tyrannical control over the people of Europe. Its power at various times rivaled the authority of kings (most of whom paid some form of homage to the Catholic pontiff, who served as the Vicar of Christ), claiming that right through ascendancy from the apostle, Peter, whom they viewed as the first *Pontifex Maximus.*

In 1382, an Englishman named John Wycliffe (1328-1384) began translating the Latin Vulgate into English. Wycliffe was very critical of the papacy and was, unfortunately for him, very outspoken in his opinions. Had it not been for the protection of the fourth son of Edward III, John of Gaunt (1340-1399), Wycliffe would have been tried for heresy and probably burned at the stake. As it was, he was excommunicated from the Catholic Church for his views, and forced into a disgraced, premature retirement.

Wycliffe's Bible, the first complete version of the Bible ever to reach the laity (as well as the first English translation of the Bible in the world) was completed in 1388, four years after Wycliffe's death from natural causes.

With the untimely death of Edward III in 1383, papal persecution of Wycliffe became more severe. The scholar was still afforded some protection by Edward's grandson, Richard II (1367-1400), who shared the throne with John of Gaunt for six years before becoming sole regent of England. When Wycliffe died, the Catholic church demanded possession of his corpse. Upon the threat of excommunication, John of Gaunt acceded to church demands and surrendered Wycliffe's remains. Wycliffe was cremated, and his ashes were thrown into the Thames River on the belief that if a believer's body was utterly destroyed by fire it could not be resurrected. That is the reason condemned heretics were always burned at the stake.

William Tyndale (1494-1536) was raised in the sheltered environment of the University of Oxford, and was exposed to the Scriptures at a very early age. Not many years after his graduation from the University of Cambridge, Tyndale, a brilliant Bible scholar—and also another outspoken critic of the papal system—was branded as a heretic by the Catholic Church in Glouchestershire. Fearing for his life, Tyndale fled from England and took up residency in Antwerp, Belgium.

In 1525, at the age of 31, Tyndale translated the Greek New Testament into English. His version of the *Pentateuch* followed in 1530. Tyndale's *Book of Jonah* followed in 1531. Four years later, in 1535, the Catholic Church formally charged him with heresy, and a warrant was issued for his arrest. He was taken into custody and remanded to Vilvorde Prison for the better part of a year, during which time church inquisitors tried to force him first, to confess his heresy, and then to recant. When their efforts failed, the Church ordered him taken to Augsburg where he was tried by a church tribunal. Found guilty of heresy, Tyndale was taken to the public square in Augsburg where, on the morning of October 6, 1536, he was tied to a stake, strangled to death, and then burned.

While Tyndale was confined in Vilvorde, his friend and fellow theologian, Miles Coverdale (1485-1569), published his own version of the Scriptures, *The Coverdale Bible.* Coverdale's version was based partially on the Vulgate and partially on Martin Luther's translation, as well as on work that he and Tyndale had collaborated on prior to Tyndale's arrest for heresy.

Within ten years still another version, *The Rogers' Bible,* was being circulated throughout Europe. This effort was essentially a reprint of Tyndale's effort. Within a few years it became known as *The Translation of Thomas Matthew.*

Jack Rogers, like Wycliffe and Tyndale before him, was vehemently opposed to the dogmas and dictates of the Roman Catholic Church, and openly preached against the papacy. Rogers was arrested in 1553 and detained in his Smithfield home for almost a year while the Church considered the charges against him. While he had ample opportunity to escape to safety in either Germany or Switzerland, Rogers refused to do so because he had a large family and could not afford to take them with him.

In the fall of 1554, Rogers was formally charged with heresy by order of the Bishop of London. He was immediately taken from his home to Newgate Prison where a futile effort was made to force him to renounce his faith. On February 3, 1555, Rogers was taken from Newgate to Smithfield. The following morning, in the presence of his wife and ten of his eleven children (the youngest, who was born while he was in Newgate Prison, was with his nurse), Rogers was burned at the stake.

Thomas Cranmer, the first Protestant Archbishop of Canterbury secured the lasting favor of Henry VIII by sanctioning the monarch's divorces from his second, third, fourth and fifth wives.

In 1539 Cranmer wrote the preface of what was to become known as *The Great Bible*—the first official Protestant Bible. The second printing of this Bible in 1562 was renamed *The Cranmer Bible* in honor of the cleric, who became one of the countless Christian victims of Mary I of England—more commonly known as Bloody Mary. In 1549 Cranmer introduced the *Book of Common Prayer* which is still used by most mainline Protestant denominations today.

Henry VIII died on January 28, 1547. His will stipulated that in the event of the death of his only son, Edward (who suffered from tuberculosis), the throne would pass first to Mary, the eldest daughter; and then, if Mary failed to produce a male offspring, to Elizabeth, his youngest daughter.

Shortly before Edward died from tuberculosis, John Dudley, the Duke of Northumberland, coerced the dying monarch into signing a decree which granted all rights to the throne to Lady Jane Grey, the daughter of the Duchess of Suffolk, whose only link to royalty resided in the fact that her mother was Edward's aunt.

Immediately upon Edward's death on July 10, 1553, Dudley proclaimed

Lady Jane Queen of England and attempted to use Edward's proclamation to enforce his claim. In one bold, decisive stroke, Princess Mary, the rightful heir, had Lady Jane Grey, Dudley, and several members of her own court arrested and declared herself Queen. Lady Jane Grey was confined to the Tower of London. Dudley and his co-conspirators were summarily executed.

When a marriage treaty was arranged between Mary and Phillip of Spain, a minor revolution broke out in England, since Spain was traditionally the enemy of the British people. When the rebellion was quelled, Mary decided it would be prudent to eliminate any competition she might have for the throne of England. On February 12, 1554, Lady Jane Grey and her husband, John Dudley's son, were executed; and Mary's own sister, Elizabeth, was confined to the Tower of London while Mary contemplated some safe measure to rid herself of that threat as well.

Mary I reigned only five years, but her reign will historically be remembered as the most bloody period in the history of England, hence the nickname, Bloody Mary. During that five years, upon order of the Queen, over 300 Christians and an assortment of personal enemies of the throne were burned at the stake for heresy. One of her victims was John Rogers. Another, previously mentioned, was Thomas Cranmer, the former Archbishop of Canterbury. Because of his criticism of the papacy during the lifetime of Henry VIII, Cranmer was stripped of his position as Archbishop, tried for heresy, and condemned to die. On March 21, 1556, he was burned at the stake.

While Mary's pogrom was disseminating the English Christian population, a group of Protestant theologians fled to the continent where they found safe haven in Geneva, Switzerland. Their combined efforts led to the publishing of the *Geneva Bible* in 1560.

With the untimely death of Mary I, Elizabeth (1533-1603), the daughter of Henry VIII and his mistress, Ann Boleyn, was crowned queen. Elizabeth immediately revoked all Catholic legislation and reinstated all of the laws her father had decreed with respect to the Church.

Largely because of Elizabeth I, the official Church of England version of the Scriptures, *The Bishop's Bible,* was published in 1568. That version was used in all of England's churches until the introduction of the *King James Version* in 1611.

Recognizing the possibility of flaws in the text of the Vulgate, the Catholic Church authorized the transcription of a new version in 1582, called the *Rheims Bible.* Twenty-seven years later, it was updated and became known as the *Douay-Rheims Bible.* Even with the introduction of the *Jerusalem Bible* in 1966 and the *New American Bible* in 1970, the *Douay-Rheims Bible* has been the mainstay of the Roman Catholic Church since 1609.

With the death of Elizabeth I on March 24, 1603, James Stuart, the king of Scotland (1566-1625) was proclaimed King of England, ending 118 years of Tudor rule. While enroute to London from Edinburgh to claim his crown on May 7, 1603, his entourage was met by a group of Puritans led by Dr. John Reynolds. Reynolds presented the new monarch with a list of grievances the

Puritans had against the Church of England, and asked the monarch if he would address them once he was crowned. James agreed to meet with all of England's church leaders as soon as he could after his coronation. The meeting took place on January 14, 1604 at the winter palace, Hampton Court, in Middlesex.

The Puritans, who came to Hampton Court seeking religious reform, suddenly discovered that the new monarch believed in the divine rights of the episcopacy—providing, of course, that episcopacy supported his own claim to absolute temporal authority. Outside of the Anglican movement, every religious leader was opposed to episcopacy, believing bishop-rule would invariably lead to a state church and a church state not unlike the situation fostered by the church in Rome.

From a perspective of reform, the Hampton Court Conference was an extreme disappointment to all but the Episcopal bishops. However, due largely to the efforts of John Reynolds, King James did authorize the body to undertake the translation of a new English version of the Bible. Later that year, 54 of England's best Bible scholars met to discuss exactly how this herculean task should be undertaken.

The task force was divided into two groups. One group was assigned to work exclusively on the Old Testament; the other on the New Testament. Each group was then divided into three teams, with each team comprised of nine members. One team from each group was assigned to work at Oxford, one at Cambridge, and one at Westminister. The two Oxford teams were headed by Dr. John Harding, Professor of Hebrew studies at Oxford. Dr. Lancelot Andrews, Dean of Westminister headed the second team. Dr. Edward Lively, Professor of Hebrew Studies at Cambridge was appointed to oversee the third team. However, before work could actually begin, Lively died. He was replaced by Dr. Robert Spaulding. Reynolds, who almost single-handedly caused the project to happen, accepted a subservient position on one of the teams under Harding.

The work actually began in the summer of 1607. The translation was completed in 1610, and the first printed version appeared in 1611, with an introduction dedicated to King James.

Prior to his death in 1656, Anglican Archbishop James Ussher, an Irish clergyman of some distinction, created the chronological dating which still appears today in many versions of the Bible. In the 1701 version of the *King James Bible,* the date, October 23, 4004 B.C., which Ussher had meticulously calculated to be the date when creation occurred, was included as a marginal reference. The month, day of the week, and hour of Ussher's creation theory have long since fallen to the wayside, but many students of the Bible still tenaciously cling to 4004 B.C. as the year in which God created Adam and Eve. Unfortunately, whatever logic or calculations Ussher applied to arrive at his theory was flawed, since there is no scriptural evidence which supports Ussher's chronology and a considerable amount of scientific evidence which contradicts it. It is important for the Christian to remember that science will always support Scripture—when the scriptural theories advanced by man are based on fact.

Ussher's assumption was that the genealogies from Adam to Abraham, recorded in the Book of Matthew, were a complete and total record of all first born offspring without exception or omission, with each occurring at a precise, measurable interval. Add to that fallacy the erroneous supposition that the world was created in six literal, 24-hour days and you have an accurate picture of the problem Ussher created for the witnessing Christian in the latter part of the twentieth century.

Since I will address the question of whether or not the world was created in six literal days, it would be repetitious to deal with the subject at this point. It is sufficient to say that I am a believer in the literal interpretation of the Bible—except when Scripture itself indicates the passages are not literal.

Speak to almost any Christian today, and ask them which version of the Bible they read, and nine out of ten will mention the *King James Version.* Ask them which version is the most accurate, and in all likelihood, the same response will be forthcoming. What percentage of the most popular Bible in the world is dependent on previous translations?

In the Old Testament, 4% of the KJV comes from *The Wycliffe Bible;* 18% from *The Tyndale Bible;* 13% from *The Coverdale Bible;* 19% from *The Geneva Bible;* 4% from *The Bishop's Bible;* and 3% from lesser known transcripts. Only 39% of the KJV was translated directly from original Hebrew manuscripts.

Approximately 85% of the *Authorized King James Version of 1611* was taken, word for word, from the Tyndale Bible. The remaining 15% came from the other versions listed above. The original Greek text did not arrive in England until 1628—seventeen years after the *KJV* was completed. Although the bulk of the text was taken from Tyndale's version, his controversial anti-papist annotations were excluded from the *King James* text.

The original 1611 version contained some 4,765 marginal notes and Scripture references concerning the literal meaning of many Greek and Hebrew words. By 1760 some 30,000 additional marginal references were added. By the early eighteen century the *KJV* had crowded out all other versions of the Bible, and stood alone as the authoritative Word of God. Although it was largely compiled from other works, the *KJV* is viewed by most as being a comparably accurate translation of the original Greek and Hebrew texts.

By the early eighteenth century the *KJV* overshadowed all other versions of the Bible, and became, in the minds of most men, the precise, literal written Word of God. In fact, to the common man today, that is still the case. Many do not see any difference between the KJV and the original Greek and Hebrew scrolls, believing the scribes who penned them actually used the archaic nomenclature of 17th century England, and that the KJV represents the most accurate translation available. In fact, that was the most immediately apparent inaccuracy with Joseph Smith's *Book of Mormon.* The document, which Smith claimed to have received from an angel, Moroni, on the night of September 23, 1823, was penned in perfect *"King James"* prose—when it was purported by its translators, Smith and Oliver Crowdery, to be a text written in 600 B.C.

Although the KJV is a beautiful translation, it is, unfortunately, neither the most scholastically accurate nor theologically correct version. The transcribers wanted to create a translation which captured the full essence of the meaning of the Scriptures they were translating, and to a very minor degree, sacrificed interpretative accuracy to achieve their objective. This was done because the translators knew they were creating an epistle for the laity—the common man—who was, in matters of interpretative theology, completely ignorant; and, who would not, in their opinion, understand the meaning the Scriptures attempt to convey. In point of fact, all modern translations, to some degree or another, do exactly the same thing. The unqualified acceptance of the *King James Version* is due less to accuracy and more to the fact that it has been in general use by the laity for over 350 years.

A few years ago, I received a letter from the principal of a small Christian school in Madison, West Virginia, who upbraided me for quoting Scripture from versions other than the KJV, adding: "...Because of the day we are living in, there are many people who are confused about which Bible is the Word of God. I have decided to write a long letter to expose the other books impersonating as Bibles. There is only one Bible—the A.V. of 1611. All others are forgeries, and this letter will prove that to any reader who wants to know the truth..."

Another writer questioned my use of a *New International Version* text in an article I had written, informing me that he "...only used the version Christ used—the authorized King James Version of 1611..." Now, I do not think the writer of that letter actually believed that Christ carried a copy of the *King James Version* with Him on His pilgrimage of the Holy Land—particularly since Christ was obviously crucified 1,578 years before the translation existed. However, I am convinced, in the mind of the writer, the *KJV* most closely approximated the literal Word of God as spoken by the literal Son of God—hence, the analogy he used.

A version called *The Literal Translation of the Bible* appeared in 1862, but failed to gain much acceptance in the Christian community. In 1885 the *English Revised Version* was published. Like the original KJV, 54 Bible scholars worked on this translation. It's commission was authorized by the Church of England, which felt the KJV of 1611 was obsolete because the meanings of so many English words had changed over the years; and, even more important, because so much more was now known about the root meanings of words in both the Hebrew and Greek languages.

In 1901 the first modern language American version was published. The translation was the product of both American and British scholarship, and was highly regarded for its scholastic accuracy. The translation was called the *American Standard Version*. In the same year *The Twentieth Century New Testament* appeared, and was touted by its publishers as the most faithful translation of the original Greek text ever made. In 1902 *The New Testament In Modern Speech* was published. Touted by the publisher as a study Bible, it contained an explanatory preface to each book, as well as the extensive use of expository footnotes throughout the text. Because of the use of annotations, this version, more commonly called *Weymouth's New Testament,* became very popular with new converts to Christianity.

In 1909 the Oxford University Press introduced *The Scofield Reference Bible,* which quickly became the most popular annotated version using the King James text. While the version contains the name of Bible expositor, pastor and teacher, C.I. Scofield, who was commissioned by the Oxford Press to edit the annotated rendering which would bear his name, several Bible scholars contributed to the 1909 edition. Among these were Professor James Barrellet of the Theological Faculty of Lausanne; Professors Sayce and Margoliouth of Oxford University; Professor C. R. Erdman of Princeton University; and Walter Scott, an eminent Bible scholar of the day.

The *Scofield Reference Bible* was revised in 1917, 1941, and again in 1967. The two early revisions dealt primarily with the aesthetics of the rendering—the use of larger, more readable type faces; the substitution of arabic rather than roman numerals; the addition of several new annotations, as well as clarification of earlier ones; and finally, the addition of a panorama view of the Bible which the editors thought was necessary because "...no portion of the Scripture is to be intelligently comprehended apart from some conception of its place in the whole....The Panoramic View of the whole Bible will, it is believed, show the unity of the book—a fact in danger of failing to be perceived in face of the other and more evident fact that it is made up of many books..."

In other words, because Scofield's annotations provided the reader with so much theological information about the verse, or text, under consideration, it was felt people might begin to mentally disassociate each book from the balance of the tome, treating each as a separate book within a volume of writings—such as a profusion of short stories, by different, unrelated, authors, compiled within a common cover. For that reason, the editors at *Oxford Press* decided because "...the Bible story and message is like a picture wrought out of mosaics: each book, each chapter, verse and even word forms a necessary part..." of the whole picture; and, a comprehensive understanding of *all* of the Word of God was necessary for man to fully understand and appreciate the Scriptures.

While aimed at advancing theology, the 1967 Scofield rendering was more of a scholastic effort. Ussher's chronology, or that part of it prior to 2100 B.C., was removed; obsolete and archaic words, as well as those words whose general meaning had changed (i.e., in Elizabethan times, an apothecarist was a person who made perfumes, not pharmaceuticals), were clarified. Scriptural typology was designated, and care was taken to distinguish between *types, illustrations* and *examples.* And, most important, archeological discoveries in Egypt, Mesopotamia, Palestine, and other areas in the Holy Land, which support and otherwise corroborate biblical accuracy, were added, in summary form, in the appropriate places.

Today's Bible student is much more fortunate than those in earlier days, since there are now several comprehensive study Bibles available which present the reader with authenticated archæological data as well as in-depth and accurate annotations concerning the meaning of the text.

The *Scofield Reference Bible* remains the most popular reference Bible available. Many of Scofield's annotations have become so universally accepted they have been added to other versions, in particular, the *New International Version.*

In 1908, a version which would quickly become known as the pastor's bible was assembled by a prominent American theologian, Frank Charles Thompson, D.D., Ph.D. This rendering, like Scofield's, utilized the traditional King James text. It's publisher, *B.B. Kirkbridge Bible Company* of Indianapolis, Indiana, called it the *Thompson Chain Reference Bible.* The popularity of the *Chain Reference Bible* with pastors was found in a topical chain index which linked subject matter, providing the pastor with almost effortless topical sermon material. The *Thompson Chain Reference Bible* was updated in 1917, 1929, 1934, 1957, 1964, and again in 1982 when *Zondervan* co-published a *New International Version* text which contains an archæological supplement edited by G. Frederick Owen, D.D., Ed.D.

Like the *Oxford University Press, B.B. Kirkbride* addressed the spiritual attitude of the reader, and cautioned the reader not to treat the Bible as one might view ordinary literature. Its cautionary statement said, "...It may be read, or studied, in the same spirit as a volume of Milton, Shakespeare, or as an historical work and it will be found interesting and profitable; but the merely literary student, or critic, however scholarly and persistent he may be, will never discover its choicest treasures. Paul says, 'The natural man receiveth not the things of the Spirit of God: for they are foolishness unto him; neither can he know them, because they are spiritually discerned...'" Over the past one hundred and fifty years, natural man—including the feminists who abound in society today—have attempted to eviscerate the Word of God through the creation of a multiplicity of humanistic versions of the Bible which either demasculinate God, or attempt to negate the deity of Jesus Christ through the deification of man. The latest of these attempts, published in 1995 by the *Oxford University Press,* is called *The New Inclusive Bible.* It is an ultra-liberal, politically correct version of the Bible which addresses God, Christ and the Holy Spirit in neutral gender—and, because its author, a feminist, is left-handed, it eliminates any mention of anyone sitting on the *right hand* of God.

Dr. James Moffatt introduced his annotated version of the New Testament in 1913 and an Old Testament translation followed in 1924. A combined volume was printed in 1935. While initially popular, the *Moffat Bible* has fallen into disuse. This is due in part to the fact that *Moffat's New Testament* was translated from Greek manuscripts of an origin later than those manuscripts traditionally used, and contains terminology not found in the more ancient texts.

Riverside's New Testament and *The Godspeed Bible* were published in 1923, followed by the *Montgomery New Testament* in 1924. In 1937 The International Council of Religious Education (of which forty of the largest American denomination belong) commissioned the translation of a new version. In 1952, after fourteen years of work, the *Revised Standard Version* appeared. This version has all but replaced the KJV in the pulpits of many mainline Christian churches in America. While it has been acclaimed for its simplicity, the RSV translation is viewed by most Christians as too liberal, and leaning towards the extremes of interpretation rather than following the traditional understanding of words. The *RSV* was updated in 1971, with most revisions occurring in the New Testament text. The single verse which most Christians find abhorrent in the RSV remained unchanged:

> *"Therefore the Lord Himself will give you a sign: a young woman will conceive and will give birth to a son, and will call Him Immanuel."* (Isa. 7:14; RSV)

The interpretation of the Hebrew word, *álmâh,* while assumed to be a young woman, also clearly denotes a young woman who is a virgin. The translators of the RSV made the decision to use the term *young woman* rather than *virgin* because Isaiah, in writing his inspired text, did not use the distinctive word, *b^ethûwiâh,* which was usually applied to virgins (as seen in Gen. 24:16, 24:43 and Gen. 34:3), with the added reference of *na'ärâh* in 24:16 to further described Rebecca as a "virgin who had known no man." The RSV translators decision was based, at least in part, on the application of the Greek word, *parthenos* (young woman about to enter womanhood) instead of the more narrowly defined word, *neanis*, in the *Septuagint.* It is important for the student of Scripture to realize that both terms, *b^ethâwiâh* and *álmâh,* were alternately applied to either young women or virgins. While the historic chronology of the virgin birth of Jesus Christ does not rise or fall on the phraseology of Isa. 7:14, the RSV text unnecessarily dilutes the prophecy concerning the virgin birth—one of the two most important supernaturally significant events in the entire Word of God. The other is the physical resurrection of Jesus Christ. For the Christian to obtain eternal life, both of those statements must be true. It is for that single reason that many Christians today view the RSV as an abomination.

In 1954 *The Amplified Bible* was published. This version, while not actually a version, was an important addition to the theological edification of the novice Christian and Bible student alike, since its focus is on the amplification of the meanings of the various Greek and Hebrew words found in the original text. Its proper application is its use in conjunction with some other study Bible. *The Amplified Bible* is impractical and tedious as a reading text by itself.

During the following two decades, the floodgates of theological diversity opened, and a multitude of new study Bibles began to appear. *The Emphasized Bible* which, like *The Amplified Bible,* was created to provide enlightenment with respect to the meaning of particular words and verses of Scripture, was published in 1954 as well. *The Berkeley Version* was printed in 1959; and in 1966 a new Catholic version, the *Jerusalem Bible*, came into print. It was followed almost immediately by the *Good News Bible. The New American Bible* was completed in 1970. This version, commissioned by Pope Pius XII in 1947, employed the theological talents of Catholics, Protestants and Jews. Unlike prior Catholic efforts, the translators of the *New American Bible* did not work from, or even refer to, the Vulgate. Instead, their translation came entirely from the Greek and Hebrew texts.

The *New American Bible* was an important theological work, and should have been greeted as such by Protestants as well as Catholics. However, much of the attention which should have been paid that translation by Protestants was diverted a year later by a simplified text created by Dr. Kenneth Taylor. Taylor began his work by paraphrasing Scriptures for his own children. *The Living Bible* was the result of that effort.

The Living Bible became an overnight success. It is used so extensively today that paraphrased versions of both the *Scofield Reference Bible* and the *Thompson Chain Reference Bible* in *The Living Bible* text are now available. Also appearing in 1971 was *The New American Standard Bible.* Unlike *The Living Bible,* which utilized the talents of one man—Taylor—the *New American Standard Bible* was the product of eleven years of effort by 54 Hebrew and Greek scholars.

The *New International Version* was published in 1973. Over 100 scholars, working for eight years under the auspices of the *Christian Reformed Church,* the *National Association of Evangelicals,* and the *New York International Bible Society*, which undertook the financial sponsorship of the project, put together this contemporary language Bible. To assure there were no doctrinal errors or bias, the scholars who performed the translation were selected from the Anglican, Assemblies of God, Baptist, Brethren, Church of Christ, Evangelical Free Church, Lutheran, Mennonite, Methodist, Nazarene, Presbyterian and Wesleyan faiths, as well as the Christian Reformed movement. Understanding the importance of maintaining the essence of the original text, the NIV scholars endeavored to create one of the most accurate translations available today; and, as a result, the NIV is rapidly becoming one of the most popular versions of the Bible in print.

In 1976 *Reader's Digest,* who had for years been publishing condensed versions of popular books, decided to condense the Holy Bible, using the *Revised Standard Version* as its text. The project took eight years to complete. The *Reader's Digest Condensed Bible* appeared briefly in 1982. Of the 773,692 words which appear in the original KJV text, over 300,000 words, or some 39% of the Scriptural content, was deleted from its text. Combine that with the fact that few Christians liked the RSV from which it was created, and it is not difficult to see why the *Reader's Digest Condensed Bible* was discredited so easily. (The term "Bible" is used figuratively to describe this work. Because of its condensation, it can best be described as a theological essay.) The product which *Reader's Digest* created was attacked by almost every conservative Christian group in the nation. As a result, the *Reader's Digest* project failed to secure the endorsement of any mainstream conservative Christian groups or churches—nor was it even endorsed by the liberals who defended its creation in the press.

The last important work under consideration in this thesis was the revision of the *KJV* into contemporary, twentieth century language. This undertaking, completed in 1982, was to be called the *New King James Version.* As with the 1604 Hampton Court commission, 54 scholars, working as six teams comprised of nine scholars, carefully undertook the task of updating the KJV text, careful to maintain the beauty and dignity of the original version. Although it is theologically more accurate than the original text, the NKJV has not been able to displace the *1611 Authorized King James Version* as the Bible most Americans read and love.

It is fitting to close the Forward of this book with the mention of another paraphrased edition: *The Jewish New Testament*, which was published in 1989. While this volume is not an original translation (it is based on the United Bible Society's *The Greek New Testament*), it has one unique characteristic which makes it noteworthy in this thesis: it is linguistically, culturally and theologically Jewish. Although most Christians today view Christianity as irreconcilably separated from Judaism, they are branches from the same tree.

In the early Messianic church, the most heatedly debated question was not whether a Jew could believe in Jesus Christ, but whether a Gentile could become a Christian without converting to Judaism. Today, the reverse is true. Christianity debates whether a Jew can become a Christian and still practice Judaism.

Although the New Testament, like the Old Testament, is a Jewish book, Christian anti-semitism, albeit shrouded under a cape of holy righteousness, has infiltrated Christian theology, and many Christian practices today are based on those biases. It is important that Christians understand their Jewish roots, and the Divine link which bonds Christians and Jews into the family of God.

The Jewish New Testament offers the Christian edification in two ways. First, the Christian, in reading, becomes more acutely aware of the Jewish antecedent, together with the fact that Christianity did not replace Judaism, but rather, was grafted into it; and second, *The Jewish New Testament* provides the Christian with an additional tool with which to better understand what the Messiah said, and what those words meant in the context of the Jewish people to whom He spoke. For example, in Matthew 6:23, Christ, in the Sermon on the Mount, said: "But if thine eye be evil, thy whole body shall be full of darkness..." Most Christians would understand that statement to mean having an evil eye, casting spells, or at the very least, coveting something belonging to someone else. The reality is, in the Jewish context, it means being stingy *('âyin râ'äh).*

It should be remembered, however, that in any paraphrased Bible, *opinion* always plays a key role in determining which word or phrase is editorially substituted in a particular verse. If the author feels the current text does not project what, in his or her opinion, the text actually means, the substitution of other words may dramatically change the meaning, and could corrupt the context of the entire passage. The reader of a paraphrased Bible must keep this thought in mind, and treat the paraphrased edition not as Scripture, but rather, as a theological commentary on the Scriptures.

CHAPTER ONE

THE CREATION AND THE ANTEDILUVIAN WORLD

Did God create man, or did man create a God to worship?

Is the God we worship real? Did He create the universe and everything in it, or did our primeval ancestors create an illusionary deity to explain those things their finite minds could not comprehend? Is our God no more real than the gods of mythology, created in the minds of imaginative writers to explain such things as birth, death, and the afterlife, day and night, and the seasonal renewal of the earth?

Humanism teaches that God is a myth, created by fearful, superstitious minds. The doctrines of humanism assert that the universe was ever-existent, and that man—rather than being a product of Godly creation—slowly evolved over eons of time; and that existence, as we know it, begins and ends with the individual. The doctrine of this religion—the religion of humanism—redeems man from the moral obligation of pleasing God and grants him the right to please only himself. This position is documented in the *1933 Humanistic Manifesto:*

> *"We believe that the traditional dogmatic or authoritarian religions that place revelation, God, ritual or creed above human needs...do a disservice to the human species...We find insufficient evidence for the belief in the existence of a supernatural...As nontheists we begin with human beings not God, nature not deity...Humans are responsible for what we are or will become. No deity will save us; we must save ourselves...Promises of immortal salvation or fear of eternal damnation are both illusionary and harmful..."*

To this declaration of self, God disdainfully said:

> *"Surely, your turning things upside down shall be esteemed as the potter's clay; for shall the work say of Him who made it, He made me not? Or shall the thing formed say of Him who formed it, He hath no understanding?"* (Isa. 29:16; KJV)

Furthermore, God leaves little doubt in the mind of the man, woman or child who seeks knowledge with respect to who created whom when He declares:

> *"I have made the earth, and created man upon it; I even my hands*

have stretched out the heavens, and all their host have I commanded." (Isa. 45:12; KJV)

The seeker of the truth of the Holy Scriptures will not find, concealed within its pages, presumptive documentation of God's existence which would satisfy the intellectual skeptic, although such proof exists in abundance throughout the Bible. I know. As a nontheist, I probably spent as much, if not more, time studying the Scriptures than many of today's Christians (which does not speak well of many in the Christian community, who must have at least some of the answers the nontheist, to whom they must ultimately witness, will ask). I searched for hard, fast physical evidence of the deity of Jesus Christ, as well as supportive proof of the existence of God. I found nothing which convinced me the Bible was anything more than a book of fables. At the time I was confident that ensuing generations would view the Bible in exactly the same manner as they perceived Greek mythology, or any other ancient writing which endeavored, through parabolic analogies and similitudes, to explain our existence. I was wrong.

Scripture clearly reveals the mysteries which man must fully comprehend to have an esoteric understanding of God, and an intimate, salvation knowledge of Jesus Christ. However, by deliberate design—a mystery in and of itself—its revelations cannot be discerned with a carnal intellect. This fact is verified by Jesus Christ.

"The same day went Jesus out of the house, and sat by the seaside. And great multitudes were gathered together unto Him, so that He went into a boat, and sat; and the whole multitude stood on the shore. And He spoke many things unto them in parable..." (Matt. 13:1-3; KJV)

"And the disciples came, and said unto Him, Why speakest Thou unto them in parables? He answered and said unto them, Because it is given unto you to know the mysteries of the kingdom of heaven, but to them it is not given. For whosoever hath, to him shall be given, and he shall have more abundance; but whosoever hath not, from him shall be taken away even what he hath. Therefore speak I to them in parables, because they seeing, see not; and hearing, they hear not, neither do they understand. And in them is fulfilled the prophecy of Isaiah, which saith, By hearing, ye shall hear and shall not understand; and seeing, ye shall see and shall perceive. For this people's heart is become gross, and their ears are dull of hearing, and their eyes they have closed, lest at any time they should see with their eyes and hear with their ears, and should understand with their heart, and should be converted, and I should heal them. But blessed are your eyes, for they see; and your ears, for they hear. For verily I say unto you that many prophets and righteous men have desired to see those things which ye see, and have not seen them; and to hear those things which ye hear, and have not heard them. Hear, therefore, the parable of the sower. When anyone heareth the

word of the kingdom and understandeth it not, then cometh the wicked one, and catcheth away that which was sown in his heart. This is he which received seed by the wayside. But he that received the seed in stony places, the same is he that heareth the word, and immediately with joy receiveth it; Yet hath he not root in himself, but endureth for a while; for when tribulation or persecution ariseth because of the Word, immediately he is offended. He also that received seed among the thorns is he that heareth the word; and the care of this age, and the deceitfulness of riches, choke the word, and he becometh unfruitful. But he that received seed in the good ground is he that heareth the Word, and understandeth it, who also beareth fruit, and bringeth forth, some an hundredfold, some sixty, some thirty." (Matt. 13:10-23 KJV)

To appreciate the significance of this Scripture, it is necessary to look beyond the context of those specific verses to the historicity of that era. First, it was a common practice in that day—not only by the Jewish rabbin, but by the Arabs and other Semites in that area of the world as well—to instruct with the use of parables and similitudes. Second, prior to that day, Christ had refrained from an extensive use of similitudes when speaking to the multitudes, addressing the crowds with simple statements and even simpler truths. The fact that He was now speaking only in parables confused Christ's disciples and triggered the question: "Why do you speak to the people in parables?"

Christ's disciples questioned Him not because they failed to perceive the meaning of what He was saying. Rather, they questioned His use of parables at that moment because it was important to them—comprehending neither the nature nor the purpose of Christ's earthly ministry—that those listening should clearly understand the message He brought.

Jesus spoke in parables for four reasons. First, the religious leaders of the day had, by that time, attributed His miraculous powers to Satan (Mt. 9:32-34; 12:22-41; Mk. 3:22-30; Lk. 11:14-23), which meant most of the Jewish population would listen to the Pharisees and Sadducees and reject Christ out of hand. Second, as stated by the Messiah when questioned by His disciples, He spoke in parables to fulfill the prophecies concerning Him. Third, Jesus spoke in parables to confuse the unbeliever, since the parables concerned the judgment which would befall those who rejected Him. Finally, Christ spoke in parables in order to continue revealing the truth of the kingdom of God to those who believed in Him, and were willing to explore the truth of His message.

Think of a parable as a walnut. Inside its hard shell is the meat. To get at the meat, it is first necessary to open the shell. The lazy man either ignores the nut because the shell poses too much of a problem for him to crack; or, he crushes it, and the meat within it is rendered useless. The diligent man, on the other hand, carefully removes the shell and the meat, upon which he can now feast, remains intact for him to enjoy.

Christ's incarnation, and the entire process of redemption, is a mystery which could never be discerned by man without divine revelation. Divine revelation is given only to those who earnestly, and in good faith, seek it. Therefore, the first step to understanding the preeminence of God must be faith. Fortunately, it is not a large step. It is, in fact, a baby step: divinely inspired with an abundance of proof for baby Christians.

Faith opens the spiritual eyes of man, and the mysteries which confound and baffle the carnal man are more easily discerned, and more completely understood. To prove the validity of His word, God assured His creation He would provide prophetic signs through which man would know He was, He is, and shall forever be, God.

> *"I have declared the former things from the beginning; and they went forth out of My mouth, and I showed them; I did them suddenly, and they came to pass...I have even from the beginning declared it to thee, before it came to pass I showed it to thee, lest thou should say, Mine idol hath done them, and my carved image, and my melted image, hath commanded them...Mine hand also hath laid the foundation of the earth, and My right hand hath spread out the heavens..."* (Isa. 48:3, 5, 13; KJV)

There is no greater test of the validity of the Bible than in the fulfillment of prophecy. Several years ago a mathematician calculated that there was only one chance in 87,000,000,000,000,000,000,000,000,000,000,000,000,000,000,000,000,000,000,000,000,000,000,000,000,000,000,000,000, 000,000, 000,000,000,000 that the prophecies concerning the first coming of Jesus Christ could have been correct based exclusively on guesswork. Multiply that number by all of the fulfilled prophecies in the Bible, and the odds of guesswork playing any role becomes absolutely astronomical!

The cynic, in response to this statement, will offer, in the defense of humanism, prophecies from the likes of Nostradamus—something the nontheist has done for two hundred years—arguing that the prophecies of Nostradamus are as accurate, if not more accurate, than those found in the Bible. There is, however, no truth in their argument. The prophecies of Nostradamus are, more often than not, vague ramblings which can be applied equally to countless events throughout history. Biblical prophecy, as previously stated, is specific and relates only to the specific person or event—usually described by name or geographic area—for which it is intended.

God is real. That He is the Creator and not a creation is clearly amplified throughout the validated testimony He has given man. The fact that God holds authority over man clearly indicates He is not a creation of carnal man, who views himself as the center of authority on earth. After all, is that not the reason man denies Him?

How was the universe created?

The sheer multiplicity of theories which have been advanced over the ages to explain how the universe was created and how the planet upon which we reside was formed and developed are far too numerous to count, and too absurd to remember. Most of the theories which man has proposed to explain not only his own origin, but that of his world and his universe, were grounded neither in fact or sound mathematical probability. Usually they were based either on the prevailing point of view of whomever had the power and authority to enforce the perspective; or the view was egocentric, with man playing a key role in the creation process.

Although Isaiah described our planet as a sphere (Isa. 40:22) some two thousand two hundred years before Christopher Columbus confirmed it was; man has, from antiquity, insisted that the Earth was a flat, motionless island in a sea in the middle of the universe. Around this motionless mass man believed the sun, moon and stars revolved. The logic behind their reasoning was quite simple. Each morning the sun rose in the east; and each night it set in the west, slipping below the horizon as darkness erased the light. It was quite clear to the naked eye that the earth did not move—only the heavenly bodies moved. Supported by this reasoning, man in his ignorance, naturally concluded that the sun, moon, and stars revolved around the earth. Additionally, from the vantage of safety on land, man could also see that anyone who ventured too far into the sea risked falling off the planet when they reached the edge of the earth. Was this not, in fact, confirmed in the Holy Scriptures? Did not the Bible refer to the ends of the earth in several places (Dt. 13:7, 28:64; Isa. 5:26, 42:10, 48:20, 62:11; Jer. 25:33)? If the earth did not have an end, why would the Bible say it did?

In October, 1492, Christopher Columbus astounded the skeptics by sailing beyond the horizon without falling off the earth. Even though this voyage, together with two additional voyages the following year, caused man to reappraise his perception of the shape and nature of our planet, he still universally refused to reconsider his thinking regarding its placement in the universe. In fact, most men, believing Columbus simply hadn't sailed far enough to fall off, adamantly clung to their superstition.

Man was content with his geocentric viewpoint until 1514, when Polish astronomer Niklas Koppernigk, known to the world as Copernicus, completed a study of the heavens which verified that man's known universe was not geocentric (earth-centered) as was commonly believed, but was heliocentric (sun-centered). Although Copernicus' findings were reasonably accurate from a scientific perspective, his theory was not received well by his peers, who were largely content with the earth-centered theory, although it defied every known law of physics. Copernicus was ridiculed by the scientific community and threatened by the Roman Catholic Church. Faced with a choice of recanting his theory or facing excommunication—or worse—from the Church, Copernicus publicly withdrew his declaration, and apologized to the Church. Man is born in ignorance, lives in ignorance, and without God, dies in that selfsame ignorance which will condemn his soul to eternal damnation.

Today, man is learning more not only about the size, shape and nature of his own world, but of the universe in which our planet, our solar system, and our galaxy resides as well. Of course, that should not be surprising to the Christian, since it was prophesied by Daniel (12:4) in the sixth century B.C. Although science has done everything within its power to use scientific discovery to disprove the Scriptures, the reverse has actually happened. Instead of increasing the gap between science and religion, knowledge is drawing them closer together. Like science's *big bang theory* to explain the creation of the universe, the Bible itself begins with a dramatic declaration:

> *"In the beginning, God created the heaven and the earth."*
> (Gen. 1:1; KJV)

The Bible does not start with a philosophical argument for the preeminence of God; rather, it begins with a declaratory statement of His preexistence. He existed before the universe existed, because He spoke it into being.

> *"In the beginning was the Word, and the Word was with God, and the Word was God...All things were made by Him; and without Him was not anything made that was made..."* (Jn. 1:1; KJV)

The world may have been created six thousand years ago, six million years ago, or even six billion years ago. The timing is not important; nor does the Bible, in its original text, make any such claims or statements in that regard. Unfortunately, a Christian—who was a mortal human being like the rest of mankind—did. And, regrettably, a creation timeline—9:00 a.m., October 23, 4004 BC—calculated by Bishop James Ussher, was inserted as a marginal reference in the 1701 printing of the *Authorized King James Bible,* where it still remains in many modern day versions of the Bible.

The atheist, nontheist and agnostic will use those things prominent Christians say and do in an attempt to discredit not only the body of Christ, but the written Word of God as well. They attack Christianity and Judaism through us, through our conversations, actions and interpretative or doctrinal writings because the recorded Word of God has successfully withstood their attack for two thousand years.

Far too often Christians feel they must defend the Word of God through clarification and explanation. The Bible, in its original text, is the infallible Word of God and requires no defense. When man, in his finite wisdom, attempts to explain that which he does not understand, he does a disservice to the God he serves. But man is a curious creature who was endowed by His creator with a superior intellect which craves knowledge, and far too often, is without the patience required to prayerfully seek it; or lacks the wisdom to know what is, or is not, important in God's master plan to redeem mankind.

It should be obvious to every Christian who has ever opened a textbook dealing with the subjects of science, astronomy or physics, that proponents of the six thousand year creation theory will have a serious problem defending their position, particularly since the Bible itself does not support the theory. The Holy Spirit, who is the actual author of all of the books of the Bible, clearly tells us that in God's timeline, a day is like a thousand years, and a thousand years is like a day (2 Pe. 3:8). That is not to suggest that the Christian, in attempting to determine when creation occurred, should view each of the six creation days as a thousand years. What the Holy Spirit was saying is that when viewed in the context of eternity, time as man knows it, is irrelevant. God was not providing the Christian exegete with the spiritual calculator with which to figure it out.

Not content with a literal six thousand year creation theory which will not withstand scientific scrutiny, many exegetes now place a vast amount of time between Gen. 1:1 and 1:2. They believe it was during this period that Lucifer fell (Isa. 14:12-15), and that God destroyed a primeval heaven and earth, making the world waste and void *(tôhûw wäbôhû)*. This conclusion was reached by assuming the word *was* (i.e., "...And the earth *was* without form..."), *hâyâh* (to exist; to be; to become), is more accurately *hây*[e]*'tâh* (became). There is apparently no scriptural basis for the substitution of a past tense word for one of the present tense, so we must conclude the correct word in Gen. 1:2 is *hâyâh.* While the use of *hâyâh* does not preclude the eon theory, neither does it lend support.

The Word of God is mute—deliberately mute, I believe—on how long ago the universe was created. And, for that matter, at precisely what time during that process God created man. We, as Christians, have become so fixed on arguing about the chronological timeline that we have missed the essence of what this Scripture is actually saying: the universe and everything in it was divinely created by God at a particular time appointed by Him for its creation. Nothing else is relevant. Christians seem to be of the opinion if they cannot establish a reasonably accurate chronological timeline, they do not have a supportable position on the issue of an instant creation.

To compound the Christian's dilemma on the issue, German physicist Rudolph J. E. Clausius (1822-88) advanced the First Law of Thermodynamics in 1850. The thesis of the First Law is simple: *something* cannot be created from *nothing.* The establishment of this mathematical reality led scientists of that day to conclude that the *First Law* supported the humanists' view that the universe had existed forever. This led to the steady state theory of the universe. Thus, if the universe had existed forever, God could not have created it.

The fact is, scientific evidence now overwhelmingly supports the *big bang* or *instant creation* theory. Residue of the *big bang* was discovered by observers at the Kitt Peak Observatory in Arizona is the mid-1970's. The long held view that the universe has always been here in its present state has fallen to the wayside, discounted by scientists who have discovered through the use of microwave electromagnetic radiation that our universe is still expanding.

Since it has now generally accepted that the universe has not been in existence forever, and that it is currently in a state of expansion, some scientists reason that the universe has been expanding and contracting forever. The expansion/contraction theory, its advocates strenuously insist, is absolutely mandated by the First Law of Thermodynamics. Since we now know for certain that the universe was created from a primeval explosion, those scientists insist the explosion occurred when all existing matter collapsed in upon itself and a thermonuclear chain reaction occurred.

However, the Second Law of Thermodynamics excludes that as a possibility. The Second Law deals with a mathematical expression known as entropy. Everything which is subject to change possesses entropy. Entropy measures the deterioration of expended energy over a period of time.

The expanding/contracting theory is based on the unscientific notion that anything which expands also possesses the ability to contract. This theory violates the principles of the Second Law. For the universe to be able to contract it would necessarily have to cool. As it cooled, it would lose energy. The lost energy could not change back into matter and would therefore not be available again as energy when the remaining material collapsed and created a second, third, or fourth big bang. The matter which burned off with each expansion cycle, as well as that which would escape the gravitational tug of each contraction, would soon be depleted, and the entire process would simply cease. Each cycle would be less forceful than the preceding one as more and more energy escaped.

As Christianity examines the current scientific theories (which remain *unproved* hypotheses) concerning the creation of the universe compared to the Scriptural accounting of the event, no irreconcilable discrepancies exist. The Bible confirms that the universe (i.e., the heavens and the earth) was spoken into existence by the Word of God. The big bang was the voice of God.

In the fourteenth century, William of Ockham, an English scholar, formulated what has become known as Occam's Razor. This slice of logic declares that the simplest theory that fits the facts is usually the one that most closely corresponds with reality.

Science teaches that our solar system was created from gaseous materials which resulted from a primeval explosion in the voids of space, and that over eons of time those gases condensed and eventually solidified, forming planets which, trapped in the gravitational field of the sun, began to revolve around it. The scriptural account supports the scientific view. In Gen. 1:2, we see "...and the earth was without form..." In a gaseous state, the world would be without form. "...And darkness was on the face of the deep..."

Scientists believe the supernova collapsed into a spinning disc called a nebula. The gravitational field of the spinning nebula pulled much of the gaseous cloud into the disc of solar debris, creating a thermonuclear fire which became our sun.

> *"And God said, Let there be light; and there was light..."*
> (Gen. 1:3; KJV)

It is interesting that the Biblical account of the creation of what we now know as our solar system parallels the scientific account of how it necessarily evolved. The same is true with the geographic formation of the Earth. At one time scientists tell us, all of the land masses of the world were joined as one large, supercontinent which science named Pangaea. The single universal sea, of which the Pacific Ocean is a remnant, was called Panthalassa.

> *"And God said, Let the waters under the heaven be gathered together unto one place, and let the dry land appear, and so it was..."* (Gen. 1:9; KJV)

The molten, semi-liquid core caused the earth's crust to crack in scores of places and large, slow moving continental plates were formed. As those plates came together, pressure built, earthquakes occurred and resulted in the formation of hills and valleys. As the continental plates moved apart, fissures were created as the land masses separated. Pressurized lava from the interior of the planet broke through the weakened crust around those fissures with volcanic eruptions and mountains were created.

From the mid-point of the Pacific Ocean the continental masses move away from each other at the rate of some four centimeters each year. In other words, each year the Pacific Ocean becomes four-tenths of an inch wider and the Atlantic Ocean becomes four-tenths of an inch more narrow. The continental plates do not, however, shift at a uniform rate or in a uniform direction. The earthquakes we experience today are the result of those plates rubbing against, and up and over, each other. These things are all part of the creation mode set into motion eons ago when God spoke the world into being. The shifting of the continental plates also plays a key role in the endtime when, the Bible informs us, earthquakes and volcanic eruptions will increase in both frequency and force (Matt. 24:7), serving as a sign of the times.

Before continuing, it is important to point out to the reader that I am not advancing Genesis 1:1-27 as a model for scientific creationism, although many Christians, seeing the scientific parallels of this straightforward creation narrative, might be so inclined. To do so would open the text to criticism from skeptics since there is an obvious discrepancy in the sequence of events depicted in Gen. 1:14-19 when compared to what must logically be the scientific order of events. Light from darkness—i.e., the sun—is created on the first day (1:3-5); the distinction behind the sky (and the water vapors within the clouds—a phenomenon which, by the way, requires heat to create evaporation) and earth are established on the second day (1:6-8); land and ocean are created on the third day (1:9-13); and, on the fourth day, we see what will be argumentatively interpreted by the skeptic as the formation of the moon and the stars—events which scientifically, would have occurred in conjunction with the formation of the earth from a gaseous state. It must be noted that the description of the events of the fourth day (1:14-19) had nothing to do with the physical creation of the sun and the moon, which would have been an ongoing process from Gen. 1:1. Rather, Gen. 1:14-19 is describing the distinction between day and night through, quite possibly, the placement of the moon in an orbit around Earth.

It is interesting to note when the Word of God begins to discuss the creation of living things, life springs forth first in the sea (Gen. 1:20, 21). Again, science concurs with the Biblical account by affirming its belief that life on earth started in the primeval sea. It is not until we reach Gen. 1:21 that science and scripture begin to disagree.

> *"And God created great whales, and every living creature that moveth, which the waters brought forth abundantly, after their kind, and every winged fowl after its kind..."* (Gen. 1:21; KJV)

What exactly is God telling us in that verse? Quite simply, God is affirming that nothing evolved from one species into another similar or dissimilar species. God created each species after its own order. Life did not slowly develop through an evolutionary spiral, with higher orders evolving from lower orders, with an evolutionary eraser called natural selection correcting nature's errors. Contrary to the claims of the evolutionist, there is absolutely no scientific evidence which supports the theory of evolution! Evolution, like religion, is a philosophy. Unfortunately, evolution is a philosophy which is taught in our schools and universities as fact. Because it is a widely accepted theory that is mistakenly accepted as fact by most of the scientific communities of the world, evolution is perceived as fact by a majority of the population. Perception, unfortunately, has a habit of becoming reality—whether or not that perception is supported by truth.

Over the years, Christian groups have unsuccessfully attempted to have the Biblical creation theory included in the science textbooks used in our public schools as an alternate view of creation, only to have members of the scientific community insist that the Biblical view does not meet the minimum criteria required to be technically classified as a theory. Surprisingly, the arguments advanced by the scientific community to prevent creationism from being included in scholastic textbooks should also preclude evolution from being included.

Theories are advanced by observers of particular processes or events that, upon examination, establish the premises from which a logical conclusion is drawn. For a philosophical concept to be termed a theory it must meet certain criteria. First, the premise must be examined for demonstrable truths. Second, it must be supported by observations which explore and examine the properties or processes through which the theory was advanced. And third, proof which, under the proper conditions, will confirm the conclusion of the theory, must be offered. Once the theory is confirmed, it then becomes fact. Needless to say, neither the Biblical view of creation nor the scientific view can be confirmed, and hence, both remain theories.

The diary of evolution, archæologists, anthropologists and paleontologists alike will admit, is the fossil records which abound throughout all of the lands and seas of the world. These are the observable records of the evolutionist. What exactly do these records say?

Fossil records emphatically deny evolution.

Most evolutionists claim that matter evolved very slowly through minute genetic mutations which favorably advanced the species over a long period of time. Granted, the premise is logical since a dramatic genetic mutation would, in all likelihood, be so disruptive that the plant or animal to which it occurred would not survive, and the mutative process would end. It would logically require a series of mutations before a successful transformation from one species to another could occur. For the sake of argument, I will concede that these things might have actually occurred, even though such a transformation actually violates the principles under which the evolutionary theory is advanced. What favorable advantage would lungs provide the fish which, by necessity, lives under water? Would the evolutionist have us believe the fish decided it could fare better on land? Or that a fish developed legs, and much later developed lungs because it could no longer outswim the predators which fed on it? Is nature so precise that it can selectively target one particular class or species for evolutionary upgrade, and then perform a linked series of mutations on that specific class or species over a long period of time to achieve that objective—particularly when the first mutation in a series of transformation events, rather than being advantageous, would place that species at an environmental disadvantage? To do so, nature would have to have intelligence—and a long term game plan.

Scientists have always had a tendency, when examining fossil records, to make evolutionary leaps which are not supported by either fact or sound judgement. During the famous 1925 *Scopes Monkey Trial* in Dayton, Tennessee, Clarence Darrow, an American Civil Liberties Union attorney, offered the court physical evidence to prove his argument that Scopes was teaching supportable scientific fact. The exhibit Darrow produced was a representation of what became popularly known as Nebraska Man, a hominoid that Henry Fairfield Osborn, one of the country's leading paleontologists, named *Hesperopithecus haroldcookii,* after Harold Cook, the man who discovered the fossil—a single tooth! An imaginative illustration of Nebraska Man—constructed from that single tooth, which Osborn insisted combined the characteristics of the chimpanzee, *Pithecanthropus* and Man—was aggressively defended by the American scientific community which desperately wanted to believe that prehumans stalked prehistoric game on the North American continent. Defending their position, the scientific community argued that when other skeletal remains of Nebraska Man were found, they would bear witness to the accuracy of the artist's conception. When a complete skeleton was discovered in 1927, Nebraska Man proved to be a prehistoric pig.

The single greatest fallacy with evolution as a scientific theory is that it begins with a conclusion rather than a premise. The laws governing the establishment of scientific proofs have never been successfully applied to the theory of evolution, because evolution actually requires a much greater leap of faith than creationism. The idea that nature could, and would, selectively isolate specific plants and animals and set them on an evolutionary spiral to advance life suggests that nature has both an intelligence and a master plan. The view of the evolutionist is so narrowly focused that they eagerly grasp any evolutionary straw which appears on the surface to support their opinion—without applying theoretical logic to that evidence to determine whether or not it is likely to be true.

Like the Christian, eager to construct a chronological timeline, the evolutionist has constructed an imaginary phylogenetic model to support evolutionary linkage between the various life forms. The major problem with their model is that it infers not only that minor variations necessarily occurred within particular classes, resulting in the creation of other species within the classification (i.e., a dog and a cat having the same ancestral parent) but that fundamentally different classes arose from the same ancestral form (i.e., an amphibian or a reptile from a fish).

In the evolutionary chain, paleontologists offered *coelacanth*, a Devonian Period *crossopterygian* (lobe-finned fish) as the transitional link between fish and tetrapod. Coelacanth was believed to have become extinct sometime during the Cretoceous Period—some 65 million years ago. However, in 1938 a living coelacanth was netted off the coast of southeast Africa. Since that time several have been caught in the waters between Africa and Madagascar. At first an embarrassment to the evolutionist, coelacanth—which has remained unchanged during the past 350 million years has since regained its vaunted position as the evolutionary link after underwater movie footage of coelacanth was shot in 1987. Instead of explaining why contemporary coelacanth—whose ancestors supposedly breathed air through internal nostrils into membranous lungs when they rose to the surface of the primeval sea—does not currently possess those preadaptations to life on land, paleontologists refer to the 1987 movie footage which shows, in their opinion, that coelacanth swims, not like a fish, but rather, like a four legged animal. While observation is fundamental to science, it is also the least reliable premise upon which to establish a conclusion.

The evolution narrative is based entirely on assumption, and is not supported by any existing fossil evidence. Paleontologists have diligently searched the fossil records in vain for any evidence which links the invertebrates to the vertebrates, amphibians to fish, reptiles to amphibians, amphibians to mammals—and apes to man. Furthermore, since the transition from invertebrate to vertebrate, fish to tetrapods, nonflying animals to birds and cold-blooded creatures to warm-blooded mammals would require major transformations—which would necessarily have occurred over thousands, and perhaps millions, of years—there should be abundant fossil records to confirm these transitional forms. None exist.

Because they do not, evolution experts like Stephen Jay Gould and Richard B. Goldschmidt, formerly a zoologist at the University of California at Berkeley, have rejected the neo-Darwin theories believed by most evolutionists in favor of an instantaneous, accidental transformation theory which argues that after long periods of genetic stability, a species can undergo a radical change that is not recorded in the fossil history book. This theory metaphorically suggests that a reptile could somehow lay an egg from which a feathered bird hatched; or that a horse could give birth to a cow. (For this theory to have any merit, the ancestral creature would have to give birth to two such mutants—one male, and one female.) While the theory itself is ludicrous, it does offer the evolutionist an explanation—ridiculous as it is—why no transitional forms exist within the fossil records—something that has puzzled every paleontologist in the world. The absence of transitional forms is a universal phenomenon which has been noted in every phylum, class, family and species—including plant life!

Because of the absence of fossil records, the evolutionist has turned to a new device to prove his case: molecular biology. The fundamental tenet of molecular evolution is that all genes contain a coded protein DNA sequence, and that mutations can be traced through hybridized DNA typing because protein similarities and differences have been preserved by natural selection.

The theory behind DNA hybrid matching is that an evolutionary link is most likely to exist when mismatches in the 1.1% to 1.5% range are found.

When the nuclear DNA of man and the African apes (the gorilla and the chimpanzee) were hybridized, a base mismatch of 1.1% resulted. When tested against the orangutan, the mismatch was 2.4%, convincing molecular geneticists that they had firmly established an evolutionary link between ape and man. However, another DNA hybridization study, using a baboon type C virus transcript, contradicted the earlier find, and suggested instead that man was more closely linked with the orangutan. Since DNA hybridization is still an unproven science, DNA geneticists can manipulate results pretty much at will. Taken at face value, DNA hybridization is no more reliable than the fossil records which fail to prove the case of the evolutionist.

The evolutionist will continue his pursuit of the missing link not because sound scientific evidence suggests it exists; but rather, because the religion of the atheist—humanism—demands a satisfactorily convincing explanation to refute the Biblical creation it denies. The Genesis creation would be much easier for the evolutionist to understand if he could answer one simple question: "What came first, the chicken or the egg?"

The Christian, knowing God created everything from nothing, easily accepts the fact that the chicken came first. The evolutionist, who flatly rejects the Genesis creation theory, must also reject the most natural response to the question, leaving him in somewhat of a quandary. He has no alternative but to defend Goldschmidt's instantaneous accidental transformation theory, arguing that something other than a chicken laid at least two eggs containing chickens—one of which would had to have been a chicken, and the other a rooster. Needless to say, the odds of this happening are absolutely astronomical.

Was the world really created in six literal, 24 hour days?

There is probably no more controversial topic in the entire Word of God than the question of whether or not the world was actually created in six literal, 24 hour days. There is more strife among the body of Christ over this issue than the four most commonly debated issues which separate the brethren from fellowship with one another: absolution of sin after death, the promise of eternal salvation, the spiritual gift of tongues, and baptism as a means of salvation. The theological debate over this question is more controversial than the others simply because it transcends denominational barriers.

What does the Bible say on the subject? Gen. 1:1-2:2 describes what many Christians view as a literal six-day creation. However, Gen. 2:4 says:

> *"These are the generations of the heavens and of the earth when they were created,* in the day (emphasis added) *that the Lord God made the earth and the heavens."* (KJV)

This verse suggests that the creation was an event which occurred in a single day.

While those Christians who oppose the literal six-day creation theory view this verse as evidence that contradicts the timeline in Gen. 1:1-2:2, others insist the first chapter of Genesis deals with the creation of the universe, while Gen. 2:4-25 deals specifically with the creation of mankind. Advocates of this argument suggest the term *in the day* merely denotes that creation occurred within the prescribed time frame established by God, and is not to be taken literally. The phrase *in the day (b^{e}yôm)* is an idiom for *when.* In the NIV text, the word *when* is correctly used instead of *in the day,* eliminating the conflict. Gen. 1:1-2:2 is, in fact, a capsulated view of the entire creation of the universe. Gen. 2:4-25 is a specific record not only of the creation of mankind, but more important, of God's first covenant with man. That, in and of itself, merits the expanded view.

Because much of the Genesis narrative deals with primordial events, many Christians question the historicity of those chapters dealing with the antediluvian period (one through eleven). Some view the chronicles of both Adam and Eve and the Flood as either myth or etiology, and accept only the delineation from Abraham forward as historic fact. Most who hold that view believe science has put forth a convincing argument that the world is millions, if not billions, of years old.

However, it should be understood that while pagan mythology also records similar supernatural activities (such as a divine creation and, in most cases, a primordial flood) science has confirmed that the world did experience a universal flood sometime in its primordial past. In other words, as a Christian, you can be certain the events and explanations offered in the Genesis account are true.

The question which now remains unanswered is simple: does the terminology of Genesis 1:1-2:2 suggest the *days* of creation were literal 24-hour days, or do they merely impart divisions of time without specific cyclical reference? The first clues are found in Gen. 1:27:

> *"So God created man in His own image, in the image of God created He him; male and female created He them."* (KJV)

This is an important verse because it establishes an indisputable cyclical reference to time. Most Christians read Gen. 1:27 as a continuous, unbroken creation act which occurred in the waning hours of the sixth day, after the creation of the reptiles and the land animals. However, we must be careful not to apply the rule of *absolute literalism* if absolute literalism was not intended.

As we examine Gen. 2:4-25, we can view the creation story in much greater detail; and, in doing so, we are treated to a revelation which is not obvious in the creation overview depicted in Gen. 1:27. An unspecified period of time elapses between the creation of Adam and that of Eve.

After forming man from the dust of the earth and breathing life into his nostrils (Gen. 2:7), God took the man and placed him in the Garden which was in Eden, to till the earth and maintain the garden (Gen. 2:15). Adam was made caretaker of the Garden, with the added responsibility of naming all of God's creatures which were in the Garden (Gen. 2:19-20).

While not explicitly stated, the scriptural content supports the conclusion that a span of time elapsed between 2:7 (the creation of man) and 2:22 (the creation of woman). In verse 20 we see that Adam had just completed the task of naming all of the animals. Carl von Linne, the eighteenth century Swedish botanist (known to the world simply as Linnæus) required several decades just to name the plants and animals found in Europe. Granted, Linnæus named everything by kingdom, phylum, family, class, subclass and species. It is, of course, much less time-consuming to simply call a cow a cow, rather than an animalia/chordata/mammalia/theria/antio-dactyla/bovine. While it may not have taken Adam as long to name the animals in the Garden as it took Linnæus to name all of the plants and animals in Europe, logic suggests it would have taken longer than the few minutes, or perhaps hours, which remained in that literal 24-hour sixth day.

Since we can now see something which appears on the surface to be a discrepancy in the Scriptures, we need to examine the terminology used in the earlier verses because Scripture always confirms Scripture. There are no discrepancies in the Word of God. At times we, as humans, fail to discern what the Lord is telling us; but at no time is God ever confused, nor does He ever contradict Himself.

Looking at Gen. 1:5, we need to examine the Hebrew rendering of the phrase, *the first day* as it is applied in that text. The Hebrew words are *yôm éhad. Yôm éhad* actually means *day one* rather than *the first day (hayyôm harison),* and more literally could be interpreted, in this context, as *at one time.* It would seem if God meant Gen. 1:5 to be literally interpreted as the first physical day rather than the first division of the creation process, either *hayyôm harison,* or *rö'sh* (the word used in Gen. 8:13 to specifically describe the first day of the month) might have been used. (*Rö'sh* means *first* or *head,* but is most commonly recognized by many Christians as a prophetic symbolism for Russia.)

Continuing our original thought, the second day (verse 1:8) is *yôm seni,* literally the second division rather than *hayyôm hasseni,* the second day—and so on, through the seventh day. It should also be noted that the definite article, "the," is not used in any of these verses, suggesting that Gen. 1:5-31 is not detailing specific time frames in terms of human hours, but rather, the Scriptures are merely outlining the sequence in which that creation occurred.

Advocates of the literal six-day creation see further evidence to support their theory in Gen. 1:3-5:

> *"And God said, Let there be light; and there was light. And God saw the light, and it was good: and God divided the light from the darkness. And God called the light Day, and the darkness He called night. And the evening and the morning were the first day."* (KJV)

Those advancing this argument are quick to point out that the use of the words *evening* and *morning* confirms a literal, 24-hour solar day. The fallacy of that argument is that the solar day was part of the fourth creation act.

> *"And God said, Let there be lights in the firmament of the heaven to divide the day from the night; and let them be for signs, and for seasons, and for days, and years. And let them be for lights in the firmament of the heaven to give light upon the earth; and so*

it was. And God made two great lights; the greater light to rule the day, and the lesser light to rule the night; He made the stars also. And God set them in the firmament of heaven to give light upon the earth. And to rule over the day and over the night, and to divide the light from the darkness; and God saw that it was good. And the evening and the morning were the fourth day." (Gen. 1:14-19; KJV)

Before continuing, it is important to make an observation for the edification of the reader. While the modern world views the start of each new day at 12:01 a.m., from God's perspective, the solar day actually begins in the evening, at sundown. The previous day no longer exists once the sun vanishes below the horizon. This thought is emphasized repetitively in verses 1:5, 8, 13, 19, 23, and 31. God was not delineating creation day frames in those verses. He was establishing time frame perimeters which would play a major role in the worship practices of His people, the Jews. In Judaism each new day begins at sundown. As we explore the death and resurrection of Jesus Christ later in the book, this observation will be imperative to our understanding of how Christ could be in the grave for three days and three nights and rise on the third day.

That the six days of the creation process were undefined periods of time, characterized with a beginning and an end, and not solar days, seems evident in both Ps. 90:4 and 2 Pe. 3:8.

"For a thousand years in Thy sight are but as yesterday when it was past, and as a watch in the night." (Ps. 90:4; KJV)

A watch is approximately four hours.

"But beloved, be not ignorant of this one thing, that one day is with the Lord as a thousand years, and a thousand years as a day." (2 Pe. 3:8; KJV)

Time, in the eyes of God is not necessarily the same as time as defined by man. Remember, God's time is eternal, man's isn't.

Whether God created the universe in six literal 24-hour days, or six days in God's time is not important. What is important is that God did create the universe—and everything within it!

Does the Bible teach that a vast millennia exists between Gen. 1:1 and 1:2, and that Lucifer fell during this period when a primeval catastrophe, which destroyed the earth, occurred?

Although the Bible offers no scriptural evidence that the fall of Lucifer (Isa. 14:12-15) was associated with a primeval catastrophe which destroyed the earth, advocates of this theory are again growing in number. The *Genesis gap theory* enjoyed a large degree of popularity for a great many years. However, a better understanding of the ancient languages of the Bible have caused the theory to fall to the wayside in recent years.

The gap theory was predicated on the belief that a vast millennia separates Gen. 1:1 from 1:2. Adherents of this concept see the "...without form and void..."

(chaos) of Gen. 1:2 as being inconsistent with a perfect, orderly creation which a perfect God would have created.

> *"In the beginning God created the heaven and the earth. And the earth was without form and void (töhû wäböhû); and darkness was upon the face of the deep. And the spirit of God moved upon the face of the waters."* (Gen. 1:1-2; KJV)

Töhû wäböhû is variously understood to mean a formless waste, or an empty place; or, possibly even a state of confusion (i.e, *chaos*). To further confirm their theory, gap adherents quote a portion of Isaiah 45:18:

> *"For thus saith the Lord who created the heavens, God Himself who formed the earth and made it; He established it. He created it not to be in vain..." (töhû)* (Isa. 45:18; KJV)

Because God did not create the world *töhû,* gap theorists insist that an original creation was implied, although not specifically stated, in those verses; and, that it was destroyed when Lucifer rebelled against God (2 Pe. 2:4; Jude 6; Rev. 12:4) and was cast out of heaven. However, Isa. 45:18 does not imply a new creation. The concluding words of the verse clearly state that God created the world to be inhabited—by man.

To make their theory appear more theologically sound, gap advocates interpret Gen. 1:2 as it was translated by Joseph Bryant Rotherham for the *Emphasized Bible* (*Kregel Publications,* 1959):

> *"Now the earth* had become *waste and wild, and darkness was upon the face of the deep.."* (Gen. 1:2; EB, emphasis added)

By interpreting *was* as *had become,* the meaning of the verse significantly changes from a universal condition to one that had been some other way before becoming waste and wild. The term *hay^e^tah* (was) is literally transformed to *had become.* For *hay^e^tah* to be acceptable as *had become,* the phrase "...was without form and void..." would have to appear as *l^e^töhû wäböhû hay^e^tah* in the original text. However, it appears as *töhû wäböhû hay^e^tah,* clearly indicating the meaning is "...was without form and void..." instead of "...had become without form..."

Gap theorists insist it was God's intention to create a perfect world, but He was forced to destroy it because Lucifer, the highest archangel, rebelled against His authority. God then, according the gap advocates, restored earth to a second state of perfection (Gen. 1:3) after the fall of Lucifer, and that it is this creation which is described in Genesis. The underlying logic of the gap theory is based on perfection—that a perfect God would not create anything less than a perfect world. (The gap theory also provides a convenient explanation for the fossil records of a primeval existence on earth.)

The Word of God, however, does not support the theory that God intended to create a perfect world in Gen. 1:1, or that He viewed His completed work as perfect. In fact, He did not refer to Creation as perfect—He said it was good. To confirm this, one needs only look at the original text. The word for perfect is *tämîm,* and occurs first in Scripture not in reference to the Creation, but rather, to describe Noah as "...a just man and perfect in his generation..." (Gen. 6:9). The Hebrew word for *good* is *tôb.* It is this word which God used to describe the Creation.

It is difficult to accept the notion that God would create a perfect world in Gen. 1:1, destroy it for imperfection when Lucifer fell in Gen. 1:2, only to recreate something less than perfect—and find that less than perfect condition acceptable. It is much easier to accept the idea that the *töhû wäböhû* of Gen. 1:2 has nothing to do with a second creation; but that it simply points to the fact that Earth, like all of the planets in the universe was, in the beginning, a shapeless mass of gas—without shape or form.

Does nature support Charles Darwin's theory of evolution, or does it support the Biblical view of creation?

Charles Robert Darwin (1809-1882) was born in Shrewsbury, in Shropshire, England. He was greatly influenced in his early years by his paternal grandfather, Erasmus Darwin. The elder Darwin was a physiologist, a poet, and an amateur botanist. He published an essay called *Zoonomia* in 1795 which anticipated many of the evolutionary theories which would be advanced by French naturalist Jean Baptiste Lamarck (1744-1829) concerning the principles of acquired characteristics—the backbone of Darwin's theories which were published in his essay *On the Origin of the Species by Means of Natural Selection* on November 24, 1859.

Darwin followed his grandfather's example by enrolling in Edinburgh University in Scotland, although he later transferred to the University of Cambridge in London, where he graduated with a baccalaureate degree in botany.

Shortly after his graduation in 1831, Darwin signed on the H.M.S. Beagle, a British surveying ship which was preparing to embark on a five year zoological expedition to the South Pacific. The Beagle's skipper, Captain Robert Fitzroy (1805-1865), signed the 22-year old Darwin on as the ship's naturalist.

Darwin's theories, like those of his friend and fellow naturalist, Alfred Russell Wallace (1823-1913), were influenced by two other men. The first of these was Thomas Robert Malthus (1766-1844), who wrote *Essay on the Principles of Population.* The second was Sir Charles Lyell (1797-1875), who wrote *Principles in Geology* in 1833 and *Essay of Geology* in 1838. The extent to which these writings influenced Darwin is not documented, but Wallace, in writing his recollections, said that after reading Malthus and Lyell while sick in bed, the idea of natural selection came to him "in a flash."

Darwin's diaries reveal that he began compiling data on the transmutation of the species in 1837 from his *H.M.S. Beagle* notes, completing his work in 1858. At that time, according to Darwin, he learned that Wallace, while living in the Malay Archipelago, had been working on substantially the same theory. Wallace's work, an essay entitled *On the Tendency of Varieties to Depart Indefinitely from the Original Type,* was offered to the Linnean Society for publication at the same time as Darwin's *Origin of the Species.*

Evolutionists are quick to point out that because of the distance between them, neither Wallace nor Darwin knew of the work of the other. This, in their minds, somehow made evolution a more palatable theory. However, the premise is not true. Darwin and Wallace were close friends and did communicate with each other through letters during the period when each was advancing his own theories. A letter written by Darwin to Wallace in 1851 still exists. Likewise, a portion of the content of a letter from Wallace to Darwin was published in essay form in 1855. In it, Wallace affirmed his belief that each species had descended from some other species, adding that shortly after the new species was created, the old one died off.

In 1858, Wallace, knowing Darwin was completing *On the Origin of Species,* wrote his friend that he was preparing to present his own paper on natural selection to the Linnean Society in order, one might imagine, to learn if Darwin would object to his submission prior to Darwin's. Darwin decided to withhold his essay until Wallace presented *On the Tendency of Varieties to Depart Indefinitely from the Original Type.* Lyell and botanist Sir Joseph Hooker convinced Darwin that the essays should be presented together—suggesting that both works were common knowledge to just about everyone. On July 1, 1858, both papers were presented to the Linnean Society, and were published the following year in it's *Proceedings of 1858.*

The publication of *On the Origin of Species* caused a widespread sensation, particularly in the religious community, since Darwin's views contradicted the Scriptural account of creation. In fact, Darwin, shortly before his death, compared his observations of nature with the Biblical account of creation, and declared that the Bible offered a manifestly false history of earth.

Early in 1925 the Tennessee state legislature passed the nation's first Creation Law, making it a criminal offense to teach any theory which denied Divine creation. The *American Civil Liberties Union,* founded in 1920 and still floundering in the waters of obscurity after five years, saw the Volunteer State's new creation law as a means to gain national attention for their organization.

During the spring of 1925 the ACLU began running classified ads in many of the rural Tennessee newspapers, seeking a school teacher who would be willing to help them test the new law in a court of law. The resulting court action, more commonly known as either The Scopes Trial or The Monkey Trial, was probably the first court case in American jurisprudence where the defense prepared its case before the crime was actually committed!

John Thomas Scopes (1901-1970), a 24-year old freckle-faced teacher who taught science at Dayton High School, answered the ACLU advertisement. It is still not clear to those who currently live in Dayton, Tennessee whether Scopes agreed to be the ACLU guinea pig out of a conviction for their cause or because he was in desperate financial straits and needed the stipend they offered as payment. Most believe Scopes simply needed the money. A few days after Scopes answered the ad, three ACLU attorneys arrived in Dayton and interviewed Scopes over soft drinks at Robinson's Drug Store on Main Street. Whether Scopes was the ideal candidate (or the only candidate), interviewed by the ACLU for this vaunted position, we will probably never know. Finding him an acceptable candidate for the job, the ACLU engineered the crime.

On May 25, 1925, Scopes entered the history of the United States. Stepping in front of his science class with a copy of *Hunter's Civic Biology,* he said: "We have learned that animal forms can be arranged so as to begin with the simple one-celled forms, and culminate with a group which includes man himself..." Within days of that statement, a special grand jury was impaneled, listened to the evidence, and summarily indicted Scopes.

William Jennings Bryan (1860-1925), former Secretary of State under Woodrow Wilson, and a three-time Democratic candidate for the presidency of the United States, volunteered to prosecute the case because, he informed the press, of his staunch Christian upbringing. ACLU attorneys Clarence Darrow, Dudley Field Moore and Arthur Garfield Hays defended Scopes.

In his opening statement to the jury, Darrow (1857-1938) said: "With flying banners and beating drums, we are marching backwards to the glorious age of the sixteenth century, when bigots lighted fagots to burn men who dared to bring intelligence and enlightenment and culture to the human mind..." In summation, Darrow announced it was "...bigotry for public schools to teach only one theory of the origin of man..." Today, the ACLU uses every weapon in its humanistic arsenal to prevent any view other than the scientific argument it first promoted, and then defended in the Scopes trial from being taught in the schools of America.

An *Associated Press* poll, taken over a decade ago revealed that some 76% of those surveyed believed schools should present both the Biblical and scientific views of creation. As a Christian, I must disagree. Only one theory—that which is best supported by scientific evidence—should be taught in our classrooms. The question is, which theory does science best support? Does science best support the theory of evolution through the gradual transformation of the species, or does it best support the Biblical account of creation?

Surprisingly, most people—Christians included—assume evolution is an established fact, and do not question the scientific *evidence* offered by evolutionists to support their theories. However, based on scientific evidence alone, evolution does not even qualify as a valid argument—let alone a valid theory!

The theory of evolution presupposes that all living matter arose from some less sophisticated lifeform completely by chance and, at some point, that animate life was miraculously created from an inanimate source. For the theory of accidental evolution to work, science must be able to substantiate that certain prerequisite conditions existed at the moment of molecular conception in our primeval world: that our atmosphere did not contain any measurable amount of oxygen; that it consisted, instead, of ammonia, hydrogen, nitrogen, water, methane and carbon dioxide. This is important, because in laboratory experiments, the synthesis of complex molecules of those ingredients is possible, and has been artificially achieved in an environment devoid of oxygen.

The theory which supposes the accidental creation of life is not based on empirical evidence, since scientists do not know to what degree these chemical compounds existed on our primeval planet. Rather, it's based entirely on speculation. Biochemists believe the necessary chemicals: CH_4,H_2,N_2 and H_2O, which are in abundance throughout our solar system, had to be present on Earth during the formation of life. Furthermore, since oxygen is biologically manufactured by plantlife, it is an element which could not have existed in our primeval atmosphere in amounts greater than 1%. However, because the theory of accidental creation requires an oxygen-free atmosphere, it cannot be used to explain evolution, since the life created in an oxygen-free environment could not survive once it was created. All known lifeforms on earth have always required an oxygen-rich atmosphere in which to live and propagate.

But let us suppose for a moment that is not the case. Assume instead that Darwin was correct, and that life advanced through a progression of increasingly more complex organisms to more superior beings. Would the mutations Darwin imagined be so disruptive that they could not survive in the environment which created them? What are the odds that the astronomical number of necessarily sequential mutations needed to advance any species up just one rung of the evolutionary ladder would occur in precisely the order needed? And finally, if such chains of events did occur, where is the fossil evidence to support it?

In 1890 a Dutch physician, Eugene DuBois, greatly influenced by Darwin's *The Descent of Man,* noted that man, "...being a hairless animal, probably arose in the tropics, and that the most likely place to look for early human fossils should be in Africa where there is a wide variety of non-human primates, including the two apes, gorilla and chimpanzee, which show the greatest structural and behavioral similarities to modern man" (*Man's Evolution: An Introduction To Physical Anthropology;* Macmillan; 1965; pg. 143; C.L. Brace & M.F. Ashley Montagu).

Lacking any scholastic credibility in the scientific world, DuBois was unable to raise the money required to fund an expedition to prove his theories. Certain he could prove his contentions if he could find some way to get to the tropics, DuBois joined the Dutch army in exchange for an assignment in Sumatra where he was given ample freedom to search for his missing link in the evolutionary chain.

In 1891 DuBois found a skull cap along the Solo River near Trinil. A year later, about fifty feet from where he found the first specimen, he found a femur. Still later, in the same general area, he found three teeth. While the skull cap contained anthropoid eye ridges, the femur appeared to be essentially human. Dubois decided all of the finds were the remains of the same individual, and announced to the world that he had discovered the missing link, which he called *Pithecanthropus erectus:* the erect ape man, or, as it is known today, Java Man.

DuBois' find, which was exhibited at the International Congress of Zoology in 1895, was greeted by the scientific community with more than a little skepticism, and a greatly divided opinion on the merits of the discovery. Some of the zoologists present felt the skull cap and the femur came from two entirely different beings. Others felt the fossils were from an ape. Still others believed they were human. Only the French delegation felt DuBois had stumbled across a significant paleontological find. Because he conveniently failed to mention it, none of the delegates at the 1895 convention knew that DuBois had also discovered two decidely human skulls at the same archæological level at nearby Wadjak, a year before his Java Man find.

DuBois, in fact, concealed the information until 1927 when Dr. Davidson Black (1884-1934), Professor of Anatomy at Peking's Union Medical College announced the discovery of a new species of fossil man, which is called *Sinanthropus pekinensis (Peking Man).* A year later, an anterior skull portion and fragments of a lower jaw were discovered at the same site. Later discoveries of skull fragments of both *Sinanthropus* in China and *Pithecanthropus* in the East Indies revealed one similar trait. All were victims of cannibalism.

Because the remains of cooking hearths and stone tools were found around the *Sinanthropus* and *Pithecanthropus* fossils, it was assumed both were reasonably intelligent sub-humans and that both were directly related to man. However, evidence collected over the past twenty years supports the point-of-view that both Java Man and Peking Man were animals: gibbons, gorillas, chimpanzees or orangutans. Whatever they were, it is clear they were not the toolmaking hunters—they were the food!

Sinanthropus and his Java cousin *Pithecanthropus* were both victims of modern man—who co-existed with them in the primeval world. In fact, just before he died, DuBois himself refuted his earlier claims that *Pithecanthropus* was the missing link by declaring his find was nothing more exciting than a large gibbon.

Science, however, refused to acknowledge DuBois' confession. Today, both *Pithecanthropus* and *Sinathropus* stand as indisputable evidence of the evolution of man from the ape. It suits the purpose of the evolutionist to use only that portion of the fossil records which best supports his view, and ignore all of the evidence which questions it.

Both DuBois and Black discovered the remains of Homo sapiens in the same archæological strata as their sub-human finds. In each instance, both concealed the fact. Yet most textbooks today place Java Man and Peking Man in the evolutionary chain between ape and man. The evolutionist is hard-pressed to surrender that which he wants so desperately to be true—even when faced with overwhelming physical evidence which clearly establishes the fact that it is not.

Most textbooks show an evolutionary chain which extends from *Pliopithecus* (a primitive gibbon) to *Proconsul* (another gibbon) to *Dryopithecus* (whose only fossil remains consist of a few teeth and a jaw fragment) to *Oreopithecus* (an ape), to *Ramapithecus* (whose only remains, like those of *Dryopithecus*, consists of a few teeth, a palate and a jaw fragment), to *Australopithecus,* to *Pithecanthropus* and *Sinanthropus,* and finally, to man.

As fast as the evolutionist adds a new link in his evolutionary chain, a prior link is broken. Almost three decades ago, paleontologists were forced to concede that *Oreopithecus* was an aberrant anthropoid. As previously mentioned, more recent investigations have established that *Pithecanthropus* and *Sinanthropus* were also apes. Even more recently, evidence was presented which suggests *Ramapithecus* was a chimpanzee. Yet the text books our children study in school still present these primates as collateral evidence that Darwin's theories concerning the descent of man were correct.

Whenever suggested evolutionary links are studied in an unbiased manner, with all of the available evidence found at the fossil site considered in the evaluation of the fossil record, each prospective progenitor of man has proven to be an anthropoid.

If Darwin's observations in the Galápagos Islands concerning acquired characteristics were correct, proof would be available in the form of fossil records which would show at least some transitional forms. It is interesting, as stated earlier, that in 8.5 billion fossils which have been found and examined, not a single transitional form has ever been discovered!

In *Science World* (Feb. 4, 1983), Dr. Betty Farber, a entomologist for the American Museum of Natural History, observed that fossilized cockroaches from the Carboniferous Age appeared pretty much the same as those found throughout the world today. Anthropologists studying the fossil records from the middle Devonian through the Carboniferous Age have found that other than with respect to size, insects have remained virtually unchanged for 275 million years. And, as discussed earlier, Coelacanth—theoretically a transitional model—has remained unchanged for well over 350 million years.

In the face of so much data which disputes evolution as a viable scientific theory, one might wonder why Darwin's theories are even *considered* in the scientific community, let alone *accepted* as fact. Evolution is accepted as fact because evolution is essential to the philosophy of humanism. If man is the byproduct of evolution, he is the master of his own existence, and is answerable only to himself. If, on the other hand, he is a created being, then God, not man, is the Master and man must ultimately answer to Him.

The humanist does not seem to understand that God does not rule by the consensus of man, He rules because He is God, the Creator. In my humble opinion, Darwin, the progenitor of modern evolutionary thought, discovered the error of his theories on April 19, 1882. Unfortunately, it was too late for him to do anything about it, because Darwin did not discover his error until the moment he passed from life to death.

Where was the Garden of Eden located?

Because contemporary scholars cannot precisely pinpoint the location of all four of the rivers which came out of Eden to water the Garden, they tend to view biblical Eden as imaginary. However, since the Word of God declares Eden to be a real place, we know it was (Isa. 51:3; Ez. 28:13, 31:9; Joel 2:3).

The name Eden, like Nod (the land to which Cain was exiled), is thought by many to be a generic word rather than a specific place because Nod *(nôd)* is derived from the Akkadian word *nûd,* which basically denoted migration. Additionally, the derivative *Nôd* parallels the root word as a place of homeless wandering. God cursed Cain (Gen. 4:2) and condemned him to suffer the life of a fugitive, to wander aimlessly throughout the land as a nomad. For that reason, Gen. 4:16 could be correctly paraphrased to read: "And Cain deliberately rejected God, who sent him forth into the land to wander homelessly as a fugitive."

Eden is derived from the Akkadian word *edinu,* which is itself based on the Sumerian word *eden,* which means a fertile plain or steppe. It is also associated with the Hebrew word *ádan,* which means garden of delight.

Based on the geographic description in Genesis, men have searched for the precise location of the Garden of Eden for almost 2000 years: some to confirm its existence, others to find gold, and still other because they believed within the Garden they would find a foundation of perpetual youth, or at least, of eternal life. The Garden, according to Gen. 2:10-14, is thought by many students of Scripture to have been located in the Persian Gulf area, based largely on the names of two of the four rivers which water the delta area of the Arabian peninsula before flowing into the sea: the Tigris *(Hiddekel)* and the Euphrates. The first river mentioned, Pishon, is said to have been in the land of Havilah *(häwilâ),* a land where gold, bdellium (believed to be either a pale, semi-precious stone or a pearl) and onyx could be found. However, it has been difficult to locate this area, which is believed to be anywhere from India, to Ethiopia, to Yemen to northern Sinai—or somewhere in between. The name Havilah may be derived from *hôl,* and may imply a sandy area, like a desert.

The second river, Gihon (which means gusher, bubbles, or fast-moving spring), flowed through the whole land of Cush during the Edenic period. It is likely that an earthquake or some other natural calamity caused the river to dry up, since it is only mentioned once in Scripture as a river (Gen. 2:13), and five times as a spring (1 Ki. 1:33, 1:38, 1:45; 2 Ch. 32:30, 33:14). The reference to Cush in Gen. 13 actually refers to the land of the Cassites. Because it is believed this river originated in the eastern mountains and descended down to the Mesopotamian plains, some have identified Gihon as the Kerkha River.

Needless to say, since only the Tigris and the Euphrates exist today, it is literally impossible to pinpoint the exact location of the Garden of Eden by tracing those rivers back to their common source, since Genesis clearly states only one river, Pishon, came out of Eden, rather than four rivers flowing into the Garden (Gen. 2:10). Outside the garden, the river parted and became four heads—*Pishon, Tigris, Euphrates* and *Gihon,* forming, it is believed, the arable tract known as the Fertile Crescent.

If the rivers of Eden did create the Fertile Crescent, it may well be that the Jordan River is possibly a remnant of Pishon. Shifting land masses have brought about many topographical changes on the faces of every continent. It is believed by many students of Scripture that the massive upheaval which created Mount Seir in Edom also diverted the Jordan River from its original course, emptying it into the Dead Sea.

The headwaters of both the Tigris and the Euphrates are found in the mountains of Armenia. From Scripture, we can surmise that the headwaters of the

Pishon and the *Gihon* originated there as well:

> *"And a river went out of Eden to water the Garden; and from thence it parted, and became four heads. The name of the first was Pishon; that is it with compasseth the whole land of Havilah, where there is gold...And the name of the second river is Gihon; the same is it that compasseth the whole land of Cush. And the name of the third river is Hiddekel (the Tigris); that is it that goeth forth toward the east of Assyria. And the fourth river is Euphrates."* (Gen. 2:10-11, 2:13-14)

The ancient Akkadian name for Armenia is *Uratu*. Its Hebrew equivalent is Ararat. Ararat is both a land (2 Ki. 19:37; Isa. 37:38) and a mountain range. When the flood waters receded, you will recall, Noah's ark came to rest on the mountains of Ararat (Gen. 8:4). After 377 days in the ark, Noah and his family came forth and offered a sacrifice to the Lord. Pleased by its sweet savor, God blessed Noah and his sons, and said to them:

> *"Be fruitful and multiply, and fill the earth."* (Gen. 9:1; NASB)

Was it irony, coincidence, or divine intent that God's instructions to Noah and his sons were the same instructions He gave to Adam and Eve:

> *"Be fruitful and multiply, and fill the earth..."* (Gen. 1:28; NASB)

in the same approximate place, on Mt. Ararat in what is now a forsaken stretch of mountainous terrain which separates modern day Turkey from Armenia. Mt. Ararat (Turkish *Agbri Dagbi*) consists of two mountainous peaks, Great Ararat (16,804 ft.) on the west, and Little Ararat (12,782 ft.) which is located to the east, on the Aras Plain. According to tradition, Noah's ark came to rest on Great Ararat. It should be noted, however, that Scripture does not specifically state which peak the ark came to rest on, stating only that:

> *"...the ark rested in the seventh month, on the seventeenth day of the month, upon the mountains of Ararat."* (Gen. 8:4; KJV)

Whether the Garden of Eden was located on Great Ararat, Little Ararat, or on the Aras Plain, mankind will not know until whatever petrified remnants of Noah's ark which remain are found. We can be reasonably certain from Scripture only that the ark came to rest in this general region—and not, as many suppose, in the southern area of the Arabian peninsula near the Persian Gulf. I believe the ark will pinpoint, more precisely, the location of the Garden, since I believe it was God's purpose to initiate the replenishment of the earth from the same spot He originated it.

If Cain was the first offspring of the world's first couple, Adam and Eve, and Abel and Seth were second and third, who did Cain marry when he was exiled to the land of Nod?

Adam and Eve had several children (Gen. 5:4)—both sons and daughters—of which Cain was merely first. In our current age of feminism, it is perhaps difficult to understand, but daughters were neither counted nor mentioned in Hebrew genealogies because the seed of inheritance always passed from first born son to first born son.

In Jude 14 Enoch is mentioned as the seventh from Adam. He was not the seventh person born of Adam, or even the seventh born from Adam's seed. Enoch was the first born son of Jared (Gen. 5:18), seven generations removed from Adam.

If you were asked to picture Enoch in his antediluvian environment, I suspect you might think of him walking and commuting, alone with God, in a quasi-edenic setting uninterrupted by mankind, much like that which Adam might have enjoyed before he allowed himself to be enticed by Satan. The picture, however, would be by no means accurate. Although only 280 years had passed since the Creation (and assuming an average of six offsprings per union), there could have been as many as 131,220 people on earth when Enoch was born ([A&E + C] X D^6). Taking that logic one step farther, three generations later when Noah built the ark, there could have been as many as 3,542,940 people living on earth ([A&E + C] X D^9) when Noah entered the ark.

Matthew Henry, the noted seventeenth century Bible scholar dealt with the question of Cain's siblings very well:

> *"Many other sons and daughters were born to Adam, besides Cain and Abel before this; but no notice is taken of them, because an honorable mention must be made only in those whose loins Christ...was..." (A Commentary on the Whole Bible;* Revell)

Hebrew tradition claims that Adam had thirty-three sons and twenty-seven daughters.

Before continuing with the purpose of this narrative, it is important to address one other question which is directly related to the issue, and which is usually introduced by the skeptic when this particular question is raised with the brethren. Although the question has already been answered, the question needs to be broached so that both the question and the answer may be viewed in continuum.

Cain, when he was being driven from the land, expressed concern to God that he would forever be a fugitive and that anyone who found him would kill him. Since he was being driven from the land in which all of his known relatives lived, who else need he worry about? Was his fear expressed because he thought one of his sisters would follow and slay him? Or, did he think Adam, distraught over the loss of Abel, would track him down?

Because the Bible only mentions Cain, Abel, and after the death of Abel, Seth as the offspring of Adam, we have been taught to assume that that was an accurate record of all of Adam's children at that time—without omission or exception. However, we must understand that at the time Cain killed his brother, he would have been approximately 129 years of age; and Abel, anywhere from 110 to 125 years of age, because Seth was born shortly after the murder (Gen. 4:25), and Adam was 130 years old (Gen. 5:3) at the time of Seth's birth.

It is logical to assume that both Cain and Abel had taken wives. And, although Scripture suggests that, up to that point, Cain did not have any children (Gen. 4:17), I am inclined to believe Abel did. It was, perhaps, fear that one of his nephews would hunt him down to avenge the death of his father which caused Cain to express his fear of assassination to God. In any event, in the three and a half forty-year generations which had passed since the birth of Cain, we can assume the human race had propagated to at least three thousand people.

While there is no mention in either the historic or aprocryphal writings of the Jews of any history associated with Abel, the Second Book of Adam and Eve, an aprocryphal fourth century A.D. writing, names Cain's wife as his sister, Luluwa (1:6) and Seth's wife as Aklia (7:4-5). The Books of Adam and Eve, as well as several other writings which date back to the first four centuries A.D., are a collected work of Hebrew traditions, folklore and myths. These writings are, needless to say, not divinely inspired. They have little or no value from either a historic or scriptural perspective, and are mentioned here purely for their value as Hebrew folklore.

Were the "sons of God" in Gen. 6:2 really fallen angels?

Almost from antiquity, the *sons of God* mentioned in this verse were thought to be angels who had not kept their first estate (Jude 6,7). This opinion was expressed by Flavius Josephus, the first century Jewish historian in his *Antiquities of the Jews*:

> *"...for many angels of God accompanied with women, and begat sons that proved unjust, and despisers of all that was good, on account of the confidence they had in their own strength, for the tradition is that these men did what resembled the acts of those whom the Grecians called giants."* (1:3:1)

Christian exegetes have found this issue much more problematic than their first century Hebrew counterparts. A more logical, although contradictory, opinion, but more in keeping with the Word of God is outlined here.

First, angels—heavenly or otherwise—are spirit beings with spiritual, rather than human, bodies. As spirit beings, they could not cohabit with women (Mt. 22:30). Observed from this perspective, we know the *sons of God* in this verse were not fallen angels, they were godly descendents of Seth. The daughters of men represent the ungodly descendents of Cain.

While the latter opinion almost totally precludes the former view from consideration today, there are questions raised by the first which are not completely answered by the second without diligent scrutiny.

> *"And it came to pass, when men began to multiply on the face of the earth, and daughters were born unto them, That the sons of God saw the daughters of men that they were fair, and they took them wives of all which they chose."* (Gen. 6:1-2;KJV)

The problem with this verse, and comparative verses such as Job 1:6, 2:1, 38:7; Ps. 29:1, 89:6, and Dan. 3:25, is one of confusion for many students of Scripture who were largely taught the Bible, with only exiguous exceptions, is a literal work—which it is—that means precisely what it says, and says precisely what it means. For this reason, most students of Scripture ascribe to the rule of uniform interpretation which, theoretically, will accurately guide his or her quest for knowledge in the Scriptures. There is, however, only one universal rule of interpretation which must be observed at all times when studying the Bible, and that is the rule of absolute inerrancy.

The rule of uniform interpretation mandates that the *word* used means exactly the same thing every time it is used, regardless how it is used. There is no scriptural basis for this opinion, which resulted not from the limited vocabularies of the Hebrews or Greeks; but rather, from our use of the English language, which is comprised of a virtually endless litany of words. (Each word in our language has a precise meaning, and means specifically the same thing each time it is used.) If you have ever used a thesaurus you know, at times, anywhere from ten to fifty or more different words may mean, with slight endemic variations, the same thing. The reason for the multiplicity of words in our difficult dialect should be obvious: through the use of words, we can even more narrowly define the precise meaning of the statements we utter or write. Uneducated in linguistics, the layman assumes the same to be true when reading translations of other languages.

In the Hebrew text, in Gen. 6:2, the phrase, sons of God, is *b*^{e}*nê* ^{e}*löhim*, and literally means sons of God, implying angelic beings. The same word, *b*^{e} *nê* ^{e}*löhim*, is used to describe what could only be angels in Job 1:6 (as well as the other verses cited above):

> *"Now there was a day when the sons of God came to present themselves before the Lord, and Satan came also with them..."* (KJV)

Because of this verse, many exegetes—who clearly understand that spirit beings cannot have carnal relations with humans—believe the sons of God in Gen. 6:2 were humans who were demonically possessed; citing, as evidence, the phenomenon of giants—who, in pagan mythology, were usually gods or descendents of unions between humans and gods. Others feel the sons of God were the rulers of the antediluvian communities, who in many cases, were viewed by those whose lives they virtually controlled, as deities. The reality is, there was common occurrence of giants in those days, and continuing to the time of David in 1000 B.C. In all likelihood, this abnormality was the result of genetic inbreeding.

Furthermore, if the sons of God in Gen. 6:2 were fallen angels who had communed with the daughters of men (an impossibility), they would most likely have been referred to as *b*^{e} *nê'hâsstan* or *b*^{e} *nê'helel*—both of which denote fallen angels. Nowhere in Scripture are fallen angels ever referred to as sons of God. Once departed from their first estate, they would no longer have any part with God, nor He with them.

We can safely conclude that *b*^{e} *nê* ^{e}*löhim* refers to the descendents of the godly line of Seth. The tragedy of the union between the descendents of Seth and Cain meant a rejection of the moral values which God established through the seed of Seth. It was the repudiation of these values that caused man to become totally depraved in the eyes of God, and brought about the Great Flood.

Man, a base character at best, has refused to learn from history. The conditions which brought about the flood existed in abundance when God destroyed the five cities of the Valley of Siddim, of which Sodom and Gomorrah were a part, with fire and brimstone. It was those same conditions which brought Jonah, the unwilling witness, to Ninevah to warn its 120,000 inhabitants that if they did not immediately repent, God would destroy Ninevah in forty days. Ninevah repented, and was spared judgement until 612 B.C., a period of some thirty-eight to eighty-eight years.

Those same corrupt conditions, best described in the ninth chapter of Genesis, universally exist within the world today. In fact, current levels of godlessness in our world of materialistic political correctness make the conditions which incurred God's wrath in Sodom and Gomorrah pale in comparison. Likewise, the judgment which befell Sodom and Gomorrah will also pale in comparison to the soon-coming retribution God has promised at the end of the period known as the *times of the Gentiles* (Mt. 24:3-28).

Like Ninevah, mankind has an opportunity to repent of its abominations. Unfortunately, like the residents of Ninevah, man's grace period to repent will soon expire. Our churches have become lukewarm like Laodicea, and man's deity has become himself. Judgment shortly awaits us somewhere down that yellow-brick road which the world's political, religious and economic leaders promised would direct the world to a humanistic utopia.

Did's Noah's grandfather, Methuselah, drown in the Flood, or did he die prior to Noah's entering the ark?

Methuselah was 369 years old when Noah was born (Gen. 5:25, 27). Scripture informs us that Noah entered the ark in the six hundreth year of his life (Gen. 7:11). Methuselah died when he was 969 years old. By combining the age of Methuselah at the time of Noah's birth with the age of the patriarch when he entered the ark, it is obvious that Methuselah died during the year of the Flood. The only question which remains unanswered is whether Methuselah perished in the Flood, or died of natural causes during the seven day period immediately preceding the deluge.

Gen. 7:1 suggests Methuselah, who was obviously counted among the godless rather than the godly, died during that seven day period, rather than drowning with the godless society which was swallowed up by the waters which covered the earth for 300 days.

> *"Then the Lord said to Noah, 'Enter the ark, you and all of your household; for you alone I have seen to be righteous before Me in this time."* (Gen. 7:1; NASB)

The key word in this verse is, needless to say, *all.* In the Hebrew text emphasis is placed on the phrase "...you and all your household...," stressing God's promise to Noah that because of his faithfulness, all those in his household would escape the flood which would destroy mankind within a matter of days. Noah's family was set apart from judgment. The fact that Methuselah—a patriarchal member of Noah's household—did not enter the ark with Noah, says something not only about Methuselah, but offers a valuable clarification concerning the promise of salvation as depicted in Acts 16:31 as well.

As few as they are, references to Methuselah in the apocryphal writings of the first to fourth centuries A.D. suggest that he, like Noah, was a godly man in the order of Seth and Enoch; and as such, Methuselah was a man who attempted to evangelize the corrupt society in which he lived. It is much more probable that Methuselah, like his antediluvian counterparts, ridiculed his grandson for building a boat the size of the ark in the midst of dry land and that he was more philosophically likeminded to his contemporaries than his grandson. God did not tell Noah that his household was exempt from judgement because of the righteousness of Methuselah. He said to Noah, "...I have found you righteous in this generation..." clearly implying there were no others in that state of being. Many linguists feel Methuselah's name, *mi-thoo-ze-la,* implies violence and wickedness; others suggest the last syllable, *selah,* indicates divinity, and implies that Methuselah was a practitioner of idolatry. Conversely, *mi-thoo-ze-la* may also be interpreted as a hunter; or, with respect to the syllable, *selah,* a godly person.

My opinion is based not on linguistics, but rather, on scriptural logic. One week before the Flood, Methuselah was living. Perhaps God decided Methuselah was simply too old and frail to make the trip, and would have been too much of a burden on Noah and his sons, since Methuselah was 969 years old. However, I seriously doubt it. It is more likely that Methuselah, as part of Noah's household, was divinely set apart from those who were destined to perish in the flood only because of God's promise to Noah. Yet Methuselah, as a part of that corrupt and godless generation, could not be allowed to live beyond the Flood where his pagan ideologies could influence the offspring of Shem, Ham and Japeth.

In Acts 16:31 Simon the jailer asked Paul and Silas what he needed to do in order to be saved. They replied, "Believe on the Lord Jesus Christ, and you and your household will be saved." Does that verse suggest Simon's salvation was transferrable to the members of his household? Or does it merely state that because of Simon's righteousness, his family would be set apart to be spiritually dealt with by the Holy Spirit individually? Of course, it means the latter, since salvation is not a transferrable condition. Each who seeks salvation must, through faith, believe to be saved.

Methuselah, the grandson of Seth, who walked with God, was the son of Enoch (who was translated to heaven without experiencing death) and lacked the faith of his forbearers. Because he did not believe in the God of his father, Methuselah, who—because of Noah's righteousness—was set apart from the judgment which was about to befall mankind, but nevertheless died in his sins just prior to Noah's entering the ark.

CHAPTER TWO

THE AGE OF THE PATRIARCHS

Why did God allow Abraham to disinherit Ishmael, his firstborn, and cast him from his household?

Ishmael, the father of the Arab nations, was born of the union between Abraham and Sarah's handmaiden, Hagar. Because Sarah was barren, she offered Hagar to Abraham as a surrogate wife to bear her husband's children. It was a legal custom of that day, based on the *Code of Hammurabi* (circa 1700 B.C.). According to the law, the offspring of such a union were considered to be the legal children of the husband and wife, not the maidservant. Through Hagar, Sarah intended to fulfill God's promise to Abraham that he would be a great nation (Gen. 12:12).

> *"And Sarai said unto Abram, Behold now, the Lord hath restrained me from bearing; I pray thee, go in unto my maid; it may be that I may obtain children by her. And Abram hearkened to the voice of Sarai. And Sarai, Abram's wife, took Hagar, her maid, the Egyptian, after Abram had dwelt ten years in Canaan, and gave her to her husband Abram to be his wife. And he went in unto Hagar, and she conceived..."* (Gen. 16:2-4; KJV)

It is amazingly conceited on the part of man to suppose he must—or, for that matter, even could—help God fulfill what man views as an impossible promise. It is difficult for the finite mind to comprehend that absolutely nothing is impossible for God, who created the universe and all substance within it. Not only did Sarah resolve to personally intercede to bring to pass that which God said He would do, so likewise did Sarah's granddaughter-in-law Rebekah when she helped Jacob wrest the birthright of the first-born from his brother Esau (Gen. 27:1-46). The historic rift between the Arabs and the Jews is rooted in those two acts of human intervention.

When Hagar became pregnant, a conflict arose between Hagar and Sarah. Hagar, because she could bear children, saw what she ambitiously believed was an opportunity to assume a role in Abraham's household which was at least equal to Sarah. Consumed with both fear and jealousy, Sarah went to Abraham:

> *"And Sarai said unto Abram, My wrong be upon thee: I have given my maid into thy bosom; and when she saw that she had*

conceived, I was despised in her eyes: the Lord judge between me and thee. But Abram said unto Sarai, Behold, thy maid is in thy hand; do to her as it pleaseth thee. And when Sarai dealt harshly with her, she fled from her face." (Gen. 16:5-6; KJV)

Fearing it was Sarah's intent to kill her, Hagar fled into the wilderness where she was found by an angel of the Lord who convinced her to return and submit herself to Sarah. Hagar conceded, and returned to Abraham's tent. However, the animosity between the two women did not abate, and in fact, continued to grow and fester for fourteen years—from the birth of Ishmael to the birth of Isaac, Abraham's heir apparent.

Because God wanted man to understand He was deliberately creating a people unto Him, He held Sarah barren until such time in her life, and the life of her husband, that childbearing was an impossibility. To have a man of eighty-six—Abraham's age when Hagar, who was much younger, gave birth to Ishmael—produce offspring may have been uncommon, but it was not miraculous. However, when a woman in her nineties and a centenarian man, produce an offspring—that, in and of itself, can be termed something of a scientific rarity if not a miracle.

The jealousy which Sarah had experienced over Hagar throughout most of her life was now transferred to Hagar's son, Ishmael, who viewed the birth of Isaac as a threat to his birthright as the firstborn of the patriarch. When Sarah witnessed the animosity of Ishmael towards her son in the form of mockery (Gen. 21:9), she feared both for Isaac's life and his birthright, and demanded that Abraham expel the Egyptian and her son from his camp (Gen. 21:10).

Sarah's demand might appear hard-hearted and callous in a contemporary society, but such harsh practices were quite common in the days of Abraham. And, while Sarah's exaction distressed Abraham greatly, Scripture clearly shows that her demand was actually God's will at that time (Gen. 21:12-13). It was actually necessary to expel Ishmael so the rights and privileges of the first-born could be fully granted to Isaac, the rightful heir. Isaac, the son promised to Abraham by God, was divinely appointed to be the father of the nation Israel.

"Through Isaac your descendents shall be named..."
(Gen. 21:12; NASB)

Symbolically, Ishmael represents the bondage of the law. Ishmael was born of a bondservant. Although he was born of the seed of his master, he was still under bondage—a possession of his master. When Sarah abrogated the surrogacy of his birth, Ishmael was viewed only as Hagar's son. As such, he was not acceptable to inherit Abraham's possessions, since he was technically one of them. If we place ourselves under the law, we are also technically not acceptable to inherit the kingdom of God.

Ishmael was cast out as the law itself was cast out when Jesus Christ, the seed of promise (represented in this analogy by Isaac), came. Isaac represents the promise of grace through faith (Gen. 18:10-14). He was born free of the law of bondage—just as we are free of the shackles of the law through the atoning blood of Jesus, who is Himself the Seed of Promise typified by Isaac.

Did God destroy only Sodom and Gomorrah with fire and brimstone, or were other cities in that area destroyed as well?

God has been dealing with the baseness of man since the time of Adam, and man has quickly forgotten the retribution which God always exacts for humanistic corruptness, believing perhaps, since those catastrophes were initiated against societies in another age, the lessons which should have been learned were no longer relevant.

No human being over the age of twelve living on earth today—theist, nontheist or atheist, aboriginal or educated—can say, with any degree of integrity, they have not heard stories of a primeval flood which covered Earth during antediluvian days, virtually destroying all life, except that which lived within or upon the universal sea. To some, the story of the Flood was presented as folklore, to others it represented mythology, and to still others, it was presented as biblical history. But in each instance it was presented in the form of a deity, or deities, punishing a willful mankind for its transgressions against that deity or deities. Every society on Earth, and every society which has ever existed on Earth, knows of the Flood. Granted, as I said, some attribute the Flood to a pagan deity, or groups of deities. Others, while acknowledging the information received, simply deny it took place.

Mankind universally knows of the Flood because the Flood was a historic event which God, through Noah, etched in the memory of man as an indelible warning that godly retribution always follows human corruption.

For 317 days Noah and his family drifted aimlessly in the ark. How much of that time, do you imagine, was spent remembering the fearful screams of their former neighbors—many of whom were cousins, nieces, nephews, uncles and aunts—as the flood waters which erupted both from heaven and the bowels of the earth swallowed them? Noah and his family had witnessed firsthand the terrible wrath of God, and it was a lesson Noah would certainly have instructed his sons to teach to their children, determined that mankind not forget, lest they be revisited with God's wrath. The *Pseudepigrapha* records, in the Apocalypse of Adam, the following:

> *"Then Noah will reply, 'I shall bear witness before Your might that it is not from me that the race of these men has come, not from my sons... [5 lines missing] "...knowledge...'"* (Adam 3:16)
> *"Then Noah...divide(d) all the earth among his sons, Ham and Japeth and Shem. He (said) to them, 'My sons, hear my words. Behold, I have divided the earth among you. But serve Him in fear and subjection all the days of your life. Do not let your seed depart from the face of God the Almighty..." [5 lines missing] "Then Shem, the son of Noah (said), 'My seed will be pleasing before you and your power. Put a seal on it with your strong hand in fear and commandment, so that all the seed that has come forth from me will not be inclined away from you and God the Almighty, but they will serve in humility and fear of their knowledge...'"* (Adam 4:1-6)

God understood and, desiring to alleviate Noah's fear, promised the patriarch He would never again destroy mankind with a universal Flood. As a token of that covenant, God created the rainbow, whose sole purpose was to remind men not only of His covenant, but the reason for it. Noah did not interpret God's promise as a covenant which precluded some other future cataclysmic judgement—only that such a catastrophe would not come in the form of a universal flood.

Scripturally, uncleanliness and sin can be purged through one of only two methods: either by water (baptism is a water symbol) or fire. Since God promised not to destroy mankind again with water, we know fire will be the instrument He will use in the endtime. Likewise, fire was God's choice when Sodom and Gomorrah became a stench in His nostrils.

The morally bankrupt people of Sodom introduced mankind to a new form of debauchery: homosexuality. The term sodomy, which typifies any unnatural or perverse sex act, comes from that place. Sodom, whose ruins most likely lie under the waters at the southern extremity of the Dead Sea, was the largest of five cities located on the Jordanian rift, and was believed to be the economic hub of the area. The names of those cities were: Sodom, Gomorrah, Admah, Zeboiim and Bela (which was also known as Zoar).

When Lot, Abraham's nephew, came into that area, he settled with his wife and two daughters in Sodom where he, like most of the residents of Sodom, prospered. Although Lot knew the God of Abraham, and was a moral man who despised the lifestyle of Sodom, he could not bring himself to leave the prosperity, position, and power he had acquired. He did not wish to return to the humble existence which had previously been his fate when he was a nomadic shepherd like his uncle. Sodom controlled him, influencing everything he did. Lot represents the perfect example of the man who feels he can give his heart to Lord and allow his mind and spirit to remain in the world.

Had God not destroyed Sodom, Sodom would have destroyed Lot, as it destroyed his wife. Lot's wife had become so like the Sodomites, she could not turn away from the lavish lifestyle to which she had become accustomed without looking back. She now remains a permanent memorial to that catastrophe, enshrined with others who attempted to escape the fiery holocaust, in a five mile long ridge of crystalline salt just to the west of the southern edge of the Dead Sea, where one of the many free-standing crystalline salt pillars is appropriately named Lot's Wife.

What is most interesting in the records of the destruction of Sodom and Gomorrah is the verbal debate between Abraham and three angels—one of whom is believed to be a theophany (an appearance of the pre-existent Christ), which God sent to Abraham at Mamre. Abraham, convinced there were righteous people in Sodom and Gomorrah, became the world's first intercessor as he bargained clemency for Sodom and Gomorrah.

The corruptness of Sodom and Gomorrah was so pervasive that it had spread well beyond the walls of those cities, and had likewise afflicted Admah, Zoar and Zeboiim. Knowing God's plan to destroy all of the cities affected with Sodom's plague, Abraham pleaded with the angels, insisting there were righteous people within those cities who would be killed along with the guilty. Although Abraham abhorred the wickedness of the Sodomites, he prayed that the righteous among them—including his nephew—might be spared. Abraham, who first asked if fifty righteous people could be found, would God spare the city, eventually pleaded his case on ten just people. God agreed, if ten righteous people were found in Sodom, the city would be spared. Only one, Lot, existed.

While Gen. 19:1-29 depicts only the destruction of Sodom and Gomorrah, other scriptural references indicate at least four of the five plains cities were destroyed by the fire and brimstone which rained down from heaven (Jude 7) on Sodom.

Zoar, the smallest of the five cities (Gen. 19:21-22), was actually spared, not because it was innocent of the charges leveled by God against it's sister cities, but because Lot pleaded with the angels of destruction to spare Zoar so that he might find a place of sanctuary. However, the absolute devastation which Lot witnessed along the way to Zoar, combined with the likelihood that the people Lot found in Zoar were not unlike those who had just been destroyed in Sodom, frightened Lot so much that he did not feel safe there, either. From Zoar, Lot and his daughters fled into the mountains.

It is difficult to believe that once Lot left Zoar it would be exempt from the retribution which befell the other cities which incurred God's wrath. One additional verse suggests God may have destroyed Zoar as well after Lot and his daughters escaped:

> *"So when God destroyed the cities of the plain, He remembered Abraham, and He brought Lot out of the catastrophe that overthrew the cities where Lot had lived."* (Gen. 19:29; NIV)

The destruction of Admah is mentioned in Dt. 29:23, and again in a joint reference to Zeboiim in Hos. 11:8, where the prophet refers to the fate of Admah and Zeboiim as a warning to Israel to turn from its sin.

The scriptural account of the destruction of Sodom, Gomorrah, Admah and Zeboiim is still viewed by skeptics, like the Biblical account of the Flood, as folklore. However, in 1924 an archeological expedition led by Dr. William Foxwell Albright and Dr. Melvin G. Kyle found, in the southeast corner of the Dead Sea, artifacts and the remnants of five fresh water oases. The artifacts, which include great quantities of potsherds, flints and other items, date back to 2500 B.C. The society which created these artifacts ended abruptly around 2000 B.C. Archeological evidence further indicates the region was densely populated prior to that cataclysmic event which apparently destroyed all vegetation. While biologically desolate today, the land was once a fertile plain which would have supported a variety of crops.

Interestingly, explorations in that area by several American oil companies, including Standard Oil, revealed the presense of petroleum in this region. Whether it exists in profitable quantitites is debatable, but oil and asphalt do exist in the region at the southern tip of the Dead Sea. Geologists will usually be quick to acknowledge that wherever oil and asphalt are found, there is also likely to be highly flammable pockets of gas as well. The reference to bitumen (i.e., slime pits) in Genesis 14:10 suggests large quantities of surface oil and asphalt existed. Combined with the high levels of sulfur found in that region, a readymade catastrophe was waiting to happen. The ruptured strata in that area suggests an earthquake may have triggered the holocaust which devastated the cities of the plain. This supposition has been borne out to some degree since geologists have discovered that the valley lies along the path of a fault line which extends deep into Africa.

The scriptural significance of Sodom and Gomorrah, as it relates to the endtime, must neither be overlooked nor minimized by the Christian world today, since homosexuality, which is an abomination to God, expressly portends much of what is wrong with our post-Christian society that has proven, in many ways, to be more debase than Sodom and Gomorrah. Neither city, even in the heights of it's debauchery, offered its unborn as sacrifices at the altar of self-gratification. The world community of which we are a part is a much more corrupt society, and because of this, will one day face the greatest devastation imagined by man since the days of Noah.

> *"For as in the days that were before the flood they were eating and drinking, marrying and giving in marriage, until the day that Noah entered the ark, And knew not until the flood came, and took them all way, so shall also the coming of the Son of Man be."* (Mt. 24:38-39; KJV)
>
> *"For then shall be great tribulation, such as was not since the beginning of the world to this time, no, nor shall ever be. And except those days be shortened, there should no flesh be saved; but for the elect's sake those days shall be shortened."* (Mt. 24:21-22; KJV)

Who were the Shepherd Kings of Egypt?

Even before the days when Joseph, the eleventh son of Jacob, was sold into slavery, the land of Egypt was ruled by the Hyksos pharaohs. The Hyksos were a tribe of nomadic Semite warriors who conquered Egypt sometime between 2160 and 2000 B.C. According to Egyptian historian Manetho, the Hyksos appeared in Egypt during the reign of a pharaoh called Timaus (Greek translation) some 500 or more years before the Exodus. Manetho's chronicle states the Hyksos subdued Egypt without engaging in any major military campaigns. Their easy conquest of Egypt was attributed to the use of chariots and the compound bow. Because flocks of sheeps and goats accompanied their armies, the Egyptians called them the shepherd kings.

The biblical account of Joseph's years in bondage tell us that he was purchased by Potipher, an Egyptian (Gen. 37:36; 39:1), who served as the captain of Pharaoh's guard. Most people who read the Bible simply ignore this clarification, seeing nothing unusual about the fact that an Egyptian served as the captain of the royal guard in ancient Egypt. However, it was unusual since

Pharaoh was not an Egyptian. Also, it clearly shows the degree of trust which must have been exhibited by the royal family to Potipher, who was responsible for the security of Pharaoh. Most biblical scholars believe that very few important government positions were held by natural Egyptians during the reign of the Shepherd Kings. Potipher's was an exception worth scriptural noting because it clearly indicates he was an Egyptian in an otherwise non-Egyptian government.

While the Hyksos conquered all of Egypt, they ruled only Lower Egypt. A puppet government was created in Upper Egypt, and was administered by Theban princes. The inner circle of the Hyksos regime probably consisted entirely of Semites. The Hyksos rulers of Egypt were extremely unpopular with the Egyptian people. They were harsh rulers who burned Egyptian cities, demolished many pagan temples and enslaved the Egyptian population. When they were finally overthrown by the viceroy of Thebes, Ahmose I (sometime between 1580 and 1567 B.C.), the Egyptians destroyed every obelisk, stele and monument reminiscent of that period of Egyptian history. Because of that, little is known not only of the Hyksos, but also of the late and middle kingdoms of Egypt.

It was the Pharaohs of the middle period, the 18th dynasty, who oppressed the Jews. Thutmose III (reign: 1501-1447 B.C.) is believed by many Bible scholars to have been the Pharaoh of the Exodus. Others feel the distinction belongs to Thutmose IV who reigned from 1420 to 1411 B.C. Still others recognize Ramses II as the Pharaoh of scripture.

It is more likely that Thutmose III was the Pharaoh of the Exodus for several reasons. First, Thutmose III had an older sister, Hatsheput. When Thutmose I died in 1514 B.C., Hatsheput, who was fully grown at the time, and her younger brother, Thutmose II, ruled jointly until his death in 1501 B.C. Since Thutmose II was only thirteen years old at his death, Hatsheput, while sharing the title of regency with her brother was, for all practical purposes, an absolute monarch during that period. Thutmose III had no desire to share the throne of Egypt with his sister and brought about her downfall. When he became co-regent in 1501 B.C., Thutmose III capitalized on Hatsheput's sympathies for the Hebrews in order to strengthen his own position and successfully undermined her in the Egyptian court. Fearing assassination, Hatsheput was forced to abdicate her right to the throne, and went into seclusion. Thutmose III ordered the obliteration of her inscriptions from the obelisks of Egypt which recorded her accomplishments, thereby erasing even more of the history of the eighteenth dynasty.

Since Thutmose I's great-grandfather, Ahmose I, delivered the Egyptians from the Hyksos, the memory of Hebrew rule was still vivid in the minds of the ruling caste during the time Hatsheput shared the throne with her brother. The feeling in Egypt towards the Hebrews was one of both hatred and fear. The Egyptians feared that the Hebrews, who were growing large in numbers, would rise up and overthrow the Egyptians a second time. To prevent the Hebrew population from growing strong enough to accomplish this end, the Pharaoh, most likely Thutmose I, ordered the deaths of all newborn Hebrew males. If Thutmose III was the Pharaoh of the Exodus, then Hatsheput was the Egyptian princess who pulled

Moses from the Nile and raised him as her own son (Ex. 2:5-10). This was an offense which, combined with the fact that Hatsheput, unlike other Egyptians of the day, was a monotheist, would have provided Thutmose III with everything he needed to discredit his sister and perhaps even bring about her death.

Additional evidence which supports Thutmose III as the Pharaoh of the Exodus can be found in a seemingly unrelated scripture:

> *"And it came to pass in the four hundred and eightieth year after the children of Israel came out of the land of Egypt, in the fourth year of Solomon's reign over Israel, in the month of Ziv, which is the second month, that he began to build the house of the Lord."* (1 Ki. 6:1; KJV)

Solomon died in 931 B.C. after ruling forty years (1 Ki. 11:42). He became regent in 971 B.C., which means the fourth year of his reign was 967 B.C. Using those dates as a guide, we can precisely date the Exodus as an event which transpired in 1447 B.C. Assuming the date of Solomon's death is correct, and since we know Moses was eighty years old when he led the exodus out of Egypt, he would have been born in 1527 B.C.—during the reign of Thutmose I.

Most contemporary scholars feel Ramses II, based primarily one verse of scripture, was Pharaoh during the time of Moses. If Ramses and not Thutmose III was the Pharaoh when God called Moses, then the Exodus would have occurred sometime around 1290 B.C. The verse, certainly a powerful argument in favor of Ramses, is Exodus 12:37:

> *"And the children of Israel journeyed from Ramseses to Succoth, about six hundred thousand on foot that were men, besides children."* (KJV; see also Gen. 47:11; Ex. 1:11; Nbrs. 33:3-4.)

The name, Ramseses, itself suggests Ramses was Pharaoh, since it is unlikely the Egyptians would be building a treasure city for a Pharaoh who would not even be born for another 200 years. However, the historic and archæological evidence in favor of the earlier date is much too strong to either overlook or discount. It is quite possible, since the city of Ramseses was also known, in different times, as Tanis, Avaris, and Zoan, that Hebrew scribes inserted what would have been a more commonly known name at a later date. It is most likely that Ramseses was called Tanis during the period of the captivity, since one of the principle temples of ancient Egypt, the Temple of Tanis, was located there during the time of Moses.

Confusion and conflict between various theological camps over biblical dating, particularly during the period when the Exodus took place, stems from three factors. First, and probably most critical, was the practice of the Egyptians to erase those portions of their history they did not want ensuing generations to acknowledge. Almost all records of the 18th dynasty were eradicated. Second, because the Hebrew year was considerably different than the solar year as the Gentile historian knew it, adjustments were made to reconcile them. And finally, to add to the confusion, two overlapping methods of dating were used by the Jews themselves to record the ascensions and reigns of their kings.

The Amarna Letters, written to Amenhotep III around 1400 B.C. suggest

1447 B.C. as the most likely date of the Exodus; and that Thutmose III was the pharaoh of the Exodus since the letters, from the Canaanites in Palestine, were a plea for help:

> *"...The Habiri* (Hebrews) *are capturing our fortresses; they are taking our cities; they are destroying our rulers. They are plundering all of the country of the king. May the king send soldiers quickly. If no troops come this year the country is lost..."* (Paraphrased text from one of the Amarna letters.)

In addition to the plea for help, the letter also presents a parallel description of Joshua's conquest of Canaan. During the period from 1930 through 1936, Dr. John Garstang, Director of the British School of Archæology in Jerusalem, and a member of the Department of Antiquities of the Palestine Government, conducted extensive excavations in the ruins of Jericho. Amid those ruins he found pottery and scarabs bearing the inscription of Amenhotep III that suggest the fall of Jericho occurred sometime between 1411 and 1375 B.C. Additional archæological finds in Palestine verify that Jews from the tribe of Asher lived in that area prior to the 13th century B.C. (Since tribal divisions did not manifest until the Exodus, it is difficult to believe that the Palestinian finds were created by Israelites who did not go into Egypt with Jacob.) Another interesting discovery made by Garstang concerned the manner in which the walls of Jericho fell (Josh. 6:20).

The walls of Jericho were double, consisting of an outer wall which was six feet thick, and an inner wall, which was twelve feet thick. Garstang's excavation revealed the walls were built on a faulty, uneven foundation of brick and mud mortar. The walls were linked together by houses that were built on top of the wall. In Garstang's scientific opinion, the outer walls, which fell outward, "flat down," were shaken by an earthquake, and because they were linked to the inner wall by the houses, pulled the inner wall down as well.

In 1580 B.C. the Thebean prince, Ahmose I, the Hyksos' puppet ruler of Upper Egypt, rebelled against the Shepherd Kings. After thirteen years of conflict, the Hyksos were defeated, and Ahmose I became Pharaoh. The eighteenth dynasty began in 1567 B.C. with the coronation of Ahmose I and ended in 1358 B.C. with the death of Amenhotep IV. All of the Pharaohs who may have figured in the oppression of the Israelites reigned during this dynasty.

Based on the genealogies outlined by Josephus, Joseph was sold to Potipher in 1706 B.C., at the age of seventeen (Gen. 37:2). From that date, we can assume Joseph was born in 1723 B.C. Since he lived 110 years (Gen. 50:22, 26) it is likewise reasonable to assume he died in 1613 B.C. Within 33 to 46 years of Joseph's death, the ruling caste of Hyksos became a nation of slaves.

In dealing with the prophecies outlined in Genesis 15:13-14 and Exodus 12:40-41, the 430 years of affliction must be viewed not as having started with the death of Joseph as many suppose, but rather, when Abraham went down into Egypt around 1877 B.C., or at least, with the mocking of Isaac by Ishmael (Gen. 21:9). The logic of this argument should be obvious. If we are to suppose that the 430 years began with the death of Joseph, then the Exodus would have necessarily taken place during the reign of Ramses II. However, if you believe the Bible is the inerrant Word of God, then 1447 B.C. (or an approximate date) is the only acceptable date. Since we know from the Amarna Letters that Jericho fell sometime between 1411 and 1375 B.C., as well as from artifacts that establish Asher as a tribe in Canaan prior to 1300 B.C., the 430 years of affliction could not have commenced with the death of Joseph and must, therefore, be associated with one of the other two events.

We know from Scripture (Ex. 11:5; 12:29) that the first born of Pharaoh died the night the death angel passed over Egypt (Ex. 12:3-30) and that Pharaoh himself, in all likelihood, perished during the chase into the Red Sea (Ex. 14:21-30). If she had been alive, Hatsheput, as the first born of Thutmose I, would have died the night of the Passover. However, she died a disillusioned and broken woman sometime around 1487 B.C., perhaps at the hand of either Thutmose III or the court princes, who saw the rebirth of the Shepherd Kings through her and Moses. Persecution of the Israelites became much more severe after her death.

Little is actually known about Hatsheput since only one obelisk that stands 97 feet tall and weighing 150 tons remains in Thebes to remind history of her existence. It is likely she believed in the Hebrew's God, and worshipped Jehovah at the Temple of Serabit el Khadim in the Sinai, about three days journey into the wilderness (Ex. 3:18). The temple, probably built by the Midianites (Gen. 25:1-2), was constructed for the worship of the God of Abraham. Later it became the primary worship center for the Egyptian goddess Hathor, whom skeptics insist was the single deity worshipped by Hatsheput.

In his early writings concerning the history of the Jews, Manetho refers to the Hyksos as the Shepherd Kings. In his later accounts, which deal specifically with the captivity, the term *hyksos* was still used in reference to the Jews. In the later writings, the meaning of the term had changed. Hyksos no longer meant shepherd kings. From that point forward, it meant *the captive shepherds.* The Hyksos were so despised by the Egyptians that it was not enough to simply obliviate the steles and obelisks which referenced them. The Egyptians wanted to completely dominate and punish them forever. The period of the Hyksos ended only when Thutmose III allowed the Hebrews to leave Egypt.

Why did God inflict ten plagues on the Egyptians when killing the first born of Egypt would have been sufficient to secure the release of the Hebrews from bondage?

Why did ten plagues befall the Egyptians before Pharaoh consented to release the Israelites? Why did God harden Pharaoh's heart seven times (Ex. 7:13; 8:19; 9:7, 12, 34; 10:20, 27) when the Egyptian ruler might well have released the Hebrews earlier than he ultimately did if God had not intervened? Did God deliberately harden Pharaoh's heart, or did He merely allow Pharaoh's human nature to manifest itself to the point that his hatred of the Israelites simply overrode his better judgment?

There can be little doubt God deliberately hardened Pharaoh's heart, thereby ensuring that all ten plagues would necessarily be manifested before Pharaoh relented and gave the Hebrews their freedom. In Ex. 7:3-5, God said to Moses:

> *"And I will harden Pharaoh's heart, and will multiply My signs and My wonders in the land of Egypt, and will bring forth Mine armies, and My people, the children of Israel from among them. And the Egyptians shall know that I am Lord, when I stretch out My hand upon Egypt and bring the children of Israel from among them."*

In Ex. 20:4, as He gave the Ten Commandments to Moses, and again in Ex. 34:14, God clearly declared He is a jealous God and would not tolerate the worship of pagan deities by the Israelites, whom He had chosen as His people—the people through which the Messiah would enter humanity.

In the minds of idol worshippers, gods controlled both prosperity and disaster. More than 100 different gods were worshipped by the Egyptians. Approximately 30 of these were primary deities. Although the God of Abraham is clearly a jealous God, He is not a spiteful tyrant who elicits obedience through terrorism. God did not seek exaltation through the destruction of the lands and people of Egypt. Rather, God knew Pharaoh would not relent until He had sufficiently proven all of the Egyptian gods were powerless against Him and that He alone, the God of Abraham, was God!

It is doubtful that archæologists, bibliologists and historians will ever fully understand why the Egyptians worshipped so many different deities, particularly when two, three or more deities were overlords of the same realms. It is most likely because the Egyptians themselves were a diverse people with a variety of cultural differences and distinctions. Both *Hapi* (the fertility god) and *Sobkh* (the crocodile) were gods of the Nile. Three gods, *Amon, Ra* and *Osiris* were worshipped as the supreme deity. Both *Mut* and *Neith* were acknowledged as the goddess who created the universe (we know this goddess today as Mother Nature). *Hathor* was the goddess of the underworld, and *Wepwawet* was the god of the dead.

The Egyptians worshipped several triune godheads, but unlike the Christian Trinity, which consists of Father, Son and Holy Spirit within one Godhead, the pagan trinities all consist of a father, a mother and a son (three separate and distinct gods joined as a family unit). The first Egyptian deities worshipped as a triune god were *Ra* (the father god), *Neith* (the mother god) and *Geb* (the son). Probably the most well-known pagan trinity consists of *Osiris* (the father) *Isis* (the mother) and, depending upon the legend, either the reincarnated *Osiris* or *Horus* as the son-god. Others include *Ptah, Sehket* and *Imhotep* (a deified Pharaoh), as well as *Amon, Mut* and *Knonsu. Amon* and *Knonsu* are depicted by the ram—the symbol of Satan.

Secular critics of the Bible dispute the historicity of much of the Scriptures, particularly with respect to the patriarchs (Adam to Abraham), because many of the events recorded in the book of Genesis are duplicated in the pagan mythologies of ancient societies which clearly predate Israel's conquest of Canaan sometime around 1400 B.C. (the date of which is clearly confirmed by the Amarna Letters).

As previously mentioned, Noah would have taken great pains to make certain his sons and their sons, and their son's sons would teach their children about the Flood. A universal flood would necessarily be recorded in the mythologies of all ancient societies; and those who knew of the destruction of Sodom and Gomorrah would include that supernatural event as well. With respect to a pagan trinity which presented a reincarnated *Osiris* as the son god head some 1500 years before the crucifixion and resurrection of Jesus Christ, it must be understood that long before the birth of the Messiah, a spiritual battle for control of Earth was being waged. Satan, the archenemy of Jesus, was once Lucifer, the highest, most powerful archangel in Heaven (Isa. 14:12-17). Lucifer wanted to be God. When he was cast out of Heaven, Lucifer became the god of this planet—a position he still holds today.

Satan knows how the Book ends, and because he was there when it all began, he knew the history which would be recorded when the Book was penned by men inspired of the Holy Spirit (2 Ti. 3:16; 2 Ptr. 1:20-21). Satan has been aware since the fall of Adam that a Redeemer would appear somewhere in the history of man. To make it more difficult for man to recognize the Messiah, Satan created an abundance of counterfeits along the way. Pagan triune deities were only some of the ploys Satan has used.

Because of their diverse nature, several plagues were required to usurp all of the Egyptian gods. Scripture does not specifically state, nor suggest, that the plagues were either directly or indirectly intended to destroy the Egyptian deities. However, when the plagues are compared to the roles these deities served in the minds of the Egyptians, the parallels become obvious. Even before the first plague was leveled, at least one Egyptian deity was incapacitated by the God of Abraham. This happened when Aaron was commanded to throw his staff down before Pharaoh and it became a serpent, which devoured the serpents which were created from the staffs of Pharaoh's sorcerers (Ex. 7:9-12). One of the earliest gods worshipped by the Egyptians was the cobra.

The first plague God brought upon the Egyptians was the turning of the Nile into blood (Ex. 7:14-25). This plague proved that *Sobkh* and *Hapi,* the Nile gods, were both inferior to the God of the Israelites. *Hekqet,* the frog-headed goddess of fruitfulness was completely ridiculed when frogs covered the entire land of the Egyptians (Ex. 8:2-11). The fourth plague, manifested by swarms of flies, proved the pagan deity *Khepera* was powerless against the great *I Am.*

When God struck down the livestock of the Egyptians (Ex. 9:3-12), several deities fell. Among those were *Amon, Atum, Hathor, Herishef, Horus, Khnum,* and *Ptah.* Each of these deities were depicted by either cows, bulls or rams. *Ptah,* the apis bull, was the golden calf fashioned by the Children of Israel (Ex. 32:1-35).

The judgment by hail and fire (Ex. 9:13-26) was directed primarily against *Anibus,* the jackal-headed god, who held the scales of justice and determined right and wrong in the Egyptian society. The plague of locusts (Ex. 10:3-20) destroyed the credibility of *Serapia,* the god of the land who protected the grain fields of the Pharaohs from the locust. *Ra,* the sun god, and *Neith,* the sun goddess, both proved to be ineffective when God darkened the land of the Egyptians for three days (Ex. 10:21-23), but allowed light to shine in the homes of the Hebrews.

When God cast judgement on the first born of Egypt, He destroyed the remaining gods. *Taurt,* the goddess of childbirth, *Thoth,* the ibis-headed god of healing, and particularly *Athor,* the spotted calf goddess of the first born were crushed as the anguished cries of death echoed throughout the land. Even *Horus,* the personal god of Pharaoh, could not keep death from visiting the first born of the king.

Concerning the worship of idols, God said:

> *"Don't act like the people who make horoscopes and try to read their fate and future in the stars! Don't be frightened by predictions such as theirs, for it is all a pack of lies. Their ways are futile and foolish. They cut down a tree and carve an idol, and decorate it with gold and silver and fasten it securely in place with hammer and nails, and there stands their god like a helpless scarecrow in a garden! It cannot speak, and it must be carried, for it cannot walk. Don't be afraid of such a god, for it cannot harm nor help, nor do you any good...The wisest of men who worship idols are altogether stupid and foolish. They bring beaten sheets of silver from Tarshish, and gold from Uphaz, and give them to skillful goldsmiths who make their idols; then they clothe these gods in royal purple robes that expert tailors make...Say this to those who worship other gods: your so-called gods, who have not made the heavens and earth shall vanish from earth, but our God formed the earth by His power and wisdom, and by His intelligence He hung the stars in space and stretched out the heavens...But foolish men without knowledge of God how before their idols...All are worthless, silly; they will be crushed when their makers perish. But the God of Jacob is not like these foolish idols. He is the Creator of all, and Israel is His chosen nation. The Lord Almighty is His name."* (Jer. 10:2-16; LB; paraphrased)

Why did God order the complete annihilation of the Amalekites to the last man, woman and child?

As Moses led the Children of Israel from Elim (Ex. 16:1) into the Wilderness of Sin in southern Sinai, they were attacked by the Amalekites (Ex. 17:8-13). While the Bible is mute on the reason for the unprovoked attack, Josephus, the first century Jewish historian offers an explanation in *Antiquities of the Jews* (3:2:1). Josephus noted that, fearing the Israelites would grow strong, prosper and subdue the descendents of Esau, Amalek exhorted the other Edomite kings (Gen. 36:9; Ps. 83:6-11) as well as Moab and Ammon (the descendents of

Abraham's nephew Lot) to join him in the destruction of the Hebrews before they could overtake the land.

Amalek, ten generations removed from Esau (Gen. 36:16), apparently hated the descendents of Jacob as much as Esau himself hated Jacob over the loss of his birthright (Gen. 25:27-34; 27:1-41). The matter of Esau's birthright has been a matter of contention between the Arabs and the Jews since the days of Jacob, and is still hotly disputed today. When Amalek came down against Israel at Rephidim, Scripture confirms that God had to divinely intercede to keep the Israelites from being destroyed in that battle (Ex. 17:11-13). When Joshua, the son of Nun, finally defeated Amalek, God decreed that He would utterly erase the memory of Amalekites from under heaven (vs. 14) because Amalek tried to destroy the people God had set apart as His own (1 Sam. 15:2) when He brought them out of the land of Egypt.

While encamped south of Canaan in the Wilderness of Paran, God told the Israelites to go up and possess the land which He had promised them. Because the land was inhabited, and because they had been an oppressed people for 430 years, the Israelites were afraid. Through Moses they entreated God to let them send a vanguard before them (Dt. 1:21-22) to search out the land of the Amalekites, the Hittites, the Jebusites, the Amorites and the Canaanites (Nbrs. 13:2, 29) before entering. To prove to them that the land was good, God allowed Moses to send twelve men (one from each tribe) into the land of milk and honey.

God told the Israelites to possess the land without regard for those dwelling there. He assured Israel He would fight their battles as He had done when they were leaving Egypt (Dt. 1:29-30) It would appear that a people who traveled under the divine protection of God—accompanied by a pillar of clouds by day and a pillar of fire at night—would neither doubt His presence, nor His power. But the reports of strong cities and giants influenced the Israelites more, and being more afraid of mortal humans than God, they rebelled (Dt. 1:19-43). To punish them, God condemned them to wander in the wilderness of Sinai for forty years (until the entire generation that disobeyed Him had died). Had they trusted the Lord to fight their battles as He did in Egypt, the Amalekites would have been destroyed by Joshua and Caleb when Israel took possession of Canaan around 1400 B.C. Instead, Saul was faced with the same charge in 1030 B.C. Ten years after Saul was anointed king of Israel by Samuel, God said:

> *"I remember that which Amalek did to Israel, how he laid in wait for him in the way, when he came up from Egypt. Now go and smite Amalek, and utterly destroy all that they have, and spare them not, but slay both man and woman, infant and suckling..."* (1 Sam. 15:2-3; KJV)

Saul did according to the Word of God, except he spared Agag, the king of the Amalekites (1 Sam. 15:8, 20). Because Saul disobeyed God's instructions to completely destroy the Amalekites, his kingdom was taken from him (vs. 28) and given to David. Fearful of the wrath of God, Saul then slew Agag (vs. 33) with a sword. Nineteen years later, in the year Saul died, David was still fighting the remnants of the Amalekites (1 Sam. 27:8; 30:1, 17; 2 Sam. 1:1-16). Four hundred Amalekites escaped.

Sometime between 715 and 686 B.C., during the reign of Hezekiah, Simeonites killed the last of the Amalekites, with the single exception of the seed of Agag. Scripture indicates that by 480 B.C. the Amalekite population had dwindled to a single household—that of Hammedatha, the Agagite. According to Josephus, Ahasuerus (Xerxes I) favored Hammedatha's son Haman (who was, in his own right, an Amalekite prince). Because Haman was very popular with both the Persian citizens and those living in captivity in that land, Ahasuerus made Haman prime minister of his empire (Est. 3:1).

Haman, like his ancestors, hated the Jews. His hatred seems to have been originally channeled in the direction of Mordecai, a descendent of Saul through Sheimei (1 Sam. 9:1; 2 Sam. 16:5; Est. 2:5). Mordecai, who was a civil servant that sat at the king's gate (a tax collector). Haman's contempt for Mordecai may have been caused by Mordecai's refusal to bow before Him, as was the custom for commoners in the presence of kings and other royal dignitaries. It is not clear if Mordecai's unwillingness stemmed from a knowledge that Haman was an Amalekite, or if it was simply because kings and princes were sometimes worshipped as deities, and bowing before Haman might be construed by a jealous God as Mordecai's offering obeisance to a pagan deity.

In any event, when Haman saw that Mordecai would not pay homage to him, he became incited and decided to kill the old man as an example of his power over the Israelites. However, Haman's advisers warned him that if he killed Mordecai (who was viewed as a leader of the Jews), Haman would probably incite a rebellion of the Jews. According to Josephus (11:6:5), Haman went to Ahasuerus with an indictment not only against Mordecai, but against the entire Jewish population. Haman believed Ahasuerus would view him as a small, prideful man for seeking the life of one Jew who refused to pay him homage. Instead, Haman depicted the Jews, as a people, to Ahasuerus as

> *"...an ill-natured nation intermixed with all mankind that is adverse to Persian law, and not subject to kings, and of a different conduct of life from others, that hated the monarchy, and of a disposition that is pernicious to Persian affairs..."* (Ant. 11:6:6).

Haman offered Ahasuerus 10,000 talents of silver (approximately $5,280,000 of today's dollars) for permission to destroy the Jews (Est. 3:9). Believing Haman had the kingdom's best interests at heart, Ahasuerus waived the monetary payment and granted Haman's petition.

To determine the day that Haman's petition would be carried out, lot *(pur)* was cast. The decree, which Ahasuerus signed on the thirteenth day of *Nisan,* was to be carried out on the thirteenth day of *Adar* (Est. 3:7, 12). Ahasuerus' decree was sent to every province in Persia. The decree specified that on the prescribed day, the Persians were to

> *"...destroy, to kill, to cause to perish, all Jews, both young and old, little children and women [on that day]..."* (Est. 3:13; KJV)

Haman did not know of the promise God made to Abraham, and the seed of Abraham through Isaac and Jacob:

"I will bless them that bless thee, and curse them that curse thee..." (Gen. 12:3; KJV)

With that, Haman was doubly cursed, for of his ancestors, God had already said:

"I will utterly put out the remembrance of Amalek from under heaven." (Ex. 17:14; KJV)

The plot which Haman contrived to destroy the Jews came back on the descendents of Amalek (Est. 8:5, 11; 9:1-16). The gallows, which Haman constructed for Mordecai became the instrument of his own death (Est. 7:7-10).

At a feast prepared by Esther for her husband, Ahasuerus, and his Prime Minister Haman, she revealed to the king for the first time that she was a Jewess. As such, she pointed out, she was also subject to the king's decree concerning the extermination of the Jews. It should be noted that once a decree or statute was enacted by a Persian king it could not be recanted or repealed—even by the monarch who enacted it (Dan. 6:15). Realizing he had been duped by Haman, Ahasuerus, who was in a state of utter confusion, left the banquet chamber and retired to the palace garden. Haman, who had hoped to secure permission from Ahasuerus that night to hang Mordecai, suddenly realized his own life was hanging in the balance. He began to intercede with Esther for his life.

When Ahasuerus re-entered the banquet chamber, Haman had prostrated himself across the bed upon which Esther reclined (Est. 7:8). Apparently still in a state of confusion, Ahasuerus believed Haman was attempting to rape his queen, and accused him. Before Haman could respond, one of the king's chamberlains reminded Ahasuerus of the gallows which Haman had constructed for Mordecai. Without giving Haman an opportunity to defend his actions, Ahasuerus ordered him hung. Haman was taken out and immediately executed.

In the month Adar, on the prescribed thirteenth day of the month, the Jews, due to a new decree issued by Ahasuerus, gathered together in all of the provinces to defend themselves (Est. 9:2). Because of the strange turn of events which placed a Jew, Mordecai, in the position of Prime Minister (Est. 8:2), the Persians aided the Jews in the destruction of Haman's allies.

To permanently cut off the seed of Amalek according to God's word, the ten sons of Haman were also hung from the same gallows which their father had prepared for Mordecai (Est. 9:13-14). When Haman's sons died, that which God commanded of Saul almost over 600 years earlier was done. With the fall of the House of Haman, the last Amalekite was destroyed, and Amalek, who vowed to destroy the people of God, passed from the remembrance of man.

How could Moses have written the Pentateuch when his death is recorded within its pages?

It is truc that the death and burial of Moses is recorded in Dt. 34:5-6, and it is also true that Moses wrote the first five books of the Bible which make up the Pentateuch. Moses' commission to write the Pentateuch, or the Torah, as it is known to the Jews, is found first in Ex. 17:14:

"And the Lord said unto Moses, Write this for a memorial in a book and rehearse it in the ears of Joshua..." (KJV)

Further evidence of his authorship is found in Ex. 24:4; 34:27; Nbrs. 33:2 and Dt. 31:9, as well as 1 Ki. 2:3; 2 Ki. 14:6, 21:8; Ez. 6:18; Neh. 13:1 and Mal. 4:4. Christ assigned the authorship of the Pentateuch to Moses in Jn. 7:19 when He said:

"Did not Moses give you the Law?"

The charge to complete the Pentateuch was assigned by God to Joshua, who would have been schooled in writing by Moses, who was himself educated in Pharaoh's court (Josh. 1:8).

Skeptics do not seem to realize that the true author of Scripture is not the man who recorded the events which were described within the scrolls. Rather, the author is the Holy Spirit who provided the words which were transcribed. When you dictate a letter to a secretary, who is the author of the correspondence? The person who dictates the words, or the secretary who puts them on paper? The person who dictates the words which were penned, of course.

Man has discovered hundreds upon countless hundreds of ancient texts throughout the world during this century alone. None of them, other than the Bible, are viewed as anything more than historic writings. The Bible is absolutely unique among all writings because it is God-inspired. And while skeptics are quick to point out that many of the events and characters of the Bible have not been historically proven, none of them will readily admit that absolutely no Bible text has ever been disproven with contradictory historical evidence! And it has not been for the lack of trying!

In 1920 William Foxwell Albright, who was also a professor of Semitic languages at John Hopkins University, created most of the procedures which have made Biblical archæology a disciplined science. Using Bible text as a guide, Albright attempted to confirm, or refute, through archæological evidence, the truth or fiction of the Scriptures. Albright completed a chronology which suggested Abraham, Isaac and Jacob lived around 1800 B.C. He was the first to date the Exodus, and Joshua's victories in Canaan, around 1200 B.C.

As previously stated, the Amarna Letters, discovered in 1891-92 by Sir Flinders Petrie, contained messages sent to Amenhotep III by the Canaanites in 1400 B.C. who were seeking military assistance to defeat the Habiri (Hebrews). They indicate Albright's timeline was off by about two hundred years. Some skeptics insist the term *habiri* does not refer to the Hebrews but to some other warring tribe of whom no record exists. However, further proof that the Amarna Letters refer to Joshua's conquest of Canaan was unearthed when Garstang discovered the ruined walls of Jericho during his depression-era excavations. Garstang concluded that Jericho fell around 1400 B.C., independently supporting Petrie's conclusions concerning the dating of the Amarna Letters. Others argue that the presense of the Tribe of Asher in Palestine around 1400 B.C. repudiates Scripture, suggesting in agreement with Albright's opinion that since the Exodus took place around 1200 B.C., the presense of tribally divided Hebrews in Canaan means that neither the captivity nor the Exodus were factual events.

Since most Biblical archæologists agree with Albright's time frame in regard to the Exodus (because of the Ramseses references), placing it anywhere from 1290 to 1250 B.C., they also conclude that Petrie's *habiri* were not Jews and Garstang's battle of Jericho either occurred much later or it was representative of some other struggle—the fact that the walls of the city fell in exactly the manner described in Josha 6:20 notwithstanding.

Bible skeptics, in an effort to discredit Scripture, have insisted for years that all of the Old Testament was written well after the captivity, placing the text at the very earliest between 575-435 B.C. Yet in 1979 Israeli archæologist Gabriel Barkay discovered two tiny silver scrolls inside a tomb he was excavating in Jerusalem. The scrolls have been archæologically authenticated as pre-Solomon. On one of the scrolls was a benediction from the Book of Numbers. Not only did the discovery prove the existence of the Bible before 575 B.C., it proved at least portions of it were being copied long before most skeptics believed any part of it was written!

The problem most skeptics have with Moses is as you might have guessed, the miracle of the parting of the Red Sea. If Moses was a historic person, then the events he recorded in Exodus are likely to be real as well. If those events, the ten plagues of Egypt, the parting of the Red Sea, and the divine destruction of the Egyptians as well as the Canaanite defeat by Joshua, are real, then God, likewise, is real. If Moses was a historic person, then it is likely that Abraham was one as well. And if Abraham really lived, then it is likely that Noah was real also. That conclusion is totally unacceptable to the skeptic, because if Moses, Abraham and Noah were historic figures, then it follows that the Flood—of which abundant evidence clearly exists—really happened as well. For that reason, archæologists have expended much effort searching the Sinai for physical remnants of the Exodus. The consensus of the scientific community is that since the Bible suggests a vast number of people, some 600,000 excluding women and children (which would actually bring that total to around two million souls) wandered forty years in the Sinai, there would be some evidence of the journey somewhere.

Most likely, the number found in Exodus 12:37 was a scribal error which happened when the original text was translated into either Greek, Latin or English, because the word for *thousand* in Hebrew, *'élap,* is also the word for *clan* or *family.* Two isolated Old Testament verses support the view that neither Joshua nor Moses in writing this record, stated that 600,000 men, excluding women and children, embarked on the journey, but rather that 600 clans or families trekked into the desert—bringing the total number of people involved in the migration down from approximately two million to somewhere in the neighborhood of 5,500.

The confirming sentence in Judges states: "...Behold, my family *('élap)* is poor in Manasseh..." (Jud. 6:15; KJV). Needless to say, this verse could not be read as "...my thousand is poor in Manasseh..." In 1 Sam. 10:19, we see "...So now present yourselves before the Lord by your tribes and your clans...*('élap)*" (NIV). What is most interesting is that the *King James Version* translation uses the word *thousands* in this verse rather than *clans,* although it is obvious when the two renderings are viewed side-by-side that Samuel is telling the Israelites to present themselves to the Lord by tribe and clan, and not by tribe and *thousands.* There is a major difference between thousands and millions, particularly to the archæologist who is seeking confirmation. Physical evidence of the Exodus exists somewhere beneath the shifting sands of the Sinai, waiting for man to stumble across it. Less than five years ago, archæologists insisted that David, the father of Solomon, like Abraham and Moses, was not a historic figure because while they had unearthed secular evidence of Solomon's existence, none had ever been found detailing the exploits or reign of David. In 1993 a team of archæologists, digging in an ancient mound in Tel Dan in northern Israel, found a basalt inscription referring to the House of David, and more specifically to David as the King of Israel. David can no longer be disputed as a historic person.

Secular archæologists and paleontologists, who are prone to accept scientific theories as fact without any substantative supporting evidence, are far too quick to dismiss bibliology out-of-hand—even if the biblical theory fits the jigsaw puzzle more precisely than the scientific opinion! The biblical archæologist must have hard, physical evidence to support his theory before the scientific community will consider it. The secular archæologist needs nothing more than a supposition to have his opinion lauded as a valid scientific breakthrough!

The reason, as I have already pointed out, is obvious. Man, a created being, was granted a free will by his Creator; and with that free will, the ability to choose. Among the choices available to man is the prerogative to either accept or reject the Creator who fashioned him. To accept God as the Creator, man must then abide by the rules God has established, or suffer the consequences. Carnal man does not like the available options and instead seeks to eliminate God from the minds of His creation, somehow believing if God is erased from the minds of all men He will no longer exist (a technique used by pagan societies to change the future by eliminating the past from the memory of men).

Taking this discussion to its natural conclusion, we can reasonably assume that if the historicity of the Bible is true, the as yet unfulfilled prophecies dealing with the apocalyptic eschatology of mankind will continue to unfold according to God's plan, as the *times of the Gentiles* come to an abrupt end in the not too distant future.

CHAPTER THREE

SYMBOLISM IN THE OLD TESTAMENT

What are "types," and what is their purpose in Scripture?

A *type* is an Old Testament person, object or event which prefigures a New Testament person, object or event. An *anti-type* is a New Testament fulfillment of an Old Testament type. For an Old Testament person or event to be considered a *type* (such as Melchizedek) there must be an appropriate New Testament *anti-type* (such as Jesus Christ).

The Bible abounds with prophetic *types*. Some are fairly obvious; others are not, and require a degree of study to decipher. Many are all but lost because of an effort on the part of the early Christian church to disassociate Jesus from Judaism. For example, the Church changed the day of Christ's resurrection from the third day of the Passover to a pagan event which falls forty-three days after the vernal equinox. Many Renaissance painters depicted Jesus with blond hair and blue eyes in an obvious attempt to gentilize him.

To more fully understand and appreciate what God is trying to teach us through His word we must be able to recognize Biblical types when they are presented to us and understand their significance in relation to Christ. The Paschal Lamb (Ex. 12:3-11; Lev. 23:5) represents the sacrificial death of Jesus. Every Christian acknowledges Jesus as the Lamb of God, but few associate that lamb, or the Messiah Himself, with the Passover—of which He is an *anti-type.* When John the Baptist looked upon Jesus after His baptism in the Jordan River, he proclaimed:

> *"Behold, the Lamb of God, who takes away the sins of the world."* (Jn. 1:29; NASB)

Of Jesus, the apostle Paul said:

> *"Clean out the old leaven, that you may be a new lump, just as you are in fact unleavened. For Christ, our Passover, also has been sacrificed."* (1 Cor. 5:7; NASB)

As Christians, we have dutifully learned the Easter Story. We acknowledge that the Messiah came to Jerusalem for the Passover in 32 A.D., knowing He would be betrayed by Judas Iscariot, tried first by the Sanhedrin and the Pharisees and then by Pontius Pilate, who sanctioned His crucifixion by surrendering him back to Caiphias, the high priest. We learned that Jesus was crucified, died, was entombed. On the third day He rose from the dead. Other than understanding that the Passover was a Jewish rite practiced in remembrance of the Exodus from Egypt, most Christians do not realize the powerful significance of each and every event which transpired that week, and exactly how important many of these events were in the confirmation of Christ's identity as the Son of the Living God—and His authority to act as our propitiation. Likewise, few practitioners of Judaism realize these events, like so many Semitic traditions, were actually *types* which prefigured Christ's coming.

Our study for this text will deal with only one *type* with its corresponding *anti-type:* the Passover and the Paschal Lamb. By concentrating on only one *type* in this section dealing with *types,* rather than superficially touching on many, I hope to encourage the reader to more deeply explore the Scriptures for others. (In other sections of this book I will address other *types* and *anti-types* as they pertain to the subject matter under discussion.)

As you ponder this topic, one thing should become both quickly and abundantly clear: to recognize *types* when they appear in Scripture and to correctly match them with their fulfilled *anti-types,* the reader must have more than a cursory understanding of both Christianity and Judaism. Nothing in Scripture more clearly confirms the divine linkage which exists between Judaism and Christianity than the biblical application of *types* and *anti-types.*

On the tenth day of Nisan (the first month of the religious Jewish calendar), Christ entered Jerusalem by the East Gate for the last time:

> *"Then Jesus, six days before the Passover, came to Bethany, where Lazarus was, who had been dead, whom He raised from the dead."* (Jn. 12:1; KJV)

Most Christians read that passage without realizing that an important *type* was presented. The Passover lamb was to be examined for blemishes from the tenth to the fourteenth of Nisan, since it must be absolutely perfect in every sense to qualify as a perfect sin offering (Ex. 12:5-6). The last four days of Christ's human life are closely scrutinized by Scripture, and He is likewise found to be without spot or blemish (Lk. 11:53-54; Jn. 8:46, 18:38; 1 Pe. 1:18-19).

The Passover lamb was slain on the fourteenth day of Nisan (Ex. 12:6-7). The blood of the lamb was the symbol (a *type*) of redemption from the death angel who passed over the land of Egypt that night. Christ was crucified on the fourteenth day of Nisan (Mt. 26:2; 27:45-56; Mk. 15:33-41; Lk. 23:44-49; Jn. 19:30-37). Our sins are washed away with His blood (Rom. 3:25; Heb. 9:12-14, 11:28; 1 Jn. 1:17; Rev. 1:5)—and only through Christ can they be erased.

The Passover lamb was to be eaten in one household. It's bones could not be broken, nor could its body be divided and shared with neighbors:

> *"In one house shall it be eaten; thou shalt not carry forth any of the flesh abroad out of the house; neither shall ye break a bone of it."* (Ex. 12:46; KJV)

When Christ was crucified, not one of His bones was broken (Jn. 19:36) although it was a Roman custom to break the legs of crucified criminals to speed up the process of death by asphyxiation. The soldiers broke the legs of the two thieves (Jn. 19:32), but saw that Jesus had already expired (Jn. 19:33) and did not break his legs.

> *"For these things were done that the scripture should be fulfilled, a bone of Him shall not be broken..."* (Jn. 19:36; KJV)

Scripture verifies that the Passover typifies Jesus Christ—and only Jesus Christ! It is interesting to note that in John 1:11 the Passover is described as the *Lord's Passover.* In John 2:13; 6:4; and 11:55, it is specifically referred to as the *Jews' Passover.* When the Jews rejected Jesus Christ as their Messiah, they rejected the sacrifice of the Lamb.

Christ, the Paschal Lamb, was our sin offering to God. In Old Testament times, the sin offering was presented to the priests at the East Gate of the Temple (Ezek. 46:1-9). After the High Priest was consecrated with oil, the sin offering was sacrificed, and its remnants were taken from the city through the West Gate, and burned. As our sin offering, Christ entered Jerusalem for the last time through the East Gate. As our High Priest, He was consecrated with a spikenard of costly oil (Mt. 26:1-12; Mk. 14:3-8; Jn. 12:7) by Mary of Bethany before entering the city. It was because of the significance of this act that Christ said of her:

> *"Verily I say unto you. Whenever this gospel shall be preached in the whole world, there shall also this, that this woman hath done, be told for a memorial to her."* (Mt. 26:13; KJV)

After His arrest and mock trial, Jesus was taken from the city through the West Gate to Golgotha, where He became the Sin Offering for our sins.

What is the meaning of Ezekiel's vision of the four living creatures, and how does it relate to a similar vision experienced by John?

Ezekiel, the son of Buzi (the family of Zadok), was a Levite. As such, he was part of the aristocracy. Ezekiel was among the Judeans[1] taken into captivity by the Babylonians when Benjamin and Judah fell in 597 B.C.[2] Ezekiel was probably 25 years of age when he and his wife were taken captive. The Book of Ezekiel opens with the vision which begins his ministry during the fifth year of captivity. (Levite ministries traditionally begin in the 30th year of life.) Interestingly, the similar vision witnessed by the Apostle John on the Isle of Patmos occurred in John's old age, at the end of his ministry.

Because the intense love Ezekiel had for his young wife was apparently common knowledge within the Judean community in Tel Abib, God informed

---

[1] *Hence, the post-exilic name, Jew, by which the returning Israelites were called. At the conclusion of the Exile in 538 B.C. (coinciding with the fall of the Babylonian Empire), it was the Judeans who returned to Palestine.*

[2] *The ten northern tribes fell in 722 B.C., around the time the Assyrian king, Shalmaneser, died. Sargon, the son of Shalmaneser, claimed credit for the defeat and took 27,500 Israelites into captivity. The ten northern tribes were assimiliated into the Assyrian society. While the Samaritans in Palestine descended from the ten northern tribes, those Israelites taken captive did not return to the land of their forefathers.*

the prophet He was going to take her from him. Her death, combined with God's instructions to Ezekiel that he could not mourn her, would serve as a sign to the nation of Israel.

After her death Ezekiel, who was viewed as priest, prophet and teacher by the Judeans, began physically acting out many of the prophetic messages he received. Because of his strange behavior many of his contemporaries believed he was addled—and many historians view his writings with the same skepticism. However, Ezekiel was a major prophet who enjoyed a very special relationship with God. The phrase, Son of Man, which Jesus used to describe Himself, was used by God to describe Ezekiel 85 times, emphasizing the transcendence of God through him.

Ezekiel's first vision came to him as he stood with other captives along the Chebar River:

> *"And I looked, and, behold, a whirlwind came out of the north, a great cloud, and a fire enfolding itself, and a brightness was about it like the color of amber, out of the midst of the fire. Also, out of the midst of it came the likeness of four living creatures. And this was their appearance: they had the likeness of a man. And every one had four faces, and every one had four wings. And their feet were straight feet; and the soles of their feet was like the sole of a calf's foot; and they sparkled like the color of burnished bronze. And they had the hands of a man under their wings on their four sides; and they four had their faces and their wings. Their wings were joined one to another; they went every one straight forward. As for the likeness of their faces, they four had the face of a man, and the face of a lion, on the right side; and they four had the face of an ox on the left side; they four also had the face of an eagle. Thus were their faces; and their wings were stretched upward; two wings of every one were joined one to another, and two covered their bodies. And they went every one straight forward; wherever the spirit was to go, they went; and they turned not when they went. As for the likeness of the living creatures, their appearance was like burning coals of fire, and like the appearance of lamps; it went up and down among the living creatures; and the fire was bright, and out of the fire went forth lightning. And the living creatures ran and returned like the appearance of a flash of lightning."* (Ezek. 1:4-14; KJV)

Ezekiel saw and recorded in vss. 4-28, the Shekinah Glory of God surrounded by cherubim (10:10), a special order of angelic beings who minister to God and are the bearers of God's throne-chariot, described as a sapphire throne that was propelled by four brilliant crystal wheels that allowed it to maneuver in any direction without turning. Above the throne Ezekiel describes a vision in the appearance of a man—the precarnate Christ. From Him came the appearance of fire, and from around Him, the aura of the rainbow (Ezek. 1:22-28). The focus of our discussion, however, is not on the Shekinah Glory of God, but rather, the symbolism of the cherubim, which has significance to the Christian today in his or her understanding of the character of Jesus Christ that was manifested by the physical appearance of the cherubim.

Aside from Ezekiel, who experienced this vision twice, only John, the beloved Apostle, witnessed this symbolic vision. The description, and therefore the symbolism, of the cherubim differ in each of the three recorded idioms. Since I have recorded Ezekiel's first vision above in the KJV text, I will set the remaining two here, in the same text, for your consideration. The emphasis, added to highlight the characteristics of each facet, is mine.

> *"And every one had four faces; the first face was the face of a CHERUB (k^erumb), and the second face was the face of a MAN, and the third, the face of a LION, and the fourth, the face of an EAGLE."* (Ezek. 10:14)
>
> *"And the first living creature was like a LION, and the second living creature was like a CALF (moschos), and the third living creature had a face like a MAN, and the fourth living creature was like a flying EAGLE."* (Rev. 4:7)

In these revelations we can clearly see four facets of the triune God. In these facets we see similitudes of Christ's earthly ministry: the face of the MAN represents the humanity of Jesus as depicted in Luke's gospel. The image of the man is found in each of the three visions. The face of the LION delineates the kingship of Jesus Christ as depicted in the Gospel of Matthew. (It is interesting to note that the human nature of our Savior is recorded by a physician—Luke; and Christ's legal claim to the throne of David was recorded by a government official—Levi, the tax collector.) The image of the *lion* is present in each vision. The face of the EAGLE represents the deity of Jesus Christ, and is clearly illustrated in the Gospel of John. Again, the image of the eagle is present in each vision. It is only when we look at the fourth face of the CHERUB that we see any differences. And, those differences are stark enough for us to ask what those differences represent:

Ezek. 1:10	Ezek. 10:14	Rev. 4:7
Man	Man	Man
Eagle	Eagle	Eagle
Lion	Lion	Lion
Ox	Cherub	Calf

As these verses are paralleled, something interesting comes to light: the ox *(showr)* of Ezek. 1:10 becomes the cherub *(k^erumb)* of Ezek. 10:14, which then becomes the calf *(moschos)* of Rev. 4:7. What significance could we possibly glean from the distinctions between the ox, the cherub and the calf? When the Christian discovers what each face prefigures, the reason for the variations becomes obvious.

From the likenesses of their faces, we see (as noted), three facets of Christ found in the testimonies of His apostles. In Ezekiel 1:10 we see the fourth facet which was recorded by Mark in his Gospel. The ox is a beast of burden, a servant to mankind. John Mark clearly depicted Jesus as the Servant of all who follow Him. This thought is clearly amplified by Christ in Mark 9:35:

> *"...If any man desires to be first, the same shall be last of all, and servant to all..."* (KJV)

To make certain His disciples understood that true greatness is measured in humility, Christ humbled Himself even more by washing the feet of Peter.

Each of these visions presents us with a four-dimensional view of the Messiah—the man who was God in human flesh and the king who became a servant (Ezek. 1:10). Ezekiel's second vision portrays, instead of the servant, the resurrected and ascended God (Ezek. 10:14). And finally, in John's vision, instead of the servant, we see the sacrifice of the new covenant (Rev. 4:7), who died that we might have eternal life.

Was Melchizedek a theophany, Shem the son of Noah, or a Gentile king from the land of Canaan?

A theophany is a manifestation or physical appearance of God in a human or, sometimes, angelic form (Gen. 3:8, 12:7, 16:13, 17:1, 18:1; Ex. 3:2, 24:10, 40:34-38; Josh. 5:13-15; Jud. 2:1-5, 6:11, 13:2-8; 1 Ki. 8:10-11 and Isa. 6:1-9). Many early theologians felt Melchizadek was a theopany because the writer of Hebrews symbolically described him as being:

> *"Without father, without mother, without descent, having neither beginning of days nor end of life..."* (Heb. 7:3; KJV)

This phrase describes only someone without human origin. And although Jesus had a human mother and experienced both human birth and human death, His precarnate Being had neither beginning of days nor end of life.

The legend of Melchizedek—without father or mother—as something other than a theopany poses quite a dilemma for Christian and Jew alike. Melchizedek, as a human with the same antecedral credentials as Christ, would conflict with the Christian tenet that Jesus was God's only legitimate priest from Heaven and with the Jewish belief that the descendents of Aaron (through Zadok) were the only legitimate priests on earth. The problem is not quite so severe for the Jews, however, since the Levitical priesthood did not commence until the Israelites returned from Egypt. Be that as it may, the fact that Abraham paid tithes to Melchizedek would make his priesthood more superior to that of Levi, who descended from Abraham.

Hebrews 7:3 does not necessarily indicate that Melchizedek had no human origin. Rather, the writer of the epistle to the Hebrews is exploiting the silence of the Scriptures concerning Melchizedek to make a point. Because the Word of God does not record any mention of his father, mother, genealogy, birth or death, Melchizedek's priesthood is not dependent upon any legal stipulation or natural succession but purely upon God's appointment (see 7:15). Melchizedek had no predecessor or successor (or at least, none that were recorded), and as such, his priesthood was singlular and permanent, unlike the Levitical priesthood. Thus, the silence of the Scriptures concerning Melchizedek provides us with one of the most profound types of Christ found in the entire Old Testament. Christ's priesthood was established by God's oath (7:21; Ps. 110:4) and not through legal requirement or physical descent. Because He suffered death as an obedient Son and was then raised up to God's right hand, He is perfected (i.e., qualified) to be our great High Priest in perpetuity, like Melchizedek. (See further, 5:5-10; 7:15-28.)

Rabbinical tradition holds that Melchizedek, who is described in Genesis 14:18 as the king of Salem, was actually Shem, the first born son of Noah and it was, tradition holds, because of that ancestry that Abraham paid tithes to him. As Shem, Melchizadek would have been the theoretical king of his tribe, and the high priest of all those, including Abraham, who descended from him. However, Shem had both a father and a mother. He was born, and his death is noted in the Bible. Therefore, it could not be said of him that he had neither beginning of days nor end of life.

In fairness to the rabbinical theory, it is important to determine whether or not the assertion has time-frame merit. If Genesis 11:10-26 records actual next generation genealogies, then Shem, who lived 600 years, could have been living when the events described in Genesis 14:18-20 came to past. Shem would have been 490 years old when Abraham was born, 565 years old when Abraham and Lot left Haran, and only 576 years of age when Ishmael was born. Since the encounter between Abraham and Melchizedek occurred prior to the birth of Ishmael—assuming again that the Genesis 14 genealogy represent an actual father/son genealogy—then Shem would have been living when Abraham paid his tithes to Melchizedek.

Is that genealogy an actual father/son chronology? Granted, Bishop Ussher, who created the chronological timeline from Adam to the birth of Christ, thought it was. But was it? Do the words beget or begat *(yälad)* specifically imply next generation descendents? Perhaps, but not necessarily. *The Theological Wordbook of the Old Testament* (*Moody Press,* 1980; Vol. I; pg. 379) states: "...The word does not necessarily point to the generation immediately following. In Hebrew thought, an individual by the act of giving birth to a child becomes a parent or ancestor of all who will be descended from this child. Just as Christ is called a son of David and a son of Abraham, *yälad* may show the beginning of an individual's relationship with a descendent..."

In the genealogy of Jesus in Matthew 1:1-17, we read that Johoram (Joram) begot Uzziah (Azariah) (vs. 8) when in fact he was Uzziah's great-great-grandfather. Johoram fathered Ahaziah (2 Ki. 8:25), who fathered Joash (2 Ki. 13:1), who fathered Amaziah (2 Ki. 14:17), who in turn fathered Uzziah (2 Ki. 15:1). We may therefore logically conclude that Arpachshad (Gen. 11:10) was not Shem's literal son, but was in fact a descendent of Shem through whose seed Abraham was born.

Furthermore, as we examine Genesis 6:3-7, it appears God associated the wickedness of man's imagination with his longevity, and closed the antediluvian age with both a flood and a curse (Gen. 6:3) that limited man's future longevity to 120 years.

Adam lived 930 years. Seth lived 912 years, and Enoch walked the earth 365 years before he was translated to Heaven without experiencing death.

Methuselah lived longer than any human—969 years, and died the year of the Flood. Noah lived 950 years, and Shem, his firstborn, lived 600. Arpachshad lived 438 years, Peleg lived 239 years, and Nahor, the father of Terah, lived 148.

Abraham, the patriarch of the Jews, lived 175 years. Moses, who brought the children of Israel out of bondage, lived 120 years. Aaron, the older brother of Moses, died in the desert at age 119 and Joshua, who led the Israelites into the Promised Land, lived 110 years. When the lifespans of man lost their theological significance, they were no longer recorded in the Scriptures. However, the scriptural records suggest that a man bordering on 600 years of age would have been out-of-place in a world when 200 would have been considered a unique rarity. It is logical to conclude that Shem died many, many years before the birth of Abraham.

The *Arabic Catena,* an ancient history of Ishmael's people, claims Melchizedek was the son of Heraclim, a son of Peleg (who was the son of Eber). According to the *Catena,* Eber's mother was Salathiel, one of the daughters of Gomer. Gomer (Gen. 10:2) was the son of Japeth, who fathered the Gentile nations. The single largest problem with this genealogy is that, instead of being Japeth's genealogy (with the exception of Gomer), it is the chronology of Shem.

When the Dead Sea scrolls were discovered in 1947, archæologists unearthed a virtual library of ancient leather scrolls wrapped in linen cloth from earthen jars, the most recent of which was dated around 70 A.D. The Arab/Israeli War of 1948 caused archæological activity around Wadi Qumram to cease for over a year. From 1949 until 1956 over 200 such scrolls were found. Among these scrolls, the complete Book was Isaiah (1QIs[a]) was discovered. Also found about the same time as was a Commentary on Habbakuk (1QpHab). In 1956, archæologist working with Ta'amireh Bedouin in cavesite 11Q in Khirbet, discovered several complete manuscripts, among which was a scroll centered around the person of Melchizedek. In the text, Melchizedek is described as *elohim, the head of the son of heaven.* He is further characterized as a judge, presiding over the final judgement and the condemnation of Satan—i.e., a prefigurement of Jesus Christ. It is clear from the text that the Qumram Community viewed Melchizedek as a theophany.

Who Melchizedek was is not satisfactorily answered anywhere in Scripture, nor in any of the apocryphal works which abound throughout the world. He remains a mystery. However, the fact that his identity is not revealed suggests it is not important to know precisely who he was. What is important is what he represents. His appearance in Scripture is uniquely theological. He appears suddenly—as did Jesus, who was dramatically announced with a star which pointed to His birthplace in a manger in Bethlehem. Melchizedek was God's spokesman to Abraham—Christ was God's spokesman to humanity. Melchizedek is described as *apator, ametor, agenhalogaytos:* without human origin. Jesus was conceived by the Holy Spirit, and does not have human origin. Melchizedek was imputed as righteous, the king of peace. Jesus is Righteouness, the King of Peace.

Melchizedek presented Abraham and his soldiers with bread and wine for the refreshment of their bodies. Christ presented bread and wine as His body and blood for the renewing of our spirits.

Although the Bible presents Christ as "...a priest forever after the order of Melchizedek..." (Ps. 110:4; Heb. 5:6, 6:20, 7:21), Jesus is the model from which Melchizedek was cast, not the other way around. Christ is the *anti-type* of Melchizedek, who is portrayed in Scripture as a *type* of Christ.

What were Urim and Thummim?

The breastplate which was first worn by Aaron (Ex. 28:15) was called the breastplate of judgement. That which is worn by the Christian is called the breastplate of righteousness (Eph. 6:14). It is part of the whole armor of God (Eph. 6:11). In the case of the high priest, the breastplate was part of the ephod he wore whenever he entered the Holy of Holies to make intercession for the people. Within the breastplate were two stones, the urim and the thummim (Ex. 28:30; Lev. 8:8; Dt. 33:8; Ezra 2:63; Neh. 7:65).

The breastplate contained four rows of three precious stones. These twelve stones represented the twelve tribes (Ex. 28:21). The stones in the first row were a ruby, a topaz and a beryl. (Beryl is beryllium aluminum silicate, a hexagonal crystal gemstone, most commonly found in granitic rocks. Beryl can be emerald green to deep green, pale blue-green, helidor yellow to morganite pink. Emeralds, sapphires and aquamarine stones are beryllium.) The second row consisted of an emerald, a sapphire and a turquoise. The third row contained an amethyst, an agate and a jacinth (a zircon). Finally, the breastplate contained a chrysolite (a form of beryllium), an onyx and a jasper (silicon dioxide), a fine grained, opaque gemstone with characteristics similar to flintstone (Ex. 28:17-20) The breastplate was attached to the ephod by two onyx stones which were worn upon the shoulders of the high priest. The names of the twelve tribes (six on each stone) were inscribed on the onyx shoulder stones.

Josephus, the first century Jewish historian believed the shoulder stones were the urim and thummim (Antiquities of the Jews, 3:8:9), but that is apparently not true. The breastplate was fashioned to form a pouch (Ex. 28:16), into which the urim and thummim were placed (Ex. 28:30). Most Bible scholars believe urim and thummim were a pair of flat stones, dark on one side, light on the other. The light side was urim; the dark side, thummim. Advocates of the light/dark theory maintain urim *('ur)* means light (or revelation; knowledge), although thummim *(tom),* they concede, instead of dark, means perfection, completeness, integrity or truth. Others insist the correct definition of urim comes from *'ädar,* meaning to *curse;* and thummim, from *tämam,* is more correctly interpreted as *to be perfect.* Needless to say, if the scholars cannot agree on either the origin of, or more specifically, the meaning of these words, it becomes even more difficult to understand their purpose. It is more logical that the latter definition is correct since urim begins with the first letter of the Hebrew alphabet, and thummin with the last. Creation begins with Adam—who carried the curse of mankind; and it will end with Jesus Christ, who is Perfection.

The purpose of urim and thummim was to verify that the words spoken by the high priest were the revealed word of God. How this was accomplished has been the center of debate for centuries. Advocates of the flat rock theory insist the stones were cast as by lot *(pur)*. If the urim side of both rocks came up the request was refused. If the thummim side of both rocks came up the request was granted. If one urim and one thummim side turned up it signified that God was either undecided in the matter or did not wish to deal with it at that moment.

Proponents of this argument defend their position by citing Saul's inability to get an answer from God concerning his upcoming battle with the Philistines at Gilboa:

> *"And when Saul saw the host of the Philistines, he was afraid, and his heart trembled greatly. And when Saul inquired of the Lord, the Lord answered him not, neither by dreams, nor by urim, nor by prophets."* (1 Sam. 28:5-6; KJV)

Scripture clearly suggests urim and thummim were not limited to *yes, no* and *ask me again later* answers. In Judges 1:1-2, the Israelites, using urim, asked God specifically which tribe was to go up against the Canaanites. In response, God replied: "Judah shall go up; behold, I have delivered the land into his hand."

According to the Talmud, the Shekinah Glory would fall upon the stones, and a brilliant heavenly light would illuminate the letters in the names of the twelve tribes, spelling out the words which God wished to convey. This does not seem likely either since five of the twenty-two letters of the Hebrew alphabet do not appear in any of the tribal names. Pre-mishnaic literature, particularly the aporcryphal Talmudic Pseudo-Jonathan scroll insists that to the letters for the tribal names were added the names of Abraham, Isaac, Jacob, as well as the tribes of Jeshurun, completing the Hebrew alphabet. While this serves as a convenient explanation, Scripture does not support the contention.

The Septuagint text of 1 Samuel 14:41 which is largely accepted as extremely accurate by most Bible scholars, implies that either urim or thummim—but not both—was drawn from the pouch, again suggesting urim and thummim provided only *either/or* or yes/no answers.

In *Antiquities of the Jews,* Josephus states that the Holy Oracle stopping giving forth its miraculous light during the brief reign of the Maccabees, when John Hyrcanus (the last righteous priest) fought Antiochus IV Epiphanes. However, it seems more likely that the breastplate containing the urim and thummim was part of the plunder taken back to Babylon when Nebuchadnezzar sacked the Temple in 586 B.C., since the oracle is mentioned only one time in Scripture after the captivity. The same verse is found in both Ezra 2:63 and Nehemiah 7:65. Recently returned from Babylon, the Jews were trying to re-establish the priesthood through the line of Zadok in accordance with God's word (1 Sam. 2:35, 10:1, 12:3, 16:31, 24:6). Because the priestly line had been polluted with those who did not rightly belong there, the question was raised whether or not the priests should risk eating the shewbread or meat offerings of the Temple, a practice which was reserved only for those divinely appointed to the priesthood.

> *"These sought their register among those that were reckoned by genealogy, but it was not found: therefore were they, as polluted, put from the priesthood. And the Tirshata (governor) said unto them, that they should not eat of the most holy things, till there stood up a priest with urim and thummim."* (Ezra 2:62-63; Neh. 7:64-65; KJV)

The eating of the shewbread and burnt offerings were suspended in the second Temple because the Jews were waiting for the high priest with urim and thummim to appear. While he was prophetically anticipated, and the Jews anxiously awaited his arrival, they failed to recognize Him when He came, not as the priest/warrior they were expecting, but rather, as a servant of man. He, of whom urim and thummim was a *type,* was the Light of the world. He who was perfect (thummim) became sin (urim) for us, and bore those sins to Calvary that we might have eternal life. Jesus Christ is our Urim and Thummim.

What significance do the Levitical feast hold for the Christian today?

Out of the ten feasts which the Jews celebrate annually, seven of them (eight, counting the Sabbath) are sanctified by God (Lev. 23:4-7). The remaining three: *Hanukkah, Purim* and *Tisha b' Av* came into practice long after the Pentateuch was written.

The best know Jewish holiday, or feast day, to most Christians is *Hanukkah* because of its proximity to the Christian holiday of Christmas. Strangely enough, most Christians regard *Hanukkah* as the Jewish Christmas although nothing could be farther from the truth.

Hanukkah is an eight day feast which begins on the 25th day of Kislev (which corresponds with a date which may fall anywhere between November 15 and December 15 on the Julian calendar). This event, known as either the *Feast of Dedication* or the *Feast of Lights,* commemorates the victory of Judas Maccabee over Antiochus IV Epiphanes, which culminated with the recapturing of the Temple in 165 B.C. Over the years, two different explanations for the origin of Hanukkah have arisen in the Jewish community. In 2 Maccabees 1:9 and 10:6-8, the scribe wrote that because the Maccabees were in hiding during Succoth *(Sukkot)*, they were unable to properly observe the feast. When they defeated Antiochus, they celebrated the feast belatedly, calling it the *Sukkot of the month of Kislev.* It became a memorial to that victory.

The *Talmud* attributes the feast to a miracle. According to Talmudic tradition, it was the intent of the victorious Jews, after they cleansed and purified the Temple, to rededicate it with a lighted *mennorah* for eight days as Solomon had done when he dedicated the original Temple. However, when Antiochus entered the Temple, he defiled all of the Holy oils. When the Maccabeans completed a search of the Temple, they found only one cruse of pure olive oil, which was capable of keeping the lamp lighted for one day only. Miraculously, the oil burned for eight days and nights, hence the reason for celebrating the *Festival of Lights.*

Purim is celebrated on the fourteenth day of *Adar* (corresponding to a date between February and March 15). *Purim* is a one-day feast day, and commemorates the deliverance of the Jews from the hands of Haman. The name *Purim* is derived from the Hebrew word *pur,* which means lottery. Haman used a lottery (Est. 3:7) to determine upon what date the Jews would be destroyed.

Tisha b'Av is a day of mourning, and commemorates the destruction of the first Temple by Nebuchadnezzar in 586 B.C. It also commemorates the destruction of the second Temple by Titus in 70 A.D. (on the same day, some Jewish scholars maintain). For the Gentile mind, *Tisha b'Av* can best be described as the Jewish Memorial Day. All of the suffering the Jews have experienced throughout history is memorialized on this day—particularly the holocaust of World War II when over one-third of the entire world's Jewish population was exterminated by the Nazis as the world watched with blinded eyes and listened to the screams of the dying with deaf ears; after which most insisted they had no knowledge of the genocide.

The seven feasts which God ordained (excluding the Sabbath), are *Pesach* (Passover, Lev. 23:5); *Hag Hamatozot* (Unleavened Bread, Lev. 23:6); *Omer* (First Fruits, Lev. 23:10-11); *Sheuvot* (Pentecost, Lev. 23:15-17); *Rosh Hashana* (Trumpets, Lev. 23:24-25); *Yom Kippur* (Day of Atonement, Lev. 23:27-28) and, finally, *Succoth* (Tabernacles, Lev. 23:34-36). As Christians, it is important to understand the significance of these feasts, since every major milestone in the Christian faith is based on them. It should come as no surprise to the Christian world that each of these events are Christ-centered.

The first feast, celebrated on the fourteenth day of Nisan is Passover. There is probably not a Christian anywhere who does not associate this event with the crucifixion of Jesus Christ. Since Christianity actually begins with the crucifixion, death and resurrection of Jesus, it should not come as a surprise that the first feast the Jews celebrate each year is anticipatory of that event (Ex. 12:6/Jn. 12:12; Ex. 12:46/Jn. 19:36; Ex. 12:13/Heb. 10:10, 14; 1 Jn. 1:7; Rev. 13:8). Christ is our Passover. Just as the death angel passed over the houses of the Jews in Goshen the night the first born of Egypt died, so will judgement and damnation pass over those who are covered with the blood of Jesus Christ.

The Feast of Unleavened Bread represents the sinless, holy walk of our Lord. It is also our communion with Him. Combined with Passover, we have the body and blood of Jesus Christ (1 Cor. 11:24-25). The Feast of First Fruits represents the resurrection of Jesus Christ on the third day (Jn. 2:19; 1 Cor. 15:4). Christ was the first to be resurrected (1 Cor. 15:20-46), the first to ascend into Heaven, and the first to possess a glorified body (Mk. 16:19; Lk. 24:37-43, 49-53; Jn. 20:17, 19-29; Acts 1:6-11). (For those who may believe Lazarus was the first to be resurrected, it is important to note that Lazarus was restored to life, not resurrected from the dead. This distinction is important, because Lazarus died at a later date after he was restored to life. Had he been resurrected from the dead, he would not have been subject to death. Christ was resurrected incorruptible, as will those who share in the first resurrection.)

Pentecost represents the birth of the Christian church (Acts 2:1-47). Two wave loaves containing leaven are used in the Pentecostal offering. The loaves represent spiritual Israel, the saved Jews and Gentiles (Gal. 3:28), which is the true church of Jesus Christ.

We need to pay particular attention to the command of the Lord to use leavening in this offering. Leavening represents sin (Mt. 16:6-12; 1 Cor. 5:5-8; Gal. 5:7-9). By commanding the use of leavening, God is warning the believer that the church will not be free of sin.

The Feast of Trumpets symbolized the translation of the church (1 Cor. 15:52-53; 1 Th. 4:15-17; Rev. 3:10). From the Christian perspective, there are two significant things to be observed in connection with this feast. First, it should be noted that an interval of three months separates this feast from the previous one. This period represents the entire Church Age—*the times of the Gentiles*. Second, as we examine the previous Levitical feasts, we can clearly see when the event typified by the feast occurred historically, it happened on precisely the same date as the feast which prefigured it was celebrated.

For example, Leviticus 23:5 tells us the fourteenth day of the first month is the Passover. History confirms that on Monday, April 6, 32 A.D., Jesus of Nazareth entered Jerusalem by the East Gate for the last time. Four days later, on the fourteenth of Nisan, He became our Passover. On the first day of the week (Lev. 23:7) following the Passover, the believer is instructed to bring a sheaf of the first fruit to the priest at the Temple (Lev. 23:10) as an offering. On Sunday, April 12, 32 A.D., Christ became our First Fruit offering when He arose from the grave.

Forty-nine days from First Fruits (the seventh Sabbath) is the Feast of Pentecost (Lev. 23:15-16). Pentecost was an important feast day for the Israelites because it marked the beginning of the early harvest. On May 31, 32 A.D., fifty days after the Sabbath preceding First Fruits, the Christian church was born when the Holy Spirit came down from Heaven like a mighty rushing wind and filled the upper room where the disciples were gathered. Three thousand souls were saved that day. It was truly an early harvest for the early church.

When we examine the Scriptures that deal with the Feast of Trumpets, we quickly discover there has been no specific event, as yet, which has fulfilled that which *Rosh Hashana* represents. This should not surprise us, however, since the Feast of Trumpets prefigures the rapture of the church. While the event is celebrated on the first day of the seventh month, it is done so, unlike the other feasts, as a memorial to the event it forecasts. This, also, should not come as a surprise to the Christian, since the Word of God clearly informs us only God knows the day and hour when Christ will return for His church (Mt. 24:36).

God's timetable continues with the Day of Atonement. Opinion seems somewhat evenly divided whether this feast deals with the Rewards Judgment of the believers at the bema seat of the Lord, or if it prefigures the Sheeps and Goats Judgment which will take place during the forty-five day period between the end of the Great Tribulation and the commencement of the millennial kingdom.

The Rewards Judgement (1 Cor. 1:8, 4:5; 2 Cor. 5:10; Phil. 1:6, 2:16; 2 Tim. 4:8) will be a public manifestation to examine the character and motives of the believer. The believer's works (not the believer himself) will be brought into scrutiny at this time to determine if they are worthy of reward. Unlike the Sheeps and Goats Judgment, the Rewards Judgment is not conducted to chastise the believer for any sins committed, since those sins have been forever placed under the blood of Jesus Christ, and cannot be seen. The sole purpose of this judgement is to determine if rewards are to be received or lost. The believer's salvation (affirmed by the fact that he or she is present in Heaven at that time) is secure.

The Sheeps and Goats Judgment, which will be discussed in much greater detail later, takes place at the East Gate of Jerusalem, and deals with those living at the end of the Tribulation. Since all of the other Levitical feasts deal with earthly events, we may rightfully conclude that the symbolic prefigurement of the Day of Atonement applies to the Sheeps and Goats Judgment rather than the Rewards Judgment, which takes place in Heaven.

The final Levitical feast is that of Tabernacles. Tabernacles prefigures the Millennial Reign of Jesus Christ on earth (Amos 9:11; Rev. 20:4). At the conclusion of the Millennium, the Great White Throne Judgement will take place. All of those judged here will be condemned to the Lake of Fire (Mt. 7:22-23; Rev. 20:11-15). This is the judgment of the damned. It will be *tisha b'av* on that day for all those who have rejected Jesus Christ as their Lord and Savior.

Pentecost: the birth of the Christian church

"You shall also count for yourselves from the day after the Sabbath, from the day when you brought in the sheaf of the wave offering; there shall be seven complete Sabbaths. You shall count fifty days to the day after the seventh Sabbath; then you shall present a new grain offering to the Lord." (Lev. 23:15-16; NASB)

One of the first things to become obvious to the Christian concerning the study of the Feast of Pentecost is that it, like First Fruits, Pentecost was celebrated on a Sunday. Advocates of the seventh day Sabbath conveniently ignore the fact that Christ was crucified on the eve of the Sabbath (which was Friday) (Mk. 15:42; Lk. 23:54) and that He arose on the first day of the week (which is Sunday) (Mt. 28:1; Mk. 16:1-2; Lk. 24:1; Jn. 20:1, 19). Seven Sundays later, on the fiftieth day, the Feast of Pentecost was celebrated.

To the Christian, Pentecost correctly represents the birth of the church. To the Jew, *Shevuot* commemorates the giving of the law on Mt. Sinai seven weeks after the Exodus from Egypt. It should also be noted that the Exodus began on First Fruits, the second day after Passover (Ex. 12:29, 41, 51). Forty-nine days later, Moses went up into Sinai to receive the Law from God. The Ten Commandments are the foundation not only of Judaism and Christianity, but Islam as well. To many Christian, the Ten Commandments represents the entire Law; to the Jew, they are just ten of 613 commandments which make up the Jewish *Taryag Mitzvot.*

Pentecost, in the Hebrew prayer book *(Siddur)* is called *zman matan Torateinu,* or the season of the giving of the Torah. The Jewish Talmud refers to

Pentecost as *atzertet,* which means a concluding festival. Many Hebrew scholars view Pentecost as the conclusion of the Feast of the Passover. Interesting enough, so do many Christians. Each of the feasts between Passover and Pentecost are inexplicably linked. The bond between these events is clearly established by Christ, who told His disciples:

> *"Nevertheless, I tell you the truth: It is expedient for you that I go away; for if I did not go away, the Comforter will not come unto you; but if I depart, I will send Him to you."* (Jn. 16:7; KJV)

thereby linking Pentecost into His own death, resurrection and ascension to Heaven.

Grain farmers in Israel call Pentecost *Hag Hakatzin,* the festival of the harvest. Fruit farmers call it *Yom HaBikkurim,* which means the day of the first fruit. Pentecost marks the beginning of both the spring grain and fruit harvests. The first harvested grains and ripe fruit were traditionally brought to the Temple as a first fruit offering to the Lord.

> *"You shall bring in from your dwelling place two loaves of bread for a wave offering, made of two-tenths of an ephad (approximately one bushel); they shall be of fine flour, baked with leaven as first fruits to the Lord."* (Lev. 23:17; NASB)

The two loaves represented, as previously stated, those who were saved by the sacrificial blood of Jesus Christ (Rom. 10:12; Gal. 26-29; Col. 3:11). The creation of the Church actually began ten days after Christ's ascension, concluding on the Day of Pentecost that which was set in motion on Passover.

As we earlier compared the wave offerings for Pentecost with that of First Fruits, we could not help but notice the absence and/or presence of leavening. Since the First Fruits wave offering represented Christ, there was no leavening since Jesus was without sin. The wave offering of Pentecost, which represents the human entity within the church, contains leaven. From that we can reasonably conclude there is sin within the church.

Now we will consider a second offering which also takes place on Pentecost:

> *"Along with the bread, you shall present seven one year old male lambs without blemish, and a bull of the herd, and two rams; they are to be a burnt offering to the Lord, with their grain offering and their libations, an offering by fire of a soothing aroma to the Lord. You shall also offer one male goat for a sin offering and two male lambs one year old for a sacrifice of peace offerings. The priest shall then wave them with the bread of the first fruits for a wave offering with two lambs before the Lord; they are to be holy to the Lord for the priest."* (Lev. 23:18-20; NASB)

Again, comparing the Pentecostal sacrifice to that of the First Fruits, the following distinction becomes apparent: when the wave sheaf is offered, only one lamb "...a he-lamb without blemish of the first year..." is offered. This lamb, like the wave sheaf, typifies Christ, the Lamb of God.

A sin offering was required for the perfecting of the community during

Pentecost. Before the Church could be formed, a sin offering was also required: Christ became that sin offering when He surrendered humanity on the cross (2 Cor. 5:21). The Church Age, which was announced by Christ Himself (Mt. 16:18; 18:15-20), was activated with His shed blood (Rom. 3:24-25; 1 Cor. 6:20), and actually became the Church ten days after His ascension, when the day of Pentecost had fully come.

The Bible tells us in addition to the twelve apostles (Matthias had recently been elected to fill the position vacated by Judas' suicide), there were 108 other disciples in the Upper Room (Acts 1:15) when they were all filled with the Holy Spirit and began speaking in other tongues (actual contemporary languages). Word of this happening spread like wildfire throughout Jerusalem. Thousands flocked to the location where the apostles were gathered and heard the first sermon of the new church preached by Simon Peter. As a result of that sermon, 3,000 accepted Christ and were baptized.

The 3,000 who were saved on Pentecost (Acts 2:41) parallel the 3,000 who died after making the golden calf in the wilderness (Ex. 32:28) at the first Pentecost.

How does the ancient Jewish marriage custom typify Jesus Christ?

According to Jewish custom, the marriage contract was made sacred and binding when the bridegroom agreed to pay the required dowry for the bride (1 Cor. 6:20, 7:23). Prior to the Assyrian captivity, a verbal contract was sufficient, providing it was executed before witnesses (Jn. 19:35).

As the Jews were dispersed throughout the various nations of the earth and became exposed to other cultures, the rabbis began to fear that the oral traditions which had been practiced by the Jews since the days of Abraham would be diluted with the customs of the lands in which they dwelt. For this reason, Rabbi Yehudah ha-Nasi, around 250 A.D., began transcribing the oral traditions into written form. The completed work became know as the *Mishnah.* From that time forward the marriage contract, which had previously been oral, was written. (Christ's written contract with His bride, the Church, is frequently called the New Testament.)

Because the Jewish marriage covenant typifies Christ and the Church it must be viewed as a permanent, lifelong union. For this very reason, God frowns on divorce, except for adultery. It is interesting to note that the relationship God has enjoyed with the Jews since the beginning of time has been fractured only when the Jews became adulterous and fancied pagan deities instead of Him.

The Church is the Bride of Christ. It is a marriage which will be consummated at the end of the age in Heaven, just prior to the Battle of Armageddon (Rev. 19:7-16). This convenant relationship is irrevocable. Unlike the traditional betrothal agreement, it does not contain a divorce clause which will allow the groom to put the bride away in the event she is unfaithful. The sins of the bride are to be forgiven—covered by the blood of the groom.

In Hebrew tradition, divorce after the consummation of marriage was extremely rare, even in cases of infidelity. More commonly, the adulterous spouse was simply stoned to death for adultery according to the Law (Dt. 24:1-4), and the matter ended. Divorce beyond betrothal was never an issue under Hebrew law. Marriage was an absolutely irrevocable institution. However, in the first century A.D. the Roman custom of divorce crept into the Jewish society, and it was this issue which Christ raised (Mt. 19:3-12; Mk. 10:1-12; Lk. 16:18; Rom. 7:1-3; 1 Cor. 7: 1-14). Unlike modern marriage engagements, the Hebrew was deemed to be married from the moment the proposal of marriage was proffered. There were no broken engagements or cancelled weddings, except in the case of infidelity.

Such was the case with Mary, the mother of Jesus. It was during the betrothal period that Mary was found to be with child (Mt. 1:18-25; Lk. 1:26-35). Her marriage to Joseph had not yet been consummated (and would not be until after the birth of Jesus), since the required waiting period of a year had not yet passed. Joseph could have legally put her away at that point, or publicly accused her of infidelity. Had he accused her publicly, she would have been stoned to death (Dt. 23:13-30). Had he chosen instead to divorce her, she would have been disgraced for life. No reputable Jew would have ever married her.

It is clear from the response of Christ's disciples in Matthew 19:10 "...if the case of the man be so with his wife, it is not good to marry..." they knew the divorce Jesus spoke of, for adultery only, was allowed only during the betrothal period. They clearly understood Christ as saying that if the unfaithfulness of the wife was not discovered until after the marriage was consummated, they would be inseparably yoked. Because the notion of being tied to an unfaithful woman was so repugnant to them, they concluded it would be better for the man if he had never married.

A lengthy interval might elapse between the betrothal and the actual marriage ceremony, sometimes periods of as much as a year or more. It was seldom less than nine months, and in many cases might exceed two or more years. The duration of the betrothal period was determined neither by the groom nor the bride. Rather, it was determined by the groom's father, who alone decided when the wedding would take place (Mt. 24:36). During the betrothal period, it was the responsibility of the bride to be ready for the unexpected arrival of the bridegroom (Mt. 25:1-13). As custom would have it, the bridegroom might well arrive in the middle of the night (1 Th. 5:2; 2 Pe. 3:10). Because of this, the bride was charged with the responsibility of keeping a filled oil lamp beside her bed (Mt. 25:6-7) in the event the bridegroom came in the darkness of night.

Paralleling this thought with respect to the Church, it is obvious the Church could not become the bride until Christ (the groom) paid the required dowry (the crucifixion). The transfer of the dowry was performed before witnesses (Lk. 23:48); and was written (the New Testament) as well. The marriage will actually take place when the Church is translated at the end of this age (representative of the parable of the ten virgins, [Mt. 25:1-13]), and joins Christ in the heavenlies (1 Cor. 15:52-53; 1 Th. 4:15-17).

It is interesting to note that in the first century Semitic world the intended groom, upon signing the marriage contract, immediately returned to his father's house to prepare a wedding chamber for his bride (Jn. 14:2). Unlike today's newlyweds who move out of their parents homes and set up housekeeping on their own, newlyweds in the Semitic world of Christ's day moved into rooms built directly onto the home of the groom's father, constructed by the groom and his friends or the bondservants of the father. Because the groom was understandably eager to bring his new bride home and consummate the marriage, his father alone possessed the authority to decide when the wedding chamber was sufficiently prepared to receive a bride (Mt. 24:36). When Christ attempted to prepare His disciples for His imminent death, and to offer assurances that He would return, His words paralleled this practice:

> *"In My Father's house are many mansions; if it were not so, I would have told you. I go to prepare a place for you. And if I go and prepare a place for you, I will come again, and receive you unto Myself..."* (Jn. 14:2-3)

Likewise, when the bridegroom returned for his bride he would provide only a moment's notice of his coming (giving that warning, perhaps, only because he did not want to catch his bride still in her nightclothes with cold cream on her face). The best man would appear mere moments before the groom, shouting, "The bridegroom is coming! The bridegroom is coming!" as the bridegroom approached the house,

> *"For the Lord Himself shall descend from Heaven with a shout, with the voice of the archangel and with the trump of God..."* (1 Th. 4:16).

and the bride is taken immediately to the bridegroom's home:

> *"...and the dead in Christ shall rise first; then we who are alive and remain shall be caught up together with them in the clouds, to meet the Lord in the air; and so shall ever be with the Lord."* (1 Th. 4:16-17)

Before the wedding feast (Jn. 7:37; Rev. 19:9) took place the marriage was consummated. While the bride and the bridegroom were in the wedding chamber, the best man stood outside the door waiting to hear the groom's voice announce the marriage had been consummated and it was time to prepare the Marriage Supper (Jn. 3:29).

Is Jesus mentioned by name as the Messiah anywhere in the Old Testament?

Skeptics of Christology insist if Jesus was the Messiah, He would be mentioned as such—by name and not by reference only—in the Old Testament. Skeptics further suggest that an all powerful, all-knowing God, who insists that the integrity of the Bible is irrefutably supported by the prophetic character of His Word, would be obligated to provide the actual name of that Messiah somewhere, prophetically, in the Old Testament before He actually appeared on the scene in Galilee. It is a valid point, as well as a logical argument. As such, it has merit and needs to be discussed since, properly applied by the skeptic to the newcomer to Christ, it could be a stumbling block which would hinder the growth of that baby Christian. To the novice, there is just so much which can be accepted on faith alone.

Although most Christians are taught that Jesus Christ is mentioned in the Old Testament by character only, and not by His given name, the reverse is actually true. Jesus is mentioned by His given name as *the branch,* the Messiah. The prophecy that identifies Him is found in Zechariah. The prophet is told to crown Joshua, the son of Jehozadok the high priest, symbolically to represent the Branch.

> *"The take silver and gold, and make crowns, and set them upon the head of Joshua, the son of Jehozadok, the high priest; And speak unto him saying, Thus speaketh the Lord of hosts; saying, Behold the man whose name is THE BRANCH; and He shall grow up out of His place, and He shall build the temple of the Lord; even He shall build the temple of the Lord; and He shall bear the glory, and shall sit and rule upon His throne; and He shall be a priest upon His throne; and the council of peace shall be between (His two offices)..."* (Zech. 6:11-13).

Because the Scriptures were originally penned in different languages (i.e., the Old Testament in Hebrew, and the New Testament in Aramaic and Greek), we see what appears to be entirely different names in the two texts. Few Christians realize that Mary, the mother of Christ, was actually named Miriam; or that Moses' sister, Miriam, would have been called Mary if the Old Testament had been penned in Greek.

The actual Hebrew rendering of the Greek word, Jesus *(Ieous),* is Joshua. In the Hebrew language Joshua is *y^ehoshua-Yeshua,* which means *Yahweh is salvation.* The name Jesus is merely a transliteration of the Hebrew name, Joshua. In the Greek language Jesus means *Jehovah is salvation.* To support this transliteration, we need only look at Acts 7:45 in the original KJV text. (Most current editions have now substituted the name Joshua in footnoted brackets to reinstate the original meaning of the verse since the use of Jesus served only to confuse the lay reader. However, more linguistically correct versions still use the name Jesus rather than Joshua.)

> *"Our fathers had the tabernacle of witness in the wilderness, and He had appointed, speaking unto Moses, that he should make it according to the fashion that he had seen; Which also our fathers that came after brought in with Jesus into the possession of the Gentiles, whom God drove out before the face of our fathers, unto the days of David."* (Acts 7:44-45)

The verse clearly describes Joshua, who was selected by God as Moses' successor to lead the Israelites into the Promised Land.

It is important to remember that the scribes who penned the original text were not theological scholars, deliberately intent on creating a linguistically correct eschatology for later generations to follow. They were largely simple men who recorded the words they were given by the Holy Spirit, in the common language they spoke and wrote, for others of the same period to read and comprehend. It is doubtful that any of the prophets or scribes even remotely imagined what they placed on parchment would be read and revered by other men, who eagerly awaited the same Messiah they sought, two or three thousand years after their deaths.

As we examine Zech. 6:11-13 there can be no doubt that it was God's intent that Joshua, the son of Jehozadok, be crowned symbolically to represent someone else who possessed the same name and of whom he, Joshua, was to symbolically depict: Jesus of Nazareth, the Son of David, the Son of God—the Branch (Jer. 23:5). The crowns described in these verses were clearly not Joshua's, for the crowning was to be memorial of a future event. We may rightly conclude, therefore, that this Old Testament Joshua/Jesus is a *type* of the New Testament Jesus/Joshua and that the prefigurement was neither accidental nor coincidental. It was, rather, divinely portended to identify the name of the Messiah in order to evidence, prophetically, His name for all believers to see and recognize.

CHAPTER FOUR

JESUS, THE MESSIAH

What does the word "Messiah" mean?

In the Hebrew language Messiah is *mäshîah,* and literally means a king or other consecrated person who has been anointed with oil. Interestingly *messiah* in Greek *(messias)* means the Christ. The phrase *Jesus Christ* means "Jesus, the Messiah." When the Sanhedrin asked Jesus, "Are you the Christ, the Son of the Blessed One?" they were very pointedly asking Him if He was, in fact, the Messiah (Mk. 14:61). Whereas in previous encounters with the Jewish religious community, Jesus had avoided answering direct questions with equally direct answers (since those queries were invariably designed to trick Him into confessing violations of oral law), now, knowing His time had come and that He was mere hours from Calvary, Jesus answered their question in the affirmative without hesitation:

> *"...I am; and ye shall see the Son of man sitting on the right hand of power and coming in the clouds of heaven."* (Mk. 14:62; KJV)

While the word *mäshîah* may be used in the context of an anointed high priest, it is almost exclusively reserved as a synonym for either a king or an anointed regent of God. The term is used less than forty times in the Old Testament, primarily in II Samuel and Psalms. While the term is frequently used to describe a regal position (1 Sam. 2:10; 2 Sam. 22:51), it is primarily used to describe the divine agent of Yahweh in the poetic writings of the psalmist—particularly the messianic 72nd Psalm, which promises that the earth, at the end of the age, would be the sole possession of the *mäshîah.*

There is a threefold theological significance to the application of the word *mäshîah* in its general sense: First and foremost, the anointed individual would be set apart from the world by the Holy Spirit to perform God's work. Second, the *mäshîah* would be a deliverer. And finally, Divine power would accompany the *mäshîah.* Moses, the perfect type, was divinely set apart from all people—Jew and Gentile alike, to save God's people. He was their deliverer. Moses was, to the enslaved Hebrews in Egypt, the *mäshîah* of his time, and as such was a *type* of the Christ who was to come approximately 1,400 years later.

One of the important aspects of the word *mäshîah* is clearly the anointing which must accompany it. The word literally means a king or other consecrated person who has been anointed with oil. Christ, or *Christos,* means one who is consecrated and anointed with oil. The Hebrew root of *mäshîah* is *mäshâch.* The Greek root of *Christos* is *Chrio.* Both root words mean to smear, rub or anoint with oil. Clearly, Christ's anointing was Divine, as was the call of Moses; and, for that matter, so was David's, from whom the physical seed of Jesus arose. However, under the Law, the anointing with oil was an important sign It was a priestly ritual that acknowledged the Divine manifestation of the Holy Spirit.

Why is there a discrepancy between the genealogies in the gospels of Matthew and Luke?

The Bible details two separate and distinct genealogies of Jesus Christ. The first, the legal genealogy, is presented in Matthew 1:1-17, and includes forty generations from Abraham to Jesus. The second, the Messianic genealogy, is recorded in Luke 3:23-38, and includes seventy-six generations starting with Jesse and going backward to Adam.

There has been much discussion throughout the ages concerning what appears to be discrepancies between these two distinctly different registers. Are both the genealogies of Joseph, as many otherwise competent theologians claim, or is the Lukan account viewed through Mary, as others claim?

Those who claim both genealogies are Joseph's are quick to point out that if the Lukan account was really Mary's genealogy, she would have been mentioned as the daughter of Heli and the wife of Joseph, as she is designated in Matthew's accounting (Mt. 1:16). Advocates of this perspective further argue that Luke records the physical descendents of Joseph back to Adam, and Matthew records the throne ascensions, taking the kingdom back to Abraham, from whom the nation of Israel arose. The Matthew genealogy lacks the historic value that many see in the Lukan chronology. Matthew's aim, many claim, was not to establish the lineage of Christ, but merely to prove that Jesus, as a direct descendent of Abraham, through Isaac and David, was the legal heir of the House of David.

In Matthew 1:17, the genealogy put forth is broken into three segments of fourteen generations:

> *"So all the generations from Abraham to David are fourteen generations; and from David to the carrying away into Babylon are fourteen generations; and from the carrying away into Babylon unto Christ are fourteen generations."*

However, a physical count of the generations listed within the genealogy indicates that while Matthew lists fourteen generations from Abraham to David, he lists only thirteen each from David to Jeconiah and from Jeconiah to Jesus. This apparently deliberate contradiction is puzzling, since Scripture clearly suggests that more than thirteen generations existed between David and Jeconiah, and also between Jeconiah and Jesus. In fact, Scripture verifies that some generations were deliberately omitted between Abraham and David to arrive at fourteen. For example, Uzziah (Mt. 1:18) is not the son of Joram, but is instead his great-great-grandson. Joram [Jehoram] fathered Ahaziah (2 Ki. 8:25), who fathered Joash (2 Ki. 13:1), who fathered Amaziah (2 Ki. 14:17), who in turn fathered Uzziah [Azariah] (2 Ki. 15:1). This discovery raises the question: Why does Scripture limit the generations shown to fourteen—particularly in light of the fact that no such restrictions appear in the Lukan genealogy?

Several theories have been advanced over the years, but none have been universally accepted by the theological community. In Hebrew numerology the value of the name David is fourteen. It has been suggested that by using numerical symbolism Matthew is emphasizing that the Messiah, the promised son of David, had come in the personage of Jesus. Whatever the reason, the genealogy presented by Matthew was not intended to be read as an actual father/son genealogy. Advocates of the dual-Joseph genealogy view maintain this discrepancy additionally supports their position.

To make this theory work, we must first assume that Matthan (Mt. 1:15) and Matthat (Lk. 3:24) are different spellings of the same name. Matthan or Matthat would have to have been the father of both Jacob (Mt. 1:16) and Heli (Lk. 3:23). Jacob, who would probably have been older, would have been the legal heir to the throne of David and would have necessarily had to die childless. Heli, who would necessarily have been the younger brother, would have been obligated under the law of levirate marriages (Dt. 25:5-10) to provide a legal successor to the throne in Jacob's name, through Jacob's widow. This theory, farfetched as it is, almost satisfies the discrepancy in the genealogies as well as the curse God placed on the seed of Jeconiah (Coniah or Jehoiachin) (Jer. 22:28-30). It does not, however, satisfy God. This theory would place Jesus in the line of succession only through default.

Additionally, if it were true, the name of Heli would not appear in either genealogy since the children born of that union would be considered the children of Jacob. Also, since the law of levirate marriages specifically deals with childless widows and the inheritance of the property of the deceased husband, the widow would normally be assumed to have been childless for several years before one of her husband's brother would assume the surrogate role of providing his brother with the seed of inheritance.

Jesus was not the Messiah through default. God's covenant with David (2 Sam. 7:12-16) stipulated that one of his direct and irrefutable descendents, not a surrogate, would establish his throne forever. Who would believe the Messianic claims of an individual whose legal right to David's throne could be even remotely contestable? Rabbi Hillel (60 B.C.–10 A.D.), upon whose teachings modern orthodox Judaism was built, was also a direct descendent of David. If Jesus' only claim to the throne of David came through a surrogate, the Jews might easily have disputed His claim in favor of someone like Hillel, who more accurately fit the mold cast by the Sanhedrin with respect to the Messiah and whose teachings were more in line with the Sanhedrin's traditional beliefs and dogmas.

While the throne of David was promised in perpetuity to the seed of Solomon, the messianic line which leads from David to Jesus was not. Solomon's seed (not Solomon's throne) was cut off at Jeconiah (2 Ki. 24:8-9; 2 Ch. 36:9; Jer. 22:28-30). Matthan provides the legal genealogy, the throne ascension, from David to Joseph through Solomon. Joseph represents the surrogate, in name only, who provided the legality of name to Mary; and who later became the father of her other children. Scripture very clearly notes that while Joseph was the husband of Mary, he was not the father of Jesus Christ:

> *"And Jacob begat Joseph, the husband of Mary,* of whom was born Jesus, *who is called Christ."* (Mt. 1:16; KJV, emphasis added)

In the thirty-nine generations detailed in Matthew's chronology, we see the seed promulgation from father to son (or grandson as the case may be) with the exception of the fortieth generation where the seed comes from the woman and not the man. Luke's genealogy, on the other hand, presents the seed succession of the royal blood line from David to Mary through Nathan.

Those who have a problem with Luke 3:23-38 as Jesus' genealogy through Mary based on the fact that only Joseph's name is mentioned in Luke 3:23 should consider the law of levirate inheritance (Nbr. 27:1-11; 36:8). The inheritance of the woman is imputed to be the inheritance of her husband. Because the woman could not inherit, a surrogate inheritor, her husband, assumed her family name. For that reason, Joseph's name supplanted Mary's in Luke's genealogy. As Jesus' surrogate father, Joseph was imputed the son of Heli through which the promise of the inheritance would be passed.

Why did Jesus refer to Himself as the "Son of Man" rather than as the "Son of God"?

All of Christianity acknowledges Jesus Christ as the Son of God, thereby affirming His deity. The biggest problem man has with Jesus is His identifying Himself as man. Christ used the title *Son of Man* in reference to Himself in order to constantly remind us of His humanity. The use of the phrase in Hebrews 2:6 establishes the humanity of Christ as an essential nature of our High Priest and Messiah.

Of all the titles by which Christ was addressed or addressed Himself, the epithet *Son of Man* is as important as those addressing Him as the Son of God. Except for the mention of Christ as the *Son of Man* in Acts 7:56 and Hebrews 2:6 (and an apocalyptic reference in Revelations 1:13 and 14:14), the term *Son of Man* is used exclusively by Jesus to describe Himself. By accepting this title Christ became representative of mankind, our surrogate before God. He came in the only form allowable to take back from Satan that which man had previously given away. The very nature of His mission on Earth demanded an incarnate being.

By stressing His humanity rather than His deity throughout His earthly ministry, Jesus continually reminded us that it

> *"...behooved Him to be made like His brethren, that He might be a merciful and faithful high priest in things pertaining to God, to make reconciliation for the sins of the people. For in that He*

Himself hath suffered being tempted, He is able to help them that are tempted." (Heb. 2:17-18; KJV)

It was the humanity of Christ (the human nature) and not the God-nature of the Messiah which was subject to temptation. While Scripture reveals that Christ had a sinless nature, and did not succumb to temptation, the possibility had to exist. Christ faced the same proposition of choice that we, as Christians, face today.

Jesus referred to Himself, or was thus referred by someone else, as the Son of Man *(bar'nas)* (Son of mankind) a total of 87 times. The phrase occurs thirty times in Matthew, fifteen times in Mark, twenty-six times in Luke, twelve times in John, once in Acts and Hebrews, and twice in the Book of Revelation. Interestingly, the prophet Ezekiel is also called son of man *(ben'adam)* (descendent of humanity) by God 85 times. In addition, the term son of man is used on two other occasions in the Old Testament to describe the Messiah—once in Psalm 8:4 and again in Daniel 7:13, for a total of 87 son of man references in the Old Testament as well.

Christ needed to firmly establish in our minds that His spiritual mission on Earth could only be fulfilled through His humanity. He had to come as a man, be tempted as a man, and defeat the adversary as a man. God had already defeated Satan—man had not. And finally, since His mission was spiritual in nature and not political, Christ took upon Himself the name which best suited His humanity.

Was Christ really tempted in the wilderness?

Was Christ really tempted in the wilderness (Mt. 4:1-11; Lk. 4:1-13) as we have been sometimes taught, or was He, as God, immune from temptation (Jas. 1:13)? On the surface, it would seem that the question is clearly addressed and answered in Hebrews 2:18, when the writer declares: "For in that He Himself hath suffered being tempted, He is able to help them that are tempted" (KJV). Yet uncertainty lingers in the minds of many Christians, young and old alike. Being God, could Christ really be tempted? James 1:13 emphatically states: "...God cannot be tempted with evil..." (KJV).

Are these verses contradictory? Or is it that we mortals equate temptation with sin to such a great degree that we do not believe it is possible to contemplate temptation outside of the realm of sin? "You know," a husband might say to his wife after an absolutely scrumptious feast, "I'm stuffed, but I just can't resist another serving..." Or a wife might say, "I know we can't afford this right now, but I just have to have it..." In both cases the subject is faced with temptation and succumbs. While the issue of temptation usually deals with the element of sin, we can be tempted outside the realm of overt sin. It is in this area that Satan first tried to entice Jesus.

As the second Adam, Jesus took upon Himself all of the frailties of man. He was made like His brethren, and took upon Himself a position "...a little lower than the angels for the suffering of death..." (Heb. 2:9; KJV)

As we study the Word of God we must recognize two things: first, as God, Jesus did not have a sin nature, and therefore could not sin. Second, Christ, according to Scripture, was tempted. It was the humanity of Jesus—the man-nature—not the spirit-nature of Christ that was subject to temptation. And while Jesus did not succumb to temptation, we must be prepared to acknowledge that His human nature had to be such that temptation could occur, since Jesus could not have been placed in such a position without possessing a genuine option to choose that with which He was being offered.

The human nature of mankind is easily tempted. Adam was tempted; Adam sinned. David was tempted; David sinned. Judas was tempted; Judas sinned. Simon Peter was tempted; Peter sinned. However, it must be understood that our sin nature can be triggered only if our spiritual nature is weak and allows that temptation to mature into fruition. We succumb to temptation because we do not activate the spiritual shield which protects us from the manifestation of our imaginations.

Because Jesus' spirit nature was Divine (since God cannot sin), His sinless spiritual nature completely shielded His human nature, protecting it from the barbs of Satan. This is precisely what we, as Christians, are also expected to do since we possess the power through the Holy Spirit to do so. As long as the Holy Spirit dwells within the Christian (1 Jn. 3:9), his spirit nature will protect us from the lusts of our corruptible flesh.

The same was true of Jesus. He was born flesh as were each of us. His physical characteristics and attributes were no different than ours. He was subject to the same worldly temptations and the same physical limitations which were faced by His contemporaries in Galilee. When it was hot, He perspired; when it was cold, He shivered. If He did not eat, He hungered; if He did not consume liquids, He thirsted. If He stubbed His toe, He felt the same type of pain other human beings felt. Although God, He was essentially man. And as man, Jesus allowed Himself to be subject to all of the biological rules which govern man. As a man Jesus proved man could defeat Satan. Our lives, like His, must be controlled by our spirits. If our spirit natures are Godly, we will be Christ-like in our daily walk. If that nature is corrupt, we will walk in sin. We cannot walk in the flesh and not sin.

Satan was very much aware that Jesus, although a man, was Divine, and as such could not be tempted to sin. Because of that knowledge, Satan's first two attempts to test Christ did not entail overt acts which we would construe as sin. Satan knew Jesus could function as our *kinsman-redeemer* (Ruth 4:1-9) only as a man. His ploy was to entice Jesus to act outside the realm of humanity; in other words, perform some miracle that a mortal human could not do—like changing a stone into bread.

After fasting forty days, Jesus hungered. Satan's first attempt was to try to lure Christ into changing a stone into bread to satisfy that hunger. When he failed, Satan then tempted Christ with the Scriptures themselves. Had he succeeded in either attempt, Satan would have successfully thwarted God's plan of redemption.

Realizing he could not entice Christ to act outside the realm of humanity, Satan knew he was defeated. At that point, Satan made his final appeal. Until the resurrection of Jesus Christ, Satan held title to planet Earth. Adam relinquished that title to him when he sinned in the Garden of Eden. Knowing Jesus was the *kinsman-redeemer* who was sent to save the world with His blood, Satan offered Jesus what He had come to die for—without the necessity of dying. The third temptation entailed Jesus bowing to Satan—an act of blasphemy against the triune Godhead.

It might seem that the simple act of turning stone into bread, or testing God (something all of us, as Christians, do at one time or another), would not constitute such a grievous sin as to thwart God's plan of redemption, but that was precisely the case—and Satan knew it. Considering what He had come to do, Jesus had to live completely within the limitations of man. He had to live in perfect obedience to the will of God to prove that we, as Christians, can do likewise. The moment He exalted Himself above the human system He had come to redeem, or used His omnipotence to save, or otherwise benefit Himself, He would have disqualified Himself as our Redeemer. Jesus had to defeat Satan in precisely the same manner that we must defeat him today. He could not, and did not, use extraordinary methods.

When we are tempted, the trials we endure always come in one of three areas: (1) our physical senses, (2) our imagination, or (3) through our reasoning. It was in these precise areas that Satan attempted to entice Jesus. Christ hungered (Mt. 4:2). Hunger is one of our physical senses. Satan failed to tempt the physical body of Jesus. Pride and ego were the characteristics Satan attacked next (Mt. 4:6). Interestingly, it was in this area that Lucifer was tempted and fell (Isa. 14:12-15). Satan failed in his effort to tempt Christ's spirit. Finally, Satan attempted to reason with Jesus (Mt. 4:8-9). Using logic, Satan offered Jesus that which He had come to die for, thereby eliminating the need for Christ's blood to be shed. Satan failed to tempt the very soul of the Messiah.

Was Jesus tempted in the wilderness? Yes. Remember, temptation is not the act of submission to an enticement—it is the contemplation of the offer. Could Christ sin? As the perfect and obedient Son of the Father, He could not—and did not.

If Christ was in the grave for three days and nights, how could He rise from the grave on the third day?

Did Jesus physically rise from the grave on the third day, or was His resurrection merely an allegorical symbol of an endtime resurrection? While His resurrection is well documented in each of the Gospels (Mt. 28:1-15; Mk. 16:1-14; Lk. 21:1-32; Jn. 20:1-9) many liberal mainline denominations appear to be having a problem accepting the resurrection as a literal, historical event (is it, do you suppose, because liberal archæologists have not physically confirmed it through fossil records which could not possibly exist since Christ physically ascended to Heaven from Mt. Olivet [Ac. 1:9-12] forty days after His resurrection?).

Shortly before his own crucifixion at the hands of Nero, Peter, who was a witness to both Christ's crucifixion and His resurrection, said:

> *"For we did not follow cleverly devised tales when we made known to you the power and coming of our Lord Jesus Christ, but we were eyewitnesses to His majesty."* (2 Pe. 1:16; NASB).

In 1 Corinthians 15:12-23 Paul stressed that the physical resurrection of Jesus was essential to our salvation. If Christ was not raised from the dead, we are still in sin, and our faith is in vain.

> *"But if it is preached that Christ had been raised from the dead, how can some of you say that there is no resurrection of the dead? If there is no resurrection of the dead, then not even Christ has been raised. And, if Christ has not been raised, our preaching is useless and so is your faith. More than that, we are then found to be false witnesses about God, for we have testified about God that He raised Christ from the dead. But He did not raise Him if the dead are not raised. For if the dead are not raised, your faith is futile; you are still in your sins. Then those also who have fallen asleep in Christ are lost. If only for this life we have hope in Christ, we are to be pitied more than all men. But Christ has indeed been raised from the dead, the first fruits of those who have fallen asleep. For since death came through a man, the resurrection of the dead comes also through a man. For as in Adam all die, so in Christ will all be made alive. But each in his own turn: Christ, the first fruits; then, when He comes, those who belong to Him."* (NIV)

Had Christ not risen from the dead, Christianity would have perished in the Upper Room before it was ever born. After Jesus was crucified the Apostles locked themselves in the room for fear of the Jews (Jn. 20:19), believing they would also be hunted down and killed. Before Christ rose from the grave on the third day (1 Cor. 15:4), there wasn't enough power in the Upper Room to light a 40-watt electric light bulb, let alone light up the world! If Christ had not risen from the grave, if He had not visited the disciples who huddled in fear in that room, Christianity would have died with His physical death. The disciples would have scattered throughout Judea, returning to their former occupations, and Jesus would have been nothing more than a memory.

More than a few converts to Christianity have a problem accepting the concept of a physical resurrection, choosing to believe instead that the resurrection is meant to be interpreted as an allegorical representation. Their problem, fanned by skeptics who believe they found an inconsistency in the Word of God which somehow invalidates the resurrection, is centered on the burial timeline: if Jesus was in the grave *(mnemeion)* for three days and three nights (Mt. 12:40), how could He possibly rise on the third day (1 Cor. 14:4)?

To fully appreciate the importance of this dilemma, we must recognize the fact that if Jesus was in the grave for three literal days and nights, we are faced with a fourth day resurrection, which contradicts the Bible. On the surface, it would appear that, if Matthew 12:40

> *"...For as Jonah was three days and three nights in the belly of a huge fish, son the Son of Man will be three days and three nights in the heart of the earth..."* (NIV)

is correct, then the tax collector's writings contradict 1 Corinthians 15:3-4:

> *"...that Christ died for our sins according to the Scriptures, that He was buried, that He was raised on the third day according to the Scriptures..."* (NIV)

Somehow, it does not seem possible that both statements could be true and accurate—yet they are! Christ was in the grave for three days and nights—and He rose on the third day! In both the Hebrew and Greek societies of that day, when a person referred to a period of time, say, three days and three nights, only a portion of the first and last days might be involved. Those contemporary to the Apostles would have understood the reference, and would not have seen an inconsistency in the two statements.

An example is found in 1 Samuel 30:12. David, in the heat of battle, complained that he had not eaten in three days and nights. The Hebrew text renders his statement (as well as verse 13 of the same chapter) as *hayyom u^e losah*, which literally means the day before yesterday. The same applies to the text of Jonah 1:17:

> *"And the Lord appointed a great fish to swallow Jonah, and Jonah was in the stomach of the fish three days and three nights."* (NASB)

Again *hayyom u^e losah* is used. We must therefore conclude the meaning is the same. Jonah was in the belly of the whale for one complete 24-hour day, and portions of two others.

This interpretation substantiates both Matthew 12:40 and 1 Corinthians 15:3-4. History confirms that Christ gave up the ghost around 3 p.m., Friday, April 10, 32 A.D. Before the sun set that evening, He was placed in a borrowed sepulcher (Mt. 27:60). This period of time, between 3 p.m. and sunset, constituted the first day and the first night. Saturday, April 11 was the complete 24-hour period, making up the second day and the second night. Jesus arose Sunday, April 12, 32 A.D.—the final time frame representing the third night and the third day. Understanding the Semitic view of day and night, we can now readily understand how Jesus could be buried for three days and three nights and rise on the third day.

What is so significant about the anointing of Jesus with a spikenard of costly oil that the woman who performed the act should be mentioned in all of the Gospels?

A variety of explanations to this question have been offered over the centuries. Some say Mary of Bethany (Jn. 12:3) anointed Jesus as an expression of *agape* love. No doubt it was, but that does not appear reason enough for an eternal memorial of the act to appear in Scripture, nor was it the reason why Christ said:

> *"...whenever this gospel is preached throughout the world, what*

she has done will also be told, in memory of her." (Mt. 26:13; NIV)

Many Christians feel Mary anointed Christ with the costly oil because He restored her brother Lazarus and that she is remembered in Scripture because of the size of the gift, which was reputed to be the equivalent of a full year's wages (Jn. 12:5), about 300 denarii.

There appears, however, to be a much more significant reason. As we examine Leviticus 8:6-12 we are instructed that before the high priest could perform the sacrifice of atonement for the people, he needed to be consecrated with anointing oil. It should also be noted that the priest could not anoint himself. The anointing had to be performed by someone else, acting on behalf of the priest. In this instance God chose a woman: Mary of Bethany.

Christ, who was both High Priest and Sacrifice, was consecrated for that which He was about to endure for mankind. *Based on Levitical law, Jesus could not have been sacrificed as a propitiation for our sins without the oblation of anointing oil.* So, while there is no doubt the anointing of Jesus by Mary of Bethany was an expression of her love and devotion to the Messiah, the crucifixion could not have taken place without it. Therefore, the importance of the pre-sacrificial anointing of Jesus cannot be overlooked, nor could it be ignored by Scripture.

Why did Christ have to lay hands on the blind man from Bethsaida twice before the man received his sight?

The posing of such a question actually implies an inability on the part of Jesus to heal the sick under some circumstances. Nothing could be farther from the truth. Jesus could have healed the blind man completely with the spoken word, but such an act probably would not have healed the man's spiritual blindness.

Bethsaida was one of three cities (together with Chorazin and Capernaum) which Christ ultimately condemned for their disbelief. When Jesus cursed those cities He declared that if the miracles which had occurred there had been performed in Sidon, Tyre or Sodom, those cities would still be standing (Mt. 11:21-24).

The blind man, like Bethsaida itself, was spiritually blind as well as physically sightless. The spittle Jesus used was an ointment used more to heal the spiritual blindness of the man than to restore his vision. Christ knew that lasting faith is built by degrees. It was for that reason that, after laying hands on the blind man the first time, Jesus asked the man if he could see anything. It was not the Lord's intent to completely heal the man in that instant. Hope needed to be kindled first—because through hope, faith is built. Once the mustard seed of faith appeared, Christ laid hands on the man the second time. In that instant, both spiritual and physical sight were given.

Because Jesus had already abandoned Bethsaida, Chorazin and Capernaum to judgment by that time because of their stiff-necked rejection of Him, He would not perform healings within those cities, nor allow testimony concerning the miracles He performed to come forth from them.

Why did Christ curse the barren fig tree?

On the sixth day before His crucifixion (Jn. 12:1) Jesus and His disciples went to Bethany to visit Mary and Martha, the sisters of Lazarus, whom He raised from the dead. The following day Jesus drove the money changers and merchants from the Temple courtyard (Mt. 21:12-13; Mk. 11:15-17; Lk. 19:45-46; Jn. 2:13-16). Jesus came to Jerusalem at that time not only to celebrate the last legitimate Passover, but to fulfill it.

We carefully note that the Passover, which was originally called the *Lord's Passover* (Ex. 12:27; Lev. 23:5), is called the *Jews' Passover* in the New Testament (Jn. 2:13, 11:55) because while the Jews celebrated it outwardly, they had rejected He who had come to scripturally fulfill it.

> *"On the next day...* (the fourth day before the Passover)*...when they were come from Bethany, He was hungry. And, seeing a fig tree afar off, having leaves, He came, if perhaps He might find anything on it: And, when He came to it, He found nothing but leaves; for the time of the figs was not yet. And Jesus answered and said unto it, No man eat fruit of thee hereafter forever. And His disciples heard it."* (Mk. 11:12-14; KJV)

This event happened in the first month of the Jewish sacred year. The date was April 6. It was still early for figs, but the leaves suggested some fruit would be present unless the tree had been picked bare by other travelers who happened by before Christ's procession.

The presence of leaves, either large or small, would be indicative of fruit, since the fig tree bears fruit before the leaves appear. The leaves would have either been the large, full leaves from the preceding season, or they were small, spring leaves. If the leaves were large, it would indicate to the wayfarer that the tree might contain large, plum colored autumn figs, called *kermouses*, which can be found on the tree throughout the winter months. If the leaves were new, there would be tender fig buds, called *bakkooroth,* or early figs, as they were commonly known.

It takes a fig tree approximately three years to bear fruit. Christ's earthly ministry was roughly three and one half years, or about the same length of time the fruitless tree had been allowed to stand. From the parable of the fig tree (Lk. 13:6-9) we learn that God was prepared to cut off His chosen people because they were stiff-necked and refused to repent. The cursing of the fig tree parallels that parable, and the action Jesus took was performed to illustrate the fate of the fruitless generation which had rejected Him.

> *"...A man had a fig tree, planted in his vineyard, and he went to look for fruit on it, but did not find any. So he said to the man who took care of the vineyard, 'For three years now I've been coming to look for fruit on this tree and haven't found any. Cut it down! Why should it use up the soil?' 'Sir,' the man replied, 'leave it alone for one more year, and I'll dig around it and fertilize it. If it bears fruit next year, fine! If not, then cut it down."*
> (Lk. 13:6-9; NIV)

Jesus had been calling Israel to repentance for three years, but the nation failed to heed His warnings. The parable warns that judgement always follows sin. Just as God's admonition to Adam

> *"...in the day that thou eatest thereof... (from the tree of the knowledge of good and evil) ...thou shalt surely die..."*
> (Gen. 2:17; KJV)

did not mean that death would occur on the selfsame day in which the deed occurred, Christ's condemnation of the fig tree, which symbolically represented the nation of Israel, did not mean judgment would fall on the Jews that specific day, either. Judgment was postponed for 38 years. In 70 A.D., Flavius Titus sacked Jerusalem and destroyed the Temple. Today, only one wall of that Temple, the Wailing Wall, remains standing.

Other than someone saying He was, how do we know Jesus Christ is the Son of God?

The evidence which clearly points to Jesus as the Son of the Living God is so overwhelming that the skeptic has a problem dismissing it with anything except irrational paralogism. The skeptic employs two basic arguments to mitigate the volume of evidence which clearly confirms the deity of Jesus. The first syllogism is centered on the Jews themselves; the second is focused on the Scriptures whose prophecies point only to Jesus as the Messiah.

The humanist argues, Scripture notwithstanding, if Jesus was the Christ, why would the Jews, who were at that time anxiously seeking a Messiah, not be able to recognize Him as the Christ while He walked among them, performing one miracle after another? Who better to pinpoint the Messiah, the humanist argues, than those who contemporaneously walked the land of Galilee with Him? Surprising as it may seem, while His disciples recognized Jesus as the Messiah, they did not immediately realize He was also the Son of God. This fact had to be revealed to them by the Holy Spirit. Peter was the first to acknowledge Jesus as the Son of God:

> *"When Jesus came into the borders of Cæsarea Phillipi He asked His disciples, saying, 'Who do men say that I, the Son of man, am?' And they said, 'Some say that Thou art John the Baptist; some, Elijah; and others, Jeremiah, or one of the prophets.' He saith unto them, 'But who say ye that I am?' And Simon Peter answered and aid, 'Thou art the Christ, the Son of the living God.'*
> (Mt. 16:13-16; KJV)

In response to Peter's declaration, Jesus confirms it was not of the disciple's own intellect that he spoke those words, but rather, that Peter was divinely inspired by the Holy Spirit to utter them:

> *"And Jesus answered and said unto him, Blessed art thou, Simon Barjona; for flesh and blood hath not revealed it unto thee, but My Father, who is in heaven."* (Mt. 16:17; KJV)

It is at times difficult for both humanist and Christian alike to understand that discernment of spiritual matters comes not only exclusively from the Holy

Spirit, but that it comes solely from the Holy Spirit, by appointment only. The logic behind this reasoning is valid, since it is central to the law of redemption.

We, as Christians, are accountable only for what we know, do, or fail to do. Knowledge is foremost, since it is either through knowledge or ignorance that we act or fail to act. We are not held accountable for those matters of which we have no knowledge, only that which we know. That is not to suggest that a person who successfully sidesteps the question of salvation throughout his or her lifetime will, because of good works, be imputed as righteous in the afterlife and granted admission to Heaven. We are saved by faith, through grace (Rom. 3:23; Eph. 2:5), and not through works. Faith and grace are action words. Faith requires something from the believer; grace requires something from God.

Coming to Christ requires a step of faith on the part of the believer. This first step must necessarily be accomplished with human intellect only, since God instilled in mankind the right of choice specifically for that purpose. We must choose to follow Him on faith (Rom. 3:28; Gal. 2:16)—not by a preponderance of evidence. Once the believer takes that step of faith, God is then required, according to His promise, to accept the believer—without reservation or qualification—shielding the believer with His grace, which is the redemptive blood of Jesus Christ. It is only at this time, by appointment, that the Holy Spirit begins to work within the believer.

If the Scriptures required no special discernment, all of mankind, knowing Jesus was the Son of God, would have been obligated to bow down and worship Him, thereby eliminating man's right to choose—something which is antithetical to God's purpose. When choice does not exist, rebellion almost certainly follows.

Lucifer, an angelic being created specifically to worship God, rebelled (Isa. 14:12-17). Lucifer *(Hêlël),* whose name means *daystar,* has been described as the most beautiful angel in Heaven; an archangel created for a position of leadership, second only to the triune Godhead in authority. Denied the initial choice of whether or not to freely worship God, Lucifer, together with a third of the angels—who willingly elected to follow him— rebelled against the authority of God and were cast from Heaven. Lucifer's name is a *hapax legomenon* used by Isaiah to describe the rebellious King of Babylon, through which, a prophetic syllogism of Antichrist is also brought into view.

Faith does require some evidence since blind faith many times leads down blind alleys to false messiahs. For that reason, the Word of God provides an abundance of prophecies which point directly to Jesus Christ. It is a road map which requires little faith to follow.

Imagine, if you will, that you are planning a trip. You have in your possession a road map which precisely details the route you are to take; and your destination is clearly marked. Your road is not as wide nor is it as well paved as the other roads on the map. But although it is narrow, it is a straight road. When you begin your journey you notice that there are many other motorists on the road as well. You recognize some of the travelers as they pass you, and you know they had planned to visit the same place as you. When you reach a fork in the highway, however, you notice many of the cars, some containing those you know, take a different fork, which your map indicates will lead to an altogether different location. Do you assume, because they reached that fork in the road before you that they suddenly have some special insight you do not possess? Or do you continue to follow your own map? The humanist would have you believe that since the first century traveler reached the fork before you, they somehow know the route better. The reality is, the humanist believes that if everyone gets detoured, and nobody shows up for the Marriage Feast, God's day of reckoning will somehow be indefinitely postponed.

God uses prophecy to confirm not only His Word, but His reality—and the reality of Jesus Christ as the Son of God. These prophecies confirm both His identity and His deity. Among them are:

PROPHECY	FULFILLMENT
Gen. 3:15	Mt. 1:20, Gal. 4:4
Gen. 22:18	Mt. 1:1; Gal. 3:16
Gen. 49:10	Lk. 3:23-24
Nbrs. 24:17	Lk. 3:23-24
Ps. 2:6	Mt. 27:37
Ps. 2:7	Mt. 3:17; Mk. 9:7; Lk. 9:35, 22:70; Jn. 1:34, 39; Ac. 13:30-33
Ps. 16:10	Mt. 28:6; Mk. 16:6; Lk. 24:46; Ac. 2:31, 13:33
Ps. 22:1	Mt. 27:46
Ps. 22:7-8	Mt. 27:31
Ps. 22:16	Lk. 23:33; Jn. 27:31-32
Ps. 22:17	Lk. 23:35
Ps. 22:18	Jn. 19:23-24
Ps. 34:20	Jn. 19:33
Ps. 35:11	Mt. 26:59-6
Ps. 41:9	Mt. 10:4, 26:49-50; Jn. 13:21
Ps. 68:18	Ac. 1:9
Ps. 69:21	Mt. 27:34; Jn. 19:28
Ps. 72:10	Mt. 2:1-11
Ps. 78:2	Mt. 13:34
Ps. 109:24-25	Mt. 27:31-32; Lk. 23:26; Jn. 19:17
Ps. 109:25	Mt. 27:39
Ps. 110:1	Mk. 16:19; Ac. 2:34-35; Heb. 1:3
Ps. 110:4	Heb. 3:1, 5:5-6
Ps. 118:22	1 Ptr 2:7
Isa. 7:14	Mt. 1:18, 23, 24, 25; Lk. 1:26-35
Isa. 9:1	Mt. 4:12-17
Isa. 11:1	Lk. 3:23-24
Isa. 11:2	Mt. 3:16-17; Mk. 1:10; Lk. 4:15-21; Jn. 1:32

PROPHECY	FULFILLMENT
Isa. 33:22	Jn. 5:30
Isa. 35:5-6	Mt. 9:32-35, 11:4-6; Mk. 7:33-35; Jn. 5:5-9, 9:6-11; 11:43-47
Isa. 40:3	Mt. 3:1-3, 11:10; Lk. 1:17; Jn. 1:23
Isa. 50:6	Mt. 26:67
Isa. 53:3	Lk. 23:34
Isa. 53:5	Mt. 27:26
Isa. 53:7	Mt. 27:12-19
Isa. 53:9	Mt. 27:57-60
Isa. 53:12	Mt. 27:38; Mk. 15:27-28
Isa. 53:12	Lk. 23:34
Isa. 60:3	Ac. 13:47-48
Jer. 23:5	Mt. 1:1, 9:27, 15:22, 20:30-31, 21:9-15, 22:41-46; Mk. 9:10, 10:47-48; Lk. 3:23, 3:31, 18:38-39; Ac. 13:22-23; Rev. 22:16
Jer. 31:15	Mt. 2:16
Amos 8:9	Mt. 27:45
Mic. 5:2	Mt. 2:1, 2:4-8; Lk. 2:4-7; Jn. 7:2
Zech. 9:9	Mt. 21:6-11; Lk. 19:35-37
Zech. 11:12	Mt. 26:15, 27:3
Zech. 11:13	Mt. 27:5
Zech. 11:13	Mt. 27:7
Zech. 12:10	Mt. 27:31-32; Lk. 23:33
Zech. 12:10	Jn. 19:34
Zech. 13:7	Mt. 26:31; Mk. 14:27, 14:50
Mal. 3:1	Mt. 21:12

Two of the most commonly known prophecies concerning Jesus are found in Isaiah 7:14 and Micah 5:2. Isaiah 7:14 deals with the virgin birth, an event that is absolutely necessary for Jesus to be deity.

"Therefore the Lord Himself shall give you a sign; Behold a virgin shall conceive, and bear a son and shall call His name Immanuel."

Most Americans, even those who do not profess Christianity, are familiar with the Christmas carol *O' Little Town of Bethlehem,* and mentally acknowledge Bethlehem as the birthplace of the baby Jesus. Most do so without realizing that Micah's ministry began during the reign of Jotham (742-735 B.C.) and continued until 687 B.C. with the fall of Jerusalem. Micah's prophecy concerning the birthplace of the Messiah occurred during this period—almost 700 hundred years before the birth of Christ!

It is not until the humanist realizes exactly when some of these prophecies were originally made that he or she attempts to employ paralogism to refute the biblical dating of the Scriptures. Surprisingly, for their defense, they actually use the very thing they argue against: the uncanny accuracy of biblical prophecy. Using the likes of Nostradamus as a model example of a prophet, they insist prophecy cannot be as accurate as that found in Scripture—therefore, something must be wrong with the Scriptures. What exactly? Of course, they have an answer. Clearly, the Scriptures, they argue, must have been written much later than the content of the text supposes. In fact, many argue that evidence exists that supports the theory that most Bible prophecies were actually penned after the fact!

Again, there is no evidence to support such humanistic wishful thinking. What the humanist really means is that there are still portions of the Old Testament which have not yet been substantiated archæologically. However, it must be noted that, to date, not a single verse of Scripture has been refuted or contradicted through archæological discovery!

With respect to New Testament scholarship, the humanist insists that the text was written no earlier than the end of the first century, A.D., and more likely, sometime well into the second century. Date changing is a necessary ingredient in the secular theology of the humanist, who insists that Christ's own disciples did not believe He was the Son of God, and that the New Testament text was written much later, long after the last of the twelve Apostles had died, when the myth of Jesus Christ had become perceived reality.

According to a 1995 *Newsweek* article on the histriocity of the Bible, a portion of Mark's Gospel was recently found which suggests not only that Mark's Gospel was the earliest of the four, but that it was very likely written prior to 40 A.D. The scroll was found among other artifacts that were dated around 40 A.D., only eight years after the crucifixion. Clearly, this indicates the original Gospel was penned even earlier—perhaps within months, or at the least, within a year or two after Christ's resurrection and ascension into Heaven. Prior to this discovery, most of those debating the age of the New Testament, theological as well as secular, believed most of the New Testament canon was written anywhere from 70 to 150 A.D. at the earliest. While it is the subject matter and not the dates of particular Gospel text upon which Christianity stands or falls, the skeptic focuses more on the dating of the testaments than the integrity of the Word of God because those are the only straws of uncertainity which can be grasped. The farther the text is established to be from the historic events which are described, the more plausible is their argument that the historical picture of Jesus was clouded by the myths of the Messiah, which would quite naturally be enhanced by those who knew the disciples who were personally acquainted with Christ.

When Jesus made His final appearance to His disciples at the Sea of Tiberias (Jn. 21:1), He signified the manner of martyrdom through which Simon Peter would glorify God. Peter, like his Master, would be crucified (Jn. 21:18-19). From that day forward there was no doubt in Peter's mind that to follow the teachings of Jesus Christ meant he would someday lay down his life for that belief. Had Peter and the other Apostles followed cunningly devised fables which were promoted by Jesus to deceive the population (for whatever reason, since Jesus did not accumulate any wealth—unlike the megaministries of the twentieth century, whose pastors have amassed what can only be described as personal fortunes while peddling the Gospel of Jesus Christ), it is not likely they would have continued the practice after the crucifixion, since doing so would have meant almost certain death—particularly if they themselves had been instrumental in either creating or promoting the myth that Jesus was the Christ.

For that reason, there are probably no testimonials which affirm the Godhead of Jesus Christ more clearly than Paul's second letter to Timothy, and Peter's second epistle to the church at large. In both instances the Apostles knew their deaths were imminent. Both were, in fact, in prisons, awaiting their executions. Paul affirms this when he writes:

> *"For I am already being poured out like a drink offering, and the time has come for my departure. I have fought the good fight, I have finished the race, I have kept the faith. Now there is in store for me the crown of righteousness, which the Lord, the righteous Judge, will award me..."* (2 Ti. 4:6-8; NIV)

Peter further affirms this thought in his final epistle:

> *"I think it is right to refresh your memory as long as I live in the tent of this body...* (ref. 1 Cor. 6:9) *...because I know that I will soon put it aside, as our Lord Jesus Christ has made clear to me..."* (2 Pe. 1:13-14; NIV)

Had Jesus not been the Christ, the Son of the Living God, Peter emphatically declares that neither he nor any of the others would have followed Him:

> *"We did not follow cleverly invented stories when we told you about the power and coming of our Lord Jesus Christ, but we were eyewitnesses of His majesty..."* (2 Pe. 1:16; NIV)

To further confirm the deity of Jesus, Peter recalls the Transfiguration (Mt. 17:1-13; Mk. 9:2-13; Lk. 9:28-36):

> *"For He receiveth honor and glory from God the Father when the voice came to Him from the Majestic Glory, saying, 'This is My beloved Son; with Him I am well pleased.' We ourselves heard this voice that came from Heaven when we were with Him on the sacred mountain."* (2 Pe. 1:17-18; NIV)

Peter then warned the believer against false teachers (2 Pe. 2:1-2), as did Paul (2 Tim. 4:3-4). Both men knew the day would come when man would reject the Bible as the infallible Word of God and find teachings which would be more gratifying to them. We know that doctrine today as humanism.

In mute testimony to the Godhead of Jesus Christ, every Apostle except John, the beloved, was martyred. John escaped death twice at the hands of the Roman Emperor, Domitan. First, an attempt was made to poison him. When that failed, Domitan ordered John boiled in oil. When that failed as well, Domitan became afraid. Believing the stories which had circulated about the Apostle, that he could not be killed, Domitan exiled John to Isle of Patmos where the Book of Revelation was written.

In 44 A.D., Herod Agrippa, in an attempt to ingratiate himself with Cæsar Caligula, initiated a strong persecution of the Christians in an attempt to rid the world of them. James, the brother of John, was beheaded for his faith. As was the custom, a witness was hired to falsely accuse him so that he might be condemned. At the execution site the accuser came to James and begged his forgiveness for the perjury he had committed. James and his accuser were beheaded together, and became martyrs for their Messiah.

Phillip of Bethsaida was martyred in 54 A.D. at Heliopolis. He was scourged, thrown in a prison, and later, crucified. Matthew, the tax collector, followed six years later. Matthew was slain with a battle-axe for his witness to the pagans in Nadabah, Ethiopia.

According to Jerome, the first century Christian historian, Simon Peter was taken to Rome where he was personally sentenced to death by Nero. His death occurred sometime between 66 and 68 A.D. Feeling unworthy to be crucified in the same manner as his Master, Peter asked to be crucified upside down. His request was granted, and Peter died head down, feet up, for the cause of Jesus Christ.

Matthias, whom the Apostles appointed to replace Judas, was stoned to death in Jerusalem. While the date of his martyrdom is not recorded, it has been suggested it is likely he was stoned with James, the brother of Christ, in 62 A.D. James' death came at the hand of Annas, the high priest of the Sanhedrin, who seized his opportunity to rid Judea of the Christians shortly after the Roman proconsul, Festus, died, and before a replacement could arrive from Rome. Since the Sanhedrin had no authority to take a human life without Roman consent (Jn. 18:31), Annas assumed a great personal risk in doing so. However, since James was "...the principle disciple of Jesus Christ (and) had been for many years the only Christian bishop of the believing Jews..." (Dissertation 1:2; see also Acts 14:26-15:2; Gal. 2:12) Annas felt it was a risk worth taking. With James and his followers dead, the Sanhedrin logically concluded Christianity would quickly wane and die.

Some conclude that Matthias could not have met his fate with James, since while both men were stoned to death, Matthias was also beheaded. It is generally believed that since James was recognized as the leader of the Christian movement at the time, it would have been more likely that he, not Matthias, would have been beheaded if the two had been executed together, or, at the very least, that both men would have suffered the same exact fate.

Paul, the Apostle God appointed to replace Judas Iscariot, was beheaded sometime between 66 and 68 A.D. in Rome. Like Peter, he was condemned by Nero. However, unlike Peter who as a citizen of a captured land had no legal rights under Roman law, Paul claimed the rights of a Roman citizen. As such, Paul had the legal right to appeal his conviction, yet he made no attempt to do so.

Judas, the brother of James the Lesser (who was commonly called Thaddeus), suffered martyrdom in 72 A.D. Two different views of his death have been recorded. The traditional view holds that Judas was crucified at Edessa, near the Euphrates River, after healing many and causing many Arabs to come to Christ. The other view is that he was shot with poisoned arrows and died near Mt. Ararat in Turkey.

In 74 A.D., Simon the Zealot was crucified in Britain. James the Lesser, the son of Alpheus, became a martyr when he was sawed to pieces (like the prophet Isaiah) for his faith. Andrew, the brother of Simon Peter, was martyred in Achaia. When the wife of the governor, Aepeas, was healed of a disease and converted to Christianity through Andrew's ministry, Aepeas had him crucified. Andrew, like Simon Peter, felt unworthy to be crucified in the same manner as Christ, and begged Aepeas to crucify him on a different type of cross. Andrew was crucified on an X-shaped cross, which is now commonly referred to as St. Andrew's Cross.

Bartholomew (Nathanael), who translated the Gospel of Matthew into the language of India, was martyred in that country. He was flayed alive with knives but did not die fast enough or painful enough to suit his torturers, who then crucified him. Thomas, called Didymus, also preached the Gospel to the pagans of India. Because he refused to believe that Jesus had really risen from the grave until he could insert his fingers into the wounds in Christ's body (Jn. 20:25-29), he is remembered as Doubting Thomas. After he saw the risen Savior, Thomas never doubted again. Knowing his God lived eternally gave Thomas the courage to die for Him. Pagan spears took his life.

Barnabas, who brought Paul to the other Apostles, is thought to have perished with his nephew, John Mark, in Alexandria. Mark was dismembered as a sacrifice to the pagan deity *Serapis*. Mark is remembered as the frightened disciple who, when grabbed by one of the multitude who came with the priests and elders to take Jesus into custody, fled naked into the night leaving his garment behind in the hand of those who grabbed him (Mk. 14:51-52). Mark is also remembered as the disciple Paul thought to be so spiritually weak that he refused to take him on his second missionary journey (Ac. 15:36-39). Yet, in the end, Mark was faithful, affirming with his own blood that Jesus was the Christ.

The eyewitness accounts of the Apostles, sealed with the testimony of their deaths, loudly confirms their personal belief that Jesus of Nazareth was exactly who the Word of God declared Him to be—the Son of the Living God. He who was first with the Father (Jn. 1:1), became flesh (Jn. 1:14), and walked with man. His incarnation is unquestionable.

> *"That which was from the beginning, we have heard, which we have seen with our eyes, which we have looked at and our hands have touched—this we proclaim concerning the Word of Life. The Life appeared; we have seen it and testify to it, and we proclaim to you what we have seen and heard, so that you may fellowship with us. And our fellowship is with the Father and with His Son, Jesus Christ..."* (1 Jn. 1:1-3; NIV)

How can we be absolutely certain in our own minds that Jesus Christ is the Son of God? It's fairly easy: take a simple step of faith and seek Him! He is who He is because of who He is. We are whoever we are because of, or in spite of, Him. We will either enjoy eternal life because of Him, or we will suffer eternal damnation in spite of the fact that He has already paid the price for our salvation. That choice belongs to each of us. All that is required to gain the evidence needed to confirm His deity is one small step of faith. Once we take that one step, the rest is up to Him. What could be easier?

CHAPTER FIVE

SALVATION

What must we do to be saved?

Nicodemus, the Pharisee, came to Jesus by night (Jn. 3:1) and asked the Lord what he needed to do to be saved.

"Jesus answered and said to him, 'Truly, truly, I say to you, unless one is born again, he cannot see the kingdom of God." (Jn. 3:3; NASB)

Nicodemus, of course, was greatly distressed at these words, immediately thinking Jesus was telling him it would be necessary for him to somehow find his way back into the womb, and then be reborn, knowing such a thing was impossible. We, of course, understand the meaning that we must experience a spiritual rebirth. Nicodemus, who was himself a teacher, asked Christ how this could be. Christ replied that

> *"...Except a man be born of water and of the Spirit, he cannot enter into the kingdom of God. That which is born of the flesh is flesh; and that which is born of the Spirit is spirit."*
> (Jn. 3:5-6; KJV)

Since this statement is a key in understanding salvation, it is important to explore exactly what Jesus was and, conversely was not saying. Before discussing what Jesus meant, it is important to understand what He did not mean. Advocates of salvation through baptism use this verse to support their position that a person who has not been baptized cannot go to Heaven regardless of faith or commitment to God. *Born of water* means, to them, water baptism. This view, however, contradicts those verses which clearly state we are saved by faith and not works. Baptism, as an *action*, is something we are required to do—i.e., a work. Since Jesus completely atoned for our sins, there is no action we can take which will mitigate either our sins or our circumstances other than the simple step of faith required to accept Jesus Christ as our Lord and Savior. Further, the argument of salvation through baptism is completely invalidated by Christ's actions on the cross, when He promised the penitent thief he would be with Jesus that day in Paradise (Lk. 23:43). Since God is not a respecter of persons (Ac. 10:34), He would not make an exception for the admittance into Heaven for one individual and not grant that right to all. The penitent thief was not baptized. Because he was not, and was still granted access to Heaven, we know baptism, although a requirement from Jesus, is not absolutely essential for admittance into the Kingdom of God.

Some students of Scripture view the phrase "...born of water and the Spirit..." as referring to the natural birth versus the spiritual rebirth as based, one might imagine, on the fact that while we were in our fetal, pre-birth stage of life, we lived within a sea of prenatal fluid. However, that clearly was not Christ's meaning. Others maintain *water* refers to the Holy Spirit, since the Holy Spirit uses two means of purification: water and fire. That is not likely either, since the Scripture would then read "...born of the Spirit and the Spirit...", rendering it even more ambiguous and confusing. Still others insist the reference to water is an admonition to read the *water of the Word* (Eph. 5:26), and that salvation is achieved through reading the Word of God with the assistance of the Holy Spirit. None of these views are scripturally acceptable.

Sin must be purged. As stated earlier, God uses two methods to purge sin from the world: fire and water. Needless to say, since Jesus Christ atoned for our sins and purged them with His blood, unregenerated water cannot wash them away.

Nicodemus was likely reminded of John the Baptist (Mt. 3:1-7), whom he probably witnessed baptizing converts along the Jordan River after preaching his message of repentance. Jesus Himself came to John, and although pure, was baptized and symbolically purged of sin. The act of being *born of water* is not the actual baptism, it is what the baptism portrays, the act of repentance. Baptism symbolically portrays the washing away of sins which was accomplished with the blood of Jesus Christ. Likewise, immersion in water symbolically represents, first, the death and burial of Jesus; and second, the resurrection. We enter the water as an old creation—a creature of the flesh. We rise from the water a new creation—a being enpowered by the Holy Spirit. Baptism without repentance is merely a cold water bath in which we are completely submerged. Such an action may well have some cleansing effect on our flesh; but it will not cleanse our unregenerated spirit. The act of baptism is symbolic of a more important event: our repentance, which leads to the regeneration of our souls. Once we have become a clean vessel, the Holy Spirit then dwells within that vessel, and we become a new creation in Christ. In that sense, we have been born again.

To those who are spiritually lost, the question remains: how do we arrive at that point: what must we do to be saved?

Paul, in Romans 10:13, tells the reader that whoever calls on the name of the Lord shall be saved. The *whoever* Paul speaks of is completely and universally unqualified, clearly suggesting that anyone, regardless of their sin, or crime, or theological bent, may call upon Him in repentance and be saved. This verse does not suggest that only those of a particular denomination or theological persuasion have access to the *bema seat* of the Lord. The statement is unequivocal! Anyone who calls upon the Lord, seeking salvation, will be saved! That means you; and it means your best friend and your worst enemy! It means anyone; and it unequivocally means everyone!

But what if we are not believers in Jesus Christ? What if the doctrines we have followed teach that Jesus was merely a dynamic Rabbi who changed the world with His message of peace? What if we don't believe that Jesus Christ was actually the Son of God? Then, we have a serious problem, since salvation and eternal life follow only those who follow Him. Jesus is the Way and the Life. It is only through Him that man can be born again; it is only through Him that we can obtain eternal life. Paul deals with that question in the following verse, when he asks:

"How, then, shall they call upon Him in whom they have not believed...?" (Rom. 10:14; KJV)

Needless to say, we must first believe. This step begins the process through which salvation is obtained. Fortunately, the first step is a small one, and requires only the faith of a mustard seed. In my case, the first step came in the form of a question to God. Since I did not know Jesus, nor was I even convinced that God existed, my question to the Redeemer started with the word *if.* "...If you are real, God, then..." (Did I actually say it was a *small* step?) It is a small step in that all that is required is faith—the faith to believe. This grain of mustard came, believe it or not, from the Christian walk, not the Christian talk, of my wife. She was the perfect, silent witness of a perfect God. She embodied what Christianity is, and because of her Christlike spirit I opened my spirit to receive. (Far too many times spouses, eager to see their loved ones saved, attempt to use the words of the Scriptures rather than the Spirit of the Scriptures to reach those loved ones, and miserably fail in their efforts to see those loved ones come to Christ.)

Introductions are always the most difficult part of building any relationship. Once the ice is broken, it becomes easier and easier to communicate with God, and for Him to communicate, via the Holy Spirit, with you. Many times believers mistakenly believe that because they were raised with a knowledge that God is real, were baptized as an infant or child, obey the Ten Commandments, and because they religiously attend church, they are saved. Being an institutionalized church member does not necessarily mean you are saved or that you have achieved salvation. Nor does it signify you are not, and have not, since none of those things actually has anything to do with obtaining salvation! Each of these elements are things the Christian does after salvation.

The Word of God clearly and emphatically teaches that we are saved by grace through faith, and not from anything we ourselves do (Eph. 2:8-9). We cannot buy salvation, nor can we earn it through good deeds or other works.

The Hollywood stereotype of the greedy rich man who achieves salvation simply by giving his fortune away to the poor moments before the grim reaper knocks on his door is pure movie fantasy. The admonition of Jesus to the rich young ruler (Mt. 19:16-22; Mk. 10:17-27; Lk. 18:18-27) to give up his wealth has mistakenly been construed as meaning the possession of wealth is tantamount to eternal damnation. Conversely, those verses have also been construed to mean that the surrender of wealth imputes salvation. Neither supposition is correct. There is nothing we can do in the flesh to earn salvation.

What then, must we do we do to earn salvation? Simply stated, all that needs to be done is to

"...confess with thy mouth the Lord Jesus Christ, and believe in thine heart that God hath raised Him from the dead.."

And, in doing so,

"...thou shalt be saved. For with the heart man believeth unto righteousness; and with the mouth, confession is made unto salvation." (Rom. 10:9-10; KJV)

As we break these verses down, we can see the order of events which must necessarily take place before salvation occurs. Just knowing that Jesus Christ is the Son of God is not enough.

"Thou believest that there is one God; thou doest well. The demons also believe, and tremble." (Jas. 2:19; KJV)

Satan knows who Christ is, and that knowledge has not saved him. If you've read the end of the Book, you know Satan will ultimately be cast into the Lake of Fire (Rev. 20:10) to be tormented by fire forever. Unfortunately, millions upon millions of our loved ones will also be cast into that same Lake of Fire at the Great White Throne Judgement (Rev. 20:11-15). Those so condemned will be found guilty because they chose to be judged by their own works rather than to be imputed righteous by the shed blood of Jesus Christ (Rom. 4:8, 11, 22-24; Jas. 2:23). Nobody, absolutely nobody, will enter the Kingdom of God through their own works. Christ made this very clear when He said:

"I am the Way, the Truth and the Life; no man cometh to the Father but by Me." (Jn. 14:6; KJV)

Since it is obvious we cannot get there on our own, it is important to understand what the Word of God tells us we must do. First, we must exercise a measure of faith: we must believe that Jesus Christ is the Way, the Truth and the Life. We have been assured by Almighty God that if we have the faith (Rom. 12:3) to believe that Jesus is the Son of God (Mt. 3:17; Jn. 3:16), that He died for our sins (Rom. 3:23-25; 1 Jn. 4:10), that He rose from the grave (Jn. 20:1-7), bodily ascended into Heaven (Ac. 1:9-11), and now intercedes on our behalf with the Father (Heb. 7:24-25), we will be saved.

Faith is fueled by the Word of God:

"Faith comes from hearing, and hearing by the Word of God." (Rom. 10:14)

We have been assured by the Word of God that if we confess with our mouths (not to man, but to God) that Jesus Christ is Lord, and believe in our hearts that He was raised from the dead, we shall be saved (Rom. 10:9):

"For with the heart man believeth unto righteousness, and with the mouth, confession is made unto salvation." (Rom. 10:10; KJV)

It is very important to understand that the *confession* mentioned here is not the specific detailing of all of the sins one has committed. Rather, it is a *confession of faith*. Once you have accepted Christ as your Lord and Savior, all of your past sins are covered by the blood, and are no longer remembered by God. We are not saved by a public delineation of our transgressions. God knows every sin we have ever committed. In fact, He knows every sin which was conceived in our imagination but never carried out. He does not have to be reminded of them, nor does He wish to call them to our remembrance. Once under the blood, our sins are forgiven and forgotten.

What must we do to be saved? Exercise that measure of faith which was given to every man, woman and child; read or listen to the Word of God; believe in your heart and confess with your mouth that Jesus Christ is Lord and you will be saved.

What does it mean to be "born again"?

Does salvation require a special experience? Is it necessary to feel goose bumps or have a lightning bolt Holy Ghost experience before we know we are saved? Can we experience salvation without emotionalism? The Bible does not describe the born-again experience as necessarily emotional—only necessary.

> *"Marvel not that I said unto thee, ye must be born again."* (Jn. 3:7; KJV)
>
> *"Except a man be born again, he cannot see the Kingdom of God."* (Jn. 3:3; KJV)

Many believe that the born-again experience is found only in the New Testament, since it is, most feel, a new covenant practice without Old Testament antecedents. However, that is not true. The prophet Ezekiel spoke of the born-again experience on two different occasions. The first is found in Ezekiel 11:19-20. The second, quoted here from the NKJV, is found in Ezekiel 36:25-27:

> *"Then will I sprinkle clean water on you, and you shall be clean; I will cleanse you from all your filthiness and from your idols. I will give you a new heart, and put a new spirit within you. I will put My Spirit within you and cause you to walk in My statutes, and you will keep My judgements and do them."*

Emotionalism is not mandated. In fact, it is not even mentioned. What is clearly indicated, however, is that we are not to rely on *self* in the matter of salvation. Instead, we are to trust in Him who saved us (2 Cor. 1:9-10, 5:17-21; Heb. 2:13-18). When we trust in our own intellect, we usually deceive ourselves.

> *"Indeed, in our hearts we felt the sentence of death. But this happened that we might not rely on ourselves but on God, who raises the dead."* (2 Cor. 1:9; NIV)

Whatever else it is supposed to accomplish in the believer, the born-again experience brings about a physical and spiritual regeneration which is usually quite apparent to the observer. The old nature is gone and a new spirit nature takes it place. It was this transformation Christ referred to when He told Nicodemus he needed to be born again. The reason, Christ explained, was that if our human nature does not change, we will be constantly given over to the flesh. Our sin nature cannot regenerate itself into sinlessness.

> *"That which is flesh is flesh; and that which is born of the Spirit is spirit."* (Jn. 3:6; KJV)

Christ's words were particularly meaningful to Nicodemus, who because he was a Pharisee, believed his salvation was secured by the Semitic bloodline which connected him through Jacob to Abraham. Although he was both a teacher and a member of the Sanhedrin, Nicodemus knew absolutely nothing about regeneration and could not therefore distinguish between natural and spiritual birth. To enter the Kingdom of Heaven man must be sinless. Absolute sinlessness can be achieved only through a parent with a completely sinless nature, since parents inherently transmit to their children the nature they themselves possess. Our natural parent is Adam. Since the sin-nature of Adam was inherent in all men, it is impossible for mankind, through physical ancestry, righteous standing, or good works within the community, to enter the Kingdom of God. Only Jesus, our spiritual father was born and lived without sin. It is only through Him, by adoption (Rom. 8:15-17) as our *kinsman-redeemer,* that we are imputed heirs of righteousness.

> *"But when the fullness of time had come, God sent forth His Son, born of a woman, born under the Law, to redeem those who were under the Law, that we might receive the adoption as sons. And because you are sons, God has sent forth the Spirit of His Son into your hearts, crying out 'Abba Father!' Therefore you are no longer a slave but a son, and if a son, then an heir of God through Christ."* (Gal. 4:4-7; NKJV)

The Bible further describes the born-again experience as something which cannot be seen, only recognized through its power:

> *"The wind blows where it wishes, and hear the sound of it, but cannot tell where it comes from or where it goes. So is everyone who is born of the spirit."* (Jn. 3:8; NKJV)

Although we can't see the wind, we can hear it; and we can witness that which it does. The power of the wind is evidenced by its sound (Ac. 7:2), and by that which it invisibly accomplishes. We can also feel the wind. It may be a gentle caress or a gale force. As the Holy Spirit deals with us, we may feel His presence, or we may not. Regardless, the evidence of His manifestation will show from within.

We may see a haughty, gossipy woman suddenly become a humble, silent prayer warrior who would die rather than reveal a confidence. It may be the man or woman who works next to you on the job, who abruptly changes from cursing God to praising Him. Or it could very well be a vain and corrupt businessman or politician who suddenly turns his life over to Christ and totally abandons his former lifestyle. (Such a man who immediately comes to mind is Charles Colson, President Richard Nixon's former White House chief of staff. Colson, as you remember, like many in Nixon's inner circle, became deeply involved in the cover-up of the Watergate break-in, and ended up serving time in a federal penitentiary. In prison Colson found the Lord, and upon his release, formed a prison ministry which now touches over 50,000 incarcerated men and women. Colson's group has also become a much respected conservative advocacy force on the national political scene.)

None can see the wind. However, we recognize the power of the Holy Spirit at work. No bells, no whistles, no goose bumps or lightning bolt experiences. Just the gentle touch of the Holy Spirit working within us to make us what God would have us become.

Can we lose our salvation once we have accepted Christ?

This is, without a doubt, the toughest theological question in the entire Word of God because it is the only trick question answered by Scripture. As such, it must be answered very carefully. Quite frankly, this question can honestly be answered either yes or no, depending entirely on who asks the question—and the motive behind the query. Before continuing, it is important to stress that the Bible is not ambiguous in this area. Scripture is very clear in dealing with this most important issue. Unfortunately, those who previously created the denominational doctrines which separate Christians today have opted to interpret Scripture much too broadly when dealing with this question, assuming those who read the Bible are truly saved individuals who have dedicated themselves to walking the narrow Christian path without straying.

The Bible implicitly teaches that salvation is a free gift of God (Rom. 6:23; Eph. 2:8-9). We cannot buy salvation, nor can we earn it (Gal. 2:16). Salvation is freely imparted to the believer by grace through faith in Christ Jesus. It would therefore appear that once we have been admitted into the family of Jesus Christ (Jn. 1:12-13), we can never lose our membership. What faith provides, grace accepts gratuitously. We are justified freely by grace through the redemption of Jesus (Rom. 3:24-25).

Identification with the family of Christ begins at regeneration with the infusion of the Spirit in the believer (Eph. 1:13). As the believer grows spiritually, he or she is more able to deal with the sin nature which remains within each of us. We are still accountable for that nature and each of us must individually accept the responsibility for any sin we commit. Left unrequited, sin will nullify the gift of grace, alienate the believer from God, and ultimately result in spiritual death.

It is taught in some quarters that sin is not imputed against the believer because salvation is an irrevocable gift, which it is. Advocates of this theory point to two verses of Scripture to support their contention:

> *"For by grace are ye saved through faith; and that not only of yourselves, it is a gift of God—not of works, lest any man should boast."* (Eph. 2:8-9; KJV)
>
> *"Whosoever is born of God doth not commit sin; for his seed remaineth in him, and he cannot sin because he is born of God."* (1 Jn. 3:9; KJV)

Before contemplating what 1 John 3:9 actually says, it is important to understand what it is not saying. It is not telling us that once we have accepted Christ it is no longer possible to sin. We can, and will, sin—probably daily—because we still have a carnal sin nature (1 Ki. 8:46; 2 Ch 6:36; Rom. 3:23; 1 Jn. 2:1). Second, it is not telling us that sin committed after salvation is not held against us. It is (Isa. 59:2; Rom. 6:23; 1 Cor. 6:9). Finally, it is not telling us that offenses which were accounted as sin before we accepted Jesus as our Lord and

Savior are suddenly rendered not-sin after our salvation. Sin remains sin, whether committed by a Christian, a Jew or a pagan. And the wages of sin is death, whether paid by the Christian, the Jew, or the pagan (Rom. 6:23).

"All unrighteousness is sin..." (1 Jn. 5:17; KJV)

What then, is 1 John 3:9 telling us? Simply stated, the Apostle John is saying that when the believer is born again of the water and the Spirit (Jn. 3:6), his or her sin nature is buried with Christ in that baptism. As long as the Holy Spirit dwells within us (Eph. 1:13), we cannot sin, because our sin nature remains buried and is not active in our lives.

The key phrase in 1 John 3:9 is the statement "...he cannot sin..." In the Greek text, the word used is *dunamai. Dunamai* means "does not have the power to..." or "...is not able..." Properly interpreted, this verse might say: "...and he does not want to sin because the Spirit of God dwells within him..." 1 John 1:8-10 more clearly amplifies this thought:

"If we say that we have no sin, we deceive ourselves, and the truth is not in us. If we confess our sins, He is faithful and just to forgive us our sins, and to cleanse us from all unrighteousness. If we say we have not sinned, we make Him a liar, and His word is not in us." (KJV)

When the believer is joined in a lasting spiritual union with God, he may deceive himself into thinking he has achieved a state of sinless harmony with the Lord, one in which offenses are immediately and unilaterally covered by the blood of Christ as they are committed.

A few years ago, my wife and I rented a home we owned to a Missionary Baptist preacher who was attempting to build a congregation, and wanted to use the house as a church. We noticed around thirty cars at his first service, suggesting an initial congregation of sixty to seventy people. Over the next few weeks the number of cars rapidly dwindled, until finally, two months later, only three or four cars arrived for services.

At that time my syndicated column *Answers From The Bible,* was quite popular and reached almost a half million homes each week. Since the theological bent of *Answers From The Bible* was deliberately nondenominational, I had been invited on several occasions to teach at a variety of churches ranging from Southern Baptist to Pentecostal to Mennonite. Wanting very much to help him rebuild his congregation, I offered to allow him to use me for that purpose.

He quickly declined my offer since he knew I was a Pentecostal. Feeling he thought the mere presence of a Pentecostal in his pulpit would cause his congregation to immediately begin speaking in tongues or be healed of all known ailments and diseases, I attempted to assure him my teachings were Christ-centered on basic Christian tenets, and not on the dogmas of denominationalism, whether Pentecostal or Baptist. In other words, I assured him, I avoided teachings on the gifts of the Spirit, baptism as a means of salvation, and the question of eternal security, which are three of the four most divisive issues in Christianity.

And although I had, in five years of writing *Answers From The Bible,* successfully avoided a theological debate on the subject of eternal security, I quickly discovered it was an issue the pastor, for personal reasons, wanted very much to debate. He insisted once an individual accepted Christ, sin, even that which was currently being committed, was not imputed against the sinner, since it was immediately covered by the blood of Christ. In other words, in his view, sin committed by a Christian was simply not sin.

Not certain I understood what he meant when he spoke, I sought a clarification. "Am I correct in assuming," I queried, "that you believe, for example, a man who had previously accepted Christ as his Lord and Savior and who dies while committing adultery with his neighbor's wife, without seeking forgiveness for that transgression before he dies, will go to Heaven?"

The pastor acknowledged he would, then further amplified his belief by recounting an event concerning a relative, either a brother or a cousin, which had occurred in that area some years earlier. The relative and his wife had both accepted Christ early in their marriage, but had drifted away from the church as they became involved in the normal, everyday struggle of life. Soon, the marriage was in trouble, and the pastor's relative began to drink. Finally, his wife filed for divorce. Realizing he had lost everything, the relative decided to make one last attempt at reconciliation; and, if that failed, he determined to kill his wife and take his own life as well.

When he voiced the threat to her, the estranged wife decided to obtain a restraining order to keep him away from her home and their children. She arranged with her identical twin sister to baby-sit while she met her attorney at the courthouse to secure the restraining order. While she was out the husband returned to her home with a shotgun. Believing the twin sister was his wife he shot and killed her. He then turned the weapon on himself and ended his own life.

In the view of the pastor, because the man had, at some previous time, accepted Christ as his Lord and Savior, his relative, who had just committed two murders, was now in Heaven.

In the view of many advocates of eternal security with whom I have related this story over the past few years, because the sin was homicide, the consensus seemed to be that the murderer went to Hell; but the victim, who like her sister had strayed from the church after first accepting Jesus Christ, was granted admission through the portals of Heaven. Ignored is the fact that in the eyes of God all unrequited sin is an abomination, and the penalty for sin—any sin—is eternal damnation.

> *"Know ye not that the unrighteous shall not inherit the Kingdom of God? Be not deceived: neither fornicators, nor idolators, nor adulterers, nor effeminate (homosexuals), nor abusers of themselves with mankind, Nor thieves, nor covetous, nor drunkards, nor revilers, nor extortionists, shall inherit the Kingdom of God."* (1 Cor. 6:9-10; KJV)
>
> *"And He that sat on the throne said, Behold, I make all things new. And He said unto me, Write, for these words are true and faithful. And He said unto me, It is done. I am Alpha and Omega,*

the beginning and the end. I will give unto him that is athirst of the fountain of the water of life freely. He that overcometh shall inherit all things, and I will be his God, and he shall be My son. But the fearful, the unbelieving, and the abominable, the murderers, and whoremongers, and sorcerers, and idolaters, and all liars, shall have their part in the lake which burneth with fire and brimstone, which is the second death." (Rev. 21:5-8; KJV)

Any and all unrequited sin can and will erase the efficacious atonement from the sinner.

"For I fear lest, when I come, I shall not find you such as I would, and that I shall be found unto you such as ye would not; lest there be debates, envyings, wraths, strifes, backbiting, whisperings, conceit, turmoil; And lest, when I come again, my God will humble me among you, and that I shall bewail many who have sinned already, and have not repented of the uncleanliness and fornication and lasciviousness which they have committed." (2 Cor. 12:20-21; KJV)

And there lies the entire debate on the subject of eternal security. To walk in a perpetual state of sinlessness requires a state of perfection the Christian will not possess until he or she is sanctified before the throne of God. Christians sometimes confuse sin-consciousness with freedom from sin. When the Holy Spirit dwells within us (1 Jn. 3:9), we are free from the consciousness of sin because our sin-nature is shielded by the Holy Spirit. Sin is still ever-present, and we no less possess the ability to sin. We simply lack the desire to sin, or we possess the strength to successfully resist the temptation to transgress. Sin will remain present in the world and, since we are in the world although not of it, we remain subject to it until sin and death are finally destroyed by Jesus Christ when He casts Satan into the Lake of Fire.

If 1 John 3:9 was really telling us that a believer could not sin after salvation had taken place, the word used in the Scriptures would have been *adunated* (we cannot, or it is not possible) rather than *dunamai.*

Does this mean we can lose our salvation? No, it does not, because, quite frankly, we can't lose it once we have accepted Christ. Our salvation is clearly a free gift from God, and God is not an *indian-giver!* God will not take back what He has freely given! We can, however, surrender our salvation back to Him!

Although our salvation is clearly irrevocable, we are nevertheless admonished to stand fast in that immunity, and to avoid the entanglement with the yoke of bondage (Gal. 5:1).

It was bondage to the Law that caused the Jews to become dislodged from their rightful blessing. It was the temporary—and I emphatically stress *temporary*—rejection of the Jews which made room for the reception of the Gentiles. As Christians we need to consider the full implication of these words before dismissing its implicit message as irrelevant for our day and time. God set aside an entire nation, His chosen people, for disbelief and disobedience. Is the Christian community so naive and conceited as to believe He would not cast out a disobedient adopted child after punishing a natural one? God is not a permissive parent!

> *"For if we sin willingly after we have received the knowledge of the truth, there remaineth no more sacrifice for sin. But a certain fearful looking for the judgement and fiery indignation, which shall devour the adversaries."* (Heb. 10:26-27; KJV)

All sin is willful. There is no such thing as accidental sin. All sin is committed with a willingness to participate on the part of the sinner. While we may not consciously think about the act, we actually contemplate sin when we allow ourselves to be placed in, or remain in, compromising situations, particularly when we arm ourselves only with our carnal nature to fight off the temptations with which we are faced (1 Pe. 4:1-2). If we do not put on the whole armor of God (Eph. 6:11) we will always end up fighting the enemy in the flesh; and, flesh never wins against spirit.

When Eve was tempted by the serpent in the Garden (Gen. 3:1-6) she did not have to succumb. She became a willing participant when her mind fell into agreement with her flesh and she tasted the forbidden fruit. David did not have to seduce Bathsheba (2 Sam. 11:4), make her pregnant (vs. 5), or compound the multiplicity of his sins by arranging the death of her husband (vs. 15, 24) so he could marry Bathsheba to prevent her stoning for adultery. Even more, Judas Iscariot did not have to betray Jesus (Mt. 26:47-49; Mk. 14:43-45; Lk. 22:47-48). Contrary to the Flip Wilson adage of the late sixties, the devil did not make him do it! Satan cannot make us sin; nor will God suffer any man or woman to be tempted (Jas. 1:13) beyond that which he or she can endure (1 Cor. 10:13).

Willful sin is presumptuous sin. There is no difference. All sin renounces the efficacious atonement, some temporarily, some permanently. Unrequited sin renounces the atonement just as effectively as presumptuous sin. The wages of sin, whether small or large, permanent or temporary, is still death!

In Romans 6:23 Paul uses the word *thanatos,* not *teleute,* to describe the type of death incumbent upon the wages of sin. *Thanatos* means spiritual death, or a conscious existence in separation from God. *Teleute* means the end of life, or physical death. The punishment for sin is clearly not physical death, rather it is the eternal separation of the individual from God.

Judas Iscariot was counted among the twelve (Mk. 3:13-19). Contrary to common belief, he was counted among the saved. He, like the other eleven, was granted power from on High. He, like the other eleven, was sent forth to preach the gospel and cast out demons. While it was ordained of old that someone would betray Jesus for thirty pieces of silver (Zech. 11:12-13), it did not have to be Judas. Judas was given an opportunity to repent and refused to accept it.

Even as Jesus prepared the bread and bitter herb sauce (Ex. 12:8) for the last Lord's Passover feast, it was not too late for Judas to repent. Had he done so, some other person (perhaps Simon the Zealot, who ideologically agreed with Judas) might have betrayed Jesus (Ps. 41:9). As they accepted the bread and sop, each disciple was reminded of God's promised salvation, and in receiving, acknowledged it. This ritual was very important to the Passover. The master of the house would sprinkle bitter herbs and bits of the lamb on unleavened bread, roll it, and dip it into the sop. He would prepare the pieces of *matzoh* one by one until each guest in the house had one. The first piece would be offered to the guest who sat on his right and his left. Both of these were places of honor. Judas sat on Christ's left. John, the beloved Apostle, sat on His right.

Since the *matzoh* was representative of God's promised salvation, the offer of bread to Judas was, in fact, an offer of forgiveness. Judas took the bread (Jn. 13:26) but did not eat it. Instead, Satan entered him (Jn. 13:37) and he left the banquet. When Judas rose from the Passover table he willingly rejected Christ and surrendered the irrevocable free gift of salvation. There can be no doubt in the mind of any Christian: Judas Iscariot was condemned to Hell! He was condemned by the very words of his Messiah:

> *"The Son of Man will go just as it is written about Him. But woe to that man who betrays the Son of Man! It would be better for him if he had not been born."* (Mt. 26:24; NIV)

What is the difference between sins which renounce the efficacious atonement of Christ's death permanently, and those which renounce it temporarily? A permanent renunciation would be like that of Judas Iscariot, who publicly, in attitude and conduct, renounced his faith and rejected Jesus Christ as his Lord and Savior. This person cannot be brought back into a state of repentance again since he has denied the only way by which salvation can be obtained. A temporary renouncement occurs when we assume God automatically forgives sin. The process by which sin is forgiven is very simple. One need only ask! However, if we foolishly believe that sins committed by us are not imputed as sin against us, the opportunity exists that through ignorance, we may not ask forgiveness.

If we willingly ignore the process by which sin is brought under the blood, we are then privately renouncing the efficaciousness of Christ's sacrifice on our behalf (Heb. 10:26-27). A Christian who dies while blatantly committing sin, or dies after such an act is committed without repenting of that transgression and asking forgiveness, risks the loss of his or her eternal soul because he or she has nullified the promise of grace and surrendered back to the Lord that for which Jesus died. In other words, while God will not take back the gift of life He has granted, we may of our own volition return it to Him at any time! The blood of Jesus Christ is not a blank check which provides the Christian a license to sin. God, in His infinite wisdom, knew we would stumble and fall. In His infinite mercy, Christ provided a safety net for those instances in our lives when we do. He did not intend, however, that His promise be used to mitigate continuing carnality after we have rejected the world and accepted Christ.

What is sin?

Ask anyone what sin is and you will probably hear a recital of the Ten Commandments; or, at the very least, as many of those commandments as the respondent remembers. We equate sin with a prescribed set of rules, of biblical rights and wrongs. Everything on the list is viewed as sin; anything not on the list is construed as acceptable. While violations of those rules may rightly be viewed as sin, sin itself transcends those rules, and may even include many other things not specifically mentioned.

Those sins specifically mentioned in the Ten Commandments include murder, adultery, idolatry, theft, envy, and the lack of respect for one's parents. Today we live in a world of political correctness which is redefining not only the parameters through which God may legally act in the affairs of mankind, but the very nature of sin itself. Children are advised that it is not only acceptable to disrespect their parents, they may now divorce them! Mothers are advised it is acceptable to murder their unborn children under the guise of personal liberty, and we are all told that adultery, or any form of illicit or perverse sex, is acceptable providing we use a condom to prevent the spread of disease. In our politically correct society there is only one evil: wealth. Wealth promotes only one sin: envy. In order for those who do not possess wealth to secure it (theoretically so they do not have to covet their neighbors), our politically correct, oligarchic society has devised a method, called taxation, by which the wealth of the more productive members of society is distributed to those less fortunate members of society who lack either the initiative or ability to become more productive members of that society.

Sin, properly defined, is any rebellion against the will of God (Josh. 1:18) whether or not it is scripturally defined as a specific sin. Anyone who provokes God (Dt. 9:7), scoffs or scorns (Prov. 24:9) His will or devises evil against God or man, commits sin. All unrighteousness against man, or mankind, constitutes sin (1 Jn. 5:17). Possessing a knowledge of right and wrong—and choosing wrong over of right, is also sin (Jas. 4:17).

Jonah, the son of Amittâi, sinned when God instructed him to warn Nineveh to repent or be destroyed. Jonah, who hated the Ninevites, wanted nothing more than to see their destruction. He rebelled against God's will. Instead of taking a ship from Joppa to Nineveh, Jonah attempt to flee from God by going to Tarshish. Because of his action, God created the great storm which caused the ship's crew to throw Jonah overboard where he was swallowed by the whale that spewed him out on the shores of the land of the Ninevites a day and a half later (Jon. 1:17)—only a three day walk from the city itself. Jonah disobeyed the will of God. Each of us at one time or another has disobeyed what we clearly recognized as God's will in, or purpose for, our lives. My ignoring God's purpose in my life for the past decade, specifically with regard to the ministry He established for me, and, in particular, this book, was a sin (see Introduction).

Sin, in any form, minor or severe, is a reproach in the eyes of God, and is something He cannot tolerate or abide.

Where is "original sin" found in the Bible?

The term *original sin* is not scriptural, just as the word *rapture* is not found in the Bible. Properly defined, original sin is that unregenerated state into which all mankind is born, which is the root of man's sin nature. When Adam, the first man, disobeyed God and fell, the entire human race fell into solidarity with him, inheriting both his guilt and his propensity to sin.

When God created man, He created him with a free will which would allow him to make choices. Adam, who had no conscious knowledge of evil, chose of his own free will to disobey God and eat the fruit from the tree of knowledge of good and evil, even after being warned that such an act would result in his death. He was not tricked by Satan, as was Eve (Gen. 3:1-6), nor was he tempted to do so. He was deceived by the woman and chose of his own free will to sin against God. This was the first, or original, sin.

When Adam succumbed to his own curiosity, his spirit became corrupt. Both he and Eve became inimical to God, and Adam suddenly had first hand knowledge of both good and evil. Adam and Eve hid from God in the Garden, suddenly fearing his wrath.

It is not necessary to teach a small child to get into mischief, he does that quite naturally because the tendency to sin in inherent. Conversely, we must teach that same child to be good since goodness is not a natural trait of man. We do not have to teach the adolescent the wily ways of the devil, but we must teach him the love of Jesus Christ. Nor do we have to teach adults how to survive in the dog-eat-dog business world, they learn that in the school of hard knocks. However, we do have to learn that success can still be achieved as a child of the Most High God.

Original sin is not a blotch which appears on our souls when we are born, and will condemn us either to Hell or *Limbo* if we die before we are baptized. A baby who dies within the womb or at birth, or shortly after birth, or any child who perishes before the age of accountability, regardless of the theology of the parent, will immediately go to Heaven where he or she will be with the Lord. Original sin is not an actual sin. Rather, original sin is man's inherent nature to sin. Original sin is purged by the blood of Jesus Christ. Once purged, we remain free of its implications as long as the Spirit of God dwells within us.

What are the "seven deadly sins"?

The Bible specifically mentions seven sins which Solomon declared to be an abomination to God. Actually, all sin is an abomination to God, since He hates all sin equally. All unrequited sin, even the slightest transgression, can send the transgressor to Hell for all eternity. Only one sin, blasphemy of the Holy Spirit, is unforgivable.

The seven deadly sins delineated in Proverbs 6:16-19 are: pride, lying, cruelty in any form, connivance, a willingness to sin, slander, and gossip or backbiting. Solomon referred to these particular transgressions as an abomination because they are totally contrapositive to God's will for our lives.

These transgressions are commonly called the seven deadly sins not because they are more severe or more of an abomination to God than any other transgression, but because most Christians do not view them as real sins, and therefore may not view these transgressions as anything for which forgiveness must be sought. It is His will that all mankind refrain from all forms of mischief, and that Christians conduct themselves in a humble, honest and caring manner;

and that all believers, on *that* day, be found free of guile.

Matthew Henry sums it up very well in his *Commentary on the Whole Bible* (Revell; Vol. 3; pg. 824) when he said: "Those that, by tale-bearing and slandering, by carrying ill-natured stories, aggravating every thing that is said and done, and suggesting jealousies and evil surmises, blow the coals of contention, are but preparing for themselves a fire of the same nature."

What is the "unforgivable" sin?

After Jesus cast the demon from the blind mute (Mt. 12:22) and restored both his vision and his speech, He was accused by the scribes and Pharisees of performing miracles through Beelzebub (the lord of flies; 2 Ki. 1:2), the prince of demons (Mt. 12:24), i.e., Satan (Mt. 12:25-29; Mk. 3:20-30; Lk. 11:17-22). Because of the impossibility of the miracles Christ performed, the crowd was astonished and raised the question: "Could this be the Son of David?" The question itself indicated the crowd was ready, at that moment, to accept Jesus as the Christ, the Messiah for whom they had waited 1,500 years. They logically turned to the Pharisees, the religious scholars of the land, for confirmation. But, because the Pharisees and the Sanhedrin had already rejected Christ as the promised Messiah, the Pharisees refused to ascribe the miracles they witnessed to the power of the Holy Spirit. Instead, they attributed the miracles of Jesus to Satan:

> *"And the teachers of the law who came down from Jerusalem said, 'He is possessed by Beelzebub! By the prince of demons is He driving out demons?"* (Mt. 12:22; NIV)

This particular miracle, performed in the presence of the Pharisees, was a validation of Christ's credentials, and clearly confirmed the person of the Messiah. Because this was somewhat of a last chance scenario for the Jews, Jesus defended that which the Holy Spirit performed through Him. As usual, since He had already been rejected, He did so in parables:

> *"How can Satan drive out Satan? If a kingdom is divided against itself, that kingdom cannot stand. If a house is divided against itself, that house cannot stand. And if Satan opposes himself and is divided, he cannot stand; his end has come. In fact, no one can enter a strong man's house and carry off his possessions unless he first tie up the strong man. Then he can rob his house. I tell you the truth, all the sins and blasphemies of men will be forgiven them. But whomever blasphemes against the Holy Spirit will never be forgiven: he is guilty of an eternal sin.' He said this because they were saying, 'He has an evil spirit.'"* (Mk. 3:23-30; NIV)

> *"Anyone who speaks a word against the Son of Man will be forgiven, but anyone who speaks against the Holy Spirit will not be forgiven, either in this age, or in the age to come."* (Mt. 12:30; NIV)

Christ offered three truths to verify His Messiahship. First, if His miracles were really of the devil, why would Satan allow Him to free someone under his power? To allow it would cause division in Satan's camp, and ultimately, would bring about his destruction. Second, since the Pharisees recognized exorcism as a gift of God, Christ questioned how they could accuse him of being demon-possessed for casting out demons (Mt. 12:28). Third, Christ pointed out that before a thief could enter a strong man's house to rob him, the thief had to have sufficient strength to overpower the strong man and bind him. By this Christ meant that He could enter Satan's stronghold at will and free those held captive, proving that He was unquestionably stronger than Satan. It goes without saying, with the ego Lucifer proved to possess as an archangel, Satan would not, or for that matter could not, grant a minion more power than he himself possessed.

Offering these arguments in defense of His Messiahship, Jesus then charged the people to reject the message of the Pharisees under the penalty of eternal damnation. Why, some wonder, did Christ add that any blasphemy committed against the Son of Man would be forgiven, but blasphemy against the Holy Spirit would not?

Jesus knew His earthly ministry was rapidly coming to an end, and until His second coming, only the Holy Spirit could authenticate His word on earth. The Holy Spirit would be the final witness of both the Person and the Word. If the Spirit was likewise rejected, there would be no other way to salvation; hence, from that point forward, everyone would be lost, negating the reason for the Atonement.

Many theological scholars believe this sin was exclusively an Israelite sin, and could be committed only when the nation of Israel was being presented evidence of the Messiah through the miracles He performed in Galilee. They insist the necessary circumstances no longer exist today, and consequently, the need for such an extreme penalty for such an extreme sin no longer exists either.

However, the nature of man, the nature of sin and the nature of the Holy Spirit invalidate their argument. While blasphemy of the Holy Spirit may not be committed in precisely the same manner as was described in that instance, rejecting Jesus Christ as the Messiah after witnessing the power of the Holy Spirit can most assuredly still occur today. Advocates of this flawed theory assume the Holy Spirit stopped performing miracles when the Apostle John died. Nothing could be farther from the truth. Miracles are just as prevalent, if not more prevalent, today than they were during the first century. As we come closer to the end of the age, they will become even more so.

Blasphemy against Jesus Christ—that is, the initial rejection of Him is a sin which can be committed only by nonbelievers, and is forgiven the instant the individual accepts Christ as their Savior. Blasphemy of the Holy Spirit is a sin which can only be committed by someone with a prior knowledge of the saving grace of Jesus, manifested through the Holy Spirit. This sin occurs when the believer rejects that which the Spirit of God had formerly impressed upon him, and he denies both the Spirit and the Savior, attributing what was accomplished by the Holy Spirit to other natural or supernatural means. Once that happens and the former believer has rejected what the Holy Spirit has authenticated, there remains no other avenue by which his sins can be cleansed (Heb. 6:4-6; 10:26), and he stands condemned, both in this world and the world to come (Mt. 12:32).

Is there a literal, fire-burning Hell, and where is it?

Some years ago, popular television talk show personality Phil Donahue commented to his guest, evangelist Jerry Falwell, that he had a problem believing God, whom Donahue perceived as all-loving and all-forgiving, would condemn him to the same fire-burning Hell that had originally been prepared for Satan and his cohorts simply because he didn't measure up to Falwell's precept of a Christian.

Many people—particularly those who belong to denominations that teach works as a means of salvation—feel exactly the same as Donahue. Others simply do not believe Hell is a real place, and that death is merely the absence of existence. Still others feel whatever Hell mankind is meant to experience will be suffered here on Earth as penance for whatever wrongdoings they have done during their lifetime. Yet the Bible clearly teaches that Hell is real—and the Scriptures even suggest where Hades is located!

There are fifty-seven references to Hell in the Old Testament, and twenty-one in the New Testament. Of the twenty-one New Testament references, at least seven were made by Jesus (Mt. 5:22, 30; 10:28, 18:19; 23:15, 33; Lk. 12:5). In each instance Christ's reference to Hell comes within a warning concerning the consequences of sin in which Hell is described as a place of unquenchable fire. In the Greek text, Hell is *gehenna.* The very nature of *gehenna* is unquenchable fire.

The most commonly used Old Testament word for Hell is the Hebrew word *sheol.* While evidence is admittedly inconclusive, the word *sheol* may be interpreted as an eternal separation from God. Of all of the Old Testament references, *sheol* is translated as Hell forty-one times in the King James text. It is translated "grave" *(qeber)* three times, and three times as "pit" *(pethach).* Because *sheol* is a Hebrew word, it is understandably not used in the New Testament. However, its Greek equivalent, *Hades,* is used instead. *Hades,* like *sheol,* means separation from God until judgment.

Before the ascension of Jesus, all who died went to Hades. Those who died in faith went to paradise (which was located in Hades) to await the coming of Jesus Christ. Those who perished in sin went to Gehenna (which was also located in Hades), to await condemnation at the Great White Throne Judgment before being cast into the Lake of Fire (Rev. 20:14, 21:8). When Jesus ascended to Heaven, He released all of the saved souls in Paradise, and took them to Heaven. Since that time, all who die in Christ go immediately to be with the Lord in Heaven (2 Cor. 5:8).

Gehenna, which quite literally means eternal fire, is derived from the Hebrew word, *Ge-Hinnom. Ge-Hinnom,* or Valley of the son of Hinnom, was the spot where the pagan altar of Molech was located in Jerusalem. Idol worshippers during the reign of Manasseh sacrificed their children to the Ammonite god Molech by throwing them from the altar precipice into a raging fire below.

> *"And he...* (Manasseh) *...caused his children to pass through the fire in the Valley of the son of Hinnom..."* (2 Ch. 33:6; KJV)

When God condemned the pagan practice of Manasseh, He also declared

His divine purpose for the place in which the altar to Molech had been erected:

> *"Therefore, behold, the days come, saith the Lord, that it shall no more called Topeth, nor the Valley of the son of Hinnom, but the Valley of Slaughter; for they shall bury in Topeth until there (is no more room)."* (Jer. 7:32; KJV)
>
> *"For Topeth is ordained of old, yea, for the king...* (Satan) *...it is prepared* (Rev. 20:10) *He hath made it deep and large. The pile of it is much fire and wood; the breath of the Lord, like a stream of brimstone, doth kindle it."* (Isa. 30:33; KJV)

We have, in those verses, a physical description of the Hell that was originally prepared for Satan and his minions, but will regrettably accommodate all who die in sin (Rev. 21:8). However, many contemporary eschatologists interpret Isaiah 30:27-33 not as the embodiment of Hell, but rather as Hezekiah's supernatural victory over Sennecherib, the Assyrian ruler, in 701 B.C. Matthew Henry, who is probably the best known early eschatologist, set the pattern for this interpretation when he said:

> *"In that valley...* (Topeth) *...it is supposed, many of the Assyrian regiments lay encamped, and were slain by the destroying angel (Isa. 37:36); or there the bodies of those that were slain were burned...:* (A Commentary on the Whole Bible; Revell; Vol. 4, pg. 173)

God destroyed 185,000 Assyrians by plague as they encamped around Jerusalem, fulfilling some say, Isaiah's prophecy that the Assyrians would be smitten by the voice of the Lord (Isa. 30:31). Since the Assyrians were destroyed by the sword of God, and not of man, (Isa. 31:8) there is some merit to the argument. However, if so, such a fulfillment was partial at best since many of the prophecies of Isaiah, like those of Daniel, were dual visions: the first addressing an immediate issue, the second dealing with a future event. We see this with Isaiah's description of the fall of Lucifer (Isa. 14:12-15), which also depicts the person of Antichrist. Daniel's prophecy concerning Antiochus IV Epiphanes (Dan. 8:9-25) also prefigures Antichrist.

Isaiah's vision first addressed Sennacherib and pronounced the judgment which would befall the Assyrian army encamped around Jerusalem. Second, it reached into the distant future and calls attention to the apocalyptic significance of Topeth with respect to the endtime. Matthew Henry makes that observation as well:

> *"Our Savior calls the future misery of the damned in Gehenna an allusion to the Valley of Hinnom, which gives some countenance to the applying of this misery, as also that in the (Book of Revelation) it is often called the lake that burns with fire and brimstone. This is said to be prepared for the devil and his angels, for the greatest of sinners, the proudest, and those that think themselves not accountable to any for what they say and do; even for kings was it prepared. It is deep and large, sufficient to receive the world of the ungodly...God's wrath is sufficient to receive the world of the ungodly...God's wrath is the fire, and sinners make*

> *themselves fuel to it; and the breath of God (the power of His anger) kindles it, and will keep it burning forever." (ibid; Vol. 4; pg. 173)*

As we further examine Isaiah 30:27 through 31:9, the prophetic dualism is unmistakable. Historically, the Assyrian of Isaiah 30:31 and 31:8 is none other than Sennacherib. Prophetically, it is none other than the Beast. Sennacherib, like Antiochus IV Epiphanes, prefigures Antichrist, whose downfall will come at the hands of Jesus Christ during the Battle of Armageddon, when he will be struck down with the sword which proceeds from the mouth of Jesus, which is the Word of God.

At the conclusion of this great battle, Antichrist and the False Prophet, together with those survivors of the battle who have accepted the mark of the beast (Rev. 14:9-10), and those who are pronounced guilty at the Sheeps and Goats Judgment, will be cast alive into the eternal fire of Gehenna to await the final judgment at the Great White Throne when Gehenna itself will be thrown into the Lake of Fire.

The Sheeps and Goats Judgment will be the final judgment held on Earth. It will not be the final judgment rendered to mankind, however. The final judgment, at the end of Christ's millennial reign, will be the Great White Throne Judgment. Scripture reveals this judgment will be held neither in Heaven nor on Earth, since the Earth, as we know it, will be gone. The Great White Throne Judgment will be conducted in an intermediate place, most likely somewhere between the two, in the air. The scene will probably be somewhat reminiscent of Ezekiel's vision (Ez. 1:4-28; 10:1-22), and those judged will experience a fear heretofore unknown to mankind as judgment is rendered and those condemned, which will include all who stand before the Great White Throne, are cast into the Lake of Fire.

The Sheeps and Goats Judgment will deal only with the judgment of the living, and will determine whether those judged are spiritually saved or lost. This judgment will take place during the 45 day period between the end of the Great Tribulation (Dan. 12:11-13; Rev. 11:3, 12:6) and the commencement of the Millennium. Where, precisely, does this judgment take place? Christ will judge the nations from the East Gate of the Holy City (Lev. 16:14; Isa. 30:33; Jer. 19:2; Jn. 5:22, 27).

> *"Go forth into the valley of the son of Hinnom, which is by the entrance of the East Gate..."* (Jer. 19:2; KJV)

On the Day of Atonement (Lev. 16) the Jews presented their sin offering to the high priest at the east entrance of the tabernacle (Lev. 1:5, 16:7; Ezek. 46:1, 3). The East Gate plays a very important role in all of the blessings, and judgments, meted to the nation Israel.

When God surrendered Jerusalem to Nebuchadnezzar (586 B.C.), and the *times of the Gentiles* began, He departed from the East Gate of the city and stood on the Mount of Olives which is east of the city, before His Glory ascended to Heaven (Ezek. 11:23). When Christ entered Jerusalem for the last time before His crucifixion (Jn. 12:12), He entered the city as a sin offering through the East

Gate. When He ascended (Ac. 1:12) He ascended from the Mount of Olives.

Christ will judge the living from the East Gate of Jerusalem, at the spot where the altar to Molech stood. The Lord will command the ground to open at that place, at the base of the hill, and those condemned will be cast into the fires of *Gehenna* from the Judgment Seat outside the East Gate at that precise location. God proclaimed this to be a place of judgment, and this is where that judgment will take place.

Where, precisely, will the gateway to *Gehenna* open? According to the Word of God, the entrance to *Gehenna* is located in the Valley of the son of Hinnom, known today as the Kidron Valley, which is directly between the Garden of Gethsemane where Jesus prayed, and the East Gate, where He will render judgment.

When we die as Christians, where do we go?

Where to the souls of deceased Christians go when they depart this life? According to the Apostle Paul, to be absent from the body is to be present with the Lord (2 Cor. 5:6-8). Our bodies are only temporary domiciles. When we shed our earthly dwelling place (2 Cor. 5:11), our spirits are immediately ushered into the presence of the Lord. Since the theology of some denominations teach that the souls of all the dead, saved and lost, sleep until they are summoned for judgment, it is important to determine which view the Bible supports.

Is there a Purgatory where the saved are assigned pain and suffering until the Day of Judgment (Mt. 10:15, 11:22, 24, 12:36; 2 Pe. 2:9, 3:7; 1 Jn. 4:17; Jude 6) in order to make them worthy of entrance into the Kingdom? The Roman Catholic Church says yes; Protestant theology flatly rejects the doctrine because Purgatory negates the efficacious atonement of the blood of Jesus Christ. Through Purgatory, salvation becomes attainable through our own works: i.e., suffering. This concept is totally contrary to the Word of God. We are saved by grace through faith, and not by our own efforts (Eph. 2:8-9).

Jesus assured the penitent thief he would be with Him that day in Paradise (Lk. 23:42-43). Christ's statement to this malefactor has created a monumental theological problem in the minds of some believers who simply ignore the evidence which clearly establishes that Paradise was used as a holding area for believers only until Jesus paid the price of admission to Heaven for all mankind. Believers in Purgatory view Paradise as a contemporary interim resting place for the souls of the saved, where those ultimately destined for Heaven must first go to purge themselves of any uncleanliness (i.e., Purgatory—the place of the purging of sin). Other believers, in an apparent attempt to discredit the theory of Purgatory, suggest the name, Paradise, is merely another synonym for Heaven, offering 2 Corinthians 12:3 and Revelation 12:7 as evidence of their belief. Such a conclusion, however, is not supported by Scripture, since that would imply that Jesus went to Heaven during the three day period in which He tasted death. He did not; nor did He claim He would.

While Scripture implicitly records the fact that Christ did not permanently ascend into Heaven until forty days after His resurrection, it does not suggest that those who rested in Paradise waited forty days before they were admitted into Heaven. In fact, Scripture suggests that Jesus did ascend to the Father shortly after His resurrection, opening the gateway to Heaven for the believers in Paradise immediately.

On the morning of Christ's resurrection, Mary Magdalene went early to the sepulcher to mourn the loss of the Messiah only to discover the stone had been moved and the tomb was empty. Believing someone had removed the body, she hurried to report this to Simon Peter who, with John, had returned to the sepulcher. Upon seeing Jesus, whom she at first mistook for a gardener, Mary Magdalene was apparently going to reach out to Him (a natural reaction for anyone seeing a loved one believed to be dead) until Jesus warned her not to touch Him (Jn. 20:17). A great many theologians believe that sometime between the meeting with Mary Magdelene in the morning when He admonished her not to touch Him, because "He had not ascended to the Father," and His offer to Thomas to insert his fingers into His wounds that same evening, that Jesus had received His glorified body, which could only have occurred if He had ascended into Heaven. This thought seems further confirmed by the imparting of the Holy Spirit on the eleven that same evening as they gathered in the locked upper room contemplating the significance of what John and Peter had witnessed at the tomb site earlier that day (Jn. 20:22).

A contradictory point of view suggests that Christ's admonition to Mary Magdalene was not based on her desire to touch Him, but rather, in her desire to hold Him. Defenders of this perspective argue there was something distinctly different in His offer to Thomas. Such an opinion is not logical, since any touch would have defiled the tabernacle, of which He was, at that point, representative. Since there are no verses which either affirm or contradict His ascension on that day, it is a point which will remain disputed by differing theological doctrines. However, there is no dispute over the fact that Jesus did not ascend to Heaven from Hades during the period He was in the grave.

Before Jesus ascended on High (Eph. 4:8), He descended into the lower parts of the Earth (Eph. 4:9-10) to take the keys of Hell and death (Rev. 1:8) from Satan, and to admonish the damned in *Gehenna* (1 Pe. 3:18-20). Prior to the Ascension, Paradise and Gehenna were both located in Hades. Although many believers still insist that Paradise (or Purgatory) is the intermediate resting place of the departed saved, that is no longer the case. When Jesus ascended to the Father, He forever unlocked the portals to Heaven. Today, all Christians who die in grace are immediately ushered into Heaven.

Did Jesus actually go to Hell when He died on the cross?

After suffering physical death on the cross, Christ and *both* thieves descended into Hades. The uncontrite thief went immediately into the flames of *Gehenna,* to suffer until the Great White Throne Judgement. The penitent thief went with Jesus to Paradise. Christ ministered to the saints there, after which

"He went and preached unto the spirits in prison..."
(1 Pe. 3:19; KJV)

In studying the word *prison* in the Greek text, it becomes clear that the word prison in 1 Peter 3:19 is not *desmoterion,* which literally means prison, or prisonhouse. The word used here was *phulake,* which means *holding area. Phulake* and *phulasso,* mean *to guard or watch.* Obviously, those in Paradise would not need to be guarded or watched.

Additionally, the word *preached* (based on its traditional meaning today) is also improperly translated. The usage here does not mean to evangelize, but rather, to proclaim. Jesus did not attempt to evangelize those who were contained within the holding area of Gehenna, since there is no salvation after death. Jesus proclaimed Himself to the lost. In essence, He said, "I am the Messiah you rejected!" confirming what each of them had painfully come to know since their arrival, that there is one triune God, *Yahweh*, and Jesus Christ was *Yahweh* in the flesh! It was at this time that Jesus retrieved the keys of death and Hades (Rev. 1:8).

When Jesus ascended, whether in the afternoon of the day of His resurrection, or forty days later when His ascension was witnessed on the Mount of Olives (Ac. 1:1-11), all those in Paradise went to Heaven. Hades, from that point forward, contained only *Gehenna*, the holding pen, where the sinner awaits judgment and condemnation before the Great White Throne at the end of the age.

Will there be one resurrection, or two?

To some Christians, the parable of the tares and the wheat suggests there will be only one resurrection:

"Let both... (the tares and the wheat) *...grow together until the harvest. At that time, I will tell the harvesters; First collect the weeds and tie them in bundles to be burned, then gather the wheat and bring it into my barn."* (Mt. 13:30; NIV)

Christ explained that parable in verses 13:36-43. The wheat represents the children of the kingdom, and the tares are the children of the devil (the unsaved). The judgment referred to here speaks only of the living, not the dead. Unlike the resurrection, which raises first the saved and then the lost, this judgment deals with the bad first, then admits the godly into the Kingdom. The explanation of this parable clearly shows us it deals with the Sheeps and Goats Judgment, which is concerned only with the living.

Scripture clearly points to two resurrections. The first is the resurrection of the just; the second, the resurrection of the damned.

> *"Marvel not at this; for the hour is coming, in which all that are in the graves shall hear His voice, And all shall come forth; they that have done good unto the resurrection of life; and they that have done evil, unto the resurrection of the damned."*
> (Jn. 5:28-29; KJV)

Although the text flow of John 5:28-29 seems, on the surface, to suggest a singular event, Luke 14:14 clearly depicts the resurrection of life (1 Cor. 15:52-53; 1 Th. 4:15-17) as an event separated from the resurrection of the damned (Rev. 20:12, 21:8)—and Revelation 20:4-5 places a timespan of 1,000 years between the two events:

> *"I saw thrones on which were seated those who had been given authority to judge. And I saw the souls of those who had been beheaded because of their testimony for Jesus and because of the Word of God. They had not worshipped the beast or his image and had not received his mark on their foreheads or their hands. They came to live and reign with Christ a thousand years. (The rest of the dead did not come to life until the thousand years were ended.) This is the first resurrection."* (Rev. 20:4-5; NIV)

It should be apparent even to the novice student of Scripture, that the events which are described in Revelation 20:4 are post-Tribulational, since "...those who had been beheaded because of their testimony for Jesus" are the saints who, in refusing to accept the mark of the beast, will be martyred during the second half of the Tribulation. These saints will be among those who reign with Christ during the Millennium, 1,000 years before the second resurrection, the resurrection of the lost, occurs.

If we are deceived by someone else in matters relating to God, and die before we learn we were deceived, will God excuse our ignorance and accept us into Heaven?

Possibly the best way to answer this question is to consider the unnamed prophet from Judah, whose tragic story is recorded in 1 Kings 13:1-24. God sent him to Jeroboam (reign, 930-909 B.C.), the king of the ten northern tribes, to prophesy against the worship of idols. As Jeroboam stood before the altar of Bethel, the prophet spoke this message of God:

> *"O altar, altar, thus saith the Lord: Behold a child shall be born unto the House of David, Josiah by name; and upon thee shall he offer the priests of the high places who burn incense upon thee, and men's bones shall be burned upon thee."* (1 Ki. 13:2; KJV)

Josiah was crowned king of Judah in 639 B.C. In 621 B.C., he desecrated the pagan altar at Bethel with the bones of the heathen priests who had worshipped there. Josiah had their decayed corpses exhumed from their sepulchers on the mound and spread their ashes over the altar. The unnamed prophet, whose bones were interred in a sepulcher on the same mound, prophesied this event almost 300 years before it happened, and called the king who would perform the deed by name! Interestingly, this prophet, along with Zechariah, are the only two prophets in the Bible who prophesied the actual name of a subject of prophecy. Zechariah prophesied the name of the Messiah as Joshua, which is the Hebrew rendering of the Greek name, Jesus. The unnamed prophet was, we may assume, equally blessed by the Lord.

God gave the unnamed prophet one charge of a personal nature: he was not to eat or drink while in the land of Israel, nor leave it by the same route he had entered (1 Ki. 13:9). The prophet disobeyed God. Upon leaving the land, an elderly prophet from Bethel chanced upon him while he was resting under an oak tree and invited him to his home for a meal. The prophet from Judah refused, explaining that God had forbidden him to eat or drink in that land.

Deliberately lying, the prophet of Bethel told him that an angel of the Lord spoke to him, and instructed him to bring the prophet of Judah back to his house that he might eat bread and drink water. Because he was both hungry and thirsty, the unnamed prophet did not seek the Lord for verification. His flesh was weak. He succumbed to temptation and went with the prophet of Bethel. Because he disobeyed God and ate and drank in a forbidden place he was condemned by the very mouth which deceived him (1Ki. 13:20-21), and was killed by a lion shortly after leaving the elderly prophet's home.

While that punishment may appear harsh to us, it must be understood that the unnamed prophet was chosen as the audible voice of God and, as such, his actions were as important as his words. That which he did, as well as that which he said, would logically be interpreted by those who witnessed him as the manifest will of God.

By forbidding the unnamed prophet to eat or drink in Israel, God visibly expressed His refusal to fellowship with those He held in contempt for practicing idolatry. By instructing the prophet to leave the land by a different route than that by which he entered suggested his journey was completely random, and without planned purpose. The sins of Jeroboam were so repugnant to the Lord that He did not want it perceived by the Israelites that they were worthy of a purposeful prophecy.

We can only speculate why the elderly prophet lied to the prophet from Judah. Perhaps he was jealous that God had selected an outsider to speak against the altars of Bethel. Perhaps he was just curious about the Judean's ministry. Or, perhaps he was simply old and lonely and wanted to fellowship with someone he considered an equal. The reason matters little. What matters is that the prophet from Judah allowed himself to be deceived.

We are all accountable for everything we say and do, whether we are duped into sinning or sin deliberately. Sin is no less sin because we were tricked. Eve is a good example of that. Eve was deceived by Satan. He tricked her into tasting the fruit from the tree of the knowledge of good and evil. Adam became a willing participant when he was tempted of his on flesh. Their sins, however, were equal in the eyes of the Lord, and so was their punishment.

Jesus, while admonishing the Christians to watch for the signs which would signify the end of the age, clearly warned the believer against the myriad of false Messiahs, preachers, and perverse teachings and doctrines which He knew would rise up in the endtime:

> *"Many will come in My name, saying, I am Christ, and shall deceive many..."* (Mt. 24:5 KJV)

Just as the unnamed prophet should not have accepted the words of the prophet from Bethel at face value without seeking a sign to test its veracity, neither should we, since our salvation may very well depend on it! If you think about it, it is logical to assume that many false prophets and messiahs must necessarily precede Antichrist, because the Gospel of Jesus Christ must be sufficiently diluted to prepare the way for the son of perdition to be readily accepted.

"Let no man deceive you by any means; for that day shall not come, except there come the falling away first, and that man of sin be revealed, the son of perdition, Who opposeth and exalteth himself above all that is called God, or that is worshipped, so that he, as God, sitteth in the temple of God, showing himself that he is God." (2 Th. 2:3-4; KJV)

Countless antichrists, false prophets and false teachers already exist in the United States and around the globe. Many have already extracted a terrible toll in souls. Two of the most notable within the past twenty years have been People's Temple founder Jim Jones and Branch Davidian David Keresh, who stole the salvation of over one thousand souls (since the majority of their followers died within the encampments of these antichrists before learning the truth about their messiahs). Only the children who had not reached the age of accountability escaped the loss of salvation, although each, solely because of the gullibility of their parents, lost their lives in horrible, agonizing deaths. Most of the 913 followers of Jim Jones died from cyanide poisoning in the jungles of Guyana on November 18, 1978. A few were shot to death as they attempted to escape the mass suicide ordered by Jones. More recently, on April 19, 1993, David Keresh and 88 members of his Branch Davidian flock perished in a fiery death as tear gas, that was pumped into their Waco, Texas compound by FBI agents exploded, and quickly engulfed the wood frame buildings, preventing anyone from escaping.

Moral, legal and political issues concerning Waco will not be raised here, since the purpose of this book is not to extrapolate on human events, however tragic. My purpose is to simply discuss the spiritual questions which, if raised by members of either cult, may have saved both their lives and their immortal souls.

The Word of God presents, in a clear, easy to understand language, the simple truth not only about Jesus Christ, but His adversaries as well. Jesus Christ is the one and only Son of God and is represented as the second Godhead in the Trinity which wholly consists of God the Father, Jesus the Son, who became man, and the Holy Spirit. We, as created beings, are not gods; nor will we ever become gods! If anyone suggests you are, may be, or even remotely could be a god—run! If anyone suggests to you that he or she is the reincarnated Christ, or his end-time prophet—run! If anyone attempts to teach you that Jesus was nothing more than a perfect, obedient man who died before completing His prescribed mission on Earth, and that they, or their leader, was appointed by God to complete Christ's work—run quickly! And if anyone tries to convince you that Jesus was not God incarnate, you would be best served to distance yourself from that person, group or church!

It is difficult for the mind of carnal man to appreciate the fact that God actually walked among us as man. Because Jesus walked in the flesh, He is largely viewed by the lost as a human being like themselves. Christ's claim to deity is likewise their claim to the *rights* of deity, a right they are only to happy to share with those who follow their teachings and, of course, support them with tithes and offerings. Many times the false messiah demands all of the follower's worldly wealth and possessions, citing Christ's admonition to the rich man (Mt. 19:16-23; Mk. 10:17-27; Lk. 18:18-27) as justification.

There exists within the world today more cults and pseudo-Christian religions than legitimate, godly sects and Christian denominations. Each and every day countless hundreds of weary seekers of the *Truth,* searching for the *Way* and the *Light,* stumble off the path of salvation and fall into the clutches of false messiahs, whose counterfeit avenues of redemption appear brightly lit with fanciful and godly doctrines of love and compassion. Unfortunately, their theology usually requires a few minor adjustments in the Word of God. A word here, a verse there, and perhaps, somewhere else, the addition of a new messiah. If presented with such a doctrine—run! Jesus Christ became man for one purpose: to die on the cross as man in order to redeem mankind. He accomplished everything He came to do (Jn. 19:30).

We are living in the most spiritual era since Jesus Christ walked upon the Earth. The *times of the Gentiles* is rapidly coming to a close. We have almost reached the end of the church age, and the gospel of Jesus Christ has circled the globe a thousand times during the past decade alone, reaching even the smallest pockets of humanity in the most isolated outposts of the Earth. Who in this world has not heard of Jesus Christ? The door to the endtime is now wide open. Soon Antichrist will step through it with his message of peace, hope, and prosperity for all. His message will be electric, the delivery dynamic, and millions will march to the beat of his drum.

In reality a portion of the doctrine of Antichrist has already preceded him and is currently being taught from the pulpits of hundreds of mainstream Christian churches across the world. It is the egregious doctrine of egocentrism in which personal freedom supplants theological responsibility, and personal liberty supersedes moral character. To make this new theology more palatable it is garbed in the silkiness of political correctness. Because this new liberalism is taught from the pulpit of the local church, the believer is encouraged to accept such things as homosexual behavior and abortion on demand as sinless lifestyle decisions and not as abominations in the eyes of God.

Since far too many professing Christians appear to be confused and seemingly lack the insight to recognize sin as sin within their own congregations, particularly when it is inaugurated from the pulpit, the magnitude of the problem and the potentially devastating effect it will have on the eternal security of the overly tolerant believer has become increasingly apparent to those who are firmly rooted in the Word of God. Each of us is personally accountable to God for our action or inaction, our conduct as Christians, and our witness of Him and His Word. Because our salvation rests squarely on our own shoulders, it seems reasonable that we would want to be absolutely certain the doctrines to which we ascribe, and the theology we practice, are scripturally based and eschatologically sound.

Had the unnamed prophet taken the time to seek God's counsel before dining with the elderly prophet from Bethel, his physical and spiritual fate would not have been placed in jeopardy. Likewise, if we fail to seek the counsel of God through prayer, through fasting, and through His Word, and as a result of our own spiritual laziness, we fall prey to a false messiah, God will not overlook our ignorance with a paternal pat on the head, saying, "Well, your heart was in the right place..." He will be obligated to say, "You have negated the blood of the Kinsman-Redeemer, who was your only propitiation for sin. Remember, when He was with you, He told you He was the Way, the Truth and the Light, and only through Him could salvation be obtained. Be gone, stranger; I do not know you!"

> *"Beloved, believe not every spirit, but test the spirits whether they are of God; because many false prophets are gone out into the world. By this know ye the Spirit of God: every spirit that confesseth that Jesus Christ is come in the flesh is of God; And every spirit that confesseth not that Jesus Christ is come in the flesh is not of God; and this is that spirit of Antichrist, of which ye have heard that it should come, and even now already is in the world."* (1 Jn. 4:1-3; KJV)

Can we always expect justice from God?

The *Oxford University Dictionary* defines justice as the administration of the law, and the distribution of both punishment and reward. Mercy is described as the forbearance and compassion shown by one person to another who is under his power, and has no claim or right to receive kindness. Grace is the manifestation of good will, and is distinguished from those rights bestowed upon one who does not merit immunity.

From the Christian perspective of salvation, justice may be correctly interpreted as receiving that which we honestly deserve, although we do not necessarily want it. Those judged before the Great White Throne will receive justice, and suffice to say, none will want it. Mercy, on the other hand, may be correctly construed as not receiving that which we may richly deserve; and grace may be defined as receiving that which we do not deserve.

> *"For all have sinned and come short of the glory of God, Being justified freely by His grace through the redemption that is Christ Jesus."*
> (Rom. 3:23-24; KJV)
> *"For by grace are ye saved through faith; and that not of yourselves, it is a gift of God..."*
> (Eph. 2:8; KJV)
> *"The wages of sin is death, but the gift of God is eternal life through Jesus Christ, our Lord."*
> (Rom. 6:23; KJV)

In the original text both Romans 3:24 and 6:23 are rendered Christ Jesus rather than Jesus Christ. This transposition is important in your Bible study, since at times scripture refers to the Lord as Jesus Christ *(Iesous Christos),* and at other times as Christ Jesus *(Christos Iesous).* Jesus became our advocate to the Father with His sacrifice on the cross (Jn. 14:6; Rom. 5:10, 8:34; 2 Cor. 2:10).

"For there is one God, and one mediator between God and men, the man, Christ Jesus." (1 Tim. 2:5; KJV)

From the crucifixion forward man no longer required a priest to make atonement for his sins. This thought is amplified by the torn temple veil (Mt. 27:51) which represents the torn body of Christ. The temple veil separated the priest's place of worship from the Holy of Holies. The tearing of the veil symbolized the opening of the way to the presence of the Father through Jesus.

As we examine those verses which refer to our Lord as Jesus Christ and Christ Jesus, we find an interesting parallel. Those verses which address our Savior as Christ Jesus deal with our salvation through the earthly ministry of the Lord. Those verses referring to Him as Jesus Christ address Him as the Son of God, our propitiation, and deal with our salvation (or loss of it) through His deity. It is noteworthy that as we compare the standard King James Version text with the language of the original text we find that Jesus Christ is substituted for Christ Jesus 34 times in the following verses: Ac. 3:20, 5:42; Rom. 1:1, 2:16, 6:23, 15:16, 15:17; 1 Cor. 1:1, 1:4; 2 Cor. 1:1; Gal. 2:16, 5:6; Eph. 1:1, 3:1; Php 1:1, 1:6, 1:8, 1:26; Col. 1:1; 1 Tim. 1:1, 1:2, 1:12, 2:5, 4:6, 5:21; 2 Tim. 1:1, 1:10, 2:3, 4:1; Titus 1:4, 2:3; Phm 1 and 9.

When Christ became our mediator, mercy through grace superseded justice. Recognizing that we have all sinned (Rom. 3:23), and the whole world abounds in wickedness (1 Jn. 5:19), none of us obviously wants justice. Justice without mercy would rightfully condemn all of us, without a single exception, to Hell. Only one person on Earth, judged from a standpoint of justice alone, could have been granted admission to the Kingdom of God, and that was the person of Christ Jesus.

Unfortunately, many who base their religious beliefs on a salvation of works instead of faith in Jesus Christ (Gal. 2:16) will stand before the throne of God and demand justice for the efforts they put forth on Earth. Little do they realize that man's carnal nature is so corrupt that man's inherent sin nature, by and of itself, would eliminate any justification to grace through his own efforts. And to stand guilty before the throne of God is a horror beyond comprehension.

As clear as this should be, we still see many religious sects which, while professing Christ, retain the ceremonial rites and oblations of the law. Practiced is salvation through tithing and other good works rather than salvation through grace by faith in Jesus Christ (Eph. 2:6-8). Theoretically, works should be the natural outpouring of salvation, not the reverse. Sin still has dominion in our lives when we rely on the doctrines of self-righteousness to deliver our souls (Rom. 6:14). The law which convicts does not deliver!

Christ is our reconciliation (Heb. 2:7), our propitiation and our mercy seat (Lev. 16:2; Heb. 9:5) before the Throne. In the history of the world there has never been such an example of justice and grace in one event as there was in the crucifixion of Jesus. Finding sin in His Son (even though it was only imputed sin), God could not spare Him under the Law. Justice condemns. Through mercy, the sins of all mankind were placed on Him, and His blood covered us all. Christ became our surety, and by grace, paid our debt.

Because this debt is now paid in full, we can expect mercy instead of justice, and receive that which grace has purchased. Surprising as it may appear, many will reject the free gift of grace and will demand justice, thereby dying in their sins.

Those who accept the sacrifice of Christ's death on the cross as their propitiation for sin will be found not guilty by the Father, and will be acquitted. Those who determine to be their own advocate before the Father, to provide an accounting of their own deeds, will stand condemned as they offer their defense.

> *"But God, who is rich in mercy, for His great love with which He loved us, Even when we were dead in sin, hath made us alive together with Christ (by grace are ye saved), And hath raised us together, and made us sit together in heavenly places in Christ Jesus; That in the ages to come He might show the exceeding riches of His grace in His kindness towards us through Christ Jesus. For by grace are ye saved through faith; and that not of yourselves, it is the gift of God—not of works, least any man should boast."* (Eph. 2:4-9; KJV)

CHAPTER SIX

THE CHURCH AGE

Who headed the early church?

If you were asked who headed the early Christian church, to whom would you assign the distinction? To John, the beloved Apostle whom Jesus loved best (Jn. 12:23)? John outlived all of the other Apostles, and is the only one who died of natural causes. Perhaps you would assign the honor to James, the brother of John. Both John and James shared a special relationship with Jesus and both were present at the Transfiguration (Mt. 17:1-9). Or, perhaps you, like most Christians, would pick Simon Peter, of whom Jesus said:

> *"And I tell you that you are Peter* (petros), *and on this rock* (petra) *I will build My church, and the gates of Hades will not overcome it. I will give you the keys to the kingdom of heaven; whatever you bind on earth will be bound in heaven, and whatever you loose on earth will be loosed in heaven."* (Mt. 16:18-19; NIV)

Peter, like James and John, was also present at the Transfiguration. A superficial examination of these verses might well suggest that Peter had, indeed, been singled out as Christ's special emissary, the keeper of the keys, to admit or requit man's admittance into the Kingdom of Heaven.

Was Christ, as many Christians suppose, telling Peter that he, Simon Peter, was the rock upon which the church was to be built? Was Peter to be *primus inter pares,* first among equals, selected by the Savior Himself to be Supreme Rabbi of His church? Was Peter being given exclusive, infallible authority over the church? Was he divinely appointed the first *pontifex maximus?*

Peter was the first apostle called of the Lord (Lk. 5:1-11). He was also the first, not of his own reasoning, but through divine revelation, to proclaim Jesus, the Christ, the Son of the Living God (Mt. 16:16). Peter preached the first post-ascension gospel, and opened the door of faith to the Jews (Ac. 2:6-42, 14:27). Three thousand received the message, accepted Jesus Christ, whom they crucified, as their Messiah, and were saved. Peter was also the first to open the door of salvation to the Gentiles when the Holy Spirit directed him to Joppa, to the household of Cornelius, the Roman centurion. Cornelius and his entire household accepted Christ and were baptized (Ac. 10:1-47).

Critics of the *petros/petra* theory maintain that because the original Gospel of Matthew was written in Aramaic, the word *kepa* (massive rock) would have been used to describe both Peter *(petros)* and the rock *(petra)*. Advocates of this theory insist the masculine and feminine genders were added in a later Greek translation to distinguish people from inanimate objects. On closer examination, it does not appear, in this instance, to be the case.

In Aramaic, Peter would be *kephas,* not *kepa.* The rock upon which the Church was to be built is *kepa* not *kephas. Petros* (Greek) and *kephas* (Aramaic) are both masculine. *Petra* (Greek) and *kepa (Aramaic)* are feminine, clearly denoting a shift in emphasis from people to objects. Christ further confirms that Peter is *petros/kephas,* and not *petra/kepa* in John 1:42 when He said, in regard to Peter: "And he... (Andrew) ...brought him... (Peter) ...to Jesus. And when Jesus beheld him, He said, Thou art Simon, the son of John; thou shalt he called Cephas, which is, by interpretation, A stone..." (KJV)

Christ, not Peter, is the rock (1 Cor. 10:4) that becomes the cornerstone (Eph. 2:20; 1 Pe. 2:6-7) upon which Christianity is constructed. Peter, like the other apostles, was a building stone who represents one of the twelve foundation columns of the New Jerusalem (Rev. 21:14). That which is Spirit cannot be built upon flesh, nor can the natural become the cornerstone for the supernatural. The Church was not built on Peter, it was built on Jesus Christ. Peter, like the other Apostles, was built *into* the Church. Christ, the chief cornerstone, was the master builder.

Peter was not accorded any special position in the Church hierarchy, nor was he conveyed any special privileges or powers not bestowed upon the others. The promises outlined in Matthew 16:18-19 and 18:18 were not given exclusively to Peter—they were only given to him first!

When Jesus told Peter He would give him the keys to the kingdom of Heaven, He was not conveying special authority or leadership in the Church to the Apostle even though a key is usually a symbol of authority. The servant who possesses the keys to his master's storehouse has authority over his master's possessions. The keys described here, however, are the keys of knowledge (Lk. 11:52) by which the saved may enter the kingdom of Heaven and the unsaved are excluded. Pictures of Peter standing by the Pearly Gates with keys in hand is such a gross exaggeration that it borders on blasphemy. Christ alone controls the entrance of Heaven.

Peter never assumed any role for himself in the primeval church other than that of an Apostle (1 Pe. 1:1; 2 Pe. 1:1) and an elder (1 Pe. 5:1). He made no claims over the primary position of authority in the Church, and none were imputed on him. It could be said that Peter's second epistle, written shortly before his death at the hand of Nero, was his last will and testament to the Church. If Peter was the Vicar of the Church as many suppose, it is logical that he would have wanted to transfer that authority, as the keeper of the keys, to a successor; or at least to detail how such authority was to be transferred not only to his immediate successor, but to those who followed in the future. No such transfer of authority is indicated, because no such authority existed.

The head of the first century church was James, the half-brother of Jesus.

James and his brothers Joseph, Simon and Judas (or Jude) (Mt. 13:55) became converts at the time of Christ's resurrection and were present in the Upper Room with the Apostles on the Day of Pentecost (Ac. 1:14). James was the head bishop of the Church probably from the moment of his conversion until he was stoned to death by the high priest Annas in 62 A.D.

Although he was raised in the same house as Jesus, James refused to believe that his half-brother was the Lord incarnate (Jn. 7:5) until Jesus *appeared to James first, and then the apostles* (1 Cor. 15:7).

Evidence of the headship of James can be found in Acts 14:26-15:20. When Paul returned from Attalia after being stoned in Lystra he became involved in a dispute with some in the church over the acceptance of Gentiles into the fellowship without their first converting to Judaism through the ritual of circumcision. The issue, which became rather heated, was finally resolved by James, who made the decision to accept the Gentiles into the church without the necessity of conversion to Judaism.

Further evidence supporting the leadership of James is found in Paul's rebuke of Peter in Galatians 2:11-14. Paul could not have taken Peter to task for improper doctrine if Peter was the infallible interpreter of church doctrine. In addition, James' authority is apparent in verse twelve, which begins, "Before the apostles starting going forth from James..." As the recognized head of the group, James controlled the activities of the disciples.

No records apparently exist that indicate which disciple, of which there were now thousands, assumed the role of Church leader upon the death of James in 62 A.D. By that time, most of the other original Apostles, who had embarked on the missionary trail into distant lands, were dead. And both Peter and Paul, who were preaching the gospel in the far reaches of the Roman Empire, would soon be arrested and imprisoned to await their fate. Both would be executed by Nero in Rome sometime between 66 and 68 A.D. No heirarchial ascendency is either described in the Scriptures, nor is one sanctioned. The Church has one head bishop—Jesus Christ, and needs no other.

Is the position of an Apostle still a legitimate office in the church, or did that function cease when John, the last Apostle, died?

I suppose that depends on whether you mean apostle or Apostle. An apostle is, quite simply, a missionary. The office of the missionary is scriptural, and still exists:

> *"And He gave some apostles...* (missionaries) *...and some prophets, and some evangelists; and some pastors and teachers..."* (Eph. 4:11; KJV)

In that sense, all of the Apostles were *apostles.* On the other hand, there were only twelve scriptural Apostles. The number is limited to twelve because there are only twelve foundations in the New Jerusalem and each foundation is named after one of the Apostles (Rev. 21:14).

Since the Bible records a total of fifteen men who were appointed as Apostles, a casual student of the Bible might have a problem here. However, if we recall, the first criteria of being called an Apostle (as opposed to an *apostle*) is that the candidate must have been personally selected, ordained and instructed by Jesus Christ. Once this criteria is acknowledged, two of the Apostles are suddenly reduced in rank from Apostle to *apostle*. Matthias, who was appointed by the eleven to replaced Judas Iscariot, and Barnabas, who was appointed in 44 A.D. to replace James the Less, who was martyred, are eliminated. This now leaves thirteen who were appointed by Jesus.

It should be obvious that Christ, knowing Judas Iscariot would be possessed by Satan (Jn. 6:70), never intended the name of Judas to be inscribed on any of the twelve foundations. Scripture verifies that Jesus intended Judas' replacement to be Saul of Tarsus, the Apostle to the Gentiles. Paul was the last Apostle. During the Tribulation, Enoch and Elijah will be the last *apostles*.

It might appear that any question concerning the office of an Apostle would be meaningless in this day and age—and rightly it should. However, there appears to be in some factions of the Pentecostal charismatic church a planned revival of the office of Apostle. This is problematic, since the office of the Apostle implies the receipt of a special anointing from God which has been entirely without scriptural foundation since the end of the Apostolic era.

Those claiming the office of Apostle do so largely based on Ephesians 4:7-12:

> *"But unto every one of us is given grace according to the measure of the gift in Christ. Wherefore, He saith, When He ascended up on high, He led captivity captive, and gave gifts unto men. Now that He ascended, what is it but that He also descended first into the lower parts of the earth? He that descended is the same also that ascended up far above all heavens, that He might fill all things. And He gave some apostles; and some, prophets; and some evangelists; and some pastors and teachers; For the perfecting of the saints for the works of the ministry for the edifying of the body of Christ."* (KJV)

It must be noted that when Paul penned his epistle to the Ephesians, shortly before his martyrdom, the office of the Apostle was still an active position in the Church, as was the function of the apostle.

Apostleship was granted to the twelve by virtue of their having been selectively trained for their offices by Jesus or in Paul's case, by the Holy Spirit. Others were recognized as *apostles*: Andronicus (Rom. 16:7), Apollos (1 Cor. 4:6, 9), Barnabas (Ac. 14:4, 14; 1 Cor. 9:6), James (the half-brother of Jesus) (1 Cor. 15:7; Gal. 1:19), Junia (Rom. 16:7), as well as Silas and Timothy (1 Th. 1:1) by virtue of the gifts they had received, although they did not hold the office of an Apostle.

In the foundational Church, which did not possess a complete Bible canon from which to instruct, each office (apostle, prophet, evangelist, pastor and teacher), was critical to the development, doctrinal stabilization and edification of the congregation. The duties of the apostle and the evangelist were normally not practiced within the local congregation. Apostles were primarily itinerant preachers whose job it was to reach the Gentile world and establish congregations which could then be turned over to local pastors and teachers whom were selected and trained within the community. Evangelists and apostles engaged in spreading the Word much the same as the traditional missionary does today. The prophet worked in conjunction with both the apostle and the pastor. Unlike the Old Testament prophet whom we mentally view as someone selected by God to utter warnings of damnation to a backslidden nation, the primary function of the New Testament prophet within the church is to provide edification and exhortation to the congregation. More times than not that role is combined into one of the other offices, usually that of the apostle or the evangelist.

Finally, within settled congregations, we find both pastors and teachers. In many cases, they are also the same person. However, because we have now entered the post-Christian era, the time of the falling away of the faith, the office of the teacher has become of critical importance to the believers. Many Christians are now backing away from the local assembly, and are receiving doses of scriptural edification via the electronic church from charismatic, Hollywood-type tele-evangelists, many of whom are more concerned with the promulgation of their ministries through tithes and offerings than they are with the job of saving souls. These mega-ministries have, in many cases, usurped the role of the Apostle; and although many of these global ministries were instrumental in delivering the Gospel around the world during the past two decades, some are now promoting doctrines that are foreign to Scripture. In some cases, because of false teachings, many actually border on scriptural heresy.

There remains, within the contemporary church, apostles (missionaries), prophets, evangelists, pastors and teachers. However, it should be noted again that the office of the *Apostle* was foundational to the first century church, and no longer exists. As we proceed closer to the end of *the times of the Gentile*, which is already closer than many would like it to be, we will likely see greatly enhanced gifts of the Spirit in operation in all of the offices as the harvesters of Christ comb the fields of tares for the remaining sheaves of wheat which can still be brought into the storehouse.

Did John the Baptist fulfill the promised coming of Elijah?

Throughout much of church history, and in particular during the twentieth century, theologians have raised the question: Was John the Baptist the complete fulfillment of the Elijah promised in Malachi 4:5, or will Elijah actually return during the endtime?

When the temple priests asked John if he was Elijah, John replied he was not. However, in speaking of John, Jesus said:

> *"For all the prophets and the law prophesied until John. And, if you accept it, he himself is Elijah, who was to come."*
> (Mt. 11:13-14; KJV)

Additionally, Christ said:

> *"...Elijah is coming and will restore all things. But, I say to you,*

that Elijah already came, and they did not recognize him, but did to him whatever they wished..." (Mt. 17:11-12; NASB)

Was John actually the promised Elijah? He firmly and emphatically declared he was not; Christ confirmed he was. Even in His confirmation that John was Elijah, there seems to be a qualifier in Christ's statement by which He appears to be telling us that while John fulfilled the essence of Elijah's message with respect to His first coming, Elijah himself must still return to complete the prophecy spoken of him concerning Christ's second coming.

That an issue over this question even exists is the result of eschatological differences between the various Christian denominations. It is at times difficult for the Christian laity, in search of basic Bible truths, to understand that Christian teachers and writers are as denominationally biased as the evangelists and pastors who promote the sectarian dogmas under which they were raised. Denominationalism is Satan's curse on the church, because it is a wedge which has successfully separated the brethren for the past 300 years—in many cases, making them hated enemies who would do physical harm to one another.

The issue of whether or not John the Baptist was the actual fulfillment of Malachi's prophecy

"Behold, I will send you Elijah, the prophet before the coming of the great and terrible day of the Lord; And he shall turn the heart of the fathers to the children, and the heart of the children to their fathers, lest I come and smite the earth with a curse." (Mal. 4:5-6; KJV)

is of eschatological, if not theological, importance to the church since the literal fulfillment of this or any endtime prophecy would suggest that those who interpret the Bible allegorically would have some very serious doctrinal problems. Conversely, if the prophecy is completely satisfied allegorically, and Elijah does not return as one of the two endtime witnesses, those who believe in the literal interpretation of Scripture would have some seriously flawed tenets within their doctrinal position.

Major denominational doctrinal issues sometimes revolve around key passages of Scripture which have endtime significance; and which, in and of themselves, do not appear worthy of the debate they receive. Usually, however, the question of whether Scripture is to be interpreted allegorically or literally is centered on these key verses; and thus, issues are sometimes created where none should exist.

Therefore, the question of whether or not John allegorically fulfilled Malachi's prophecy is a significant issue, as are those dealing with a literal seven year Tribulation, the rapture of the church, and the millennial reign of Christ on Earth. If the Bible is a book which was meant to be interpreted allegorically (i.e., as symbolism) rather than as an outline of literal events which are yet to transpire, then most of the content of this, or any book, dealing with interpretative eschatology would have little value to the believer, since one man's opinion is as good as the next, and tomorrow's author may have a more fruitful imagination and produce a work which is ever so much more enjoyable to read.

If John completely fulfilled Malachi's prophecy concerning the coming of Elijah, then you may rightly assume that particular verse, as well as any dealing with the endtime, can be safely interpreted allegorically; and that it is likely that Earth will continue on its socialist path to a one-world government filled with utopian brotherly love. If, on the other hand, you decide that Elijah must come to fulfill that which Malachi prophesied, then you can rest assured that planet Earth has reached the end of the *times of the Gentiles,* and has entered into the endtime phase, and is quickly approaching that which Malachi described as "the great and terrible day of the Lord."

After the Transfiguration, Jesus instructed Peter, John and James not to tell anyone of the vision they had seen on the Mount of Olives until the Son of Man had risen from the dead. They asked: "Why then do the scribes say that Elijah must come first?" They knew Elijah was to both herald the Messiah and prepare the world for Him. However, since they knew Jesus was the Christ, the prophecy puzzled them. In response, Jesus answered: "Elijah shall truly come first and restore all things..." In saying this, Jesus confirmed Malachi's prophecy, and acknowledged that before "the great and terrible day of the Lord," Elijah would indeed come and prepare the world for the Kingdom. At the same time, confusing his Apostles even more, Christ also confirmed that John was, in essence, the embodiment of that selfsame Elijah.

> *"But I say unto you, that Elijah is come already, and they knew him not, but have done unto him whatsoever they desired..."*
> (Mt. 17:12; KJV)

John, as the embodiment of Elijah, fulfilled that which was expected of the forerunner of the first advent of Jesus Christ. However, since Christ knew He would be rejected by Israel, a dual fulfillment was not only mandated, it was an essential part of God's overall plan of redemption.

Those who advocate that Jesus was not the Christ, but was simply a charismatic rabbi who fooled not only His own disciples, but hundreds of first century Jews as well, also suggest that John the Baptist was a somewhat deranged, although well-meaning prophet, who became convinced, because of stories told to him by both his mother and his aunt, that his second cousin, Jesus (Lk. 1:34-36) was the Messiah. Skeptics further insist that because John promoted the myth that Jesus was the Messiah, it was necessary for Jesus to impute on him the premature prophetic trappings of Elijah, since that prophecy was well-known by the Jews who had been looking both for Elijah and the Messiah for centuries.

To convince the skeptic that John the Baptist was divinely chosen by God not as the one to fulfill Malachi 4:5, but to be representative of its fulfillment, it is important to look not only at John, but Elijah as well.

John, the son of Zacharias and Elizabeth, descended from Aaronic priesthood through the seed of the daughters of Aaron. His father was a temple priest through the seed of Abijah. His calling as a prophet was, therefore, legitimate according to the Law.

Zacharias and Elizabeth, like Abraham and Sarah before them, were advanced in age, and were likewise childless. While Zacharias, according to custom, was burning incense in the temple, the angel Gabriel visited him and advised him that Elizabeth would bear him a son who was to be called John. Gabriel further told Zacharias that his son would be filled with the Holy Spirit in his mother's womb and that he would be great in the sight of God. Furthermore, because Zacharias, who like Sarah, due to their advanced ages, doubted the angel's announcement of the birth a son, Gabriel advised Zacharias that he would be struck dumb, and would not be able to speak again until the day his son was born. This was a sign to confirm the supernatural purpose of this birth.

The lifestyle of John the Baptist closely parallels that of Elijah the Tishbite. Both lived in the wilderness for most of their recorded lives. Instead of the priestly garb John could have worn as the son of a Levite priest, he dressed in a garment of camel's hair which was roughly equivalent to the sackcloth worn by the prophets in Elijah's day.

John, like Elijah, subsisted on a meager diet. Both men were ascetic. Neither married. The lifestyle of both reflected their condemnation of the world in which they lived. Elijah's conflict was with the prophets of Baal; John fought the Pharisees and Sadducees. John confirmed his prophetic commission by comparing himself to Isaiah 40:3 as "...the voice of him that cries in the wilderness, preparing the way of the Lord...," a prophecy which the Pharisees clearly understood as one which would identify Elijah when he reappeared. Because John denied that he was either the Messiah or Elijah, the Pharisees challenged his right to baptize his converts. Elijah confirmed his prophetic authority by challenging the prophets of Baal on Mount Carmel (1 Ki. 18:20-24).

Elijah denounced Ahab and Jezebel. John condemned Herod Antipas and Herodias. Ahab, the king of Israel feared Elijah. Herod, the tetrarch of Judea, feared John. Neither Jezebel nor Herodias feared the prophets who upbraided them, and actively sought to end their lives.

A translation climaxed both ministries. Elijah was translated to Heaven without suffering death (2 Ki. 2:11); and Christ, after suffering death, was bodily translated to Heaven at His ascension (Mk. 16:19; Lk. 24:51; Ac. 1:9-11) which occurred 40 days after His resurrection (Ac. 1:3). John heralded the first advent of Jesus Christ; Elijah will herald His second coming. This is verified by Jesus when He said:

> *"For all the prophets and the law prophesied until John. And if you receive it, this is Elijah, who was to come."* (Mt. 11:13-14; KJV)

The substance of Christ's words was that, to those who accepted the message which John brought concerning the Messiah, he was the fulfillment of Elijah, because no other messenger was needed. The key word in the statement is *if,* which is conditional on belief. *If* you will, then John is Elijah. Circumspectly, *if* you do not, then John is not. To many who heard him, John *was* Elijah. They heard the words of one crying in the wilderness, repented of their sins, and accepted Jesus as the Messiah. Those early believers became the grass roots members of the first century church. Others heard the gospel of John the Baptist, and not believing, rejected his plea to repent. They were rejected from the promise of grace. To them, and those like them, John was not Elijah, and the promise of the Tishbite is, as yet, unfulfilled.

To this day, the Jewish world is still waiting for Elijah to come. With each Passover they celebrate, an extra place is set at the Passover table for Elijah. Because the Jews rejected their Messiah, a literal fulfillment of Malachi's prophecy is still necessary.

It is ironic that John the Baptist, who pointed the way to the Kingdom through Jesus Christ, was not allowed to enter into that Kingdom upon his death. He, like the rest of the Old Testament saints, had to wait until the gateway to the Kingdom was opened by Jesus when He ascended to Heaven after His own physical death and resurrection.

John, a New Testament character, was the last Old Testament prophet. Elijah, an Old Testament character, will be the last New Testament prophet.

What was Paul's thorn in the flesh?

Was Paul's thorn in the flesh physical or spiritual? The two schools of thought on the subject are pretty evenly divided, with both sides offering solid, scriptural evidence to support their opinion.

In Paul, God created the greatest evangelist the world has ever known. Before his conversion on the road to Damascus (Ac. 9:1-18), Paul was one of the most feared persecutors of the early church (Ac. 7:55-8:-3; 9:1-2), and actually participated in the slaying of Stephen, the first Christian martyr, by holding the garments of those whose stoned Stephen, to prevent them from being splattered with the disciple's blood.

First century tradition claims that while he was a Roman citizen, Paul was a Hebrew, born of Hebrew parents, who originally came from the Galilean town of Gischala, fleeing when the Roman army overran Palestine. Paul himself claimed the rights of a Roman citizen (Ac. 16:37-38; 22:25-29) which suggests, at the very least, his family possessed a considerable amount of wealth, because they were granted citizenship (as were many of the elitists whom previously held positions of authority in the lands which Rome conquered).

Scripture suggests that not only was Paul not an imposing figure (2 Cor. 10:10), but also that he quite likely epitomized the proverbial ninety-pound weakling. Interestingly, a description of Antichrist in Isaiah14:16 suggests the endtime messiah of the damned will possess strikingly similar physical attributes. When Paul and Barnabas preached their salvation message to the Lystrians, they were mistaken for gods. Barnabas, because of his large, stately appearance, was mistaken for Jupiter, and Paul was thought to be Mercury. While Jupiter was the chief god, Mercury, a small, slight figure, was the winged messenger of the gods. Granted, the association to those particular gods may have been due, at least in part, to the fact that Paul actually delivered the salvation message to Lystra.

Paul, after being struck blind on the road to Damascus, suffered some form of permanent eye damage which plagued him throughout the balance of his life.

Since God knows the minds and hearts of all men (Heb. 4:12), I cannot help thinking that God, knowing the greatness He was about to impart on Paul, realized the last appointed Apostle might have some problems coping with his prominence, and did what He felt was necessary to keep Paul humble before both God and man. In 1 Corinthians 10:13 God assures us He is faithful and will not allow us to be tempted beyond that which we can endure. We, as Christians, sometimes view this verse only as it relates to outward sin. But are we only tempted with evil? At times, the sins we commit are sins of self—pride and ego. We can become so blessed we lose sight of the Giver because of the abundance of the gift. God is suddenly diminished, and the man is enlarged. When that occurs man, not God, becomes the centerpiece of the ministry, and the followers of that ministry begin to worship the man instead of God.

I believe God recognized that egotism might be a potential stumbling block for Paul, and took those steps necessary for Paul to be constantly aware of his own human frailties. Paul seemed to confirm this thought in 2 Corinthians 12:6 when he said:

> *"For though I might desire to boast, I will not be a fool; for I will speak the truth. But I forbear, least anyone should think of me above that which he sees me to be or hears from me."* (NASB)

When the Holy Spirit restored Paul's sight after the Damascus Road experience, Paul was left with a permanent eye impairment. In Galatians 4:14, Paul confessed "...and my trial, which was in my flesh, ye despised not..." He confirmed, in verse fifteen, that his infirmity was in his eyes. This thought is further amplified in Galatians 6:11 when Paul, who normally used a scribe to write his epistles, wrote to the Galatians in his own hand, in large letters so he could see them as he wrote.

The scriptural aspect of the buffeting Paul received at the hand of Satan is described in 2 Corinthians 12:7-9:

> *"And lest I should be exalted above measure through the abundance of the revelations, there was given to me a thorn in the flesh, the messenger of Satan to buffet me, lest I should be exalted above measure. For this thing I besought the Lord thrice, that it might depart from me. And He said unto me, My grace is sufficient for thee; for My strength is made perfect in weakness. Most gladly, therefore, will I rather glory in my infirmities, that the power of Christ may rest upon me."* (KJV)

It is not in the least surprising that Satan attempted to use this infirmity against Paul. Satan would not be the great tormentor he is known to be if he passed up a single opportunity to denigrate anyone for any reason. "If your God is so great," Satan may well have said to Paul, "why won't He heal you—after all, you've asked three times! Hasn't He told you that anything you ask in His name will be granted (Jn. 14:18; 2 Cor. 12:8)?" Another approach might have been, "If you're even half the evangelist others think you are, you should be able to heal yourself!" Finally, Satan might have said, "If your God really loved you, He wouldn't leave you half-blind while He heals every worthless beggar in the marketplace. I mean, after all, you're the greatest evangelist the world has ever known! You've brought more souls to the old man than His son did when He was kicking up the dust down here..."

And what did Paul say to Satan when the buffeting, which had to have been both severe and constant, occurred?

> *"...Most gladly, therefore, will I rather glory in my infirmities, that the power of Christ may rest upon me. Therefore, I take pleasure in infirmities, in reproaches, in necessities, in persecutions, in distress for Christ's sake; for when I am weak, then am I strong."* (2 Cor. 12:9-10; KJV)

As we contemplate what we have just read, it is easy to see that Paul's thorn in the flesh was, without a doubt, the spiritual harassment he received from Satan because of his physical handicap—poor eyesight.

The ministerial misfortunes encountered by many prominent 20th century evangelists has been largely centered around the problems of self. Pride and ego, i.e., the sins of self, are extremely difficult to recognize within ourselves, and are sometimes more damaging to the congregation of Christ than even the most vile crimes against society.

Cult leader Jim Jones began his theological career as a legitimate minister of a legitimate Christian denomination. Because of the doting affection of many in his congregation, Jones began seeing himself not as just their pastor, but rather, as their messiah, their deliverer from the circumstances of their poverty-stricken inner city environment. At that point, heresy supplanted sound theology in his pulpit.

Traditional evangelists and pastors are not immune from the sins of self. Two of the largest Pentecostal ministries in the world toppled because of the sins of their pastors. Jim Bakker, who headed *PTL Ministries* in Charlotte, North Carolina fell, not so much because of the gross misapplication of God's tithes which drew him a thirty-six year sentence in a federal penitentiary (later commuted to twelve years); but rather, because of suspected homosexual acts committed with male staff members and a sexual liaison with Jessica Hahn, initiated, it has been suggested, to prove to Tammy Faye that he was not a homosexual. The legal blackmailing of Bakker by Hahn's attorneys was exposed by global evangelist Jimmy Swaggart—who was himself exposed as an adulterer who regularly visited a Baton Rouge prostitute. In his public confession, Swaggart insisted that no physical copulation occurred during any of these visits. However, the desire was, in Swaggart's case, no different than the actual commission of the sin.

At times neither communal crimes nor recognizable sin plays a role in the destruction of the ministry. More times than not, the sin of ego erodes the godly mission of the evangelist. It was this sin which God guarded against with Paul.

When the evangelist or pastor becomes bigger than life in the eyes of his congregation, and the miracles or signs which precede him are attributed to the man rather than the Spirit which performed them; and the man accepts the accolades, one of two things, and sometimes both, will happen. First, the evangelist begins teaching a new revelation, usually an egocentric doctrine, in which the pastor, and at times, the pastor's congregation usually plays a key role. The health, wealth and prosperity ministries are all egocentric, and specifically deal with the revelation that tithing creates personal wealth and fortune for the tither since man cannot outgive God. So too are those ministries that deal with new endtime revelations from God in which specific members of particular congregations have been singled out by God to redefine Scripture for the endtime.

Second, God brings the ministry down. Our God is a jealous God (Ex. 20:5. 34:14; Dt. 5:9, 6:15; Josh 24:19; Nah. 1:2). While He does not want credit for that which He does not do, He expects credit for that which He, or the Holy Spirit, accomplishes in the lives and matters of man.

Unfortunately, on a much less grandiose scale, I have had some personal experience in the area of sins of the ego. God commissioned me around 1980, to begin writing *Answers From The Bible,* a theological question and answer newspaper column, which ultimately was read weekly by a half million people. My ego grew in direct proportion to the column's readership as I began addressing difficult theological issues for which I had no prior knowledge, with insight provided by the Holy Spirit. Because of the success of *Answers From The Bible,* I suddenly found myself being invited to teach at various churches with distinctly different theological ideologies, all of whom found accord with the content of the column. Additionally, I began receiving letters from readers seeking pastoral advise—something well outside the realm of my commission. Whenever I was complimented on the spiritual insight of the column, I graciously accepted the platitudes, attributing my success to the fact that I religiously studied the Bible anywhere from four to six hours each day, using both Greek and Hebrew lexicons in those studies. After a period of time I actually began believing the platitudes which had been heaped upon me. I ceased praying over the column, and began using my own intellect as I wrote. Because the Holy Spirit was no longer my ghost writer, the column began to show some minor theological flaws which were quickly called into question by the column's readers. I compensated for the lack of the anointing by changing the focus of the column from addressing theological questions to dealing with conservative issues. Within six months of that decision in 1985, *Answers From The Bible* ceased to exist.

Is the professing church saved?

As recently as ten years ago, national pollsters determined that 54% of America's population affirmed a traditional belief in God, and professed to be born again. Of those, 37% belong to denominations or sects which believe at least one of the following: (a) that Jesus Christ is not the incarnate Son of God (Mt. 2:15; 3:17; 4:3, 4:6; 27:54; Mk. 15:39; Lk. 1:32, 1:35; 3:22; 4:3, 4:9, 4:41; 23:47; Jn. 1:34, 1:49; 3:16, 3:18; 6:40, 6:69; 12:26; 13:3; 14:13; 15:23; 17:1; 19:7; Rom. 1:9; 5:10; 8:3, 8:29, 8:23; 1 Cor. 1:9; Gal. 1:16, 4:4; 1 Th. 1:10; Heb. 1:2, 1:5, 1:8; 4:14; 5:5, 5:8; 6:6; 7:3; 1 Jn. 3:23; 4:9-10; 5:9); (b) that Jesus did not physically rise from the grave (Mt. 28:1-10; Mk. 16:1-20; Lk. 24:1-48; Jn.

2:19-22; 10:18; 20:1-15; Ac. 1:3-11; 3:15; 1 Cor. 15:4; 2 Tim. 2:8); (c) that He was not conceived by the Holy Spirit (Isa. 7:14; 29:14; Mt. 1:18-25; Lk. 1:26-28; Jn. 1:1, 1:24); or that (d) He will not physically return for His church (Lk. 14:14; Jn. 14:3; Ac. 1:11; 1 Cor. 15:23, 15:52-53; 1 Th. 4:15-17).

That 37% represents the tares of the Church (Mt. 13:24-30), and can best be described as those who have only an outward appearance of faith that is used to cloak an inner carnality which they refuse to surrender. In more simple terms, they are those who have mastered the art of talking the talk, but have refused to learn how to walk the walk. They are Sunday Christians: members of the social church.

The Spirit of God cannot abide carnal believers. Without the sealing of the Holy Spirit (Eph. 1:13) there can be no indwelling (1 Cor. 6:19), because the Holy Spirit cannot reside in an unclean vessel. Since the Spirit cannot abide with those who merely utter a profession of faith with no desire to be regenerated, He cannot instruct them. Since a spiritual knowledge of God cannot be achieved in the carnal state, those who make only a superficial commitment to the Lord never become rooted and their faith quickly withers and dies.

If you are a recent convert to Jesus Christ, you need to understand the born-again experience you have heard so much about is not merely the act of reforming one's own human nature to conform to the precepts of Scripture. It is a real, physical transformation, performed by the Holy Spirit within you. Your carnal spirit nature is completely regenerated (reborn into a new tabernacle of flesh) as you become a new creation in Christ Jesus. In other words, the born-again experience doesn't take place because of action you are required to take since, other than accepting Jesus Christ as your Lord and Savior, there isn't anything you can do. What transpires is an actual, supernatural transformation that occurs within each believer who takes the step of faith.

We cannot be educated into Christianity, although many have tried. Every major college and university in this country, as well as most major universities in Europe, offer a variety of courses and related degrees in theology and biblical eschatology. Most classes on religion are taught in the same secular, politically correct manner as world history, biology or physical science. As a result, it is possible to *learn* everything contained within the pages of the Bible without ever learning the Word of God or experiencing the power of the Holy Spirit, and eventually die still condemned in our sins.

We cannot hide our carnal nature within the closets of our mind, nor can we earn salvation through good works, or through the offering of tithes here on Earth. The medieval Roman Catholic Church initiated the practice of selling indulgences based on an assumed authority to bind and loose which was conferred on Peter (Mt. 16:17). Plenary indulgences promised the removal of loved ones from Hell, a right the Church determined it possessed as the rightful heir of Peter, the keeper of the keys. This practice, which theoretically assured the family members of a loved one's transfer from Hell to Purgatory, was, depending on the financial standing of the church member, a very costly proposition since once the loved one was transferred from Hell to Purgatory, many additional prayers, fasting and almsgiving would still be required to restore the loved one to fellowship with Jesus.

That the practice has no scriptural foundation notwithstanding, the sale of indulgences remains a contemporary practice with Catholics tithing to their redemption, believing good works and handsome tithes will retrieve them from the pits of Hell should they perish in an unregenerate state. They further believe, through the practice of indulgences, they will stand cleansed, purged in the temporal fires of Purgatory, before Christ at the Great White Throne Judgment. Because the Catholic view is decidedly amillennial, they believe there will be only one judgment at which their deeds will be used to offset their sins; and, at the same time, that the sheep will be separated from the goats.

When Jesus said, "That which is born of the flesh is flesh..." (Jn. 3:6), He was saying that regardless what we do in the flesh, it remains flesh. Flesh will never become spirit because of good works; and flesh will never inherit the Kingdom of God. Unfortunately, far too many of those standing in the pulpits of the churches of America are not speaking those words to their congregations. They are preaching a politically correct social gospel which compromises the Word of God in order to keep their pews—and coffers—full.

As society relaxes its ethics, the social church has felt an obligation to accommodate the new morality by redefining sin. In the May 8, 1966 edition of *Look Magazine,* Dr. Mary Calderone summed up the new morality value system in her defense of sexual freedom in America: "Nobody from on high determines this," she said concerning morality. *"Only you determine it!"* (emphasis, mine).

The social church has adopted the attitude that whatever is acceptable to society must ultimately be acceptable to God. The commandments, they contend, were written in a different age for a different people, namely, the Jews. They, like the Catholic Church, view Matthew 16:19 as their authority to loose and bind as they redefine the characteristics of sin. Ignored in their logic is the fact that sin remains sin; and sin, in the eyes of God, is punishable according to the precepts outlined in His Word.

Redefining homosexuality as a legitimate lifestyle simply because it is politically correct is not within the legislative prerogatives of the church. Because God loves the sinner, we are led to believe He will paternally overlook the sin. However, because He is sinless, and all sin is a stench in His nostrils, He can't, and He won't. God still condemns the sin (Lev. 18:22, 20:13; Rom. 1:27). Homosexuality is no less an abomination in the eyes of God even though man has become accustomed to the stench of it!

Redefining abortion as anything other than murder is contrary to the Word of God. The Bible unequivocally declares "thou shalt not kill" (Ex. 20:13; Mt. 10:19; Lk. 18:20; Rom. 13:9; Jas. 2:11). That means the taking of any human life is a violation of the commandment. The commandment is not qualified with a list of exemptions which grants a mother-to-be immunity under certain circumstances: such as wanting a boy instead of a girl, or not having the financial means to support another child, or simply not wanting to go through the inconvenience of pregnancy.

Of course, it is not politically correct to view the fetal matter which is to be aborted as a person, because if we suddenly thought of the fetus as a human being, we would have to concede the abortionist was killing a person; and, as a law-abiding civilized society, we have a constitutional obligation to protect all human life, regardless of its state of viability. While the United States Supreme Court has been conveniently unable to determine at what point life actually begins, the Bible, which has been the basis of common law for almost 2,000 years, does not. In Psalms 139:15-16, David wrote:

> *"My frame was not hidden from You when I was made in the secret place. When I was woven together in the depths of the earth, Your eyes saw my unformed body. All of the days for me were written in Your book before one of them came to be."* (NIV)
>
> Concerning Jeremiah, the prophet, God said:
>
> *"Before I formed you in the womb, I knew you. Before you were born I set you apart; I appointed you as a prophet to the nations."* (Jer. 1:5; NIV)

The reality of human life, i.e., a person, within the womb is clearly depicted by the angel Gabriel in Luke 1:15, when the archangel informed Zacharias, the father of John the Baptist, that the son his wife Elizabeth would bear would be filled with the Holy Spirit in his mother's womb. Later, when Mary, the mother of Jesus visited her cousin, Elizabeth, the baby within her womb leaped at the sound of Mary's voice, the result of which, Elizabeth was filled with the Holy Spirit. Scripture, again, the basis of European common law, recognizes the reality of human life within the womb based not on issues of viability, but rather, on the basis of both medical and theological certainty. Life begins when the egg and the sperm form a human embryo. The medical community had little problem answering the question of when life began prior to the feminist movement. Quite simply, life began at conception. Several court cases, both local and national were waged, and won, based on the legal rights of the fetus.

Society, which today places little value on life at either end of the age spectrum, would now have us believe it is a woman's constitutional right, without social stigma, to kill her unborn child. The Word of God, which is by far a higher law, contradicts that thesis. Abortion is murder whether committed at conception (the point at which human life is endowed with its eternal soul), or at full term, slaughtered in the most inhumane manner as the baby departs the birth canal. Human life has been so devalued that it is now subservient to the whims of a morally bankrupt society—and the social church has allowed it to happen!

We, the members of the Christian community, have stood silently on the sidelines and allowed the U. S. Supreme Court to rewrite and add a separation of church and state clause to the Constitution of the United States. In doing so, we have allowed the federal bureaucracy to remove all traces of Christianity from our schools, and with it, our entire Judæo–Christian ethics system. We have allowed those to whom we have granted authority to replace school prayer with free condoms for our children—something viewed by our educators as much more meaningful than religion to the youth of America. Not in the least surprising, the social church is aiding and abetting this moral debacle in the politically correct name of human rights.

The message Jesus sent to the seven churches of Revelation is as valid and meaningful for us today as it was to the first century church. We need to listen and heed the warning of His words, originally penned for the church at Pergamos, the church settled in the secular world, before it is too late:

> *"I have somewhat against thee because thou hast left thy first love...* (Jesus Christ) *...I know the blasphemy of them who say they are...* (true believers) *...and are not, but are the...* (church) *...of Satan...Thou hast those who hold the doctrine of Balaam...* (mixing humanism with Christianity) *...to cast a stumbling block before the...* (believer). *...So hast thou also the doctrine of the Nicolaitans...* (professing Christianity but living a carnal, licentious life) *...which things I hate..."* (Rev. 2:13-15; KJV, paraphrased)

Jesus, after commending the church at Ephesus for rejecting a moral departure from the Word of God, rebuked the church at Pergamos for compromising their faith and watering down their beliefs to accommodate pagan immorality.

It is important to remember that of the seven churches Christ addressed through the Apostle John in The Revelation, Satan gained a toehold in six—and totally corrupted two of them. As the social church of the 20th century relaxed the code of ethical conduct under which their congregations functioned, its theology became unclear, and morality was both challenged and compromised. Once Christian theology was successfully diluted, man's spiritual values quickly decayed, and mainstream Christianity became the Church of Laodicea, being neither hot nor cold, and bending with every whim of political correctness.

Television and its related byproducts, satellite transmitted CATV signals and VCR productions, have been instrumental not only in the creation of the mega-ministry whose followers include not only members of the congregations of the local church, and in many instances, the pastorate as well, but in the creation of a subculture of mini-denominations whose followers more quickly identify themselves with these charismatic Hollywood-type shepherds than the doctrinal tenets of the denominations which spawned them as well. While satellite CATV has done much in the global advancement of the Gospel of Jesus Christ, it has also contributed to the decay of the local church because it encourages laziness among the congregation and more easily promotes scriptural error among the followers, who many times view the television evangelist as a larger than life celebrity whose doctrinal positions are always inspired by the Holy Spirit and never of themselves.

> *"For I know this, that after My departing shall grievous wolves...* (false teachers and preachers) *...enter in among you, not sparing the flock. Also, of your own selves shall men arise, speaking perverse things, to draw away disciples after them."* (Ac. 20:29-30; KJV)

> *"Wherefore the Lord said, Forasmuch as this people draw near*

Me with their mouth, and with their lips do honor Me, but have removed their heart far from Me, and their fear toward Me is taught by the precepts of men..." (Isa. 29:13; KJV)

As humanism further erodes the taproot of the church system, social preachers will become increasingly more popular with their worldly congregations than the traditional, morals-oriented church pastor because the words they speak from the pulpit will increasingly be the words of the world, preached to a worldly congregation (1 Jn. 4:5) who will demand, through the payment of tithes and offerings, a more politically correct social gospel.

Moreover, the social gospel does not exact penalties for sin, since sin is mitigated by the changing morality of the society which spawned it. Man feared God because God was the ultimate judge who would determine both rewards and punishment. Through the mitigation of sin, punishment is denied. God in the social church is a passive parent much like the human parent who, according to the tenets of a permissive society, is expected to allow their children all of the moral freedoms of Sodom without fear of punishment!

As humanism continues its erosion of the Gospel of Jesus Christ, the social church will continue to lead its congregation through its pied piper message into the waiting arms of Antichrist.

Is the professing church saved? Only that portion which honestly professes Jesus Christ as its Lord and Savior with their minds, their hearts and their mouths. The part of the church which does not, is not.

CHAPTER SEVEN

THE ENDTIME

Are we the generation that will witness the second coming of Jesus Christ?

When Jesus described the events which would signify the end of the current age, known as *the times* (years) *of the Gentiles* (Lk. 21:24) in Matthew 24:34, He said:

"Verily, I say unto you, This generation shall not pass, till all these things be fulfilled." (KJV)

Was Jesus speaking metaphorically, or was He speaking of a literal time and of a literal generation of people who would witness the events described? If He was speaking of both a literal time and a literal people, are we the generation of which He spoke?

In the New Testament four words are translated as generation. In Matthew 3:7 John the Baptist referred to the Pharisees and Sadducees as a generation of vipers. In the Greek text, the word used was *gennema,* which means offspring. This same word is used in Matthew 12:34; 23:33; and Luke 3:7. In Matthew 1:1 generation is derived from the Greek word *genesis.* In this instance the word is used to record the genealogy of Jesus through the line of Joseph to Solomon and David. Generation is derived from *genos* in 1 Pe. 2:9. Translated literally, *genos* means kin.

In Matthew 24:34 (as well as 11:16; 12:39; 23:36; Mk. 8:12; 8:38; 9:10; 12:30; Lk. 7:31; 9:41; 11:29-32; 11:50-51; 16:8; 17:25; 21:32; Ac. 2:40; 8:23; 13:36; and Heb. 3:10) the word generation comes from the Greek word *genea,* which means a whole multitude of men living at the same or particular place at the same time. This, then, is the context in which Jesus spoke: to the entire multitude of men living at that particular place and time—the time of that age. To fully appreciate what Christ is saying in Matthew 24:34, we need to glance at Matthew 23:36, which further clarifies exactly which generation it was to which He was referring.

> *"Verily I say unto you, All these things shall come upon this (genea) generation..."* (Mt. 23:36; KJV)

A generation in Hebrew reckoning was, and still is, forty years. Christ spoke this condemnation after His rejection in 32 A.D. Flavius Titus destroyed

Jerusalem in 70 A.D. When Titus destroyed Herod's Temple, not one stone was left standing upon another (Mt. 24:1-2; Mk. 13:1-2; Lk. 21:5-6). That destruction occurred within forty years of the date Christ decreed it.

The significance of this prophecy is further amplified by examining other scriptures where the word *genea* is used. In Matthew 11:13-16 Jesus spoke to the multitude concerning John the Baptist. He said, if they accepted the teachings of John, then to them, John was Elijah, because none other was needed. Christ's statement was directed specifically at that particular generation. John was Elijah to the believers because he heralded the first advent of Jesus. To those who rejected Him, a fulfillment of Malachi 4:5 was still required.

In Matthew 12:39 the Pharisees asked Jesus for a sign by which they would know He was the Messiah. Christ answered them by saying,

> *"An evil and adulterous generation (genea) seeketh after a sign, and there shall no sign be given to it, but the sign of the prophet, Jonah..."* (KJV)

The sign referred to was the burial and resurrection of Jesus Christ. To them, no other sign was to be given. Three thousand, who understood the significance of the event, were saved when the Day of Pentecost arrived. To ensuing generations, as the Church Age unfolded, a multiplicity of miraculous signs and wonders have occurred, leaving no doubt to those who have witnessed them that Jesus Christ is Lord and Savior of all.

The writer of the Book of Hebrews speaks of the Jews who wandered in the wilderness. Again, a solitary generation *(genea)* is mentioned. That generation perished in the wilderness. Only Joshua and Caleb were exempted, and a new generation entered into the Promised Land.

Most scholars of biblical eschatology agree that the rebirth of Israel was the catalyst which triggered the ticking of the endtime clock (Ezek. 37:1-11). The rebirth of the modern state of Israel took place on May 8, 1948. If we start at that date, and add one generation of forty years, it would appear the endtime started in 1988, and the world is living on borrowed time. If the catalyst was not the rebirth of the nation Israel, but rather, the taking of Jerusalem from the Arabs during the Six Day War, then the endtime clock would have begun ticking on June 6, 1967. Forty years would be complete on June 5, 2007. This alternate date is much more logical than the former since Daniel's seventy weeks started with Artxerxes decree to rebuild Jerusalem (Neh. 2:1-8).

Since the generation of which Christ spoke is the same generation which will experience first, the rapture of the church, and finally, the horrible devastation of the Great Tribulation, no other clues are provided that will allow the eschatologist to more precisely pinpoint the date, since the Tribulation begins with the rapture of the church, an event for which only God knows the date.

However, regardless which date you select as the starting catalyst, one thing should be obvious to the believer. All of the signs for which the Christian was admonished to watch have already happened, clearly suggesting His return is imminent. Quite obviously, Jesus can return at any moment—perhaps as you sit reading, or as you slip off to sleep this very night. Perhaps Jesus will return for

His church next week, next month, or next year. Or maybe it won't happen for another ten years.

> *"No one knows about that day or hour, not even the angels in heaven, nor the Son, but only the father."* (Mt. 24:36; NIV)

What will be the signs of His coming?

Shortly after Jesus condemned the Pharisees (Mt. 23:13-16), lamented over Jerusalem (Mt. 23:37-39), and predicted the destruction of Herod's Temple by Titus (Mt. 24:1-2; Mk. 13:1-2; Lk. 21:5-6), He left the city and retired to the Mount of Olives. Disturbed by His pronouncement of judgment, Peter, James and Andrew

> *"...went to Jesus privately saying, Tell us, when shall these things be? And what shall be the sign of Thy coming, and of the end of the age?"* (Mt. 24:3; NIV, paraphrased)
>
> Christ answered his disciples, saying:
>
> *"Watch out that no deceives you. For many will come in My name, claiming, 'I am the Christ', and will deceive many..."* (Mt. 24:4-6; NIV)

On Sunday, April 26, 1982, the New Age Movement launched a worldwide advertising campaign which should have awakened even the sleepiest Christian to the fact that *the times of the Gentiles* (Lk. 21:24) was about to come to an end. Christians all over the world awoke that morning to discover a full page advertisement in their Sunday newspapers which blatantly declared that Christ was here. I'm certain that hundreds upon hundreds of sermons were suddenly scrapped at the very last minute when the pastors of a thousand churches in the communities where these ads appeared decided to preach on Matthew 24:5-6 and 24:24 that morning.

The full page ads, which ran in almost every mass circulation newspaper in the world, featured a banner headline which boldly stated: "THE CHRIST IS NOW HERE!"

Interestingly, when the ad appeared in a Muslim newspaper, the headline proclaimed that *Iman Mahdi,* not Christ, was here. In the Buddhist newspaper, it was the *Fifth Buddha,* not Christ nor the *Iman* nor *Krishna,* who had come. Only in the Christian and Jewish newspapers did the headline proclaim Christ, the Messiah.

The massive advertising campaign, which utilized almost every major newspaper in the world, was paid for by the New Age Movement hierarchy. The advertising blitz was estimated to have cost the New Agers upwards of $3,000,000.00. The Christian Church, which had largely ignored the New Age Movement, suddenly found themselves taking a closer look. Who were these people and what were their intentions?

The New Age Movement is an esoteric worldwide network of loosely knit cell groups whose avowed purpose is the total and absolute destruction of Christianity and Judaism. Their doctrine is a mishmash of theosophy, Vishva Hindu, Transcendental Meditation, Kriya Yoga, and several other forms of self-realization that are simply too complicated to explain in a text of this size. The New

Age Movement draws heavily from the occult and mysticism.

What makes them dangerous to the Christian is that like most cults, they appear to be deeply concerned only about the welfare of others as they deny their movement is grounded in any form of organized religion. While the New Age Movement appears to be a lax, disorganized network with no specific agenda, they have effectively penetrated almost every strata of political, economic and religious life in the United States. They appear to be moving on a very regimented timetable, and they are determined to achieve their objective within their prescribed time frames. Precisely what is their objective? Like many other groups which have formed over the past couple of decades, their objective is the creation of a universal, one-world religious system followed by a one-world government which the New Age hierarchy will control.

Religion aside, the formation of a one-world government is the ultimate objective of the United Nations formed in 1945 to theoretically prevent a third world war. Similar efforts were initiated at the end of World War I, and not in the least surprising, by a similar group of advocates—world bankers. The new organization, to be called the League of Nations, was proposed at the Big Ten Summit in Paris on January 18, 1919 by Sir Lloyd George, the chief representative of Great Britain.

While obstensibly created to devote itself to world disarmament, the League of Nations was also to accomplish four other objectives. Three of these objectives were short term. First, the League was to serve as an international collection agency to monitor German reparation which was set at 342 billion gold Reichsmarks. Second, the League was to be responsible for making certain German war criminals were brought to trial. Third, as the international arbitrator of the world, the League was to settle any territorial disputes within the European community which resulted from the war. Finally, the long term agenda included the drafting of a constitution that outlined the functions and responsibilities of the League of Nations as they related to solving world health problems, creating labor standards for the world, and becoming the international administrator of the will of the League members. The League of Nations was to be headquartered in Geneva, Switzerland. The first Secretary General was Sir Eric Drummond, a British diplomat.

While U.S. President Woodrow Wilson was a staunch supporter of the League, the United States Congress, recognizing that membership could ultimately curb America's ability to govern itself, repudiated Wilson's program after a protracted, and sometimes bitter political debate between the isolationist Congress and the somewhat socialist President. Since the League of Nations was artfully concealed in the *Treaty of Versailles*, the peace treaty with Germany, neither document was ratified by Congress. The League of Nations officially came into being on January 10, 1920—without American participation or financial support. It was from its inception a failure. It was unable to protect its weaker members from attack. It lacked the expertise to deal with economic problems, nor could it enforce its own decisions. It served primarily as a world bank, issuing loans to third world countries. When World War II began in 1939 the

League of Nations had lost all of its prestige and influence.

The European banking community, which earned countless billions of dollars on the human suffering of World War II by financing both the Axis and the Allies, pointed its finger of blame at the United States for the many failures of the League as well as the holocaust of war which blanketed Europe for six years. As a result, the United States government quickly signed on when the United Nations was proposed from the ashes of the ideologically bankrupt League of Nations.

Today the power of the United Nations is growing in secret. The organization has learned from the errors of its past. During the Bush Administration the UN was artfully used by George Bush to hold together an unlikely coalition of Muslims and Jews against Iraqi warlord Saddam Hussein, restoring the organization's lost prestige. In a secret Presidential Decision Directive (PDD-25) less than two years later, President Bill Clinton surreptitiously granted what many Republican members of Congress fear may be unilateral UN authority over the mightiest military force on the globe under some extraneous circumstances. If so, Clinton, in doing so, gave the United Nations more power than any nation in the world singularly possesses, thereby restoring much of its lost influence, and providing it with the ability to enforce its decisions. Soon the foundation of Antichrist's world government will be firmly established.

Not all antichrists are interested in political power, or even possess the ability to achieve it. Some become antichrists only because they possess messianic illusions. Over the past two or three decades literally hundreds of false prophets and false messiahs have risen. We mentioned the New Age antichrist, Iman Mahdi. America, however, has had its own. Three of the best known are David Keresh of the Waco Branch Davidian commune, People's Temple founder Jim Jones, and, as unlikely as it may seem on the surface, Charles Milles Manson, the mastermind of the Tate/LaBianca murders in 1969.

Manson, whose slight, scary figure more closely resembles the biblical description of Antichrist than Jesus, was believed by his followers to the be reincarnated Christ. Had he not been convicted of several counts of first degree murder, Manson would probably have gone on to be the overlord of a pseudo-Christian cult similar to that of the Children of God or the Love Family. Manson possessed all of the charismatic qualities which characterize the typical cult overlord.

Jones, who we previously mentioned, initiated the mass suicide of 913 People's Temple members in Jonestown, Guyana on November 18, 1978. Jones had such a magnetic, charismatic personality that his followers found it very easy to overlook his obvious worldly flaws. Included in his acquaintances were many state and national political figures, including the wife and sister of former President Jimmy Carter.

While most Americans do not realize it, there are hundreds of Jim Joneses, David Kereshes and even Charlie Mansons out there, drawing our children, our friends and our relatives into their webs. A few, usually through notoriety, become nationally known, but most remain obscurely hidden in the side pockets of

Americana, silently stealing the souls of our loved ones with compassionate false doctrines and promises of godhood. How many Americans outside the state of Oregon ever heard of Bhagwan Shree Rahneesh before the Hindu guru was arrested on immigration violation charges?

How many people knew the name of David Brandt Berg? Berg, a former Christian and Missionary Alliance pastor, founded the Children of God in 1971. Berg became disillusioned with mainstream Christianity and began to cultivate a following from society's dropouts in 1968 in the Huntington Beach, California area. Declaring that God had revealed to him that California was about to slide into the Pacific Ocean, Berg and his followers, numbering somewhere between fifty and two hundred, left the state and wandered aimlessly across much of the United States and Canada, collecting other dropouts as they proclaimed the imminent return of Jesus. It was during this period that Berg became known to his rapidly growing band as Moses David. By 1985 Moses David claimed to have a worldwide following in excess of two million. His theology has long since changed from Christianity to spiritualism.

Another endtime false messiah, Paul Eerdman, founded the Church of Armageddon. Eerdman believed the world had entered into the Tribulation, and his intention was to gather God's true family together "...into a place, called in the Hebrew tongue, Armageddon..." where they would be protected from the tribulation which was falling upon Earth. God's true family, of course, consisted only of those who believed Eerdman was the Christ.

Layfayette Ron Hubbard, a science fiction writer before he founded the Church of Scientology, claimed to have visited Heaven on two separate occasions, eons apart. Hubbard insisted that Heaven, which had once been a beautiful utopian garden, had fallen into a state of disrepair much like an old, deserted house. Scientologists believe in reincarnation. They have no need of Heaven and no fear of Hell. However, if reincarnation was a fact as Hubbard claimed, and Heaven, according to Hubbard, was occupied before Scientology, then who used Heaven when it was in its original, Edenic state, and how did they get there in the first place if man is constanly being regenerated into other physical human beings?

Scientology teaches that God is an irrelevant force in nature, and that man is saved not by faith in Christ Jesus, but through counseling by Scientologists—the purpose of which is to increase his IQ level over 135 through the elimination of *engrams* from within his body. (Sounds like science fiction to me.)

When Satan tempted Eve with the fruit of the Tree of Knowledge of Good and Evil (Gen. 3:1-6), an implied benefit of eating the fruit was that knowledge was the key in achieving godhood. Thus, the increasing of one's I.Q. in Scientology is necessary to obtain that level of perfection. Satan, through Scientology, has deceived over two million souls. The harvest of tares will indeed be great.

During the same period, Victor Paul Wierwille, a former Evangelical Reform minister founded a group known as The Way International, whose purpose was to re-define and re-interpret the Bible—the right of which, Wierwille claimed, was granted exclusively to him by God. Wierwille denied the Trinity, and claimed that Jesus, while perhaps *a* son of God, was not *the* Son of God. (See *Jesus*

Christ is NOT God; The Way, by Victor Wierwille.)

Most cults teach that Jesus of Nazareth was not God in the flesh. Rather, they insist that Jesus was merely a prophet or, at best, a perfect man who was crucified before He could accomplish that for which He was sent. It has been conservatively estimated by various Christian writers that there are well over 5,000 cults operating within the world today. Each of these groups have their own messiah. Some purport to be simply messengers of God with some new endtime revelation not previously disclosed in the Scriptures; some represent themselves as new messiahs, sent to complete the unfinished work of Jesus; and still others claim to be the reincarnated Christ.

The reality is, Jesus Christ came specifically to die on the cross—on the precise date upon which the crucifixion occurred—in order to redeem mankind from sin and to introduce a new covenant relationship through which man, who is inherently weak, could secure promised salvation through grace. Every biblical prophecy dealing with the first advent of the Messiah was fulfilled by Jesus during His brief period on Earth. None of those specific prophecies remain unfulfilled. All unfulfilled prophecies concern Christ's second advent at the end of the Age and specifically describe Jesus not as the sacrifice, but rather, as the warrior God who will both judge mankind and reign over the affairs of the Millennial world for one thousand years.

(It was the inability of the Jews to distinguish between the first and second advents of the Messiah during the first century which created the confusion that ultimately led to their rejection of Him. They, like the Israelites in Egypt, had been taught that the Messiah would free the Jews from the bondage of foreign imperialism and re-establish both the throne of David and the national status of Israel.)

> *"You will hear of wars and rumors of war, but see to it that you are not alarmed. Such things must happen, but the end is still to come. Nation will rise against nation, and kingdom against kingdom..."* (Mt. 24:6-7; NIV)

During the past two or three centuries, wars have increased in both frequency and intensity. From conflicts in which the dead and wounded were numbered in hundreds, we now experience wars where the victims are counted in the tens of thousands, and even millions. More people, civilian as well as military, have been killed in the wars of the 20th century than in all of the wars fought in all previous centuries combined since the creation of man.

> *"...and there will be famines and earthquakes in various places. All these are the beginning of birth pains..."* (Mt. 24:7-8; NIV)

Famine and pestilence follow war like fleas and ticks on a dog. As vital food supplies are destroyed and agricultural efforts are terminated by the ravages of war, famine necessarily results, and is one of the weapons used by man against his enemies. Likewise, when critical human services are either destroyed or seriously curtailed, sanitary conditions will rapidly deteriorate and disease will become epidemic.

War and abortion notwithstanding, the population of the world is multiplying at such a phenomenal rate that food production, using current technology, may not, according to several government sponsored studies, be able to sustain the population within fifty to one hundred years. It took the world from Adam to 1850 to reach one billion people. In 1930—eighty years later—the world's population reached two billion. By 1960 another billion was added, and in 1975 the population exceeded four billion. Even with an almost zero population growth rate in the industrialized countries of the world, the population grew by five hundred million between 1975 and 1980—and population control has now become one of the primary objectives of the United Nations. By 1985 the population of the world exceeded five billion, and is currently nearing the six billion level.

U.N. statistics suggest that over 600,000 people starve to death each year in the undeveloped countries of the world. (Since government agencies have a natural propensity to exaggerate numbers whenever it suits their purpose, it is more likely the number is no more than ten to twenty percent of their estimate, but it is still, nevertheless, a staggering number!) It should also be noted that not all of these deaths from starvation occur in third world countries. Thousands of Americans, mostly small children and the aged, suffer from some form of starvation, and receive little or no assistance from either state or federal agencies—not because the funds to feed them have not been allocated, but rather, because of the nature of the bureaucracies which administers those funds. While actual cases of death from starvation are rare in the United States, hundreds of Americans die each year from starvation related causes.

Over the past twenty years, there have been over fifty significantly major earthquakes around the globe that have resulted in approximately one million deaths. During the 16th century historical records note a total of 153 earthquakes. Three hundred seventy-eight earthquakes were recorded in the 17th century, and 640 earthquakes were recorded in the 18th century. Two thousand one hundred nineteen earthquakes were noted in the 19th century—and thus far, over 5,000 earthquakes have been documented in the twentieth!

> *"...then sudden destruction cometh upon them, as travail upon a woman with child..."* (1 Th. 5:3; KJV)

As every woman who has ever had a baby knows, labor begins with mild stabbing pains which increase in both frequency and severity as the time of birth nears. This is the analogy Jesus used (Mt. 24:7-8) to describe the signs which the Christian was to witness. Earthquakes on this unsettled Earth have been noted throughout all of history, as have wars and famine. It is not the fact that these things exist which the believer was admonished to watch—but the increased frequency and severity of them as well.

It should be noted that when Jesus addressed the question of His second coming, His answer to the Apostles was not directed at His appearance in the clouds when He returns for His Church (Lk. 14:14; Jn. 5:25; 1 Cor. 15:23, 52-53; 1 Th. 4:15-17; Rev. 3:10). Rather, His answer was focused at His second physical appearance on planet Earth (Job 19:25; Ps. 96:13; Isa. 26:21, 62:11; Dan. 7:13; Zech. 8:3, 12:10; Mt. 16:27, 23:39; Mk. 14:62; Lk. 21:27; Ac. 1:11;

Heb. 9:28, 10:37; Rev. 1:7) at the end of the Tribulation. The translation of the church must occur first. The Church, of which Jesus is the head, must be removed prior to the Tribulation. If it is not removed, it would then come under the dominion of Antichrist, something Scripture clearly indicates will not be the case since Christ will never be subservient to either man or Satan.

We, as Christians, have been assured that we will escape the time of Jacob's Trouble (Jer. 30:7) which will come upon the world (Lk. 21:36; Rev. 3:10) when the Holy Spirit is taken out of the way (2 Th. 2:6-7) and Antichrist is revealed (2 Th. 2:8). (It is important to note, in verse seven, that the Holy Spirit, the Restrainer, is taken out of the way—not taken away.) While Antichrist will not be hindered during this seven year period, the Holy Spirit will still be present on Earth and will continue to comfort and strengthen those who accept Christ during that period. If the Holy Spirit was not manifest on Earth during that period, none living at that time could be saved.

"Because of the increase of wickedness, the love of most will grow cold..." (Mt. 24:12; NIV)

Due largely to the watering down of the Gospel of Jesus Christ and the widespread acceptance of false doctrines promoted by false prophets and messiahs, the love of God is diminishing—even among ardent believers. Many Christians are now being fed a more socially acceptable gospel from the pulpits of their local churches, and unfortunately, the laity has far too much of a propensity to accept what it is fed from the pulpit as gospel. If the churchgoing Christian community has lost its fear of God, can we expect any less from the heathens and proselytes? An actual hostility for, and a contempt of, God is becoming increasingly visible in America today, and actually rivals that found by the Lord in Sodom and Gomorrah.

One evening in the fall of 1995, while driving back to the Shenandoah Valley from Washington, D.C., I found a Christian talk radio program *Janet Parshall's America* in which the host, Janet Parshall, was interviewing Pastor Phil Arms. Arms' congregation is located in Houston, Texas. The substance of that dialogue is pertinent to our discussion.

Arms is a well-known evangelist in several western states. His sermons are videotaped for broadcast on area television stations throughout a multi-state area in the west. As a full-gospel preacher, Arms does not mince his words, nor does he dilute the messages which run on television into a more politically correct, socially acceptable dialogue.

Earlier that year Arms received a telephone call from one of the local Houston TV stations carrying his program. The station management informed him they had some complaints about his program, and they were advising him it would be necessary for the station to review the text of his sermons before airing to make certain they did not include any more inflammatory remarks. The remark which apparently inflamed a viewer, a Muslim, was the statement that we are saved only through faith in Christ Jesus, and that there is no other way by which man can be received into the Kingdom of Heaven.

According to the conversation between Arms and Parshall, he refused the television station editorial rights over his sermons and continued airing his programs as before. Angered by his refusal to cooperate with them, the station, in retaliation, superimposed a banner across the screen at regular intervals throughout the broadcasts which stated the program was a paid advertisement. While Arms did not feel the Word of God could legitimately be construed as a paid advertisement, he tolerated the intrusion. Within a couple of months, however, Arms received another call from the station. This time, to learn the identity of his accuser, the pastor had to engage the services of an attorney, who ultimately learned that Arms had now offended the homosexual community. Again, the station demanded the right of censorship, threatening to cancel his contract if he refused them. Again, Arms refused, and through his attorney, advised the TV station that they could not cancel his contract since he had prepaid all of the broadcast costs when the contract was initiated. Nevertheless, the TV station canceled his program and, without refunding his money, replaced it with a half hour psychic infomerical—which did not contain superimposed banners stating the program was an advertisement.

Because the message Arms broadcasted was not politically correct, the pastor was censored. Because the message presented the clear and unvarnished Gospel of Jesus Christ, it was removed from the air. The Sodomites in that community did not want to be reminded of their sins. The society in which we live extols the morality which God condemned in Sodom or Gomorrah: abortion, euthanasia, homosexuality, the worship of other gods, and the dissolution of the institution of marriage. Which must make us ask: How much longer will God listen to the cries of the righteous before He destroys that which created the stench that offends Him?

As the last minutes of the 24th hour of the endtime clock tick off before our eyes, we can see apostasy filling not only the pews of our churches, but the pulpits as well. As the social church compromises basic Christian tenets and relaxes the moral ethics which Scripture mandates, it assumes the right to redefine the very nature of sin. Morality vanishes and ethics become subjective, vague and superficial.

Humanism teaches that if by some strange chance God does exist in some form or another, He would not condemn any of His children to an everlasting hell just for being human. The fact that humanism is deeply rooted in the church is evidenced by the parable of the ten virgins (Mt. 25:1-13). Since all ten are represented as virgins, we know they all represent the congregation of the endtime church. But, while they are all representative of the church, they are not all born-again members of that body. Five of the virgins are born-again (i.e., the oil is representative of the Holy Spirit, which indwells all Christians), and five are of the world (Eph. 1:13; 1 Cor. 6:19).

We are told that five of the virgins were foolish and carried no oil in their lamps. These are they whose profession of faith is empty and meaningless—those who talk the talk but don't walk the walk. Many in the faith refer to them as Sunday morning Christians. A Christian facade conceals an otherwise carnal nature for two or three hours every Sunday morning, but quickly vanishes for the balance of the week.

When Christ returns for His church, those who have been playacting will discover they have not fooled God—but by then it will be too late. The rapture of the church will have already happened (1 Cor 15:52-53; 1 Th. 4:15-17) in the twinkling of an eye, and they will be left behind to fend for themselves in a world in which no ethical, right-minded human being would desire to live. Salvation will then come either through decapitation (Rev. 20:4) or by enduring unbelievable privation until the end (Mt. 24:13) without accepting the mark of the beast (Rev. 13:16-17; 14:9). And that will probably prove to be difficult for those left behind because, if they could not walk the Christian walk in a quasi-Christian setting, how will they perform such a walk in a world ruled by Antichrist?

Will the church really be "raptured"?

Among the most heatedly disputed theological events in scripture is the rapture of the church. Believers in the translation of the church point to several scriptures to substantiate their position. Christians who adhere to the amillennial perspective are quick to point out that the word *rapture* does not even appear in the Bible.

Rapture is derived from the Latin word *rapere,* which was used in the Latin Vulgate in 1 Thessalonians 4:17 to describe the term *caught up.* In the Greek New Testament, the word describing this occurrence is *harpazo,* which literally means to be snatched away.

Many theologians refer to this event as the *parousia. Parousia* literally means a sudden arrival, and the consequent presence thereof (1 Cor. 15:23; 1 Th. 4:15). We, as living representatives of the body of Christ, will be caught up *(rapere) (harpazo)* and shall join the dead in Christ in the clouds (1 Th. 4:16-17). This event is not to be confused with the judgment resurrection (Rev. 20:4-6; 11:15). It is the resurrection of the just (Lk. 14:14; Ac. 24:15).

> *"For this we say unto you by the Word of the Lord, that we who are alive and remain unto the coming of the Lord shall not precede them who are asleep. For the Lord Himself shall descend from heaven with a shout, with the voice of the archangel, and with the trump of God; and the dead in Christ shall rise first; Then we who are alive and remain shall be caught up together with them in the clouds, to meet the Lord in the air; and so shall we ever be with the Lord."* (1 Th. 4:15-17; KJV)

While most Christians feel that because the rapture deals exclusively with the church, scriptures concerning it are confined exclusively to the New Testament. That, however, is not true. Isaiah 26:19-20 prefigures both the rapture and the Tribulation which follows, as well as the judgment of the Lord at the end of the age. We find this same type of dialogue in Daniel 12, particularly in verses one, two, eleven, twelve and thirteen.

The entire Church Age, from the crucifixion to the millennial reign of Christ on Earth, including the rapture of the Church, is symbolized in the Levitical feasts (Lev. 23:5-36). The first three feasts are separated from the final three by the Feast of Pentecost *(Shevuot),* which represents the birth of the church. The gap between the first three and the last three feasts is the period known as the Church Age. As the Church Age comes to an end, the final three feasts will experience literal fulfillment. The first of these three events will be the rapture of the church.

The Jews call this event *Rosh Hashana.* In Leviticus 23:24-25 the Lord called it *Trumpets.* As we read 1 Corinthians 15:52-53 and 1 Thessalonians 4:16-17 we see that the sound of a trumpet will actually signal the regathering of the elect. The trumpet which will be used to sound the call is a *shofar.* The *shofar* is a ram's horn, which in Old Testament times was used both to signal an attack or to sound the victory. It announced the reign of a new king and was used in all important religious rituals. The *shofar* was used by Joshua's priests as the Israelites encompassed Jericho (Josh. 6:1-20). It will be a blast from the *shofar* which will summon God's elect into the heavenlies.

The remaining two feasts, the Day of Atonement *(Yom Kippur)* (Lev. 23:27-38), which prefigures the Sheeps and Goats Judgement (Mt. 25:31-46), and Tabernacles *(Succoth)* (Lev. 23:34-36), which prefigures the Millennial Reign, were covered extensively earlier, and therefore need not be discussed here.

In addressing the Church of Revival, Philadelphia, Jesus said:

> *"Because you have kept the word of My patience, I also will keep thee from the hour of temptation, which shall come upon all the world, to try them that dwell upon the earth..." (Rev. 3:10; KJV)*

As we examine this particular verse, we find the words *"...keep...from..."* are translated from the Greek *tereo ek,* which literally means *to preserve out of the midst of.* The amillennialist would prefer to translate this verse as coming from the Greek words *phulasso en,* which means *to guard or watch, to protect from something within the midst of it.* With a simple substitution, this phrase no longer means to escape from it, but rather, to be protected while still in the midst of it. Fortunately for the believer, the correct usage is *tereo ek,* thereby affirming the substance and reality of the rapture.

A study of John 5:28-29 shows both the resurrection of life and the resurrection of the damned. It has been supposed in some circles that this scripture delineates only a single resurrection in which those who died in Christ and those who died in sin are resurrected together. If that thought was true, it would certainly negate the rapture. By dealing only with the resurrection of life, Luke 14:14 shows John 5:28-29 to be a depiction of two separate events, bound in one prophecy. 1 Corinthians 15:23 tells us when that event takes place:

> *"For as in Adam, all die, even so in Christ shall all be made alive; But every man in his own order: Christ, the first fruits; afterwards they that are Christ's at His coming..."*

Revelation 20:4-5 tells us the length of time between the resurrection of life and the resurrection of the damned:

> *"But the rest of the dead..."* (those not living and reigning with Jesus) *"...lived not again until the 1,000 years were finished."*

Therefore, it should be clear to those who make a serious inquiry into the Word of God that the translation, or rapture, of the Church is not only a Scriptural event, it is a supernatural event which was depicted in the Bible long before the birth of the Church.

Does the Rapture occur at the onset of the Tribulation, at the midpoint, or happen at the end of the seven year reign of Antichrist?

Among premillennialists this question is about as heated an argument as you will find, since these Christians stand in single accord on all other endtime eschatological issues except one: that of the gifts of the Spirit (a topic which will not be discussed under this heading).

The question is one of semantics since each of these factions agrees, at least in principle, that the Church will be translated at some time or another. Their dispute lies simply in when this supernatural event will take place.

For the sake of our discussion we will consider the least likely view first: that of a post-Tribulation rapture. Actually, there are two post-Tribulation views: one premillennial and one post-millennial. Both, however, are based on the denial of dispensationalism.

The post-millennial view is actually amillennial since it does not acknowledge the occurrence of the Tribulation. Aside from its denial of dispensationalism, the amillennial view also denies imminency (Jn. 14:2-3; 1 Cor. 1:7; Phil. 3:20-21; 1 Th. 1:9-10, 5:5-9; Titus 2:13; James 5:8-9; Rev. 3:10, 22:17-22) by insisting the imminent return of Jesus Christ is metaphoric rather than an actual, physical occurrence. One amillennial view insists that the early church viewed Christ's return only as a spiritual event, fulfilled on the Day of Pentecost with the birth of the Church through the infilling of the Holy Spirit. Views to the contrary, they maintain, are contemporary in nature, beginning around 1850 to the present and are, therefore, flawed theology. However, the reverse is true. The early Church held the view of imminency, and expected within their lifetimes to see the physical return of Jesus Christ. The doctrine of imminency was suppressed by the Roman Catholic Church and did not resurface until the Reformation.

The amillennial view supports a single resurrection as depicted in Jn. 5:28-29, and occurring at the end of the age. The amillenialist argues that at this single resurrection the good will be admitted into Heaven and the damned will be condemned to Hell. At that time the Theocratic Age will be ushered in on Earth. Needless to say, in the amillennial view, Jesus does not return to Earth to rule—He rules the kingdom from on high.

The post-Tribulation rapture theory of the premillennialist is not much different than the rapture view of amillennialism. The doctrinal belief of the post-Tribulationist is that the Church will remain on Earth until it is raptured to meet Jesus Christ in the air, where it will immediately return with Him to rule on Earth for a thousand years, after which the Theocratic Age is ushered in. This view has been growing in popularity over the past few years, almost in direct proportion to the growth of the social church in America.

The post-Tribulationist cites a variety of Scriptures, such as Matthew 24:11-13, Mark 13:9-13; Luke 23:29-31; and John 16:32-33 as evidence that the Church will go through the Tribulation. These particular verses, however, are specifically directed at Israel, which is distinctly separate from the Church not only with respect to judgment, but rewards as well.

The more traditional premillennial views are those which place the rapture of the church either at the beginning or the midpoint of the Tribulation.

Although I was saved in the Assemblies of God, which holds and teaches the pre-Tribulation rapture view, the mid-Tribulation rapture appeared much more logical to me, and nothing was able to sway that belief for a long time. I am not certain what I read or heard that triggered my conviction. I discussed it briefly with my pastor, but the Scriptures he pointed out to prove a pre-Tribulation rapture were precisely the same verses which convinced me otherwise. My argument in favor of a mid-Tribulation rapture was based, I imagine, on the fact that the Tribulation was divided in halves, and that nothing catastrophic occurs to the Church within the first three and one half years (Rev. 11:2, 11:3; 12:6; 13:5). All of the judgments were reserved for the second half.

At the time, as a babe in Christ, I had an insatiable appetite to be fed the Word of God. However, I was not aware of any special revelatory anointing, other than that which is imputed by the Holy Spirit on all newborn believers. I lacked even the most superficial understanding of the Scriptures. It is at that time in every new Christian's walk that he or she is most vulnerable to either false teachings or incorrect doctrine.

Finally, God revealed one Scripture, which I had read countless times, that suddenly opened my eyes and changed my view of the endtime:

> *"Because you have kept My command to persevere, I also will keep you from the hour of trial which shall come upon the whole world, to test those who dwell on earth."* (Rev. 3:10; NKJV)

While holding the mid-tribulation view, I never gave any thought to the eschatological issues involved—those were the concerns of the theologians with seventeen letters after their names and the word *Doctor* preceding it. My only concern was my salvation and the salvation of my family. It didn't really matter what this theologian thought, or that one said, if it didn't feel right in my spirit. I have a whole library of books in my home that I stopped reading after the first few pages simply because the content did not sit right with my spirit when I began reading. It should be the same with you.

When dealing with eschatology, eschatological issues need to be raised. First is the issue of the distinction between Israel and the church. By placing the Church in the first half of the Tribulation, during the *time of Jacob's troubles,* that distinction becomes muddied. Israel will experience all of the Tribulation; the Church will experience none of it.

While most eschatologists believe that the placing of the Church in any portion of the Tribulation totally denies the imminence of Jesus Christ, I am inclined, with some hesitation, to disagree, at least in part, with their argument. The mid-tribulation view supports the second advent of Jesus Christ just as clearly as the pre-tribulation view. That particular argument is, therefore, a mute point and should not be raised as either an argument or a defense by anyone since the premise which fosters it is, in and of itself, wrong.

A more correct argument presents the fact that the Church cannot experience the Tribulation since it would interfere with the ministries of the 144,000 virgin male Jewish witnesses (Rev. 14:3-4), 12,000 from each of the twelve tribes of Israel (Rev. 7:3-8), who, while protected by the Holy Spirit, preach the saving grace of Jesus Christ to the world throughout the Tribulation. If the Church was still present on Earth, these witnesses would necessarily be part of it. That fact alone would pose a dilemma during the Rapture since they are obviously left behind, thus severing both the Church and Christ's promise to protect the believer from the Tribulation. Since the entire saved body of Christ will be raptured, the Church cannot be present when the 144,000 Jews are sanctified to preach the Gospel. Thus, the rapture must occur at the onset of the Tribulation.

Another argument advanced by those who support the mid-tribulation position is that Revelation 11:3-14 depicts the rapture (vs. 12) through the symbolism of two Tribulation witnesses. The analogy is that they, being Moses and Elijah, who appeared with Jesus in the Transfiguration, represent the living and dead believers who are taken up to Heaven in a cloud. This analogy, however, does not stand up under the scrutiny of Bible exegesis, since the entire argument is fraught with error.

First, the Revelation is not written chronologically. Because an event is recorded in the middle of the text is not indicative that it will occur in the middle of the Tribulation. Clearly Antichrist is revealed at the onset of the Tribulation, since he makes a seven year covenant with the Jews. Yet he is first described in Revelation 13. Also, the 144,000 Jewish priests receive their anointing in Revelation 7, yet their ministry spans the entire period. Revelation 17 depicts the apostate church. Since it exists already in the form of the social church, it requires only the harvest to separate the wheat from the tares. Revelation 18 represents the world economy—which also exists today. Both will be present during the first moment of the Tribulation, yet neither are not mentioned until 75% of the text is expended.

Second, the two endtime witnesses are not Moses and Elijah. Although Elijah has been identified in Malachi 4:5 as one of them, Moses clearly is not the other. The very argument presented by the advocates of the mid-tribulation view is precisely the reason why Moses cannot be considered as the second witness—he is already dead. Since we can only suffer physical death once, and since the two witnesses are slain by Antichrist and lay in the streets of Jerusalem for three days before rising from the dead, Moses must be excluded from consideration since he died in Moab (Dt. 34:5). Therefore, since Moses is not the second endtime witness, the entire analogy presented by the mid-tribulationist is equally incorrect.

Finally, Revelation 11 deals squarely with the ministry of two literal Old Testament characters who had previously not experienced death, and who cannot be analogously expanded into a multitude, representative of both the living and the dead. The only symbolism depicted is representative of Jesus Christ, who died and was resurrected on the third day, and who ascended into Heaven on a cloud.

Clearly, there is only one view which meets every scriptural test, and that is the pre-Tribulation rapture. The essential argument of a pre-Tribulation rapture requires only one thing not required by a post-tribulation scenario: a literal interpretation of the Bible. It must be noted that the early church viewed Scripture literally; and expected literal fulfillment of prophecy. Whenever an allegorical interpretation is allowed, man then possesses interpretative options, which is the primary reason we now have division among the body of Christ. This division is more commonly called denominationalism. If all men interpreted the Bible in exactly the same manner, literally, there would be only one denomination, and it would be called Christianity. Even those who interpret literally sometimes use allegorical clarifications to footnote far too many verses, further dividing the body of Christ since denominationalism is, more times than not, based on those scriptural clarifications. Just as God confused the common language of man at Babel (Gen. 11:1-9), Satan has been successful in confusing the exegesis of man with the wedge of denominationalism.

The amillennialist is usually quick to admit that his differences with the premillennialist lie solely in the methodology applied in the interpretation of Scripture. And most will concur that if the Bible was interpreted literally, the premillennial view would be the correct view, and a pre-Tribulation rapture would likewise be mandated.

However, the amillennialist insists, as previously noted, that the literal interpretation of Scripture is a recent phenomenon, dating back only a hundred years or so. Again, it is important to stress this is not true. Amillennialism is the most contemporary theory, dating to the Dark Ages when a decision was made by the Catholic Church to suppress the Bible, which was viewed by the church hierarchy as too much of a mystery for common man to fathom. Because the finite minds of church leaders could not comprehend the mysteries contained within its pages, the scriptures were allegorized.

This problem is the direct result of an attempt by the medieval church to separate the man, Jesus, from the God, Christ. The Church set aside the supernatural Jesus in order to exalt His ethical teachings, concealing not only His humanity, but the humanity of both Mary and Joseph, thereby creating a sub-Trinity within the Trinity. Every plank of Catholic orthodoxy was carefully hammered into place by church fathers who jealously guarded the blueprint of faith—the Bible—through which they alone possessed the ability to control the scope, shape and nature of Christian exegesis. At that time Christianity was the mandated religion of Europe, and the Church used the Bible as a weapon against kings and other heads of state. Allegorism was essential to maintain spiritual control.

The Reformation was an indirect result of this attitude. Theologians like Martin Luther, John Wycliffe and William Tyndale, who were exposed to the Scriptures in Catholicism, recognized the literal nature of the Word of God, particularly with respect to salvation through faith. It was at that time that man began to return to the exegesis of the early church.

To confirm the timing of the rapture, it is necessary only to substantiate that the translation of the church and the second advent of Jesus Christ are two separate events. The translation happens with the removal of all believers from Earth to meet Jesus in the clouds. The second advent occurs when Jesus physically returns to Earth to deal with Antichrist during the Battle of Armageddon. The rapture is representative of Christ returning *for* His Bride, the church; the second advent is represented by Christ returning *with* His Bride, now in the form of an army, to deal with Antichrist and his cohorts, and to establish the Millennial Kingdom (as opposed to the Theocratic Age, which takes place at the end of the thousand years).

The translation deals specifically with the Church—and only the Church. The second advent deals specifically with Israel and the balance of mankind. At the rapture, the church is judged. At the second advent, Israel and the balance of mankind it judged. During the translation, the believer is judged according to his or her deeds, with rewards in mind. At the second advent, the Sheeps and Goats Judgement occurs. Israel and the balance of mankind are judged to determine if they are to be counted among the saved or the lost: with the sheep entering the Millennial Kingdom, and the goats being condemned to Hell.

Who Is Antichrist?

The word of God informs us that two men will appear before Israel in the endtime (Zech. 4:11-14; Rev. 11:3-12) as witnesses of His imminent coming. Scripture clearly identifies the first of these witnesses as Elijah the Tishbite (Mal. 4:5), who was translated to Heaven without experiencing death (2 Ki. 2:11). While many students of Scripture tenaciously cling to the belief that the other witness will be Moses because he, like Elijah, appeared with Jesus in the Transfiguration (Mt. 17:1-13; Mk. 9:2-13; Lk. 9:28-36), it is not likely since Moses died (Dt. 34:5-6) and was buried in Moab, near Mt. Nebo. Since man can suffer death only once, we can be certain the second witness is not Moses.

Likewise, Satan, the world's greatest counterfeiter, will send his own witnesses to the Jews, and the Jews will receive them (Jn. 5:43). The second of the two men described (Rev. 13:11-17) is the religious figure, the third facet of the *unholy trinity* which includes Satan as the father, Antichrist as the son, and the False Prophet, who will mirror the activities of the Holy Spirit.

The first of these two men is revealed in Revelation 13:1-10. He will be the political leader whom the post-rapture world of the Jews will herald as their messiah. It is this man whom God calls Antichrist. Many Christians, particularly those who have read Alexander Hislop's *The Two Babylons or The Papal Worship* (Loizeaux Brothers), have become convinced Antichrist will be the last pope of the Roman Catholic Church. (Unless the last Catholic pope is an Islamic Arab, it is not likely he could be Antichrist.)

Skeptics have suggested that Antichrist, in order to convince the Jewish community he is the Messiah, must either be a Jew or possess the ability to convincingly represent himself as a brethren of the Jews with a direct antecedral line to David. Although their argument may appear both logical and reasonable on the surface, the reality is that the Jews will readily accept an imposter as their Messiah simply because the False Prophet, who identifies himself as Elijah, will successfully present Antichrist to the Jews as their Messiah. The prophet's declaration will be accompanied by so many signs and wonders that few will doubt his claim. This false prophet, according to Scripture, will be a Jew (Isa. 9:14-15; Hos. 9:7-8, 13; Rev. 13:11-17). Conversely, we know Antichrist will not be a Jew simply because Scripture clearly reveal he is not.

Scripture tells us that Antichrist will be a Syrian, or more precisely, an Assyrian (Isa. 30:31, 31:8; Dan. 8:9-25, 11:21-25), and while he will assume the leadership of the European Economic Community (EEC), he will be diverse from it (Dan. 7:24). The seat of his government will not be Rome. It will be Jerusalem, which also sits on seven hills (Rev. 17:8-9, 18). We know, for at least one other reason, Antichrist could not possibly be a pope of the Catholic Church. After a very brief relationship with the apostate ecclesia, Antichrist will overthrow the church (Rev. 17:16-18) and destroy it. If Antichrist was the Pope, he would not destroy the symbol of his power.

If Antichrist is not the Pope, nor one of the EEC leaders, who is he? Throughout much of modern history, students of prophecy have attempted to apply a myriad of mathematical equations to the number six hundred threescore and six in order to learn the identity of the man of peace who will bring catastrophic havoc to the world. By assigning a variety of mathematical values to 666, countless numbers of people have been erroneously identified as Antichrist. A sampling of these names include such famous and infamous notables as: Adolph Hitler, Pope Gregory, Pope Pius XII, Pope John Paul (both pontiffs), Judas Iscariot, Antiochus IV Epiphanes, Henry Kissinger, Richard M. Nixon, John F. Kennedy, Franklin Delano Roosevelt, Jimmy Carter, Menachem Begin, Nelson Rockefeller, Moummar Ghadfay, Ayatollah Khomeini, Saddam Hussein—and even Ronald Reagan. Needless to say, none of these characters of history proved to be the son of perdition—although Hitler's treatment of the Jews precisely parallels the prophecies of Deuternomy 28:49-62.

At this moment only God knows the identity of Antichrist, although he provided us a symbol—666—by which he would, at the proper time, be revealed:

> *"Here is wisdom. Let him that has understanding calculate the number of the beast; for the number is that of a man; and his number is six hundred and sixty six."* (Rev. 13:18; NASB)

If we interpret this verse correctly, the number 666 will point only to one individual, the person of Antichrist. Our problem is in understanding the verse correctly so the clues God has supplied will work. How do we go about it?

God provided us with all of the keys necessary to unlock the mystery of Revelation 13:18. There are no missing keys, nor are there any revelations as yet unrevealed. God has given us a complete work. The first key is found in that portion of Revelation 13:18 just covered: "...and it is the number of a man, and *his number is...*"

The second key is found in Numbers 1:2: "Take a census of the whole Israelite community..." In the Hebrew text, the word *separ* is used. *Separ* means *census.* In the King James text, the terminology *"...number of their names..."* is used in verses 2, 18, 20, 22, 24, 26, 28, 30, 32, 34, 36, 38, 40 and 42. Verse 45 records the taking of a census, *by number:* "...so were all those who were numbered of the children of Israel..."

In the Greek text, we see the word *number* (or numbered as it is applied in Revelation 13:18) is *arithmos,* and means a specific number. The number of the beast, 666, is not a general term. It is the specific number of a specific person. Just as your social security number specifically identifies you and only you, so does 666 specifically identify only Antichrist. To solve the puzzle we need only determine from whom the census originates.

The third and most important key is found in the eighth chapter of Daniel. Daniel describes, with uncanny accuracy, the character and reign of the Seleucid king, Antiochus IV Epiphanes.

Daniel begins his narrative by outlining the rise and collapse of the empire of Alexander the Great (356-323 B.C.). Daniel saw, in a vision, a ram with two horns (Dan. 8:1-25). The ram with two horns represent the kingdoms of the Medes and the Persians (Dan. 8:20). From the west came a he-goat (Dan. 8:5) with a single, notable horn between his eyes. The he-goat smote the ram and broke both of its horns (Dan. 8:7), becoming extremely powerful. The he-goat was the Greek Empire, and the solitary horn represents Alexander the Great, the world's first true miliary genius. Alexander defeated Darius and conquered the Medes and Persians in 331 B.C.

The great horn of the he-goat grew until it was broken (with the death of Alexander on June 13, 323 B.C.), and became four notable horns. Out of them came forth a small horn, which grew exceedingly great, and prophetically, would overshadow the other three horns although its kingdom on earth would be brief.

The four rulers which grew from the great horn of the he-goat and divided the kingdom of Alexander were Cassander, who was given Macedonia and Greece; Lysimachus, who received the right to rule Asia Minor; Ptolemy, to whom was given Egypt; and Antigonus, who was bequeathed the balance of the Empire, which included Mesopotamia, Syria and the land of Israel.

Antigonus, who was fearfully called *Cyclops* (because he had only one eye), died fighting Ptolemy during the battle of Ipsus (310 B.C.). He was succeeded by one of his generals, Seleucus I, from whom the dynasty gained both its name and fame. Seleucus gained the throne by lining up support from the other military leaders through both threats and bribery to defeat the ascension of Demetrius, the son of Antigonus, by successfully arguing that since Demetrius had lost Syria to Ptolemy in 312 B.C., he was not worthy of the throne.

Seleucus was succeeded by Antiochus I Soter *(the Savior),* who had the former king murdered. Antiochus was the first military ruler to use elephants—that for which Hannibal is notably remembered—and defeated the Galatians by terrifying them with stampeding herds of the tusked mammals. He was succeeded by his son, Antiochus II Theos *(the god).* His son, Seleucus II, provoked the third Syrian War between the Seleucids and Egypt. Peace had settled over the Mideast during the reign of Antiochus II, who married the daughter of Ptolemy II. From Seleucus II until the reign of Antiochus III the Great in 223 B.C., the empire of the Seleucids eroded, and most of the lands captured by Antigonus and Seleucus I had been taken from them by their enemies.

Antiochus III attempted to regain the lost lands and restore the Seleucid Empire to its former glory. He was able, however, to hold only Syria. Disregarding his advisors, Antiochus launched a desperate attack against Rome and was defeated at Magnesia (190 B.C.). Antiochus died in despair and was succeeded by his eldest son, Seleucus IV Philopater *(loving his father)* who, between 187-175 B.C., gradually regained much of what his father had lost. He was succeeded by his brother, Antiochus IV Epiphanes *(god manifest),* who had his brother killed in order to ascend to the throne.

> *"And in the latter time of their kingdom, when the transgressors are come to the full, a king of fierce countenance, and understanding dark sentences, shall stand up. And his power shall be mighty, but not by his own power; and he shall destroy wonderfully, and shall prosper and continue, and shall destroy the mighty and the holy people. And through his policy also he shall cause deceit to prosper in his hand; and he shall magnify himself in his heart; and by peace shall destroy many; he shall stand up against the Prince of princes, but he shall be broken without hand."*
> (Dan. 8:23-25; KJV)

The prophetic view of Antiochus IV Epiphanes is a dual prophecy. Through Antiochus we are given a glimpse of another ruler, who was to appear in the endtime—Antichrist. Antiochus IV is a *type* of Antichrist; and Antichrist is the *anti-type* of Antiochus IV Epiphanes. It is interesting to note that his great-great-grandfather's title signifies a *Savior.* His great-grandfather blatantly called himself a god; and Antiochus IV sacrilegiously refers to himself as *god manifest,* or God walking among men—assuming for himself the role of Jesus Christ. Antiochus IV was not Antichrist. He was the *archetype* of Antichrist.

As the narrative of Daniel 8:23-25 begins, the *king* spoken of is clearly Antiochus IV Epiphanes. When the narrative concludes, Antichrist is in full view. Antichrist will usurp the authority of the world's power barons. He will accomplish this task not with his own strength, but through the power of Satan. He will magnify himself and will cause the world to worship him as God. In the end his ego will cause him to challenge God (the same as Lucifer, his master). He will stand up against the Prince of princes, egotistically believing he can defeat the Lord in battle. (As strange as that contemplation is to the believer, it must be remembered that Antichrist, as a follower of Islam, does not believe Jesus Christ was *the* Son of God, and therefore will not literally return to do battle. And Satan, whose only hope of world domination depends on him, certainly isn't going to tell him!)

After ascending the Seleucid throne in 175 B.C., Antiochus IV negotiated a non-aggression pact with Rome, freeing his hands to attack and defeat Egypt.

This was accomplished in 171 B.C. when he defeated Ptolemy VI Philomater, who proved to be a coward on the battlefield (1 Mac. 1:19).

Because the Jews befriended him of their own free will when he came against Egypt, and volunteered large amounts of provisions for his troops, Antiochus decided the Jews would make much better allies than vassals, and decided against subjugating them as he had originally intended. Instead, he allowed Palestine to function as a satellite nation, much like Egypt.

Because they were suspicious of his motives, Antiochus signed a seven year covenant with them (Ant. of the Jews 12:3:4), in which he promised Syrian assistance in the refurbishment of the Temple, which was in extreme disrepair, as well as relief from all taxes for a period of three and one half years. He further agreed to a dispensation of one third of all taxes for the remaining three and one half period.

In 168 B.C. the Egyptians forced Ptolemy VI, who had become Syria's puppet king, to abdicate in favor of his younger brother, Ptolemy VII. In return Ptolemy VII promised to free Egypt from Syrian bondage. When news of this reached Syria, Antiochus directed his troops to advance on Alexandria and reinstate Ptolemy VI. However, threatened intervention from Rome—which had signed a secret peace accord with Egypt—not only caused Antiochus to stop his Egyptian excursion short of Alexandria, but to forsake it entirely.

Fearful that Egypt, with Roman support, would launch an attack against Syria through Israel, Antiochus decided to make Israel a military buffer zone, and began moving troops into Palestine. It was now becoming obvious to the Jews that Antiochus IV was no man's friend. Deciding it was time to restore Israel to its former glory, Judas Maccabee organized the Jews, formed a small army of patriots and revolted against Syria. Under a pretext of peace, Antiochus entered Jerusalem, and without bloodshed, took the city. He declared martial law and systematically began to sack the city. Led by Onaias (Menalaus), the high priest, Antiochus' troops looted the Temple and ransacked the Holy of Holies.

On December 15, 168 B.C., Antiochus installed an idol of the god Jupiter Olympius on the altar in the Holy of Holies. Ten days later (1 Mac. 1:57-62) he sacrificed a pig on the altar and declared himself to be God. Three and one half years later the Jews drove him from Israel. Antiochus IV died of distemper in 163 B.C. after failing in an attempt to sack the treasure city of Elymais (probably biblical Pergamos) which was, like Ephesus, a temple city for the goddess Diana. On his deathbed Antiochus called his advisors together, and in a strange deathbed confession he acknowledged his belief that he was dying only because of what he had done to the Jews, and because he had plundered their Temple and contempted their God (Ant. 12:9:1).

Antichrist will replicate that which Antiochus did against the Jews. Antiochus initiated a seven year covenant with the Jews. So will Antichrist (Dan. 9:27). Three and one half years into the agreement Antiochus broke his word with the Jews. So will Antichrist (Dan. 9:27). Antiochus defiled the altar of God by offering an unclean animal, a pig, as a sacrifice, after which he declared himself to be God. Antichrist will declare himself to be God (Dan. 9:27; Rev. 13:4-8).

Antiochus ruled the affairs of the Jews for seven years, from 171 to 164 B.C. Antichrist will rule the affairs of all mankind for seven years (Dan. 9:27). Antiochus was driven from Israel by the Maccabees. Antichrist will be driven from the Valley of Megiddo by Christ and His army of saints (Zech. 12:11).

At the conclusion of the Battle of Armageddon, Antichrist will be judged by Jesus Christ at the East Gate of Jerusalem—before the eyes of the world which will be gathered there for judgment (Lev. 1:5, 16:7; Ezek. 46:1-3). Before he is cast into the Lake of Fire with the False Prophet (Rev. 19:20), Antichrist will bow down and confess that Jesus Christ is Lord (Isa. 45:23; Rom. 14:11).

When Antichrist makes his grand appearance on the center stage of Earth he will quickly become one of the most admired men in the world. Genealogists will trace his family tree, counting (as Scripture does) only the male offspring by way of a census. Antichrist will be the 666th firstborn male descendent of Ishmael, whose bloodline will pass through Antiochus IV Epiphanes to the son of perdition who, like his ancestor, will mock the Son of promise. Supposing this, why can't we, you might inquire, start with Ishmael and trace forward? Because of the polygamous lifestyle of the Arabs it would be virtually impossible within a given lifetime to know which son of which son should be traced. When the family tree of Antichrist is exposed the taproot will likely prove to be Ishmael, with direct, firstborn links through Antiochus IV Epiphanes to Esau, and finally, to the firstborn son of Abraham and Hagar. No other genealogy makes sense since Antichrist, the Syrian, will be Arabic by heritage, Islamic by choice, and an avowed enemy of the Jews for whom *the time of Jacob's Trouble* was created.

What, or whom, do the two horns of the second beast represent?

Bible scholars make much ado about the ten-horned beast (Dan. 7:24; Rev. 3:1, 17:7) because of the detail with which this beast is described. The Bible leaves little doubt that this beast represents ten endtime world leaders and/or countries which align themselves politically, militarily and economically with Antichrist. Little, however, is written about the second beast, who is less adequately described in Revelation 13:11-17, other than to acknowledge him as the False Prophet (Rev. 19:20, 20:10).

It is interesting that Antichrist does not make his grand appearance on the world stage until after the union between the ten nations takes place, strongly indicating he is not one of them. Rather, he is viewed as an outsider who woos seven of them into submission and forcibly subdues the remaining three.

> *"The ten horns are ten kings who will come from this kingdom. After them another king will arise, different from the earlier ones; he will subue three kings."* (Dan. 7:24; NIV)

Most students of Scripture have, for several years, believed the ten horns represent the original ten Common Market nations: Britain, Luxemburg, The Netherlands, Germany, Belgium, France, Italy, Ireland, Denmark and Greece. The only problem with this is found in the fact that not all of these countries were part of the old Roman Empire, which is the kingdom referenced in Daniel 7:24. The theory which suggested it was simply a theory of convenience based on the current events of the time. It is more likely these kings are collectively representative of the entire European Economic Community, although their total number currently exceeds ten nations. It will be forged as an economic union with strong, global clout, combining the industrial strength of Europe with the financial resources of the Arab world. The contemplation of such a union suggests, at least initially—again, based on current events—the adversary of this coalition might logically be America, Japan and quite possibly Germany. From this coalition rises a little horn—Antichrist—and the union, which begins and continues for three and one half years as a profitable economic enterprise, suddenly becomes political as the newcomer devastates three of the countries within the coalition, and assumes absolute control over the remaining seven—who, although fearful of him, still view him as an economic messiah (Dan. 7:25).

Sometime within this period, the second beast arises.

> *"Then I saw another beast, coming out of the earth. He had two horns like a lamb, but he spoke like a dragon."* (Rev. 13:11; NIV)

The second beast is, first and foremost, a Jew (Isa. 9:14-15; Hos. 9:7-8, 9:13). Prophetically, illustrations alluding to the land refer to Israel; those alluding to the sea refer to the other nations of world. The first beast, Antichrist, rises from the sea (Rev. 13:1). He is not a Jew, he is a Syrian, or more appropriately, an Assyrian (Isa. 31:5; Dan. 8:9-25, 11:15-45; Rev. 19:11-25), which means he could arise in any part of the Arab world, and not necessarily from within Syria as it is geographically defined today.

To understand exactly who the False Prophet will be, we need to look at what will initially appear to be unrelated events and unrelated verses of Scripture.

God will seal 144,000 virgin male Jews (Rev. 14:3-4) to preach the Gospel to the world during the Tribulation—12,000 from each of the twelve tribes. In Numbers 1:20-42, we see the names of the tribes which were counted into the inheritance of Israel: Reuben, Simeon, Gad, Judah, Issachar, Zebulon, Ephraim, Manasseh, Benjamin, Dan, Asher and Naphtali. In Revelation 7:4-8 a cursory examination will quickly reveal that Dan and Ephraim are missing from the twelve tribes. In their place we find Joseph and Levi. If you remember your Old Testament scriptures, you will recall Joseph's inheritance in the land was divided between his sons, Ephraim and Manasseh. Levi, who was to be the priest of all the tribes, was not granted an inheritance in the land. The inheritance of the Levites was God Himself (Dt. 18:1-2). As we further examine the Scriptures to find out why Dan and Ephraim are missing from this honor, you will more fully understand, and appreciate, why they represent the two horns of the second beast.

> *"You yourselves knew how we lived in Egypt and how we passed through the countries on the way here. You saw among them their detestable images and idols of wood and stone, of silver and gold. Make sure there is no man or woman, clan or tribe among you today whose heart turns away from the Lord our God*

to go and worship the gods of those nations; make sure there is no root among you that produces such bitter poison. When such a person hears and therefore thinks, 'I will be safe, even though I persist in going my own way.' This will bring disaster on the watered land as well as the dry. The Lord will never be willing to forgive him; His wrath and zeal will burn against that man. All the curses written in this book will fall upon him, and the Lord will blot his name from under heaven. The Lord will single him out from all the tribes of Israel for disaster, according to all the curses of the covenant written in this Book of the Law." (NIV)

The first to turn from the revealed will of God was an Ephraimite, Micah by name (Jud. 17:4-13). Micah's mother took 200 pieces of silver and had them melted down and fashioned into a household idol to be used for the worship of God. Micah compounded his mother's sin by hiring a wandering Levite as his household priest, thereby linking the Levitical order to idolatry. Danites, exploring the land around Mount Ephraim, took the idol and the priest (Jud. 18:17-21) back to Laish (which was later called Dan). While only one Ephraimite created the idol, the entire tribe of Dan enshrined and worshipped it. Other scriptures (most notably 1 Kings 11:26, 12:26-29 and Hosea 9:7-13) indicate a deliberate attempt on the part of Dan and Ephraim to lead Israel into idolatry.

The horns of the False Prophet are the horns of the *Judas goat,* which traditionally leads the sheep to the slaughter. The name of one horn is Dan; the other is Ephraim.

The False Prophet, as his title implies, will be a religious figure. He will be a 21st century clone of John the Baptist who pointed the Jews to Jesus. Only this *Judas Goat* will lead the Jews to the false messiah, Antichrist. This satanic prophet will possess amazing powers, and like Antichrist, will be extremely charismatic. His authority to perform miracles will replicate those performed by the Apostles. However, instead of the Holy Spirit, his power will come directly from Satan. He will be extremely successful in his deceit, and millions—both Gentile and Jew—will follow his pied piper tune into the waiting arms of Antichrist, where they will readily accept his mark and condemn their souls to Hell. The False Prophet will undoubtedly identify himself as Elijah. While that may or may not be his real name, it will be the name under which the miracles the world will witness will be performed, since Elijah is the name the Jews expect.

Who are the two tribulation witnesses?

We catch our first glimpse of the two tribulation witnesses in Zechariah 4:12-14 where we are told by the angel who interpreted Zechariah's dream that the two olive trees were representative of the two who are anointed to serve the Lord of all the earth. In a more historical sense, the two olive trees were Joshua and Zerubbabel, who themselves typified Christ, the Messiah—who is both King and high priest. The lampstand represents Israel as a light to the nations (Isa. 49:6). The complete fulfillment of Zechariah's dream will be realized in the Millennium when Jesus rules from Jerusalem.

For our study, however, Joshua and Zerubbabel are also prototypes of the two Tribulation witnesses who are described in Revelation 11:4 as

> *"...the two olive trees, and the two lampstands standing before the Lord of the earth..."* (NIV)

The ministry of the Tribulation witnesses will last three and one half years (Rev. 11:3). It will begin at the halfway point of the Tribulation and will end with their executions on the streets of Jerusalem. Three and one half days later they will be resurrected from the dead. With the whole world watching they will ascend bodily into Heaven (Rev. 11:12). An earthquake will occur at that moment, and 7,000 bystanders will perish as a tenth of Jerusalem collapses (Rev. 11:13). Within what appears to be anywhere from a few hours to a few days at the most, the Battle of Armageddon will take place in the Valley of Megiddo.

When the Tribulation witnesses first appear in Jerusalem, Antichrist will have already desecrated the Temple and declared himself God (Rev. 13:5). The Jews who had previously believed him to be the Messiah will flee into the wilderness to escape him (Rev. 12:6).

It is logical to assume that Antichrist will attempt to kill the two witnesses immediately, but will not be able to hurt them until their work on Earth is finished (Rev. 11:7). Although they come in the power of Elijah and Moses, they, of themselves, will have no power. Neither did Moses or Elijah. Their power will be the power of God—and it will be a mighty power! The power of the two witnesses will be so great Antichrist will fear them, just as Ahab feared Elijah and Herod feared John the Baptist. They will have the power to the stop the rain from falling as Elijah did, and possess the ability to change water into blood, or cause plagues to fall on the land as Moses did. God's wrath will be in their hands.

Many Bible scholars believe because the Tribulation witnesses are not identified by name in Revelation 11:2-12, they do not possess historic significance. In other words, they will not be Elijah, Moses, or any other historical Bible figure. This school of thought is founded in the belief that the two witnesses will be contemporaries of the age, born and raised in that time. They will come in the power of Elijah and Moses, but will be neither.

There is only one problem with that reasoning. When they asked Him if Elijah would, indeed, return, Jesus said he would (Mt. 17:11; Mk. 9:12). Since Jesus said Elijah would physically return, we must assume he will, or acknowledge that Jesus lied. After affirming the return of Elijah, Jesus said:

> *"...But I tell you, Elijah has already come, and they did not recognize him, but have done to him everything they wished. In the same way, the Son of Man is going to suffer at their hands." (Mt. 17:11-12; NIV)*

Christ, Himself understanding what His Apostles could not comprehend, knew two fulfillments of that prophecy were mandated, and conditionally referred to John the Baptist as Elijah. Parenthetically, He was telling them that to those who failed to recognize the Son of Man as the Messiah, John was not the fulfillment of Scripture, and a literal fulfillment would still be required at His second advent. And, because of the stubbornness of the Jews, that witness would necessarily have to be indisputable! For that purpose, God chose Elijah; and, Elijah will appear as one of the two endtime witnesses.

> *"See, I send you the prophet Elijah before that great and dreadful day of the Lord comes..."* (Mal. 4:5; NIV)

Who, then, will be the other? Could it possibly be Moses, who died in Moab before entering the Promised Land? Those who steadfastly believe the second witness will be Moses in spite of his death (Dt. 34:1-7), base their conviction on two things: (1) the two witnesses come in the power of Moses and Elijah, and (2) the appearance of Moses and Elijah together with Jesus in the Transfiguration (Mt. 17:1-8; Mk. 9:2-8; Lk. 9:28-36). However, since we know the two witnesses will be murdered at the end of their earthly ministry, Moses cannot be seriously considered as one of them, since man may suffer the penalty of physical death but once.

Skeptics of his death, based entirely on the verses which are commonly used to identify these witnesses, suggest the clues so overwhelmingly point to Moses, that perhaps he did not die in Moab. Since the only record of his death was penned by Joshua, perhaps, they suggest Joshua may have merely assumed Moses died because he failed to return to the Israelite encampment. They further point out that God did not state in His rebuke of Moses (Dt. 32:48-52) that he was to die on Mt. Nebo. God merely told Moses he would not be allowed to enter the Promised Land. However, it is important to remember that the Bible is not a contrived mystery with a plot-twister ending. The Word of God is a chronology of factual events, some past, some present and some future. It was not penned for our amusement, but for our salvation. Moses died and was buried by God on Mt. Nebo in Moab. *Moses is not the second witness!*

Elijah the Tishbite did not die (2 Ki. 2:1-11). He was translated to Heaven in a chariot of fire without suffering death. If the other witness is to be both heavenly and human, there can be only one other choice. The second witness must be Enoch, the seventh from Adam.

> *"By faith Enoch was taken from this life, so that he did not experience death; he could not be found, because God had taken him away. For before he was taken, he was commended as one who pleased God."* (Heb. 11:5; NIV; see also Gen. 5:24).

Two analogies become obvious when Elijah and Enoch are paired. First, they are representative of the olive trees, symbolized by Joshua and Zerubbabel. Elijah parallels Zerubbabel the priest; Enoch parallels the righteousness of Joshua, who was himself a *type* of Christ. Second, Elijah—the Jew—is representative of the nation Israel; and Enoch—the Gentile—is representative of all the nations, through whose seed Abraham, the father of many nations, arose. It would appear, as supernatural as it may appear to the skeptic, the two Tribulation witnesses will be Elijah and Enoch. Neither have suffered death, and both are subject to it (Ps. 89:48).

Do the seven hills of Revelation 17 describe Rome?

Scripture reveals the Harlot of Babylon as a woman adorned in purple and scarlet, decked with gold, precious stones and pearls and branded with the name *Babylon the Great, Mother of Harlots and Abomination of the Earth* across her forehead (Rev. 17:4-5). She is further described as sitting on a scarlet beast, full of the names of blasphemy, having seven heads and ten horns. The seven heads are further described in verse nine as being seven mountains upon which the Harlot sits.

Much of the confusion experienced by Christians while reading the Bible comes from the colorfully descriptive, although somewhat mysterious, verses used so abundantly in prophecy, since most are obviously symbolic in nature, and cannot be read logically or interpreted literally—nor were they intended to be. Even in a literal book such as the Bible, God—who must ultimately be recognized as the author of the entire text—decided, for whatever reason, to use symbolism in certain areas. The use of both symbolism and parables does not change the fact that the Bible is a literal book. Just as Nicodemus realized a man cannot physically return to the womb to be reborn (Jn. 3:1-5), those listening to the parable of the rich man understood the *eye of the needle* (Mt. 19:24) Christ spoke of in Judea was not a literal needle, but rather that it referred to the small gates located next to the main gates of cities such as Jerusalem, and were used to admit walking individuals into the cities without the necessity of opening the cumbersome main entrance gates. These small gates, commonly known in the first century as the eye of the needle, were precautionary security gates. They were deliberately designed in such a way so only one person at a time, usually slightly bent over, could enter. It would be almost impossible for anything but the very smallest camel, and only then without a rider, to enter the city through one. In the event the city came under seige, the eye of the needle could easily be defended by one or two men.

Symbolism in Scripture is used because symbols are constant. Science speaks in the language of mathematics because mathematics is a symbolic language that is both universal and constant. As such, symbolism is not open to interpretation. Each mathematical symbol means precisely the same thing whether formulated in the United States, China or in darkest Africa; or, for that matter, whether calculated in 1996 A.D. or B.C. When the mathematical equation is properly worked, the answer will always be the same. If we lack the knowledge to understand the mathematical principles behind the formula, we cannot hope to find the solution; or the solution we arrive at will be guesswork at best. Biblical symbolism is not much different than mathematical symbolism.

The Harlot (Rev. 17) and Babylon (Rev. 18) do not prefigure either a particular city or person. They symbolize universal apostasy. Together, they represent the religious (Rev. 17) and economic (Rev. 18) systems of the end-time world which will be absolutely corrupt at that time. The same is true of the political system which is depicted in Revelation 13. The three global systems will be totally without any fiber of moral ethics, and each will be completely under the dominion of Antichrist.

Many students of the Bible, particularly those with anti-Catholic sentiments, are quick to identify the seven hills of verse nine with the seven hills upon which the city/state of Rome was built. Those hills, situated along the channel of the Tiber River, were called Aventine, Capitolene, Caeline, Equilene, Palatine, Quirimal and Viminal. As the city/state grew, Rome spread over two additional hills: Janiculum and Pincian. Suddenly, the seven hills of Rome became nine.

Babylon and Jerusalem were also built on terraced terrains landscaped with seven hills. In ancient times, cities were always built on high ground because they were much easier to defend against attack.

Situated high in the Judean mountains, Jerusalem was segmented by two dry river beds. The easternmost was called the Valley of Kidron. It is on the east side of Jerusalem and separates the city from the Mount of Olives. On the southern tip of the Mount of Olives is the Garden of Gethsemane. When God gave over the city of Jerusalem to Nebuchadnezzar in 586 B.C., He ascended to Heaven from the Mount of Olives (Ezek. 11:23). Christ also ascended to Heaven from that Mount (Ac. 1:9-11). When He returns to judge the nations and institute the Millennial Kingdom, Christ will return to the Mount of Olives (Zech. 14:4).

The other dry river bed was known by an assortment of names, among which are the Valley of the son of Hinnom, Topeth, the Valley of Slaughter, and the Valley of Jehosaphat. The Hinnon Valley joins the Kidron Valley at the Virgin's Spring *(Ain Sitti Miryâm)*, which is also known as Job's Well.

While the Hinnom Valley appears to be geographically south of the city, it swings both east and west, connecting the Kidron Valley on the east side of the city (Jer. 19:2). It will be there, just below the East Gate, that the earth will split open, exposing the unquenchable fires of *Gehenna* (Isa. 30:33). Those found guilty in the Sheep and Goats Judgment (Joel 3:2-12; Mt. 25:31-46), as well as those found wearing the mark of the beast (Rev. 14:9-11) will, along with Antichrist and the False Prophet (Rev. 19:20), be cast into the Lake of Fire from this location.

The seven hills upon which Jerusalem was built included Mount Zion, which was captured by David from the Jebusites in 1004 B.C. (1 Ch. 11:5-8), and Mount Moriah, upon which Solomon built the Holy Temple in 967 B.C. It was to Mount Moriah that Abraham took Isaac, his only lawful son, to be sacrificed to the Lord (Gen. 22:2). On Mount Moriah God provided a substitute to be sacrificed in Isaac's stead (Gen. 22:12-14). In that same spot, 897 years later, an angel of the Lord stood between Heaven and Earth with a drawn sword, ready to destroy Jerusalem. When David repented of his sin (1 Ch. 21:1-30) God spared the city and instructed David to build an altar to the Lord on that spot. Mount Moriah was at the time the threshing floor of Ornan the Jebusite (1 Ch. 21:15). David purchased the threshing floor for 600 shekels of gold. When Israel was overrun by the Moslems, the Islamic temple, The Dome of the Rock was built upon the ruins of the Temple.

The third hill was Mount Calvary. In the Hebrew tongue, the place was known as Golgotha, the place of the skull (Mt. 27:33; Mk. 15:22; Jn. 19:17). It was here that Jesus was crucified and became our propitiation for sin—the substitute provided by a merciful Father in our stead.

Mount Acra, the fourth hill, is southwest of Calvary, and was the location of the Hasmonean palace. Antigonus II, the ruler of Judea from 40 to 37 B.C. lived there until Herod the Great was appointed King of Judea by the Roman senate. Herod the Great ruled from 37 to 4 B.C. While many believe Christ was born during the latter days of his reign, in all likelihood Jesus was born during the early years of the reign of Herod's son, Herod Archelaus, who governed Judea and Samaria from 4 B.C. to 6 A.D.

Between the southeastern hill area and the Temple mount was Mount Ophel. It was upon Mount Ophel that the east gate of the city was built (2 Ch. 27:3). It will be here, outside the East Gate, that Jesus will judge the nations during the 75 day period between the end of the Tribulation and the commencement of the Millennial Age (Dan. 12:11-12; Lev. 16:14; Isa. 30:33; Jer. 19:2; Jn. 5:22, 27).

The sixth hill of Jerusalem was called Mount Bezetha. If there is a scriptural significance for this hill, it is unknown. When Herod expanded his palace on Mount Acra, he ordered the ravine which separated Mount Acra from Mount Bezetha filled in and created one long plateau so the expansion of his palace could take place. The seventh hill, Mount Gareb, connects Mount Zion. Around 70 A.D. the name Gareb fell into disuse. Because of the close proximity of Zion to Gareb, and because Gareb was a more easily defended mound, both became collectively known as Mount Zion.

It should be obvious even to the novice Bible student that Rome will not be the seat of Antichrist's government, since he came primarily to deceive the Jews. And although Antichrist will be an Arab, the seat of his government will not be Babylon, since God has decreed that Babylon will not be rebuilt (Isa. 13:19-22). Jerusalem, which is the Holy City of Christianity, Judaism and Islam, will be the city from which Antichrist will exercise his power.

However, it is important to again note that the seven mountains of Revelation 17:9 do not refer to cities or geographic locations. Symbolically, the seven mountains refer to seven kingdoms.

> *"Here is the mind of wisdom. The seven heads are seven mountains on which the woman sits are seven kings; five have fallen, one is, the other has not yet come; and when he comes, he must remain a little while."* (Rev. 17:9-10; NASB)

The woman described is the *great whore* of verse two. She is scripturally depicted as being married. As such, she is seen as unfaithful in her covenant relationship with the bridegroom.

Before considering the scarlet beast with seven heads and ten horns (Dan. 7:7, 7:24; Rev. 13:1, 17:3), we need to take a closer look at the harlot to see exactly whom she represents. Contrary to belief in some quarters of Christianity, the harlot does not represent the papacy. Instead, she represents the total sum of Christian apostasy. She is unfaithful to her first love, Jesus Christ. Because she has been unfaithful to that love, she will be excluded from the covenant relationship, and will be left behind when Christ returns for His Church (Mt. 25:1-13). In addition to being representative of apostate Christianity, the woman also represents the total sum of all of the false religions of the world. From this system of apostasy will spring forth the one-world church.

The Harlot is not Antichrist. Rather, the Harlot, in this view, combines all of the apostate systems: political, economical and religious which Antichrist will manipulate to his own advantage. And although the universal church will be completely devoid of any semblance of Christianity, Antichrist will, nevertheless, despise the surreptitious worship practiced by its apostate ecclesia since it will serve as a reminder of the God he hates. As soon as the apostate church confers godhood on him, Antichrist will destroy it (Rev. 17:16).

Those who favor the papal theory feel John wrote from his own perspective while on the Isle of Patmos. These advocates believe the *five who have fallen* depict five of the most prominent kings of the Roman Empire. If so, who do they include, and who do they exclude? Would they include Cæsar Augustus, in whose reign Christ was born, or Cæsar Tiberious, in whose reign Christ was crucified? Would they include Caligula, in whose reign the severe persecution of the Jews began? Would Nero, who ordered the executions of Peter and Paul, be included? Would the fifth be Vespasian, in whose reign Jerusalem fell, or would it be Flavius Titus, at whose hands the destruction occurred? The one who is, quite naturally, would have to be Domitian, the emperor who exiled John to the Isle of Patmos.

The flaw with this theory is that there are just too many Roman emperors. Disregarding every emperor prior to the birth of Jesus (and those excluded would then include Julius Cæsar), we still have nine emperors between Cæsar Augustus and Domitian. For this theory to work, there could be no more than five. The Bible is not a book of multiple choices in which the reader gets to pick and choose. That's how Christianity got into the mess its currently in today! Everyone has their own opinion of what the Bible says and means; and unfortunately there are as many opinions floating around as there are pulpits expounding them!

Matthew Henry, like most Protestants of his day, was decidedly anti-papal. He believed the seven mountains were seven forms of Roman government. In his commentary, he does not elaborate on them except to say:

> *"Rome was governed by kings, consuls, tribunes, decemviri, dictators, emperors who were pagan, and emperors who were Christian. Five of them were extinct when this prophecy was written; one was then in being, that is, the pagan emperor; and the other, that is, the Christian emperor, was yet to come. This beast, the papacy, makes the eighth governor, and sets up idolatry again."* (Matthew Henry's Commentary on the Whole Bible; Vol. VI; Revell; pg. 1173)

Like so many anti-papists, Matthew Henry was so determined to make this scripture work against the Catholic Church, he overlooked the obvious. The five kingdoms represent those kingdoms which immediately preceded the Roman Empire, the one which was. Looking backwards at them, they are: Greece, Persia, Babylon, Assyria and Egypt. The final kingdom is that of Antichrist.

Are the seven churches of Revelation actual churches, or are they merely seven divisions within the church age?

The seven churches outlined in the second and third chapters of Revelation represent seven actual churches which existed during the first century, A.D. Since we know, in addition to the seven churches mentioned there, the Christian church was also established in Antioch (Ac. 11:26, 13:1), Thessalonica and Berea (Ac. 17:10-12), Corinth (Ac. 18:8), Rome (Rom. 1:7), Galatia (Gal. 1:2), Phillipi (Php 1:1), Colosse (Col. 1:2), Heirapolis (Col. 4:13), and Nymphas (Col. 4:15), why were only seven singled out as the recipients of this epistle (Rev. 1:4)? And why those particular seven out of all of the possibilities in Asia Minor?

Because, in addition to being seven actual churches, the particular characteristics of those seven perfectly described all of the phases the church was to go through during the period we now know as the Church Age. Additionally, each typified the collective body of believers to be found within each church period, and each contained elements of both sin and perfection.

The Revelation of Jesus Christ came to John while he was in exile on the Isle of Patmos in the Icarian Sea. Patmos, a volcanic atoll in the Sporades Islands, was used by the Romans as a penal colony during the first century. After an effort to poison him failed, and John survived an attempt on the part of Domitian to boil him in oil, the Roman Emperor, fearing him, exiled John to Patmos. In 96 A.D., after the death of Domitian, followers of Jesus petitioned John's release. Nerva, Domitian's successor, granted the request, and John was returned to Rome where he finished his life.

John's apocalyptic epistle first addressed the Church at Ephesus (Rev. 2:1). Ephesus was at that time the city at the crossroads of the world. The three most important highways in the Roman Empire intersected at Ephesus. However, John's dictation was due not to the economic significance of Ephesus, but rather, because Ephesus best represented a church which had lost its devotion to God. As a body, the Ephesians toiled fervently in the Lord's name (Rev. 2:2-3), and diligently tried to maintain correct doctrine. However, the *born again* Spirit no longer burned (Rev. 2:4), and the Church at Ephesus was without the Light.

Smyrna (Rev. 2:8) was the second church to be singled out. Smyrna, which exists today as Izmir, Turkey, was an important learning center of the time. Today it is the oldest city in Turkey, dating back to the third millennium B.C. It was a primary center for emperor worship. Under Domitian, Roman citizens passing through Smyrna were required to burn incense in the Temple of the Cæsars and proclaim their loyalty to Cæsar as their God. When they performed this ritual they received a certificate which affirmed their loyalty to Cæsar. If they refused they were killed. Needless to say, many Christians died at Smyrna each year. For this reason, Smyrna represents the church of martyrdom.

The name Smyrna means *myrrh.* Myrrh has to be crushed before its fragrance can be released. It was during the heyday of Ephesus, Smyrna and Pergamos that the Christians were crushed beneath the iron feet of Rome (Dan. 2:32-33). The blood of those early martyrs was as the sweet savor of myrrh to the Lord.

Pergamos (Rev. 2:12), like its sister cities of Ephesus and Smyrna, was also a cultural center. It boasted of a library which contained almost a quarter million volumes. It, like Ephesus and Smyrna, was also a center of pagan worship. Besides containing three temples for emperor worship, the Pergamons also worshipped *Asclepius,* the serpent God of healing. Whenever we see the symbol used by the American Medical Association, we fail to realize what, or who, the serpent entwined around the sword, or cross, represents. It is much easier for the Christian to associate it with the serpent of brass which God commanded Moses to fashion on the end of a pole (Nbrs. 21:8-9). Moses' serpent is representative of the saving and healing grace of Jesus Christ.

The name Pergamos means to *elevate to power through marriage.* It was during the reign of Constantine that the church was elevated to a position of world power through its marriage to the Roman state. It was also at this time that humanism, in the form of Nicolaitism, crept into the church. Constantine, emperor of Rome from 306 A.D. until his death on May 22, 337 A.D., proclaimed himself pontiff of the Church at the Council of Nicea in 325. This was the birth of the Roman Catholic Church. The first pope was Constantine, not Peter. When he assumed the leadership of the Church, and took for himself the title *Pontifex Maximus,* the church, through Constantine, divorced her first love, Jesus Christ, and extended her hand in marriage to the world.

The establishment of the papal system and the subjugation of the laity by church overlords is depicted by the church at Thyatira (Rev. 2:18). In His rebuke of the church at Thyatira Christ actually admonished the church of the seventh century for seducing believers with an adulterous and idolatrous doctrine. This church is portrayed by Jezebel (1 Ki. 21:1-23; 2 Ki. 9:3-36). We know this reference to Jezebel points to the church and not an individual because of the inverse parallel found in 2 John 1 which refers to the faithful church as the chosen lady, and the faithful believers as her children.

Sardis (Rev. 3:16), the church which represents the Church of the Reformation period, is first described as being dead:

> *"I know thy works, that thou hast a name that thou livest, and art dead..."* (KJV)

How does a church die? By abandoning its first estate, which is Christ Jesus, and by placing the dogmas of man over the tenets of God, the church is doomed. Outwardly, this church was teeming with life, but spiritually it was dead.

Sardis, with a quick and easy access to both the islands of the Aegean Sea and the primary Roman highway through the Hermus Valley, was an important commerce center. Because Sardis was so wealthy, spiritual values were easily eroded, and moral decay set in. The name Sardis means remnant. While both Thyatira and Sardis represent the papal church, the latter depicts those who came out of the Roman church in protest. In His condemnation of the Sardian church, Christ offered assurances to the true believer:

> *"He that overcometh, the same shall be clothed in white raiment and I will not blot his name out of the book of life, but I will confess his name before My Father, and before His angels..."* (Rev. 3:5; KJV)

Philadelphia (Rev. 3:7), modern Alasehir, Turkey, is known by all Christians as the church which best typifies that which all Christians are supposed to be: their brother's keeper. This thought is further amplified by Jesus, when He said:

> *"I know thy works...(thou)...hast kept My word, and hast not denied My name..."* (Rev. 3:8, paraphrased)

It is here that we see Christ's promise to remove the true believer from the earth before the onset of the Tribulation:

> *"Because thou hast kept the word of My patience, I also will keep thee from the hour of temptation...*(tribulation)*...which will come upon all the world, to try them that dwell upon the earth."* (Rev. 3:10; KJV)

The Church of Philadelphia best represents the true believer, and is the only church among the seven assured of the rapture.

Laodicea (Rev. 3:14-19) was founded by Antiochus II Theos, the grandfather of Antiochus IV Epiphanes, who made the seven year covenant with the Jews. Aside from the fact that Laodicea, like its sister cities, was wealthy, there was not much to distinguish Laodicea from any other Roman city in Asia Minor. It was not exceedingly corrupt, nor did it possess any major achievements of which to boast. It was the same with the Laodiceans themselves. By standing for little, they had little to defend.

A further note of interest (largely for the collector of Bible trivia) concerns the Laodicean water supply. Because water was scarce around Laodicea, it had to be piped into the city from nearby Hierapolis and Colosse through a series of aquaducts which connected the cities. Half of Laodicea's water came from hot springs of Hierapolis, and the balance came from the cold water streams of Colosse. As the hot and cold water met in the aquaduct, it, like the Laodicean's spiritual works, became lukewarm.

The problems mentioned concerning each of the seven churches of the first century are no different than the problems currently faced within the Body of Christ. Because the words are those of Christ, they must be viewed by all believers in this age as an admonition to them to return to their first estate: Jesus Christ.

There can be no doubt in the mind of any Christian who has seriously studied the Scriptures, or attended a Spirit-filled church: we have reached the end of the Church Age. We are in a period, the last period of the Church Age, when all seven of these churches co-exist. To which do you belong? Does your church deserve, based on Christ's admonition, commendation or condemnation? If you belong to the social church of Pergamos, the cultic church of Thyatira, the spiritually dead church of Sardis, or the lukewarm church of Laodicea, you must escape to Philadelphia before it is too late.

> *"Behold, I stand at the door, and knock; if any man hear My voice, and open the door, I will come in to him, and will sup with him and he with Me. To him that overcometh will I grant to sit with Me in my throne, even as I also overcame, and am set down with My Father in His throne."* (Rev. 3:20-21; KJV)

Does the Bible agree with the scientific view concerning the "appearance" of an endtime world involved in a nuclear war?

Sometime around 1984 (the specific date having long since vanished from my recollection), I had an opportunity to watch a very interesting program on public television hosted by astronomer Carl Sagan, who was at that time one of the nation's leading proponents of nuclear disarmament. Sagan, an avowed atheist (as are many members of the scientific community), was speaking to a very large audience on the subject of nuclear winter.

According to Sagan, who is one of the leading authorities on the subject of nuclear war aftermath, 25 percent of the world's population would be annihilated outright in a thermonuclear exchange between the free world and the (then) Soviet bloc nations. Another seven to eight percent, Sagan predicted, would die from radiation poisoning and burns within two to three weeks due to the lack of proper medical care.

Fully one third of the survivors, Sagan claimed, would perish from long-term radiation sickness, famine, pestilence and disease during the nuclear winter which would blanket the Earth like a death shroud for a period of anywhere from one to three years—depending on the severity of the thermonuclear exchange which spawned it.

Sagan, the creator of the extremely popular and equally humanistic PBS series *Cosmos,* is very well known in the Christian community for his atheistic views concerning God and creation. His description of the effects of nuclear war is, however, uncannily scriptural. While Sagan on this particular PBS special was merely citing statistics by some of the best scientific minds in the world, it was almost as if he was referencing endtime Bible prophecy as he spoke.

Sagan estimated that 25% of the population of the world would be annihilated outright. His calculation is in complete accord with Revelation 6:8, where the Apostle John wrote that, in his vision, he saw:

> *"...a pale horse, and his name that sat on him was Death, and Hades followed after him. And power was given unto them over the fourth part of the earth to kill with sword, and with hunger, and with pestilence and disease, and with the beasts of the earth..."*

Sagan further surmised that another seven or eight percent of the world's population would die from radiation sickness within two or three weeks, bringing the total dead to approximately one third of the population.

> *"The first angel sounded, and there followed hail and fire mixed with blood, and they were cast upon the earth, and a third part of the trees were burnt up, and all green grass was burnt up..."*
> (Rev. 8:7; KJV)

While this verse may appear to suggest that only vegetation is being destroyed, we must remember that prophetically, God has used both trees and grass as a symbol for man (Ps. 52:8; Isa. 40:6, 51:12, 56:3; Jer. 11:6; Dan. 4:1-22; 1 Pe. 1:24; Rev. 8:7). In his commentary on The Revelation (Loizeaux; 1976; Lecture IX; pg. 149) Dr. H.A. Ironside draws the analogy that "...grass is man in his weakness, man in his littleness; the tree is man in his dignity, in his independence—man lifting himself up against God." It is difficult not to agree with Ironside's analogy. This judgement is directed against humanity, not vegetation. The total dead, within days or weeks, will reach one-third of the world's population.

The logical aftermath of a nuclear exchange Sagan concluded, is nuclear winter. Nuclear winter occurs when particles of radiation and nuclear debris block the rays of the sun from reaching the surface of the planet, denying both warmth and sunlight, the two elements necessary for plantlife to grow. Without sunlight, vegetation, the first link in the biological chain of life, dies, and the ecological balance of the planet is abruptly interrupted.

> *"Immediately after the distress of those days, the sun will be darkened, and the moon will not give its light..."* (Mt. 24:29; NIV)

In the King James Version, the word *distress* is rendered *tribulation.* The Greek word is *thlipsis,* which more accurately means *distress* or *affliction* rather than *tribulation.* Those who have watched any docudramas on the effects of a nuclear winter should appreciate what Matthew 24:29 is saying.

Sagan theorized that a nuclear winter would affect every country on every continent in the world whether they were involved in the actual holocaust or not. The extent of this nuclear winter is outlined in Revelation 8:12:

> *"And the fourth angel sounded, and a third part of the sun was smitten, and a third part of the moon, and a third part of the stars, so that a third part of them was darkened, and the day shone not for a third part of it, and the night likewise..."* (KJV)

It would appear from this verse that fully one-third of the effective light of the sun, moon and stars would be lost to the world during a period of nuclear winter. The number of those who would perish during this period is recorded only as *many* (Rev. 8:11). Sagan suggested that conditions on Earth would be so bad under those conditions that people would actually envy the dead (Rev. 9:6).

As I listened to Sagan's argument for unilateral disarmament, I remember wondering if people like Sagan could actually make a difference in the theological scheme of things. With respect to disarmament, although many liberals believe they were at least partially responsible for the events which have been unfolding in the world since 1992, their contribution does not deserve more than a footnote in history—and that footnote will quite naturally be found largely in the secular textbooks of the secular schools of America, where the liberal alone seems to hold editorial license.

Since Sagan's program aired, the Soviet Union collapsed, completing the last of a series of events critical to biblical prophecy with respect to the Tribulation; and both the United States and the former Soviet Union have been dismantling their nuclear stockpiles. Although the Saganites of the world have been holding a victory celebration for the past four or more years, their disarmament efforts had nothing whatsoever to do with the events which took the Soviet Union to the brink of economic and social collapse. Credit for the demise of the Soviet Union must be attributed to the brinkmanship of President Ronald Reagan, since it was the Reagan Administration's vast increase in military spending, together with its Strategic Defense Initiative, more popularly known as *Star Wars,* the controversial satellite missile program, which contributed greatly to the bankruptcy of the Soviet Union, who, it seems, devoted far too much of its Gross National Product on 21st century nuclear weapons technology.

Today the former Soviet Union is no less an enemy or threat to the United States than it was prior to the breakup—there are just more independent states with which to deal. Unfortunately, the economic reform movement initiated in Russia by liberals like Boris Yeltsin, who reportedly suffered two heart attacks the summer before the 1996 Russian elections, have failed dismally. If the economic trend is not reversed, and real economic growth ensues, it is likely that ultra-conservative Communists may again grab the reigns of power in Russia, restoring the nuclear threat against not only America and Europe, but also against their former Iron Curtain satellites, most of whom are not likely to willingly surrender their newly found freedom back to Moscow in order to reunite the Soviet Union.

As I watched Sagan that evening I found myself wondering several times throughout the three hour program if disarmament could actually postpone the inevitable, promised holocaust of the Tribulation. There was at that moment no doubt in my mind that the world, if it seriously repented of its sins, could. Ninevah did, and was spared the wrath of God for almost150 years. But, I wondered, would disarmament deter the inevitable in today's high-tech, sin-filled, godless modern world? My conclusion, as I pored over the Bible later that evening, was that it would not, or for that matter, could not. The biblical clock, although similar to the scientists' doomsday clock, was set by the hand of God. Since it was, His program will logically take place according to His timing, not the timing of man. The events recorded in The Revelation will, unfortunately for far too much of mankind, take place on schedule.

Today most Americans view Russia as a second-rate nuclear power; believing the threat of the bear has dissipated. The truth is, where one threat formerly existed, there now exists a dozen. Several of the former Soviet states, which previously had no authority over the nuclear weapons stockpiled within their borders, are now sizeable nuclear powers in their own right—capable of launching a nuclear strike not only at their former overlord, but at any nation on the globe! Many of them, just as cash-strapped as their former masters in Moscow, may soon be secretly unloading parts of their nuclear stockpiles to the highest bidders in the Mideast—if it is not already happening.

Make no bones about it, the threat of a thermonuclear war is just as real today as it was a decade ago. It must happen, because the aftermath of nuclear war, or a divine holocaust which descriptively duplicates it, is clearly detailed in Scripture. The face of the adversary may or may not be same face it appeared to be ten years ago, but the resulting holocaust will be exactly the same.

As America reads its liberal daily newspapers, and watches liberal TV news coverage, it is being provided with a carefully laundered, politically correct view of the world. Yesterday's enemies are today's friends and tomorrow's trading partners. Glasnost has become global. Today the only major world power not a full partner in the world community of trading partners is China. Much of that is through choice. China is likely to remain at least partially isolated from Economic Babylon (Rev. 18) until its armies march into the Mideast on a quest for black gold, the wealth of Antichrist. This event which will almost certainly be one of the catalysts which brings about the Battle of Armageddon (Rev. 9:14-16; 16:12, 16).

Global politicians, bankers and businessmen see utopia within their grasp. Repeating former British prime minister Neville Chamberlain's 1936 policy of appeasement, combined with his cry of "peace in our time" as England made unbelievable territorial concessions to Adolph Hitler, today's global community will provide its former enemies with all the resources needed to rebuild their economies and strengthen themselves for future altercations with their new trading partners. Winston Churchill said it best, "Those who fail to learn from history are doomed to repeat it."

During the cold war of the 1960s, Secretary of Defense Robert S. McNamara convinced John F. Kennedy that Russia would disarm if the United States took the initiative and started to disarm first. Kennedy (and after his assassination, Lyndon B. Johnson) undertook a dialogue with the Kremlin to pursue such a contemplation. Kennedy agreed to limit the American nuclear stockpile to a specific number of first strike and retaliatory nuclear missiles. The first strike arsenal which contained some1,000 plus intercontinental ballistics missiles (ICBM) and 600 plus submarine-launched ballistics missiles was deliberately scaled back to an amount insufficient to achieve a first strike victory over the Soviets. This was done to prove our good faith intentions to the Soviets.

How did the former Soviet Union respond to America's good faith gesture? They tripled their production of offensive nuclear weapons! Those Americans who were dubbed hawks by the liberal press, and who advocated that the best defense was a strong offensive capability were proved, by the events of recent history, to be correct. None of the hawkish statesmen would have disagreed with the argument that there existed, at that time, enough nuclear weapons stockpiled between the United States and the former Soviet Union alone to reduce Earth to a charred cinder. Realistically, there was probably enough to do the job two or three times over.

After witnessing the devastation wrought by the single kiloton atomic bombs dropped on both Hiroshima and Nagasaki, America pledged, both to its own people and to the world, to never again be the aggressor nation in a nuclear war. Because of that stated position, the United States must have the capacity to launch a retaliatory deathblow on any country, anywhere in the world, after a massive first-strike has been launched against us. We are safe as a nation only as long as our adversaries know we have the capability to destroy them after we have been annihilated—providing, of course, that matters to the adversary.

Sagan, whose public position contradicted his personal belief of the checkmate value of a nuclear weapons stockpile was, however, correct in his belief that the former Soviet Union would not gamble on launching a first strike, since they would likely have been simultaneously annihilated. History supports his view.

In 1941 American, British and Soviet troops invaded Iran to expel the Axis troops which had overrun most of the Middle East, and cut off the supply of crude oil to Germany. On September 15, 1945, Shah Muhammed Riza Pahlavi formally petitioned the withdrawal of all Allied troops from Iran by March 2, 1946. The United States and England agreed. The former Soviet Union refused, stating it was necessary to remain in Iran to prevent American expansionism in the Mideast from interfering with Soviet interests in the area. The Soviets also occupied the provinces of Azerbaijan and Kurdistan and treated them as Soviet satellites. Iran complained to the newly formed United Nations, but like its predecessor, the League of Nations, the UN did nothing.

In April, 1946, Harry S. Truman, on the prompting of Churchill, reportedly placed a telephone call to Soviet dictator Josef Stalin and issued a brief, curt ultimatum: "Get out of Iran or face the consequences!" Truman threatened to drop an A-bomb on Moscow and Stalin backed down. By May 9, 1946, all of the Soviet troops had been withdrawn from Iranian soil.

President Dwight D. Eisenhower used the same ploy against China to end the Korean War. After several months of wasted political foreplay in the Pammunjom peace negotiations, Eisenhower made it clear to the Chinese delegation that he intended to end the war one way or another: either through the peace talks at Pammunjom or over the nuclear waste of Pyongyany, the North Korean capitol. Within two days the North Koreans were seriously committed to finding a political solution to the problem, and within a month of Eisenhower's threat a demilitarized zone was created and a permanent cease-fire agreement was signed. And although most of the American troops were brought home, and the Korean War, for all intensive purposes, was over, no formal peace treaty between North and South Korea was ever signed. A state of war, while in a state of hybernation, still theoretically exists between the two Korean governments.

According to H.R. Halderman in his 1978 book *The Ends of Power* (Times Books, (pgs. 85-94), when China entered the nuclear age in 1962, Nikita Khrushchev approached President John F. Kennedy and proposed a joint Soviet/American surgical strike on China's nuclear plants in order to prevent the sleeping giant from building a nuclear arsenal of its own. Kennedy ordered Defense Secretary Robert S. McNamara to put together a feasibility study to determine the consequences. It was determined that neither the United States nor the former Soviet Union had any nuclear weapons clean enough to knock out China's reactors without causing lethal doses of nuclear fallout to blanket Japan, Korea, Taiwan, Tibet and Siberia. The possible deaths of hundreds of thousands of innocent people did not deter the Soviet's determination to proceed. The Soviets preferred to deal with the political fallout than risk having a nuclear threat next door. It was not until Kennedy refused to participate that the Soviets abandoned the idea. The Soviet change of heart was not due to the fear of condemnation in the court of public opinion; rather, it was due to a fear that if their action resulted in a war with China, they would be weakened and the United States would become the dominant military power in the world.

In 1969 border skirmishes between Russia and China along the Ussuri River brought the issue back to the forefront. Again, the former Soviet Union petitioned the United States to participate in a joint military effort against China. Again, the United States declined.

This time, however, the Soviets did not. They were convinced they had the proverbial ace-in-the-hole. President Richard Nixon's hands were full with an unpopular war in Vietnam. Anti-war sentiment in American was so strong that Nixon couldn't gather enough support in Congress to drop conventional bombs on Hanoi. Vietnam was a wedge that divided America, and America's liberal media was the hammer which drove the wedge deeper. The Kremlin was convinced that Congress would not allow Nixon to initiate a nuclear strike against Russia in defense of America's number two enemy. Russia had enough of an edge to take the gamble.

In an attempt to avert world disaster, the State Department tried to establish a diplomatic dialogue with the Chinese, but their efforts failed. In December, 1969, U.S. Air Force intelligence chief, George Keegan, allowed the Soviets to intercept a phony message sent from Hawaii to Defense Secretary Melvin Laird in Washington, D.C. The message, transmitted uncoded, informed Laird that Strategic Air Command bombers carrying 1300 nuclear warheads targeted for specific Soviet cities were airborne and ready to strike in the event Russia launched a nuclear offensive against China. After a stalemate that lasted several days, U.S. aerial reconnaissance verified that the Russians were withdrawing from the disputed border area.

There is a particular logic which has, due to the worldwide proliferation of nuclear weaponry, been successfully applied to these types of holocaust-threatening confrontations in the past—it is a doomsday logic known as M.A.D. (Mutual Assured Destruction), which all of the participants clearly understand: in a nuclear war even the aggressor becomes a victim. In the past this knowledge kept all of the players in check because each, in it's own way, had displayed some sort of value on life—or, if not for the individual's physical life, at least towards it's own national way of life. Ronald Reagan changed not only the ground rules of the playing field, but the outcome of the Cold War as well, with the introduction of S.D.I. Under the high-tech umbrella of the strategic defense initiative a nuclear war could now be won, and won decisively. Almost overnight, even without perfecting S.D.I., the United States advanced militarily into the 21st century as the Soviet Union's fragile, and suddenly obsolete, war-based socialist economy shattered.

Unfortunately, new players have entered the game of geopolitics. These players, through prior acts of terrorism, have clearly demonstrated a total disregard for human life—including their own. The doomsday logic which has kept the major players in check since 1945 no longer applies. The war of the new players is neither the war of politics nor economics. Although their dispute appears, at least on the surface, to be territorial, as does the continuing conflict between the Bosnians, Serbs and Croats, it goes much deeper than simple territorial disputes. The disputed territory is the entire Mideast. Instead of simply a territorial dispute, the conflict will be a war of religious ideologies: a *jihad*. The key players are the Arabs and the Jews. It is an eons old conflict that deals with the historical inheritance of Ishmael and Esau, and the right of Israel, who the Arabs believe usurped their inheritance, to exist as a nation. Israel is at this point in time a nuclear power. It is, in fact, the only nuclear power in the Mideast. Currently Israel maintains the third most powerful army in the world, estimated as equal to the combined military strength of England and France. Israel's enemies have tried for years to purchase a nuclear arsenal from both the former Soviet Union and China with which to destroy the Jews. The collapse of the Soviet Union may have provided them just such an opportunity.

It will not be clear to mankind until those events which will bring us to the endtime center stage occur, that we will know precisely from whom the nuclear threat will come. But, understandably—it will come. And when that threat arises, the holocaust, and its subsequent nuclear winter, will occur.

The efforts of man cannot prevent the events which must necessarily occur to fulfill prophecy. The physical location of the trigger may pass from one enemy of God to another —but someone will ultimately pull it!

Does the Bible state that the United States will survive the Tribulation as a nation?

The United States, or anything which can be specifically construed as the United States, is not mentioned in the Bible. The only references which could even remotely relate to the United States are those which refer to the islands in the sea (Isa. 59:18; Jer. 25:22, 31:19; Ezek. 39:6; Dan. 11:18; Zep. 2:11), as a general, nonspecific reference to the Gentile nations.

It is difficult for the people of the most Christian nation in the world to accept the notion that the Word of God deals with them only superficially and, at times, somewhat indirectly. It should not surprise them, however, since God has made no secret of the fact that the Bible records both a set of instructions to, and a chronology of, His people—the Jews. The Christian is included in the promises originally granted the Jews; but even then, grace comes through adoption.

The primary theme of the Bible concerns God's redemptive relationship with the Jews first and the Church second; although most Christians view themselves as the primary focus of Christ's redemptive sacrifice. Granted, we have been the primary recipient of that grace for the past two thousand years; however, it should never be forgotten nor minimized by the Christian that the blessings we have received were first offered to the Jews.

The lands of which the Bible speaks are for the most part the lands of previous world empires that related directly to God's people. Many of those lands will share center stage with Israel in the final days. Although we are Israel's primary advocate in the world arena today, the United States, as a geographic or political entity does not exist in Scripture. This, also, should not come as a surprise, since the Bible is, again, God's chronology of His people—the Jews. During the endtime the Church, of which we are representative, is not present either, having been raptured to avoid *the time of Jacob's Trouble* which will be God's judgment on His people, the Jews.

Although the United States as a geographic area is ignored by Scripture, much of the land which encompasses the former Soviet Union is clearly present (Ezek. 38:1-39:12), since it will be directly involved in the final days of contemporary Israel—as will Egypt, Syria and the balance of the Arab and Islamic nations. So will many of the nations of Europe as well as China, which is mentioned by character (Rev. 9:14-16). With the single exception of China, which is merely an endtime intruder, the lands under scrutiny in apocalyptic literature are those lands which were part of the Roman Empire (Dan. 2:31-43), and will be active participants in the endtime affairs of Israel. It is very probable that the only references in endtime Scripture which can be construed as relating to the United States are those which refer either to God's judgment on Magog (Ezek. 39:6) or as the last confederate of Israel—who deserts the Jews when it becomes politically unpopular to align themselves with her. While not specifically stated in Ezekiel, we know from other scriptures that in the end God's people will stand alone against all of the nations of the world (Zech. 12:1-4).

Scripture indicates that Egypt, Syria and Israel will all survive the holocaust of the Tribulation as nations; although Egypt, for her deceitful treatment of the Jews, will remain desolate for a period of forty years (Ezek. 29:9-16). However, the only country in the world which is guaranteed national status in perpetuity is Israel (Jer. 30:11).

Will Russia attack Israel, and if so, when would such an attack most likely take place?

Since the collapse of the former Soviet Union many students of Scripture have retreated from previously published views that Russia is clearly depicted in Ezekiel 38:2 as the land of Magog. Scripturally, Magog was a son of Japheth and grandson of Noah. Magog's descendents, the Scythians, settled the region north of Black Sea. In his history of Israel *Antiquities of the Jews,* Josephus records the connection:

> *"Magog founded those that from him were called Magogites, but who are by the Greeks called Scythians..."* (Ant. 1:6:1)

The Scythians, a confederation of warring tribes who were also known as the *tochari,* spread throughout central Europe where their tribal society prospered. Periodically the Scythians launched raids into Israel, but no concerted effort was ever made by them to establish themselves in the area. Around the time when Demetrius I Sotor, the son of Seleucus IV, was assassinated in 150 B.C., the Scythians began exploring eastern Europe and Asia Minor. Under a chieftain named Moga, the Scythians attacked the Greeks in Bactria (135 B.C.). The Greeks successfully repelled the invasion. Scythians fought at least two battles with the Seleucids: one in 129 B.C., and the other five years later, in 124 B.C., shortly after the Seleucids were defeated by Artabanus I, while they were retreating from the field of battle. Archæological digs in India record a Scythian chieftain named Azes who fought the Yüeh-chihs around Chir Tope (the date of which is still disputed).

Future nations, which did not exist when the prophecies concerning them were uttered, are prophetically identified by antecedral tribal names, since the regions settled by those historic characters have remained extant throughout history. Magog unmistakably identifies the area north of the Black Sea which is geographically Russia.

The first contemporary scholar to identify Magog as Russia was Dr. C. I. Scofield, who did so as an annotated footnote in his 1909 Reference Bible. Most theologians who viewed Ezekiel's prophecies allegorically thought Scofield was wrong. Russia was an isolated, backward monarchy eight years before the Bolshevik Revolution, and was probably the least expansionist-minded nation in Europe. However, countries, and the fortunes of countries, are subject to change—sometimes abruptly! Today's allies may well be tomorrow's enemies; and yesterday's enemies may be tomorrow's friends. We need only look at recent world history to confirm this thought.

The dispute which periodically surfaces around the identity of Magog as Russia is based largely on an erroneous interpretation of three names which appear in Ezekiel's prophecy by those whose only scholarly attributes appear to be in the area of phonetics. *Rosh* has been phonetically interpreted as Russia; *Meshech* as Moscow, and *Tubal* as Tobolsk. Although convenient, the exegesis which spawned these opinions lacks credibility. *Rosh* is a Hebrew adjective which means head chieftain or chief prince, and never in any scriptural usage of the word, denotes a nation. Meshech and Tubal, like Magog, were sons of Japheth. Tubal is believed to have settled in the area south of the Black Sea which we know geographically as Armenia. Mechech settled the lands which now include modern Turkey. Collectively, Magog, Mechech and Tubal represent the Scythian hordes which terrorized much of central Europe and Asia Minor for hundreds of years.

As we examine the history of Israel we cannot help noting that when enemies come against Israel, they usually do so in consortiums of ten (Gen. 15:19-21; Jer. 46-51). Such will also be the case when Magog comes down against Israel. Russia will come down with nine allies (Ezek. 38:2-13). The nations which will join the Russian confederation to steal the riches of the Dead Sea, probably at the onset of the Tribulation (Ezek. 39:9), will be Turkey *(Meshech)*, Ethiopia *(Cush),* Libya *(Put),* Armenia *(Tubal),* Iraq, *(Togarmah),* Iran *(Persia),* the as yet undefined eastern Russian confederation states *(Gomer),* Yemen, Kuwait and South Yemen *(Sheba),* and Saudi Arabia *(Dedan).* These nations are identified as such solely by the geographic areas associated with the sons and grandsons of Noah. And while Saudi Arabia is currently considered a close ally of the United States, and played a key role in the defeat of Iraq during the Persian Gulf War in 1991, it is important to keep in mind that they, being Islamic, are neither friends nor allies of Israel. When it becomes more politically profitable and expedient for them to do so, the endtime Saudi government will throw its political and military support behind the efforts of its Arab neighbors against Israel.

What is even more startling than those who appear to be allies in this confederation are those who are conspicuously absent. Israel's most fervent enemies, Egypt, Jordan and Syria, are missing. While it may not be too thought provoking to those of us living during the second half of the 20th century, since we have been part of that history and have witnessed the signing of peace accords between Israel and both Egypt and Jordan, it is astonishing when viewed from the perspective that Ezekiel's prophecy dealing with this event was recorded some 2,500 years ago!

Efforts are currently underway to negotiate a lasting peace accord between Israel and Syria. Such a treaty would most likely materialize only after Israel agreed to surrender the Golan Heights, which it took from Syria during the Six Day War in June, 1967. Pressure is being consistently applied on Israel by both the State Department and the UN, who have both assured the Israeli government they will guarantee the safety of Israel's borders. At the same time a UN proposal would bring about the partitioning of Jerusalem. It was these highly volatile issues which brought about the collapse of Israel's Labor Party during the May 29, 1996 general election that ousted Shimon Peres and handed the reins of government over to newly elected Israeli Prime Minister Benjamin Netanyahu's Likud Party. Netanyahu, a conservative hard-liner, campaigned on a platform that was adamantly opposed to any form of land-for-peace proposal. Netanyahu was equally vocal in his insistence that he would not entertain any proposals which created a permanent Palestinian state, nor would he ever allow the partitioning of Jerusalem.

Daniel Pipes, editor of the *Middle East Quarterly,* closely followed the Netanyahu campaign and probably has as much insight of how Israel's new Prime Minister thinks as any Westerner. In a June 5, 1996 interview with Tom Carter, assistant foreign editor of *The Washington Times* concerning Netanyahu's attitude toward the possible surrender of Israeli territory for peace, Pipes said: "The essential dilemma of the Arab-Israeli conflict is that Israel must give up hard, concrete, useful possessions—land, water, oil—in return for assurances, for words on a piece of paper. The imbalance of this equation means that the Israelis must look very closely to strict fulfillment of agreements and, more than that, fulfillment of the spirit as well as the letter of those agreements. If they don't get that, they don't have anything.

"They've given up land, water, oil for nothing...Israeli Jews have by a considerable margin indicated in this election by something like 56% to 44%, that they don't think the Arab in general, and Palestinian in particular, record meets their criteria for going ahead to make more concessions. Should there be fulfillment in letter and spirit, then I think the Likud Party would be perfectly willing to do so...Likud has a long list of what it sees to be Palestinian abrogations, lack of fulfillment of agreements, from controlling terrorism to extraditing criminals to changing the charter and so on. These are all points which the Labor Party more or less dismissed...Likud is going to put great emphasis on..."

The reality is, political pressure from the United States as well as the UN will continue to mount. Whatever concessions are needed to bring about a Middle

East peace accord will be demanded, and ultimately extorted from Israel. Surprisingly, all of the players seem to understand this. The leaders of Egypt, Jordan and the Palestinians, in a prepared statement to the *Associated Press* made on the 29th anniversary of the start of the Six Day War, said they expected Netanyahu would soften his stance on peace once he assumed office. Egyptian President Hosni Mubarak took it one step farther when he added, "We are convinced, totally convinced, that the peace process is irreversible, that all that has been agreed upon (by former Labor Party Prime Ministers Yitzhak Rabin, who was assassinated, and Peres) will be implemented, and that work towards a comprehensive settlement will continue."

Peace will eventually descend on the Holy Land (Ezek. 38:14; 1 Th. 5:3). Israel's borders will be guaranteed by those who formerly vowed to destroy her. The agreement will be auspiciously supported by both the United States and the UN. Shortly after that event transpires, the Word of God suggests, Russia will come down against Israel (Ezek. 38:4; 38:11-15). The Russian invasion of Israel will immediately precede, or occur in conjunction with, the translation of the Church. Ezekiel clearly pinpoints this invasion at the onset of the Tribulation in Ezekiel 39:9:

> *"And they that dwell in the cities of Israel shall go forth, and shall set on fire and burn the weapons... (see also Ezek. 39:1-6) ...and shall burn them seven years..."*

The duration of the Tribulation is seven years. Israel is, in this view, clearly at peace with her neighbors since she has no need of the weaponry that is being destroyed. Therefore, it is logical to conclude that the peace treaty, which guarantees Israel's safety and security, takes place just prior to, or in precise conjunction with, the onset of the Tribulation. It can occur at no other time.

It is likely that Russia's forthcoming invasion of Israel will be triggered by a universal Arab/Israeli peace accord. When it becomes apparent to Russia that her former Arab friends are prepared to guarantee the safety of Israel, Russia will view the treaty as a threat to her interests in the Mideast. Because of their hatred of the Jews, the remaining Islamic countries and the eastern European confederation will align themselves with Russia for an assault on Israel and, if necessary, Syria, Egypt and Jordan. It is likely, however, that none of the current Arab nations, or Iran, honestly believe Egypt, Syria or Jordan would allow a single drop of Islamic blood to be shed over a Jew, causing them to make a serious military miscalculation.

As this unholy confederation comes down against Israel, God will intervene (Ezek. 39:2). Five-sixths of those who participate in this attack will be destroyed. While we tend to view Ezekiel 39:1-6 supernaturally, it is more likely what we are viewing is a thermonuclear strike, launched simultaneously on the multinational forces moving into Israel from the north.

> *"...Behold, I am against thee, O Gog, the chief prince of Meshech and Tubal. And I will turn thee back, and leave but the sixth part of thee, and will cause thee to come up from the north parts, and will bring thee upon the mountains of Israel. And I will smite thy*

bow out of thy left hand, and will cause thine arrows to fall out of thy right hand. Thou shalt fall upon the mountains of Israel, thou, and all thy hordes, and the people that are with thee; I will give thee unto the ravenous birds of every sort, and to the beasts of the field to be devoured. Thou shalt fall upon the open field; for I have spoken it, saith the Lord God. And I will send a fire on Magog and among those who dwell securely in the coastlands; and they shall know that I am the Lord." (KJV)

Verse six presents a view which suggests both a nuclear strike and a retaliatory strike have taken place, since we see fire not only on Magog, but the coastlands as well. The term coastlands is a more recent transliteration of islands of the sea, and represents the Gentile nations outside the sphere of the known world at that time. This sequence of events, including the nuclear destruction of many of the major population centers in the United States, is not only scripturally logical—it is almost mandated for an orderly fulfillment of the remaining endtime prophecies, since it is probably the only thing which would create enough chaos throughout the world to conceal the occurrence of the translation of the church.

In other words, the translation of the church, the event which opens the Tribulation, will not be seen as a sign of the end by those who are left behind. The sudden and complete disappearance of millions of people will be somehow scientifically attributed to the thermonuclear holocaust, and whatever explanation is offered by the world community will be accepted as truth by the survivors.

"And for this cause God shall send them a strong delusion, that they should believe the lie..." (2 Th. 2:11; KJV)

The United States, which became modern Sodom somewhere between 1965 and 1995 due to it's open acceptance of sin and debauchery, will, like ancient Sodom and Gomorrah, pass from the conscious memory of man as a world power. Those Americans who, in the eyes of God, represented Philadelphia (Rev. 3:7-10) will, at the moment of destruction, be removed from Earth in the twinkling of an eye. Those who represent Laodicea (Rev. 3:14-16) will remain on Earth to suffer the torment of tribulation.

At the conclusion of the Tribulation the balance of power will have shifted for the last time. Israel, God's nation—the land at the center of the world—will assume its biblical role as the leader of the world, the only country on Earth guaranteed national status forever.

Will the Tribulation Temple be built on the same spot where the "Dome of the Rock" now stands?

The *Dome of the Rock,* the Islamic mosque in Jerusalem, is second only to the mosque in Mecca, Saudi Arabia as a Moslem shrine. It is doubtful that even Antichrist would be able to prevent a full scale Holy War from breaking out between the Arabs and the Jews if the Dome of he Rock was torn down in order to erect the Tribulation Temple in its place.

For centuries archæologists and theologians alike were convinced that the

Dome of the Rock was squarely built on the original Temple site. Based on that theory, it was concluded that in order for the Tribulation Temple to be built, the Dome of the Rock would necessarily have to be torn down. Current reasoning suggests that may not be the case. The growing consensus appears to be that the Dome was not built on the actual Temple site. Measurements suggest it was built in the area which originally contained the porch, or courtyard, which was outside the Temple. Scripture even seems to support this conclusion:

> *"And there was given to me a measuring rod like a staff; and someone said, Rise and measure the temple of God, and the altar, and those who worship in it. And leave out the court which is outside the Temple, and do not measure it, for it is given to the nations; so they will tread under foot the holy city for forty-two months."* (Rev. 11:1-2; NASB)

Although the entire Holy City will be subdued by Antichrist for three and one half years, only the court area of the Temple (1 Ki. 6:3) will be given over to the nations during that period. It was in this 450 square foot area that Mary and Joseph purchased a pair of turtledoves (Lk. 2:24) which were offered as a sacrifice for the birth of Jesus according to Levitical law (Lev. 12:1-8). It was also from the porch area that Christ drove away the money changers and merchants (Mt. 21:12; Mk. 11:15; Lk. 19:45; Jn. 2:13-16). It was here that Gentiles, desiring to worship the God of Abraham, would come to pray.

Since we see the measuring of the Temple, a symbol of God's Divine claimstakes, only a hairsbreadth from the introduction of the two tribulation witnesses, we may rightfully conclude, at least for the time being, it is God's purpose that the Temple and, in particular, the holy area was to be divinely protected for His glory. During that period Jews and Arabs will worship side-by-side on Mt. Moriah.

Will "Literal Babylon" rise again?

Despite the efforts of Iraqi dictator Saddam Hussein to restore Babylon to its former glory, God emphatically states that physical Babylon will never rise again:

> *"Babylon, the jewel of kingdoms, the glory of the Babylonians' pride, will be overthrown by God like Sodom and Gomorrah. She will never be inhabited or lived in through all generations; no Arab will pitch his tent there, no shepherd will rest his flocks there. But desert creatures will lie there, jackals will fill her houses; there the owls will dwell, and there the wild goats will leap about. Hyenas will howl in her strongholds, jackals in her luxurious palaces. Her time is at hand, and her days will not be prolonged."* (Isa. 13:19-22; NIV)

Ancient Babylon, which straddled the Euphrates River, is estimated to have been somewhere between twenty to fifty miles south of modern Baghdad in Iraq. Babylon first appeared in Scripture as the kingdom of Nimrod, who attempted to build a tower to Heaven. It was there at Babel that the common language of the ancient world was confounded. In the Hebrew tongue, Babylon is *baw-bel* or *ba-bel,* and means to confuse. The Akkadian translation of the name is *bab-ili(m),* which literally means *the gate of God.* The name Babylon *(babulon),* as it is most commonly recognized today, is actually a Greek rendering of the Hebrew *bawbel.* While the word is generally used to denote the Chaldean kingdom of Nebuchadnezzar, figuratively it represents tyranny.

The Semitic Amorites (Gen. 10:16; 14:13) under Summabum established the Babylonian dynasty around 1830 B.C. Babylon flourished with grandiose temples and palaces during the reign of Hammurabi (1728-1686 B.C.). Babylon was recognized as the world's primary learning center of that day. Babylonian scholars created mathematical and astronomical cuneiforms, as well as the world's first dictionary.

Upon the death of Hammurabi, Babylon grew weak and became the prey of many Mesopotamian invaders. When Assyria became the dominant world power it captured Babylon and held it until October, 626 B.C. At that time Nabopolassar defeated Assyria, and Babylonia became the greatest empire the world has ever seen—before or since (Dan. 2:31-43). In 605 B.C. Nebuchadnezzar, the son of Nabopolassar, defeated the Egyptians at Carchemish, and extended his rule to the Nile. In 586 B.C. he defeated Judah and took the Jews captive. When he accomplished this task Nebuchadnezzar became the only ruler ever to possess among his spoils all of the land which God promised to Abraham (Gen. 15:18; 2 Ki. 24:7). It is this land that the Arabs through Ishmael, the firstborn of Abraham, claim. And, because of that abrogated birthright, the Arabs have periodically resorted to a holy war, a *jihad,* to regain their ancestral rights: the lands which are associated with that heritage.

In 539 B.C. during the co-regency of Belshazzar and Nabinodus, the Mede/Persian army overthrew Babylon in one night (Dan. 5:30-31). Fifty-six years before Babylon fell, and nine years before Nebuchadnezzar took Judah into captivity, Jeremiah prophesied the overthrow of Babylon by the Medes:

> *"Sharpen the arrows, take up the shields! The Lord has stirred up the kings of the Medes, because His purpose is to destroy Babylon..."* (Jer. 51:11; NIV)

Because of her sin God decreed that Babylon would never again be inhabited.

Alexander the Great was so impressed with the ruins of Babylon that he was determined to rebuild what Xerxes destroyed in 482 B.C. Shortly after the restoration began, Alexander died under very mysterious circumstances. His kingdom was divided into four parts and given to his generals.

Saddam Hussein, equally impressed with the aura of the ancient city, began rebuilding Babylon during the Iraqi war with Iran. Renovations continued in earnest throughout the entire eight year conflict, stopping temporarily only when Hussein was forced to focus all of his attention—and resources—in building the Republican Guard defenses which were supposed to prevent the United States from taking back Kuwait—or at least to extract such a price from the Americans that public opinion in the United States would force the Americans to sue for peace.

Many Iraqi insiders believe Hussein focused on the rebuilding of Babylon during that period to remind the Iraqi citizenry of the ancient feud which has existed between Iraq and Iran since Persia overran Babylon in 539 B.C. and at the same time, to re-establish Iraq in the eyes of the world as the cradle of civilization. Hussein's reasoning, however, went much deeper.

The Baath Party, formerly known as the Pan-Arab Socialist Renaissance Party, seized power in 1963. Through an unprecedented bloodbath of murder and political assassinations, Saddam Hussein became president of Iraq in July, 1979. The ultimate objective of the Baath Party was the reunification of the Arab nations under one flag—Iraqi, of course—and the destruction of the Jewish state.

Within one year of assuming power, Hussein launched an attack against Iran, Iraq's ancient enemy, and eight years of hostilities between the two countries ensued.

Geographically Iraq is virtually landlocked, having only twenty-six miles of coastline along the Persian Gulf. Basra, Iraq's inland port, was actually fifty miles from the Gulf on the *Shatt al Arab* waterway, the border between Iran and Iraq, with both countries claiming ownership. Also, with the fall of Shah Riza Pahlavi, Iran, under the theocratic anachary of Ayatollah Ruholla Khomeini, who also wanted to unite the Arab world under one flag—which, needless to say, would not be Hussein's—began funneling money and arms to the Kurds in northern Iraq in the hopes that Kurdish rebels who, are likewise not Arabs, would overthrow the Baath regime and oust Hussein.

Probably foremost in Hussein's mind when he launched his attack on Iran was the centuries old feud between Babylon and Persia. It is difficult for the western mind to comprehend how the Mideast mind thinks, or that the people in the Middle East could view a feud that happened almost 2,500 years earlier in exactly the same manner as one which occurred only yesterday. Yet they do. (It is exactly this same mindset which infects the Serbs, Croats and Muslims in Bosnia. And it is for precisely that reason that the United Nations, NATO, and the United States, together with the combined military strength of all the nations in Europe will never secure a lasting peace in that area of the world. The animosity the Serbs, Croats and Muslims feel for each other will simply be repressed while external forces police the area, with each faction seeking a military advantage it can exploit to quickly disseminate it's enemy once those external restraints are removed—even if those safeguards remain in place for fifty or one hundred years! No peacekeeping force or army of occupation can outlast the hatred each of these factions feel towards the other.)

Saddam Hussein is, without a doubt, a man with a vision. His vision is the restoration of Babylon to its former glory. The Butcher of Baghdad views himself as the reincarnation of the twelfth century Muslim general, Saladin—who by sheer chance was born in the village of Hussein's birth, Tikrit. Saladin expanded the Islamic empire of Mohammed through most of Asia Minor. Hussein also claims to be the descendent and legal heir of Nebuchadnezzar. As such, he views the reconstruction of Babylon as a sacred chore, one which will unite all of the Arabs under his pennant.

When Soviet-made T-72 tanks rumbled into Kuwait at 2 a.m. (Kuwaiti time) on August 2, 1990, Hussein's plans for the reconstruction of Babylon were suspended. When it became apparent that he had miscalculated America's commitment to protect Kuwait, Hussein temporarily shelved his plans for Babylon and focused his attention on the destruction of the Imperial Satan—the United States, whom he predicted would be destroyed in the mother of all battles. On January 15, 1991, Desert Storm was triggered by the sudden arrival of America's new Stealth Fighter/Bombers over Baghdad. The F-117, which successfully evaded Iraqi radar and attacked Baghdad, was only the first of several new high-tech weapons which would be successfully tested during that conflict. The land war, which Hussein promised to be the bloodiest battle in the history of mankind, was over in less than 48 hours, leaving the economy of Iraqi, and Hussein's financial resources, in shambles.

Just as Nimrod attempted to build a tower to Heaven, Saddam Hussein will doubtlessly continue his grandiose reconstruction of the fabled city, complete with its famous hanging gardens. However, since God has decreed that Babylon will not rise again, it will not. Hussein's plans will be stymied, and Babylon's construction will flounder until Christ returns to claim His Church.

Although literal Babylon will not rise again, a triune representative is already standing in the wings, waiting for its fifteen minutes of fame. Spiritual Babylon is the empire of Antichrist. It will be a composite of all the corrupt political, religious and economic systems of the world existing at that time. All endtime references to Babylon address one of these three systems.

What is endtime Babylon if not the literal rebuilding of the ancient city?

Ancient Babylon perfectly epitomized both the grandeur and the corruptness of the society of man. It was, as its name implied, truly the *gate to God.* Babylon, unlike most cities of the day which were catacombed with narrow alleys, featured wide streets and broad avenues. (Beyond the walled city of the elect, the villages of the common people which made up the balance of Babylon, were designed no differently than any other Semitic city, with narrow streets and even narrower passageways.)

Babylon's hanging gardens were fabled in the known world, and its towering ziggurats still stand as a reminder of Nimrod's attempt to reach Heaven. In its heyday, Babylon is believed to have been surrounded by a forest of date palms which provided both food and wood for building and fuel, and was frequently called *tin tir ki,* which translated literally means *life of the woods,* the name by which the area was known before the city rose near the ruins of Nimrod's tower.

Babylon was periodically used by God to chastise those who failed to heed His warnings. When Jonah was sent to prophesy against Ninevah, it was Babylon which God sent, some forty years later, to end the reign of the Assyrians. God set Nebuchadnezzar against Egypt in 605 B.C. The Baylonians defeated the Egyptians at Carchemish after a bloody hand-to-hand battle that resulted in the complete routing of the Egyptians. Nebuchadnezzar's army mercilessly pursued the stragglers as far as Hamath to make certain that not a single survivor escaped back to his own country. And it was Babylon that God chose to take His beloved Judah into captivity and to destroy Solomon's Temple. Because God's hand was on Babylon or, more specifically, on the man who took Judah captive and sacked Jerusalem, the offer of grace was extended to Nebuchadnezzar.

Nebuchadnezzar's name, quite possibly an Aramaic word disseminated from the Akkadian language, means *the god Nabu has protected my inheritance.* He was the eldest son of Nabopolassar, who founded the neo-Chaldean Babylonian dynasty. Nebuchadnezzar had at least two wives whose names were recorded in transcripts: Nitocries, whose daughter married Nabinidus, who succeeded Nebuchadnezzar when the latter became insane; and Amythis, the daughter of Astyages, a Mede king, whom Nebuchadnezzar married as part of a political alliance with that country.

Nebuchadnezzar, whose kingdom flourished with temples for the worship of the pagan deities of Marduk, Nabu, Shamash, Sin, Gula and Adad, was impressively touched by the hand of the God of Abraham. Nebuchadnezzar did not repent of his sins, choosing instead to include the name of Yahweh among the minor gods of Babylon for the purpose of worship by the Jews. Acknowledging Yahweh in a proclamation, Nebuchadnezzar testified:

> *"Nebuchadnezzar, the king, unto all people, nations, and languages that dwell in all the earth: Peace be multiplied unto you. I thought it good to show the signs and wonders that the High God hath wrought towards me. How great are His signs! And how mighty are His wonders! His kingdom is an everlasting kingdom, and His dominion is from generation to generation."*
> (Dan. 4:1-3; KJV)

After showing Nebuchadnezzar Babylon's place in history, God further revealed to the king through a vision what would befall him if he did not repent. In one year God revealed to Nebuchadnezzar in a dream that he would be driven not only from his palace, but also from among even his most menial subjects where he would spend seven years living like the cattle and oxen in his fields, eating grass and satisfying his thirst from the dew which fell at night.

At the end of twelve months Nebuchadnezzar held court in his palace, obstensibly to reaffirm his regency by recounting his accomplishments to those assembled. As he began to reiterate his deeds the Spirit of God fell upon him, reminding him of the warning. In the eyes of the court, Nebuchadnezzar, whose words were heard as incoherent rambling, was thought to be insane. Within the hour Nebuchadnezzar, who had by that time lost all ability to reason, was driven from the palace. He remained an outcast until his sanity was restored seven years later. His kingdom, however, was taken from him forever, and passed first into the hand of his son-in-law, Nabinidus and later, to Belshazzar, who was regent when Babylon was overthrown in one night by the Medes and Persians.

Because Babylon represents in the mind of God the totality of man's efforts to achieve political, economical and religious godhood, it is the most ideal scriptural parallel with which to depict the absolute corruptness of man. As such, Babylon serves as an ideal biblical *type* for all manner and form of corruption. In that light, the student of Scripture should understand that endtime references to Babylon do not deal with the physical restoration of Babylon or its resurgence as a world power since we are still in the era of the Roman Empire, depicted in Scripture as the last world empire before the Theocratic Age. Rather, all endtime references to Babylon are spiritual in nature and deal with the political, economic and religious systems which will in and of themselves rule the affairs of man in the closing days of the *times of the Gentiles.*

The three endtime world systems which will be destroyed during the Tribulation are depicted as Babylon in the Revelation. The first view, which will be the last to be destroyed, is Political Babylon. It is detailed in Revelation 13. It is the dynasty of Antichrist. Second, we see, in Revelation 17, Babylon, the Apostate Church. Because Antichrist will have little need for a religious system once that entity declares him to be God, it will be the first system to be destroyed. Finally, in Revelation 18 we have a perfect view of the destruction of Economic Babylon—the economic systems of the world. While viewed separately, two of these systems, Political and Economic Babylon, will shortly become entwined into a one-world government, which according to the logic of those supporting it, will lead mankind towards a global utopia. Instead of utopia, however, this global system will lead the world into the most terrible holocaust ever imagined by man.

This one-world government, as stated earlier, began to take shape at the close of World War I with the creation of the League of Nations. The League was first proposed by the British delegation at the Big Ten Summit in Paris on January 18, 1919. The purpose of the conference was to resolve the territorial and reparation questions surrounding the surrender of Germany. However, Great Britain, who saw it's world influence waning, created the concept of a world governing body through which the British Empire could continue to flourish. The League of Nations was theoretically proposed to serve as a neutral body which could act as the arbitrator of international territorial disputes, defusing through mediation, confrontations which might otherwise lead to armed conflict.

There would be ten charter members in the League—and not in the least surprising, they would be the same ten nations who were represented at the Summit. They would be the governing body; and they alone would determine the agenda of the League. Other nations, admitted by a vote of the majority upon referral of a current member state, would be allowed one vote on any of the matters being addressed by the League. However, the only matters discussed would be those approved by the governing body. Sitting at the head of the table, representing Great Britain, was Sir Eric Drummond, who would serve as the first Secretary General of the organization.

The United States, being somewhat of an isolationist nation from its birth, and still mourning the loss of thousands of her sons who died in places whose strange, foreign names could not, many times, even be pronounced by the widows and mothers and fathers of the dead, was interested neither in the League of Nations nor in becoming a police force for those European states who could not solve their own internal problems.

Although Woodrow Wilson signed the League of Nations charter on January 10, 1920, which was then adroitly concealed within the *Treaty of Versailles* by the charter members to prevent too much scrutiny by the other European states who were eager to end the state of war which would continue to exist with Germany until the Treaty officially ended that conflict, the United States Congress, which saw the League as an organization that was being granted legal authority to usurp America's constitutional rights, refused to ratify the *Treaty of Versailles* which brought the League of Nations into being.

From 1920 until the creation of the UN in 1945, the League of Nations was an absolute failure as an arbitrator of political disputes. It served primarily as an agent for the central banks of Europe, who actually financed it's creation, granting loans to nations. Without the military strength needed to enforce it's political decisions, the League of Nations was viewed by member and non-member states alike as merely a quasi-political world bank that even lacked the power to collect it's own unpaid debts. As a result, most of the League's economic decisions failed as well.

At the end of World War II the League of Nations, which was still recalled with bitterness by those who remembered its covert creation in 1920, simply changed it's name and was more palatably reintroduced to America as the United Nations. Tired of war, and counting the deaths caused by Hitler, Benito Mussolini and Japan's warlord Prime Minister Tojo in the sheer millions, the consequences of creating a global government were ignored, and the skeleton of the one-world government was again formalized. All that remained, like Ezekiel's Valley of Dried Bones, was the addition of flesh and muscle. Two American presidents would provide those elements, and Political Babylon would soon be ready for the arrival of Antichrist.

During the 1990-91 Persian Gulf crisis, U.S. President George Bush provided the flesh by addressing Saddam Hussein through the United Nations, thereby giving the UN a physical semblance of authority. Bush's global strategy, at least with respect to dealing with Iraq, was correct, as history will record. Using the UN for the benefit of the United States, Bush's diplomacy created one of the most unlikely coalitions in the history of mankind, one in which Arabs and Jews aligned themselves against Arabs. Unfortunately, liberal historians are already crediting the Persian Gulf War victory to the UN, which, because of Bush, now possesses a physical semblance.

Previously the UN was simply a building in New York where diplomats from around the world met to debate geopolitical developments. The voices belonged to the diplomats, and the decisions which were made, to their respective leaders. Today, due largely to the abrogation of his constitutional responsibilities, U. S. President Bill Clinton provided the United Nations not only with the podium from which to speak—but a loud voice and a big stick as well! The big stick Clinton provided is the military might of the most powerful nation in the world, granted to the UN by Presidential Decision Directive 25, a document Clinton then classified as Top Secret to prevent scrutiny by Congress.

U.S. Representative Robert K. Dornan [R-CA], Chairman of the House National Security subcommittee, which has oversight responsibilities in this area, requested the text of PDD25 when rumors began to circulate around Washington that the secret agreement abrogated American authority over its own military whenever United States troops were placed in cooperative ventures with the UN—and that the UN had the authority to call up American troops whenever emergency situations arose where the UN deemed those troops were necessary. Instead of receiving the actual text of PDD25, Dornan received only a fifteen page summary highlighting the details of the Clinton/UN Agreement. In February, 1996, Dornan, who was at that time an announced candidate for the 1996 Republican presidential nomination, was calling for Congressional hearings to determine the ramifications of PDD25. When Dornan's presidential aspirations fizzled, so did his zeal to investigate the ramifications of PDD25.

With tendons of steel attached to its scrawny skeletal frame, the UN now possesses the muscle it has lacked since 1920 to enforce its will. Within one month of assuming control of United States forces in Europe under the guise of NATO to defuse the civil war in the Balkans—with a tutorial American theoretically in tactical command—the UN, on January 16, 1996, announced it was contemplating the assessment of a global tax on travel to support its sagging coffers.

Instead of demanding to know by what authority the UN could tax American citizens, former Senate Majority Leader Robert Dole (R-KS), the 1996 Republican presidential nominee, responded the following day by saying if the UN levied a worldwide travel tax, the United States would have no alternative but to withhold funding from the organization—suggesting by his statement that the UN possessed legal authority to tax American citizens. From where does its authority to tax nations come? Apparently from its charter. Prior to 1990 the UN was merely a forum through which countries expressed their ideas and frustrations. Today the UN is a socialist global society seeking national status, and it is driving claim stakes in all of the capitols of the world. Tomorrow it will be the seat of government for Antichrist.

Because Antichrist is more closely associated with Political Babylon, he is depicted in Revelation 13, where the first major clue to his identity is revealed. However, this chapter deals as much with the global political system as it does with the man.

> *"...I saw a beast coming out of the sea. He had ten horns and seven heads, and ten crowns on his horns, and on each head a blasphemous name..."* (Rev. 13:1; NIV)

In view with Antichrist are ten nations—the same ten nations which prefigure the revived Roman Empire. Seven, scripturally, is the number of completeness, and ten symbolizes world power. Collectively they appear to represent complete world domination. It is a political alliance. We know from Daniel 7:24 that three of these rulers ultimately dispute the authority of Antichrist and try to break away. Their efforts will prove to be futile, and their attempt will be quickly subdued.

"The beast I saw resembled a leopard, but had feet like those of a bear, and a mouth like that of a lion. The dragon gave the beast his power and his throne and great authority."
(Rev. 13:2; NIV)

In view is a composite of three of the four world empires depicted by Daniel's image of Nebuchadnezzar. The leopard represents the Greek Empire (through which Antiochus IV Epiphanes arose), the bear represents the Mede/Persian dynasty, and the lion represents Babylon. The characteristics of all of these former empires will be present in the reign of Antichrist. Since the Roman Empire still exists, it did not need to be symbolized.

One of the most interesting verses in this prophecy appears next. It has probably been debated as much as the 666 which symbolizes the identity of Antichrist—and, like *the number of his name,* it will likewise remain something of a mystery until the event it describes occurs:

"One of the heads of the beast seemed to have had a fatal wound, but the fatal wound had been healed. The whole world was astonished and followed the beast." (Rev. 13:3; NIV)

Theologians and eschatologists alike have speculated as to the precise meaning of this prophecy; but the answers each have surmised are just that: speculation.

Some students of the Bible believe this verse suggests that Antichrist will be assassinated and, like Jesus Christ, will be resurrected from the dead. And because of that miracle the world will marvel, believing he is Christ, and will follow him. This cannot happen, however, because as devious as Satan is, the power of resurrection is not in him. That is a power God alone possesses. He could very likely fake his own death, and in that manner, deceive many; but he cannot be fatally wounded and return from the dead.

When Anwar Sadat, the former president of Egypt, was assassinated by Muslim fundamentalists in 1981 for signing, on March 26, 1979, the Egyptian/Israeli peace treaty, many biblical doomsayers expected him to rise from the dead on the third day according to this Scripture, and assume his rightful role as Antichrist. He didn't. He wasn't. He couldn't.

Others believe the wounded head represents the Roman Empire, since the seven heads are likely to be the same kings, or kingdoms, depicted in Revelation 17:3, one of which was the Roman Empire. However, the miraculous revival of the Roman Empire would not entice the world to follow Antichrist—an Arab.

The seven heads represent seven kings, or kingdoms. Five were past, one is current, and the other represents the kingdom of Antichrist. The Roman Empire, which is representative of the current kingdom, has been dying the everlasting death of decay for almost 2,000 years since it was never conquered by a foe. Its enemy was itself. In 486 A.D. the Roman Empire, a society which fed upon itself too often and too much, simply collapsed.

It will be the seventh head, the head that depicts Antichrist, which will receive the wound. It will appear to be a wound to the death, and will likely be reported as such by the world press. However, it will be merely a fortunate stroke of luck, perhaps even a planned stroke of luck, for Antichrist will use the opportunity to his advantage. It may be that an Israeli patriot, a political assassin, or perhaps even a mentally disturbed zealot intent on assassinating any type of celebrity, will make an attempt on his life. Since God apparently intends to use this event to tempt those who remain after the translation of the church, it is an event which must await its own fulfillment.

In any event, in addition to the sketchy view of Antichrist which is exposed here, we are also presented with a portrait of political unification, the formation of the endtime geopolitical confederacy which Antichrist will control through the auspices of the UN. This geopolitical system, together with the global economic system, will rule the world for seven years.

The Harlot of Revelation 17 is the apostate church, and will be a composite of those superficial Christians who were left behind when the rapture occurred, as well as everyone who belonged to all of the world's cults and pseudo-Christian religions—all of whom denied the singular deity of Jesus Christ. Among them will be many well-known church figures and religious leaders who, like the secular leaders of the day, will attempt to rationalize the disappearance of countless millions of missing loved ones worldwide. Because of the presence of these eclectics, most will believe whatever lie is spawned, since they, the leaders of their faiths, will still be present on Earth.

As we look at the Scriptures which describe the Harlot, we cannot help but notice the presence of the same political entities that appear in Revelation 13. Like those former societies of which the current one depicts, the economic, political and religious systems are inextricably entwined, and are absolutely controlled by the reigning monarch. Linked at conception to the political and economic systems, the Harlot, like an unwanted baby, is aborted at midterm. Since Antichrist hates God with an intense fervor, he will not be able to tolerate even a counterfeit version of religiosity for long—just long enough for the apostate church to proclaim him as God. When that is accomplished he will have no further need for the hypocrites, who stand like pious demigods in Sunday finery behind their pulpits, proclaiming their messages of peace on earth and good will to all who believe the gospel according to them.

The Harlot does not represent one particular religious sect or denomination. It is not the Roman Catholic Church, and the mention of martyrdom

> *"...I saw the woman drunk with the blood of the saints, and with the blood of the martyrs of Jesus..." (Rev. 17:6; KJV)*

does not refer to those who died for their faith during the Inquisition. I feel it is absolutely necessary to make a firm statement in this regard, since there are attributes of Babylon which in and of themselves suggest this view might be viable.

Babylon was, from the Flood to it's destruction at the hand of Xerxes, the foremost center of idolatry in the world, beginning with Nimrod, the son of Ham. Not only did Nimrod attempt to build a tower to Heaven, his wife, Semiramis (according to non-Biblical accounts) founded the secret religious society upon which Babylonian paganism was based. Semiramis claimed her son, Tammuz, was born of a miraculous conception, and as such was God in the flesh, thereby counterfeiting the promise of Genesis 3:15 in which the seed of the woman would stand between Satan and man and, through that seed, mankind would be saved. Both Tammuz and Semiramis were worshipped by the Babylonians as gods; and through them the practice of mother/son worship was initiated. According to Babylonian folklore, Tammuz was attacked and killed by wild animals. While being mourned by Semiramis, Tammuz was restored to life, creating the first pagan triune godhead. Satan, who clearly knows how the Bible ends, attempted through imitation, with the substitution of Semiramis and Tammuz for Mary and Jesus, to dilute the person and deity of Jesus Christ. Admittedly, Satan's ploy has been somewhat successful through the ages, since many who have heard of the miraculous birth, death and resurrection of Jesus Christ have opted not to believe the biblical account, believing instead that the Bible, like the Babylonian myth of Semiramis and Tammuz, is merely a Jewish fable from the same origin.

The symbolism of Babylon was selected to typify not only the endtime religious apostasy of the world, but the political and economic systems as well—not because literal Babylon will be briefly restored, since it clearly will not. Rather, Babylon best symbolizes mankind in its basest imagination, an abomination that is a stench in the nostrils of God. Also, in its heyday, Babylon was the economic, political and religious hub, the center of life, of the civilized world.

The Apostle John, in penning the Revelation of Jesus Christ, was not pointing a finger at one religious sect or endtime denomination. Instead, he was describing the egocentric politically correct religiosity of all mankind at that point of history. We see in the description of the Harlot the co-mingled trappings of both church and state:

> *"And the woman was arrayed in purple and scarlet color, and bedecked with gold and precious stones and pearls, having a golden cup in her hand, full of abominations and filthiness of her fornications..."* (Rev. 17:4; KJV)

While the garb of the Harlot may be similar to the trappings of the ritualistic church of today, it represents not the Church, but political authority. When Christ was mocked, His accusers draped Him in a scarlet robe, the symbol of kingship. Apostate Christianity is irrefutably linked with the political system which spawned both its doctrine and its abominations: abortion, homosexuality and godless worship. It will be for those sins that the Harlot is present—and not even Antichrist will be able to tolerate the stench!

The final system represented by Babylon is the global economy of the endtime world. This system, burdened with problems originating shortly after the translation of the church, will collapse towards the end of the Tribulation, devastating the economies of every nation on Earth (Rev. 18:3), from the richest to the poorest.

The promise of God assures the Christian of the removal of all true believers before *the time of Jacob's Trouble* (1 Cor. 15:52-53; 1 Th. 4:15-17; Rev. 3:10). This event, depicted by the Feast of Trumpets (*Rosh Hashana*; Lev. 23:24-25), will occur at the onset of the Tribulation.

"For this we say unto you by the word of the Lord, that we who are alive and remain unto the coming of the Lord shall not precede them who are asleep, For the Lord Himself shall descend from Heaven with a shout, with the voice of the archangel, and with the trump of God; and the dead in Christ shall rise first; Then we who are alive and remain shall be caught up together with them in the clouds, to meet the Lord in the air; and so shall we ever be with the Lord." (1 Th. 4:15-17; KJV)

Each of us came into this world naked. And in that manner we shall leave it. The garments we wore in life will be left behind as Christians, in the twinkling of an eye (1 Cor. 15:51-52), are translated from temporal to eternal life. Among those garments left behind will be the personal effects of the believer: cash, check books and a variety of credit cards, together with all of the pertinent identification needed for anyone who finds them to make use of them. And since many of those remaining on Earth will be of questionable repute, it is very likely that some will attempt to do so, creating a new problem for the world banking community, which will already be suffering from massive financial losses brought about by the brief nuclear war triggered either by Russia or one of its ten-nation confederates, obstensibly to prevent the United States from coming to the assistance of Israel (Ezek. 39:2-6).

Since it will take anywhere from three to six months for the magnitude of this problem to be appreciably comprehended by the world banking community, and another three to six months for Antichrist's program to be implemented worldwide, it will be some six to twelve months before the government can adequately respond to the rampant, fraudulent use of credit cards. Because they will also be deceived by the government's well-concocted explanation, the bankers will not understand what happened to those who formerly owned those credit and debit cards.

Fearful of a recurrence of the mysterious event which created the problem, the banks will be reluctant to simply cancel all existing credit cards and have their owners apply for new ones. Coming to their rescue, the government of Antichrist will quickly and conveniently supply the answer. Instead of issuing plastic, Antichrist concludes, with pseudo-Solomonic wisdom, the government will force

"...everyone, small and great, rich and poor, free and slave, to receive a mark on his right hand or on his forehead, so that no one could buy or sell unless he had the mark, which is the name of the beast or the number of his name." (Rev. 13:16-17; NIV)

That way, in the event another mysterious disappearance happened, there would be no remnants of cashless money to worry about. Every man, woman and child will be known by a global identification number issued by the state. Without that assigned number, combined with an additional symbol which will apparently serve to verify the valid issuance of the number, buying and selling will not be able to occur, since all global monetary units will be electronically transferred from one person to another through that assigned number. It is also likely that the events which trigger the Tribulation will additionally serve as justification to dispose of all territorial currencies, replacing them with global monetary units, i.e., *e.money*—if such an event does not occur before that time (since it is already one of the primary objectives of the global community which is currently evolving).

We see in Revelation 18 the opulence of spoiled wealth: Antichrist's global society at the moment of its demise. For almost seven years prior to that day, the world of Antichrist will enjoy unprecedented prosperity, and all of the nations of the world, from the greatest to the smallest, will share that good fortune. Utopia will have arrived! The world, preoccupied with the amassing of wealth, will again choose to ignore the persecution of the Jews—this time, at the hand of Antichrist, who breaks his covenant with Israel and attempts to annihilate them when they refuse to worship him as God. Even the plagues and natural disasters which suddenly engulf the world do not detract or deter the merchants of the world from their objective. As the bankers of the world have learned, wealth is most easily accumulated during times of world strife and disaster.

As the world's economies collapse, literally within an hour, so will the political system of Antichrist. The commerce centers of the Antichrist will suddenly be devastated by earthquakes, triggering fire and destruction all around the globe. Thousands will die. Within weeks famine and pestilence will begin to set in. The labors of men, which only weeks earlier had provided them both wealth and security, will suddenly vanish—computer bytes of buying power lost in the hard drive of an electronic monetary system completely destroyed by the global disaster. The merchants of the world who still have goods to sell will lament because, just as it was during the Great Depression of the 1930's, few will possess the means to buy what they have to sell. Only those with portable wealth: gold, silver, precious stones, food stuffs or commodities will be able to buy or sell. Wealth in the closing days of the society of man will be conducted exclusively by barter.

It will be the search for any form of portable wealth, together with the promise of global political power, which will ultimately lead all of the nations of the Earth to the Valley of Megiddo. Again, man will be deceived. Initially, it will be the intent of the world leaders to seek out and destroy Antichrist, whom they will blame for their misfortune. Antichrist, realizing time is running out, will flee to the Mideast to complete his plan for the destruction of the Jews. Satan, knowing Christ will shortly return to Earth to establish His kingdom in Jerusalem (Zech. 14:4), will, through deceit and trickery, amass all of the armies of the world in that area to stop Him.

Bribed with the offer of power and the spoils of war, the nations of the world will agree to assist Antichrist in his planned destruction of the Jews—who will have been blamed for the collapse of the economic system:

> *"Behold, the day of the Lord cometh, and thy spoil shall be divided in the midst of thee. For I will gather all nations against Jerusalem to battle; and the city shall be taken, and the houses rifled, and the women ravished; and half of the city shall go forth*

into captivity, and the residue of the people shall not be cut off from the city." (Zech. 14:1-2; KJV)

It will be the cry of His people at the brink of annihilation, which brings Christ to the Mount of Olives to battle the nations on the Plains of Jezreel at the mountain of Megiddo, which is in the Hebrew tongue, *Armageddon* (Zech. 14:3; Rev. 16:16).

Will tomorrow's global society accept the substitution of "e.money" for the traditional paper currencies used by all of the nations of the world today?

E.money, electronically transmitted currency, cybercash or digital dollars has been a reality for well over two decades. The explosive computer revolution combined with evolutionary advances in the technology hyped as the information superhighway has provided such ease of access to the Internet that new subscribers eagerly flood the on-ramps of the electronic superhighway by the hundreds of thousands through a myriad of website networks linked to the core government-created international electronic database.

The technology of the Internet, like the advent of the telephone itself, has been touted as a revolutionary, convenient, timesaving method for a busy society on the threshold of the 21st century to conduct business—across the street, across the nation, or around the world. By the close of this century every home and business in every industrialized nation of the world will be linked in some form or fashion to the Internet. Every aspect of our personal lives will be open to scrutiny not only by Big Brother, the increasingly intrusive governments of our slowly merging global society, but by anyone who owns a personal computer and a modem.

To fully appreciate the significance of e.money in the economic demise of the contemporary societies of the modern world, it is important to understand the role money has imperatively played in the development, progression and ultimate disintegration of every world society and empire to date. Money, as a tool of barter, has not always existed. Early societies, as well as many aboriginal third world societies today, rely on barter to survive. The accumulation of wealth may be determined by the amount of gold, silver or precious stones a man physically possesses: portable wealth. It can likewise be measured by the number of sheep, goats and cattle that graze in his fields. Grain, like cattle, represents physical wealth, since food is necessary to sustain life. In some areas of the world water is a bartered commodity. Anything of value can, and probably has, served as money since money is merely a universal measurement of exchange. In and of itself, money, especially the money which is circulated today, has no real transcendent value.

Coined money has been in use approximately 3,000 years. Civilizations require some form of coinage or other portable wealth with which to purchase needed commodities, since it is impractical to carry bushels of grain or bring sheep, goats or cattle to the market on shopping day.

In most societies it is the function of government to create the money supply. The coinage created by most ancient societies bore the inscription of the monarch who coined it. As each new monarch succeeded a previous one, new coinage was minted. The value of the coin was determined by both the weight and purity of the gold, silver or copper contained within it. For that reason, the coinage of some countries was worth more than that circulated in other countries.

While banking, usury, was actually invented by the ancient Babylonians, money was first coined in Sardis, the Lydian capital, around 650 B.C. Lydia, which lies in western Asia Minor, was the gateway to the Orient. As such, it was one of the major commercial centers of the world, and remained so until 547 B.C. when it came under Persian control. Greece, a neighbor of Sardis, saw the value of coinage, and at least partially attributed the wealth of the Lydian society to its monetary system. Following their lead, Greece likewise adopted a monetary system. Every society that followed the Greek Empire brought with it a monetary system. Those who maintained the integrity of their legal tender, like Greece (who quickly learned from experience not to debase it's monetary system), flourished; those who debased it, like Rome, decayed.

Henry the VIII (1491-1547 AD) changed the concept of money forever when he established the first monetary system based on fiat. By royal decree the House of Tudor recalled all coinage and recirculated newly minted coins which contained far less silver than those they replaced. The legal tender laws, decreed by fiat, forced England's subjects to accept them as full weight and purity. Outside of England the debased coinage of the Tudors had little value. As a result, inflation, almost unknown prior to that time, plagued the reign of Henry the VIII. To compensate, Henry the VIII did what many modern societies do when inflation devalues its currencies: he coined even more worthless money. This time the House of Tudor minted copper coins which were then washed with pure silver, giving them an appearance of purity. The new coins, called *groats,* quickly became known as *red-groats* as the thin silver coatings wore off, exposing the copper core.

When Elizabeth I ascended the English throne in 1558, she found a country racked with hyperinflation and near bankruptcy. She quickly commissioned an economist, Sir Thomas Gresham, to study the problem and recommend a solution. Gresham's report to Elizabeth has become an accepted law of economics: *bad money drives good money out of circulation.* Gresham's recommendation to reverse England's problem was simple: eliminate the fiat money and return to a legal tender system based on the integrity of gold and silver. Unfortunately, Elizabeth discovered Gresham's Law did not work well in reverse. Good money does not drive bad money out of circulation. Good money, gold and silver, will always be hoarded, and bad money will always remain the legal tender. It is only when all traces of bad money are removed from society through a monetary recall, that good money will again circulate as legal tender—which is what Adolph Hitler did to end the hyperinflation that destroyed the German Republic and brought about Hitler's Third Reich.

Post-war Germany deliberately destroyed the value of it's monetary system by flooding the nation with countless millions of worthless marks to offset the 342 billion gold Reichsmarks they were obligated to pay in reparations according to the terms of the Treaty of Versailles.

Since the Reichsbank had suspended the redemption of Reichsmarks in gold at the outbreak of the war in 1914, the German government could legally pay off this assessed debt with fiat money. And that is precisely what they did. By 1918 the amount of money in circulation increased fourfold. Unfortunately, the hyperinflation set into motion by the German government began to snowball.

By November 15, 1923, the Reichsbank was issuing a million new marks each day, and had, in fact, issued the astronomical sum of 92 quintillion paper marks in just five years—all of which were backed by nothing, since not even the promises of the government were worth anything in the eyes of the German population. In 1918 ten pounds of potatoes cost approximately one mark. In 1923 it cost 500 billion marks! A dozen eggs, which cost three marks in 1918, cost 960 billion marks in 1923. And a pound of butter, which also cost three marks in 1918, was priced at an unbelievable six trillion marks! The value of the German mark to the English pound fell from a value of twenty-to-one to 20 billion-to-one in December, 1923. The German trade economy all but destroyed, the German middle class turned to Hitler, who seemed to be the only person who understood why the hyperinflation was occurring. Fiat money creates inflation. Too much fiat money creates hyperinflation.

Modern banking and the fractional banking system accidently developed in England when wealthy merchants, fearful of being robbed, began to store ingots of gold and silver with goldsmiths for safekeeping. The goldsmiths, in return, would supply the depositor with an affidavit, a certificate of deposit, affirming the value of the stored bullion, and its availability to the bearer on demand. The merchants soon learned these certificates of deposit, which provided them immediate access to their funds, also served as bearer demand notes for those with whom they conducted business. Rather than carrying large, heavy ingots of gold and silver which invited both attention and theft, the merchant would simply write a bearer note, which the person to whom it was given would present to the goldsmith for payment.

At the same time the goldsmiths, who were handsomely recompensed for safeguarding the wealth of their customers, discovered that the demand notes, rather than the gold or silver which guaranteed it's value, became legal tender, and the bullion itself remained on deposit. Using their depositor's gold as a monetary reserve, the fledgling bankers began issuing demand notes of their own to other borrowers, who paid usury—not to the depositor who owned the gold which guaranteed the loan, but rather to the goldsmith for the use of those dormant funds. Modern banking was born. These early bankers, who had little or no personal wealth of their own, became rich by loaning to others funds which did not belong to them.

In the winter of 1693, England, still somewhat insolvent due to Henry the VIII's fiat money, was forced to approach a group of elitist European bankers through English financier William Paterson (1658-1719) for a much needed loan. Seizing the opportunity to gain control of the monetary system of England, the bankers demanded the right which previously belonged only to sovereign nations: the right to coin money. Faced with a real threat of bankruptcy, England was forced to concede. The Bank of England, which today creates Great Britain's money supply, was chartered as a private joint-stock association with capital of £1,200,000 on July 27, 1694. Although perceived as the government's bank, the Bank of England, much like the United States Federal Reserve Bank, was originally owned and controlled by an international consortium of bankers. However, on March 1, 1946, after 252 years of private ownership, the Bank of England was placed under government control. England now owns all of the stock.

The creation of the Federal Reserve System in 1913 stands in direct violation to the United States Constitution, which mandates that only our government, specifically the House of Representatives, has the right to coin money. Efforts by the central banks of Europe to create a system in the United States similar to that in England began to intensify in the latter days of the 19th century, and came to a head during the banking panic of 1907 when the international banking community created a major economic recession in the United States. Threatening to bring the United States economy to a complete standstill if it did not seriously entertain negotiations with the European banking community, Congress began to debate the merits of a central banking system.

At that time the United States was the only nation in the world whose currency was still based on the gold standard. As such, the American dollar was the most stable currency in the world, and less subject to inflation than the monetary systems of any of those countries who threatened it. Yet six years after the Panic of 1907, Congress, aided and abetted by Woodrow Wilson, caved in.

The *Aldrich-Vreeland Act* was quickly enacted in 1907, and in 1908 a National Monetary Commission was created. Senator Nelson Wilmarth Aldrich (R-RI), President Theodore Roosevelt's political nemesis, was appointed as its chairman to study the banking situation and make recommendations to Congress. The commission tendered its report in 1912, a few months after Aldrich left office. Congress did nothing with the report until Woodrow Wilson became the 28th President of the United States on March 4, 1913.

Wilson, who believed America was too much of an isolationist nation and needed to belong to the world community, recommended to Congress that they enact legislation which would provide America with a more elastic currency, one based on the "...commercial assets of America..." rather than on the bonded indebtedness of its government, with a theme of "...decentralization rather than centralization..." Although ideologically naive in some areas, Wilson was well aware of the power wielded by the central banks of Europe, and decided that several central banks which could compete with one another, located in key commerce centers around the nation, instead of one central bank, would better serve the needs of America and, in particular, the United States government.

Wilson's patriotic verbiage was included in *The Federal Reserve Act of 1913*. Wilson's rhetoric notwithstanding, the legislation clearly violated both the language and intent of the Constitution by abrogating the defined rights and responsibilities of the United States government in the area of monetary control.

The Federal Reserve Act divided the nation into twelve bank zones, with separate central banks located in Atlanta, Boston, Cleveland, Chicago, Dallas, Kansas City, Minneapolis, New York, Philadelphia, Richmond, St. Louis and San Francisco. Each bank theoretically serves independent of the others. Seven governors, appointed to 14 year terms, and a Fed Chairman, appointed to a four year term, were selected by Wilson to sit on the Federal Reserve Board, the ultimate, central governing body of the Fed, with offices in Washington, D.C. Since the power of the Fed remains centralized in this board, the twelve member banks are, in reality, empty voices which have, since Wilson, obediently followed the dictates and directives of the Fed chairman.

The Fed controls not only the issuance of both paper currency and coinage, but through the Federal Open Market Committee, the buying and selling of the U.S. government securities as well. These securities create the debt-base upon which the solvency of the United States dollar is founded.

As part of President Franklin D. Roosevelt's promised reorganization of the banking system—concealed in the smoke and mirrors of bank relief—New Dealers passed, in addition to *The Banking Act of 1933* which created the Federal Deposit Insurance Corporation, a joint Congressional resolution called *The Gold Repeal Joint Resolution* which, when it was approved on June 5, 1933, arbitrarily cancelled the gold clause from all federal and private obligations, and effectively removed the United States from the gold standard. The following year Congress enacted *The Gold Reserve Act of 1934* that allowed Roosevelt, in typical Henry the VIII style, to devalue the American dollar, something he promptly did. The dollar was devalued to approximately 55¢, immediately reducing the net worth of America's personal wealth by some 45%! Since the government possesses only debt, it reduced its obligation by a like amount, again, robbing the same Americans. Bondholders who invested in America with 100% dollars, were repaid with 55% Roosevelt dollars. The government won; the people lost. It was this money, taken from the public by a new form of taxation, which financed many of Roosevelt's New Deal programs.

By eliminating the gold standard and basing the issuance of money on the sale of government bonds, the solvency of the American dollar is based on its own debt. America pays its obligations with money created by additional debt—owed to the same citizens it taxes for profiting from buying the bonds our government must sell to create the money supply. Is it any wonder the United States is in debt to the tune of $5,900,000,000,000.00?

In addition to the creation of money through the sale of debt, the Fed—in what can be best described as a legal Ponzi scheme—also creates money through the use of the fractional reserve system. To more fully comprehend how the fractional reserve works, it is important to understand that, in today's society, money is merely an abstract measure of buying power symbolized by computer bytes and bookkeeping entries. The bank creates a deposit, and the funds suddenly exist—funds which are just as real as any delivered by a Brinks armored car from the Federal Reserve! Only no physical money exists. It is simply a matter of multiple deposit bookkeeping called a *money multiplier.*

Imagine, if you will, depositing the sum of $1,000.00 into your saving account. You are credited with that $1,000.00, and can withdraw it any time according to the terms of your account. Once your deposit is recorded the bank will loan to someone else whatever portion of your $1,000.00 is currently allowed by the Fed. Usually the bank is required to keep a reserve of between 10% and 20% of their deposits. (Whenever the Fed wants to tighten the money supply it raises the M1 legal reserve requirement, which means the bank must then hold in a non-interest bearing reserve, a greater percentage of its deposits, reducing the availability of funds to other potential borrowers. In this case, let's suppose the current reserve requirement is 20%.)

The bank can legally loan someone else $800.00 of your money. Let's assume the borrower spends the $800.00 which, in turn, is deposited by the merchant who received it (and, to make our scenario easier to manage) in the same bank. The bank may now loan $640.00 of that deposit to another borrower. When those funds are recycled, an additional $412.00 is created. This $412.00 creates $370.80 more. Without taking our example any farther, we find the bank has created, in four separate bookkeeping entries, $2,222.80 in additional real money from one deposit of $1,000.00—which still exists!

Wouldn't it be nice if we could create additional money in that manner whenever we needed it? Of course, if we did, it would be called counterfeiting. But if you really think about it, and as strange as this statement may sound on the surface, counterfeit money is actually worth more than the legal tender currency we receive from Uncle Sam since our legal tender is now fiat money. Neither certificate is actually worth more than the value of the paper upon which the denomination is printed, since our monetary system is not based on any commodity of value. The counterfeit bill is worth more only in the sense that the government-issued certificate carries with it the baggage of debt. A $20 bill issued by the United States Treasury represents $20 of debt, plus interest, incurred to create it. A counterfeit $20 bill is debt free! We have been taught to abhor the counterfeiter who steals wealth by creating money from nothing. What difference is there, other than a question of constitutional legality, between the Fed, who creates money from debt; or the counterfeiter, who creates it from nothing? In a practice sense, however, the Fed note is backed by the promise of the federal government that the note is legal tender and has an exchange value equivalent to its denomination. The counterfeit note, although it fraudulently claims to be legal tender, is backed by no such guarantee of exchange, and is from that perspective absolutely worthless.

Today the U.S. government is going to great extremes to protect it's currency from the high tech counterfeiter. In the past, the counterfeiter required an artisan to create the plates from which the bogus bills were struck. Now all that is required is a good computer and an illegal source of paper and ink. In 1995 the Treasury discovered the United States was being flooded with what appeared to be almost perfect counterfeit $100 bills which were reportedly being mass produced somewhere in the Middle East. The bills were so good that most American banks could not distinguish them from the genuine article. Ultimately, it was necessary for the United States to not only change the appearance of the $100 bill, but to use new high-tech inks and space-age paper as a means of protecting the integrity of our currency. Although the Treasury announced plans were underway to redesign other denominations, no other bills have thus far been introduced into the mainstream.

Obviously, the Fed has other plans. It is more likely the introduction of the new *Ben Franklin* was merely a temporary stopgap measure rather than a first step in redesigning the monetary system of the United States since, in all likelihood, the monetary system of the United States will be revamped to better serve the needs of the global trading community.

The units of exchange used by the new global trading partners will be cybercash rather than currency; e.money, the abstract legal tender of Antichrist. It will be a monetary system created without the expense of printing, handling or maintaining paper currency, or the minting of metal coins. E.money can virtually be created at will, from nothing, by a simple data entry, much the same way the Fed creates money through the use of money multiplication.

By the very nature of our evolving global society, money in its current form has become obsolete. The information superhighway has accelerated the development of a global marketplace which requires a more universal monetary system, one not measured in dollars, yens, pounds, rubles or marks. This new universal cybercash will likely be measured in digital units divisible by eight rather than ten. Global transactions in which millions of dollars change hands, occur several times every day with simple data entries on keyboards of computers located in corporate boardrooms, plush executive suites—and even private homes, bypassing the central banks of the world. This freedom will not last long. Big Brother has arrived, and will shortly be able to monitor every single monetary transaction in the world because currency as we know it will very shortly, no longer exist.

The *Associated Press* reported in a July 23, 1996 *Washington Post* article that all new Social Security recipients who sign up for benefits, beginning in August, 1996, will have their checks electronically deposited into their bank accounts, even if they would prefer to receive their benefits in the traditional manner. Moreover, those without bank accounts will be obligated to open them in order to receive earned benefits since, according to Treasury spokesman James Hagedorn, "...We can't issue (recipient benefits) by check."

Prior to that announcement by the federal government, automated deposits were optional. Approximately 61% of the 43 million people who receive Social Security payments receive their benefits by direct deposit. According to Hagedorn, current recipients without bank accounts may continue to receive paper checks until 1999. At that time, to continue receiving their benefits, they will be obligated to switch to some form of direct deposit—either a checking or savings account, or a special ATM account which will allow those without traditional bank accounts to spend their funds electronically. At that time, the Treasury announced, all federal obligations—regardless of the nature of the disbursement—will be paid electronically.

The new measure, the Treasury stated, was mandated by the need to save money; and will, the government estimated, save approximately $500 million over five years. Who doesn't want to save money? Furthermore, the government announced, it will eliminate almost 100 thousand check thefts and forgeries each year. Who isn't against crime? Before making their July, 1996 announcement, the Social Security Administration curried support for their plan from senior citizens groups, who will be the first Americans affected by the Big Brother legislation, in order to make this regulation more palatable to those affected. By the turn of the century currency as we know it will most likely no longer exist.

Central banks of the world have been involved in every single monetary transaction which has occurred in the world since 1913 that involved the use of a bank draft, money order or personal check. Tomorrow the world banking system will know every single transaction you make, regardless how large or how small, simply because every transaction by every person in the world will be done electronically.

E.money, in that respect, eliminates any possibility of kiting since account balances are instantaneously verified as electronic transfers are made. If the funds, or monetary units, do not sufficiently exist within the account, the transaction will be abruptly interrupted with an error message detailing the reason for the termination. In fact, e.money potentially eliminates all forms of check writing fraud typically perpetuated by the holder of a traditional checking account, thereby protecting both the bank and the recipient of the transaction. In fact, the use of e.money will eliminate many traditional forms of crimes since the criminal will no longer be able to conceal ill-gained profits. E.money will virtually end drug trafficking as we know it, since the drug pusher can be easily traced through his or her e.money account. Drug trafficking will likely become the first bartered crime in the history of the world, with payment being made in either portable wealth or commodities which offer legitimate resale liquidity.

On the other hand, e.money presents a whole new world of opportunity for the malefactor, who by gaining access to the database of any bank, can pilfer at will from any country in the world, without leaving any electronic fingerprints! E.money accounts can be drained of all existing funds by e.thieves, and then simply erased from the memory bank of the system to conceal the crime. Complicated personalized computer I.D. codes will likely be advertised through the Internet as safeguards to prevent break-ins by computer hackers. Eventually, these devises themselves will be stolen by the hackers who break their intricate access codes, and sold on blackmarket websites to potential thieves. Professional e.thieves, however, will not enter the e.money accounts of their victims through the front door addresses which grant access to the account owners. They will enter through the same backdoors they have been using for years to gain access to programs which are shielded by protective access codes.

When the e.money system of Antichrist fails in the closing days of the Tribulation, it will be the result of complex global monetary collapse. Any further supposition is speculation at best since Scripture is deliberately vague in this area, noting only that all of the economies of the world will crash—almost simultaneously. It is important to remember two things: first, within the next decade it is likely we will be using a universal monetary system, most likely e.money, which will link the wealth and economies of all industrialized nations into a single global marketplace. Second, if the monetary system of one nation falls, the domino theory will prevail, and the monetary systems of all of the nations will collapse as well.

Furthermore, a universal e.money system all but guarantees the advent of Big Brother. With any universal monetary system comes a universal database on those who use the e.money system—which will be virtually everyone. Much of that database already exists. Call your local credit bureau and ask to see your file and you may discover you are not authorized to view it. Theoretically you are, and most credit reporting agencies, for a fee, will provide you with a printout of its contents (or at least that portion of it the agency feels you are entitled to look at). Complete access to your file sometimes requires the services of an attorney. Within that file you may logically expect to find, in addition to your financial history, a record of your current and previous addresses, and possibly your employment history. Additionally you may find health records, marital records (even those from other states); and whether or not you have ever been charged or convicted of a felony can be included as well. The notion of personal privacy has become a dream of the past, and intrusion by Big Brother has become the nightmare of the future.

Mankind invariably adjusts to the external forces which constantly seek to govern and control its life, tolerating intrusion, restriction of personal liberty, and sometimes physical debasement and, in many cases, mentally justifying them in order to make those abuses of power by government more palatable. The Jews as a nation present a perfect case scenario of this argument. As the mass deportation of Jews, first from Germany and Austria, and then from Russia, France and Belgium intensified during the early days of World War II, the Jews obediently submitted to all forms of debasement. Even when rumors of gas chambers in places like Auschwitz, Lublin, Birkenau, Belsen and Monowitz later began to surface, together with clear evidence that the attempted extermination of an entire race was being undertaken by the Third Reich, the Jews chose not to believe it, rationalizing instead that they were too valuable to the German war effort to be profitlessly slaughtered simply for the sake of their destruction.

Americans are no different in their thinking. All of us nervously laugh at the humorless joke, "I'm from the government, and I'm here to help you..." We resent the intrusion of Big Brother, yet we keep electing the same politicians who keep growing both the size and scope of that same increasingly intrusive government, with a rationale that almost defies imagination. Intrusions by Big Brother and restrictions of constitutionally guaranteed liberties, we are told, are necessary to keep America safe. And of course, we believe it. These small sacrifices, we tell ourselves, are necessary to keep us free. Of course taxation hurts, but it is our obligation as a God-fearing people to help those who cannot help themselves. We have somehow convinced ourselves that nobody, except the unfortunate, profit from taxation; and to help the needy, we are prepared to sacrifice many of the comforts which we have earned through our labors.

Rumors have been circulating in ultra-conservative quarters for several years that a universal monetary unit was agreed upon by the leading world economic powers and their respective central banks during the administration of Jimmy Carter; but the election of President Ronald Reagan in 1980, who was viewed as a right-wing radical by the world banking community, caused the plans to be shelved. Frankly, a global monetary system could not have been successfully launched at that time even if the world banking community had pressed for it, if for no other reason than the fact that the world simply wasn't ready for it. Two key elements were missing. First, we did not actually become a coherent global community until George Bush forged his global coalition through the UN in 1992; and second, a global society requires a free and open global marketplace, something which did not occur until the collapse of the Soviet Union. Had Carter been re-elected in 1980, it is likely his economic and geopolitical missteps, like President Clinton's, may have accelerated their plans.

We as a society have been exposed to e.money for several years. Most Americans have been using some form of it all of their lives. In fact, approximately half of all monetary transactions initiated in the United States are made with some form of e.money. We have simply failed to recognize it as such. Whenever we use a credit card we are using e.money. Today most employers will electronically deposit their employees' paychecks. It is conservatively estimated that approximately 20% of all Americans now receive their pay in this manner. Also, most supermarkets today offer their customers Automatic Teller Machine access at the checkout counter—e.money for groceries. It is rapidly becoming the accepted way to shop. It is because America is rapidly becoming a cashless society that crimes at ATM machines nationwide are on the increase. America, with one of the highest crime rates in the world, is ready for e.money.

The transition from currency to e.money will not be so abrupt as to cause panic in the streets. After all, e.money has been gradually introduced into our culture for almost three decades. Each new phase of this transition is now greeted by the American public with not so much as a raised eyebrow. Like most liberal programs proposed by government, the actual shift from paper currency to e.money will be preceded by a massive amount of media hype extolling the virtues of e.money, and probably will focus on the notion that e.money will virtually eliminate many forms of crime. With this pronouncement will come reams of hard-core, if not slightly exaggerated, government statistics to support this conclusion. As previously stated, there is some merit to this argument. Crimes for money, including kidnapping for ransom, will be immediately stymied, as will the street sale of drugs for cash which, today, is the only way drugs are trafficked.

However, the feeling of security created by this reprieve from some forms of crime will be brief, if at all, since crimes involving the theft of personal property: automobiles, household goods, electronics and other valuables including food stuffs will in all likelihood increase immediately, since the personal needs of the criminal will not change simply because the monetary system has changed.

As America shifted from cash to credit cards the target of criminal activity shifted. Today a large percentage of the felonies being committed involve either the theft or misuse of credit cards, thefts from bank patrons at ATM machines (which are increasing dramatically), or the theft of personal property from the homes or businesses of its victims. Tomorrow's high-tech criminal will specialize in electronic theft. And while tomorrow's e.crimes will be less traumatizing to the victims, most of whom will not even know they've been robbed until they attempt to conduct an e.money transaction, tomorrow's felonies will prove to be much more devastating to the victims since the e.thief who is able to access your bank records will be able, with a series of keystrokes, to wipe out your entire life savings!

Many Americans recognize the dangers of e.money and are wisely transferring some of their assets into portable wealth—just in case the system does not perform as promised. Most people, however, regardless of their personal feelings or apprehensions, will accept e.money as that necessary first step into a crime-free 21st century, believing their government would not do anything detrimental to them.

Will the Battle of Armageddon be an actual event, and if so, when will it take place?

The Battle of Armageddon has all the earmarks of a typical George Lucas film production, and contains all the breathtaking panoramic action sequences which made Lucas' *Star Wars* trilogy a science fiction box office bonanza. As the nations of Earth (representing the bad guys) attack Israel (you guessed it—the good guys), and are about to destroy them to the last man, woman and child, a trumpet sounds in the distance and a heavenly cavalry gallops into town, led by our hero, who is dressed from head to foot in white. Our hero summarily trounces the bad guys, rounds them all up and makes them pay for their dastardly deeds. All of the good guys live happily ever after for a thousand years. Does that not smack of a typical Hollywood script? What could be more cinematic? However, unlike the typical celluloid Hollywood production, the supernatural battle which will climax man's era on earth will not be role play—it will be an event that will be acted out, pretty much as described above, on the centerstage of Earth. The villains are real. The good guys are real. And the event itself, Armageddon, will be so terribly real you will not want even your worst enemy to experience its horror.

The Battle of Armageddon is the war every Christian thinks about, but since the collapse of the Soviet Union, few feel it remains a threat which will be realized within their lifetimes. Strangely enough, few people seem to realize that neither the United States nor the former Soviet Union will be major players in this final conflict which pits Satan and the armies of the Syrian (Isa. 30:31, 31:8; Dan. 8:9-25, 11:21-45) Antichrist against the Heavenly Host, although the United States and Russia, like the balance of the nations of the Earth, will be represented at the Valley of Megiddo.

This conflict would probably be called World War IV if it lasted long enough to be named, or if history beyond that point was so inclined to label the last war in its history. World War III will be the nuclear exchange between Russia and her confederates (Ezek. 38:2-13, 39:1-6) against the United States (39:6). The Battle of Armageddon will pit Jesus Christ and his supernatural army of saints against all of the assembled nations of the world (Zech. 12:2-9, 14:2-3; Rev. 16:16, 19:11-17) in the closing hours of the Tribulation.

The Valley of Megiddo is located within the Plains of Jezreel in Judah, between the Mediterranean on the west and the Jordan River, which cuts off the Valley on the east. The Plains of Jezreel lie in the southeastern portion of an even larger valley which divides Galilee from Samaria. Flanked on the north by Hazor and the south by Shechem, the Valley of Megiddo is, in the words of Napoleon Bonaparte, the most natural battlefield in the world. At various times this plain has also been known as the Valley of Jehosaphat (Joel 3:12) and the Valley of Esdraelon. Many of Israel's greatest battles were fought on this terrain.

During the period when the Hyksos ruled Egypt, the Shepherd Kings invaded Palestine several times between 1788-1580 B.C. and fought the Canaanites near Megiddo. The Egyptians captured Palestine in 1479 B.C. by defeating their enemies at Megiddo. It was at Megiddo where Josiah (639-609 B.C.), who destroyed the pagan altars of Bethel and restored Temple worship, fell fighting Pharaoh Necho in 609 B.C.

It was also in the Valley of Megiddo that General Sir Edmund Allenby, the British commander of the Palestine front, defeated the Turks on September 18, 1918, fracturing the joint Turkish/German alliance and ended the Ottoman Empire, a Moslem dynasty that survived almost 600 years and influenced both the political and religious thinking of half of Europe. The German forces which fought alongside the Turks at Megiddo retreated into Transjordan when Allenby routed the Turkish army. The Germans were later defeated by Arab forces under the command of Col. T. E. Lawrence, who became known to the world as Lawrence of Arabia.

It was largely through the efforts of Allenby that the Balfour Declaration, which created a national homeland for the Jews in Palestine and Transjordan, was signed on November 2, 1917. And it was precisely because of Allenby, through his defeat of the Ottomans at Megiddo, that the text of the Balfour Declaration carried all the force and substance of law. The Declaration, with a single exception, was formally ratified by the newly created League of Nations on July 24, 1920. That exception was a provision that allowed the Jews to settle in Transjordan. It was struck from the document, allowing Jewish immigration only to Palestine.

Although Antichrist will egotistically believe he is the master military strategist who chooses Meggido for his final confrontation with Jesus Christ, its location was predetermined by God. It was in Megiddo that Israel's homeland was re-established by the Balfour Declaration in 1917, and it will be in Megiddo that Israel's homeland will be confirmed in perpetuity.

CHAPTER EIGHT

THE MILLENNIUM

What is the Sheep & Goats Judgment, and when will it take place?

When Christ returns at the conclusion of the Tribulation to set up His millennial kingdom (Ps. 2, 24, 50, 72, 96, 110; Isa. 2:24, 11:1-12:6; Isa. 65-66; Mic. 4:1-3; Dan. 2:24; Zech. 1:10-11; Mt. 19:28, 23:39, 24:3-25:46; Mk. 13:24-27; Lk. 12:35-48, 17:22-37, 18:8, 21:25-28; Ac. 1:10-11, 15:16-18; Rom. 11:25-27; 1 Cor. 11:26, 15:24-28; 2 Th. 1:7-10; 2 Pe. 3:3-4; Rev. 2:7-8, 2:25-28, 16:15, 19:11-21, 20:4, 22:20) He will first purge the world of sin and evil. Jesus will accomplish this with three separate acts.

First, He will cast Antichrist (Rev. 13:1) and the False Prophet (Rev. 13:11) into the Lake of Fire (Rev. 19:20). Second, He will chain Satan in the bottomless pit for one thousand years (Rev. 20:1-3). Third, He will judge the living nations of the world from the East Gate of Jerusalem (Lev. 16:14; Isa. 30:33; Jer. 19:2; Jn. 5:22, 27). Again, this judgment is not to be confused with The Great White Throne Judgment (Rev. 20:11-15) which will take place at the end of the Millennium, and will be the judgment of the wicked dead.

This first judgment parallels the events described in the parable of the tares and the wheat (Mt. 13:24-43). This is a judgment of the living, and determines precisely who will and will not enter the millennial kingdom. All of the sinners who survive the holocaust of Armageddon will be cut off. They will not be allowed to enter the kingdom of the Living God, Jesus Christ (Isa. 1:19-31, 65:11-16; Ezek. 11:21, 20:33-44; Mal. 3:2-6, 3:18).

Not everyone living after the translation of the Church (1 Cor. 15:52-53; 1 Th. 4:15-17; Rev. 3:10) will accept the mark of the beast (Rev. 13:14, 14:9, 15:2). Many will see through the lie (2 Th. 2:11), and upon realizing they were left behind, will accept Christ and will struggle to survive in Antichrist's e.money society, a world in which they will be precluded from buying or selling. Many of these—some Gentiles and some Jews—will be beheaded for their witness during this *time of Jacob's Trouble* (Rev. 20:4).

During the Tribulation, there will be three types of people on earth: the sheep, the goats, and the brethren. The sheep will be those Jews and Gentiles who accept Jesus Christ during that period; the goats will be all who follow the pied piper tune of Antichrist, whether or not they accept his mark; and the brethren will be a select group of Jews who stand distinctly alone, separated from the balance of mankind. While many students of Scripture view the sheep as saved Gentiles and the brethren as saved Jews, bible scholar H.A. Ironside suggested in his 1920 thesis on The Revelation that the brethren were not representative of the entire Jewish nation, but are instead the 144,000 Jewish male virgins (Rev. 14:4), selected by God to spread the gospel of Jesus Christ to Israel during that period. Ironside presents a very logical argument, since both the sheep and goats are representative of Gentiles and Jews; and the term brethren is traditionally viewed as (a) someone in fellowship with God, and (b) someone who is distinctly a Jew. Since the sheep, who will consist of both Gentiles and Jews, are also in fellowship, we must recognize the brethren as yet a different group. Since no other groups exist on earth at that time, the brethren logically represent those witnesses, and like the Christians who were translated, are exempted from The Sheep and Goats Judgment.

It is common belief among Christians that the Millennial Reign of Jesus Christ on Earth will begin immediately after the Battle of Armageddon. That is not quite true. Daniel shows us that an additional 45 days will elapse between the conclusion of the Battle of Armageddon and the ushering in of the Millennial Kingdom. It will be during these 45 days (Dan. 12:11-13) that Christ will stand at the East Gate of Jerusalem and separate the sheep from the goats.

> *"If anyone worships the beast or his image and receives his mark on the forehead or on the hand, he too will drink of the wine of God's fury, which has been poured full strength into the cup of his wrath. He will be tormented with burning sulfur in the presence of the holy angels of the Lamb. And the smoke of their torment rises forever and ever. There is no rest day or night for those who worship the beast and his image, or for anyone who receives the mark of his name."* (Rev. 14:9-11; NIV)

All of mankind from all of the nations of the earth will pass before Christ at this Judgment. Those who accepted Christ as their savior during the Tribulation, the sheep, will be admitted into His earthly kingdom, an edenic setting where life will be prolonged as it was in the days of Adam. Those who have rejected the offer of grace, the goats, will be cast into Hell (Isa. 30:33; Jer. 19:2) from the gateway to Hades which will open in the Valley of the Son of Hinnom, directly below the East Gate.

During this same period judgment will separately fall upon Egypt as a nation. The people of Egypt, needless to say, will be judged individually. But because of her historic treatment of God's people, who sought refuge within her bosom and were enslaved, Egypt, as a nation, will also be judged. Because of it's treacherous dealings with the Jews, Egypt will be found guilty, and for her crime will become desolate for forty years (Ezek. 29:12). Her people, like the Jews, will be scattered among all the nations (Ezek. 29:13) of Earth to symbolize the disbursement of the Jews.

Will Christ literally rule on Earth for 1,000 years?

The millennial reign of Jesus Christ on Earth is extensively supported by Scripture (Ps. 72; Isa. 2:1-4, 9:6-7, 24:19-23, 30:15-33, 65:17-25; Jer. 23:5-8; Ezek. 21:26-27; Mic. 4:1-3; Dan. 2:44; Zech. 2:10-11; Mt. 19:28, 23:39, 24:3-25; Mk. 13:24-37; Lk. 12:35-48, 17:22-37, 18:8, 21:25-28; Ac. 1:10-11, 15:16-18; Rom. 11:25-27; 1 Cor. 11:26, 15:24-28; 2 Th. 2:7-10; 2 Pe. 3:3-4; Rev. 1:7-8, 2:25-28, 16:15, 20:4, 22:20). It will begin exactly 1,290 days after Antichrist breaks his covenant with the Jews (Dan. 9:27, 12:11) and desecrates the Tribulation Temple. Immediately after the Battle of Armageddon (Zech. 12:1-9, 14:1-4; Rev. 19:11-20) The Sheep and Goats Judgment (Mt. 25:31-46) will take place. For 45 days Christ will sit in judgment on the living, admitting some and requiting others.

Since the earthly kingdom of Jesus is not to be confused with heaven, man will retain the sin nature of Adam, and may still fall. His urge to sin, however, will be minimal, since Satan will have been bound in the bottomless pit (Rev. 20:1-3), and will not be able to tempt him to transgress against God. The world during this period will be in a primeval natural state much like that experienced by Adam and Eve. Man, during this period, will not only have the capacity to sin without exterior motivation, but will sin. Sin, however, will be dealt with as harshly and abruptly as it was with the Jews when they were in the wilderness of Sinai (Ps. 72:1-5; Isa. 11:4, 65:20, 66:24).

Because millions of people will be born during the Millennium, it will be necessary for God to provide a final test for humanity before the onset of the Theocratic Age. For one thousand years man will live under the most utopian conditions since Adam was evicted from the Garden. With Satan bound and all of man's needs supplied, man should be found without guile. But, as stated, even with the total absence of evil, man's sin nature will prevail, proving that the corruptness of the human heart can win even in the very presence of God.

The Millennium will prove to be the utopia politicians have been promising man since the dawn of time. Peace will reign for 1,000 years (Isa. 2:4, 9:7, 11:6-9, 32:17-18, 54:13, 55:12, 60:18, 66:12; Ezek. 28:26, 34:25, Hos. 2:18; Zech. 9:10) and man will enjoy freedom from all oppression for the first time since the building of the Tower of Babel (Isa. 42:6-7, 49:9; Zech. 9:11-12). It will be a prosperous world without floods, droughts or natural disasters of any type. Every person will have enough to eat (Joel 2:26). Man will toil as he has since the days of Adam, but God will remove the curse from the Earth (Gen. 3:17) and it will give forth in abundance (Isa. 65:21-23; Ezek. 36:29-30; Joel 2:21-26; Amos 9:13-14; Zech. 8:11-12). With the curse removed and Satan bound, there will be no sickness in the world (Isa. 33:24; Jer. 20:17; Ezek. 34:16), and man himself will be healed of all deformities (Isa. 29:18, 35:5-6). Language, which God confounded at Babel (Gen. 11:9), will be unified once again (Zeph. 3:9). All of the people of the Earth will speak the language of praise, which is Hebrew, the language of Canaan (Isa. 19:18).

At the end of the Millennium, man's final test will occur. Satan will be released from the bottomless pit, and will be allowed to go forth once more to tempt the Earth (Rev. 20:3-8). This season will be allowed for the final cleansing not only of Earth, but Heaven as well.

All of God's creation which did not have the opportunity to choose between God and Satan will be afforded one last chance to make such a decision. It would seem after 1,000 years of purity and prosperity that man would know better, and would choose God without any reservation. However, the promise of power, wealth and godhood will prove to be too much of a temptation for some, because a great multitude (Rev. 20:8) will reject God and elect to follow Satan at that time. Although this last rebellion will be short-lived, countless millions of people will choose the empty promises of Satan over the prosperity they experienced under the theocratic reign of Jesus Christ, and will follow Satan's pied piper tune to their eternal damnation. This rebellious multitude will be utterly destroyed by fire, and Satan will be cast into the Lake of Fire (Rev. 20:9-10).

It should be noted that once he is cast into the Lake of Fire, Satan, like any other malefactor, holds no special rank or authority. He, like any human who dies in sin, simply becomes one of those who will be tormented for all of eternity. The idea that Satan rules in Hell is not a biblical precept. Satan's sphere of authority is on Earth.

Immediately following the final rebellion of man, the Great White Throne Judgment will take place, and the second resurrection—the resurrection of the damned—will occur. Every unredeemed human, both living and dead, will pass before Christ at that time. Excluded from this judgment are those who were part of the first resurrection 1,000 years earlier.

The two books into which the deeds of man are recorded will be opened at that time, and mankind will be judged from one of them. First, the *Book of Life* will be opened. Those whose names are not found written in this book will be judged from the second book, the *Book of Works,* according to their deeds. Regretfully, all who are judged from this book will stand condemned even before the first words of defense are uttered by them, since man's works, without the shed blood of Jesus Christ to cover their sins, are not sufficient to escape the wrath of God. All who are judged from the *Book of Works* will be cast into the Lake of Fire.

Since Jesus Christ fully atoned for our sins when He became our blood sacrifice on the cross, why will animal sacrifice be reinstated in the millennial temple?

The animal sacrifice recorded in Ezekiel 43:19-27 will be memorial in nature. The purpose of the sin offering *(hatta ot)* and the peace offering *(s^{e}lamin)* is not atonement. Under the law, sacrifices were made for the atoning of sin. Since Christ fulfilled that which the law hoped to accomplish, animal sacrifice is no longer necessary.

The function of the millennial animal sacrifice will parallel the ordinance of communion. As He celebrated the last Passover with His Apostles, Jesus took the *matzoh* (unleavened bread), broke it, and giving it to them, said,

> *"This is My body which is given to you. This do in remembrance of Me..."* (Lk. 22:19; KJV)

Christ instituted the ordinance of communion not in eternal perpetuity, but only until He returns to establish His father's kingdom on Earth.

We can see from the re-institution of the Levitical priesthood, through the seed of Zadok, that the events of the millennium were not to be fulfilled by the Church. Just as the ordinance of communion was given to the Church as a memorial, so will the millennial sacrifice be given to the Jews.

It should be noted that in the millennial worship system, there is no Ark of the Covenant, no mercy seat, no cherubim, no stone tablets of the law, no veil blocking the Holy of Holies where previously only the high priest could enter. In fact, although the priesthood has been bestowed upon the seed of Zadok, there will be no high priest except Jesus Christ Himself (Ezek. 46:1-18). The sacrifices which take place in the millennial temple are not expiatory. They are memorial of the perfect sacrifice, the Lamb of God, who removed the sins of the world.

In the New Jerusalem the twelve gates will bear the names of the twelve tribes. Since Joseph's sons, Ephraim and Manasseh are included in the Promise, there are actually fourteen tribes. Which tribes are missing? Also, counting Matthias and Paul, there are fourteen Apostles whose names could be inscribed on the twelve foundations. Whose names are missing?

In Revelation 7:4-8, the twelve spiritual tribes of Israel are outlined. In this tribal synopsis, Dan and Ephraim (who originally led the Jews into idolatry) are missing. In their place we find Joseph and Levi. (See Numbers 1:20-42.) It would seem logical to conclude that the twelve tribes who witness the name of Jesus Christ throughout the Tribulation would be the names inscribed on the gates of the New Jerusalem, through which the saved remnant of the world will enter to worship God, but that will not be the case. Scripture reveals

> *"...the gates of the city shall be after the names of the tribes of Israel, three gates northward: one gate of Reuben, one gate of Judah, one gate of Levi. At the east side, four thousand and five hundred measures, and three gates: one gate of Joseph, one gate of Benjamin, one gate of Dan. And at the south side, four thousand and five hundred measures, and three gates: one gate of Simeon, one gate of Issachar, one gate of Zebulon. At the west side, four thousand and five hundred measures, with their three gates: one gate for Gad, one gate for Asher, one gate for Naptali."* (Ezek. 44:31-34; KJV)

We are not given a correlative verse that names the Apostles in relation to the twelve foundations. However, the process of elimination is much easier in this instance. It is safe to assume that the name of Judas Iscariot will not be one of the twelve so inscribed. That leaves only Matthias and Paul. Matthias was selected by the casting of lots (Ac. 1:25). Interestingly, this is the same manner by which Popes of the Roman Catholic Church are selected from the ranks of the Cardinals. Matthias was the choice of the Apostles to replace Judas, indicative of their belief that Christ wanted to perpetuate their rank. However, that was not God's purpose. Their job, which concluded in the closing days of the first century, was to spread the Gospel and create, upon the foundation of Jesus Christ, His Church.

Jesus selected Saul of Tarsus as the replacement of Judas Iscariot. All that Jesus declared to the eleven, He declared, through the Holy Spirit, to Paul. In Matthew 28:19, Christ instructed the eleven to go forth and teach all the nations. In Acts 9:15, Christ declared to Ananias that Paul would bear His name before the Gentiles. Gentile and nations are merely different translations of the same Greek word: *ethnos.*

In Matthew 24:9, Jesus promised the eleven they would be delivered up to be afflicted, and that they would be killed for Him. In Acts 9:16 Paul is promised the same fate.

For three years Paul lived in total obscurity in Arabia (Gal. 1:11-19) while he contemplated the depths of Christianity. The time he spent in his desert retreat parallels the time during which the eleven were instructed by Jesus. According to Paul, he was instructed by the Holy Spirit during this period:

> *"For I never received it of man, neither was I taught it, but by revelation of Jesus Christ..."* (Gal. 1:12; KJV)

Based on that premise, the names of the Apostles which will be inscribed on the twelve foundations of the New Jerusalem will be: Paul, Peter, James, John, Andrew, Phillip, Thomas, Bartholomew, Matthew, James (the son of Alphaeus), Simon the Zealot, and Judas (the son of James, not Iscariot).

CHAPTER NINE

OTHER QUESTIONS WHICH BAFFLE CHRISTIANS

Is there a correct version of the Bible?

Is one version of the Bible better than another? Are there any of the traditional versions or translations which are corrupt?

Every Christian has a favorite version. Mine, for years, was the *Authorized King James Version of 1611.* It was replaced with the NIV around five years ago. My wife prefers *The Living Bible,* as does my eldest daughter. But both of them enjoy the *New American Standard Bible* as well. Just as we all have favorite versions, each have versions which, for one reason or another, we dislike. In the past I have voiced a dislike for *The Living Bible* because of the nature of the paraphrase, and because of its translation of Isaiah 7:14 from the *Revised Standard Version.* However, like most Christians, I have absolute disdain for only two *paraphrased* editions—both of which are unisex versions. *The New Inclusive Bible,* which has been on the market since the spring of 1995; and a new *Turner Publishing* edition that was released in June, 1996. Striving for what can best be described as politically correct neutrality, both attack the traditional perception of God as being male by avoiding the use of masculine gender; opting instead for inclusive, neutral gender words to describe man or mankind.

The new *Turner Publishing* edition, which utilizes the updated RSV text, artfully conceals its editorialized text behind the facade of 263 beautiful reproductions of Renaissance art from the Vatican library. *Turner Publishing* defends its use of inclusivity by insisting gender neutralization occurs only when the text suggests the masculine "he" actually refers to both sexes. On the other hand, *The New Inclusive Bible* depicts any form of the Trinity in the neutral gender because, as I understand the reasoning of its author, references to God, the Holy Spirit and Jesus in the masculine gender are offensive to feminists. The feminist does not seem to understand that changing the language of the Bible to a more politically correct position does not alter the fact that the Trinity is still masculine.

My personal dislike for the RSV, as I stated, is based on its rendering of one verse. Every modern translation—from the KJV to the NKJV, with the single exception of the RSV (and the *Reader's Digest Condensed Bible* which was taken from that text), renders *'alma* as "virgin" instead of "young woman." While the word *'alma* does not unequivocally denote only those who are a virgin, it does specifically describes a young, unmarried woman whose primary characteristic is virginity. There appears to be no instance in the Hebrew text where *'alma* is used to describe a woman who is either married or is not a virgin.

My dislike for *The Living Bible* text is based entirely on Dr. Kenneth Taylor's paraphrasing, which I feel renders this version worthless for the serious student. As I said, my wife and one of my two daughters love it, and because of the simplistic liquidity of the text, have been encouraged to read the Bible. Because it is easy to read, a great many nationally known evangelists heartily recommend it. And, while it may not be a scholarly exegesis, it is reasonably accurate eschatologically; and for that reason it is extremely beneficial to the young Christian who is having a problem with the KJV's 17th century text.

Over the past twenty years I have witnessed an extreme amount of attacks leveled by church people against some of the most scholarly translations of the Bible available. What angered me most when I heard of them is that, for the most part, the attacks were usually launched by unlearned men of the cloth who never studied the Word of God in its original Hebrew, Greek or Aramaic form. I recall a letter I received a few years ago from a lay preacher from Ranger, West Virginia in which he said "...the only Bible (he) used was the Bible Christ used—the Authorized King James Version of 1611."

Not too long after receiving that correspondence, an acquaintance gave me a bulletin which had been circulated that morning in the church he attended. The author of the bulletin, the principal of a Christian school in that community, wrote:

> *"Because of the day we are living in, there are many people who are confused about which Bible is the Word of God. I have decided to write a long letter to expose the other books impersonating as the Bible. There is only one Bible, the A.V. of 1611. All others are forgeries, and this letter will prove that to any reader who wants to know the truth. Among the 'Bibles' that I will expose are the NIV, RSV, the Living Bible, Good News For Modern Man, the Amplified 'Bible' and the other seventy-five corrupt versions...What I am going to do is teach you how to look for Satan's lies, then I will give you verses to compare..."*

He continues:

> *"Let's look at Luke 2:33. The A.V. of 1611 says, 'and Joseph and his mother marvelled at those things which were spoken of by him'. Whatever book you are using for a 'Bible' will say, 'His father and mother marvelled...' Just one word is changed, but do you see the attack by the Devil? Jesus' father did not marvel, Joseph did—and he was not Jesus' father, God is. All of the corrupt versions will read this way. They try to attribute an earthly father for Jesus, thereby attacking His deity..."*

Referring to a common Greek interlinear, I looked up Luke 2:33. The Greek word used was *pater.* The verse reads: "The father of Him and the mother marvelled..." Further, the word *pater* (meaning *nourisher* or *protector*), not Joseph, is used. The translation to which he referred did not usurp the Word of God in an attempt to deny or refute the deity of Jesus. The translators interpreted the word literally from Greek to English, and in doing so, did not detract from the deity of Jesus. The translators of the original KJV text interpreted the spirit of the verse to prevent future generations from incorrectly imputing Joseph's paternity with respect to Jesus.

About *The Living Bible,* he says:

> *"This book is full of curse words, and should be burnt immediately. Any preacher that says that this is a good book to read is an apostate preacher. If you want to read filth, try John 9:34, 1 Samuel 20:30, or 1 Kings 18:27. There are other verses, but I will not waste my time in exposing this pornographic book..."*

He continues by saying he was once given a copy of *The Living Bible* and

> *"...carried the book to the trash can and tore the pages from it before putting this piece of trash where it belonged..."*

John 9:34, in the KJV, reads:

> *"They...* (the Pharisees) *...answered, and said unto him...* (the recently healed blind man) *...thou was altogether born in sins, and dost thou teach us?"*

The Living Bible, admittedly, paraphrases this verse somewhat coarsely, trying, I imagine, to show the emotional state of the Pharisees as they rebuked the former blind man:

> *"You illegitimate bastard, you! they shouted. Are you trying to teach us? And they threw him out."*

My Greek Interlinear renders the verse thusly:

> *"They answered and said to him: 'In sin you were wholly born, and you teach us?' And they cast him outside."*

I must agree with the letter writer in this instance. Dr. Taylor's interpolation of this verse was, I believe, in bad taste; and his choice of colloquialisms poorly selected. Taylor interpolates another verse somewhat as liberally as well. In 1 Kings 18:20-40 Elijah is ridiculing the prophets of Baal because their god could not ignite the wood on their altar. As he chided them (vs. 27), he says (LB text):

> *"You'll have to shout louder than that to catch the attention of your god! Perhaps he is talking to someone, or is out sitting on the toilet, or maybe he is away on a trip, or is asleep and needs to be wakened!"*

There does not appear to be a scriptural basis for Dr. Taylor's editorialized reference to the toilet, except perhaps a very inappropriate attempt on his part to show the contempt Elijah felt for Baal and his priests. Although I was somewhat forced to agree with the letter writer's assessment of the paraphrasing of 1 Kings 18:27 and John 9:34, I found little else in his correspondence to stand in agreement with. He went on to say that the writers of the corrupt versions took the name of Christ from Romans 14:10 and replaced it with God to de-deitize Jesus.

"Did you catch it? The devil is a sly liar, isn't he? In this corrupt version, they simply take out the word 'Christ' and replace it with 'God'. It seems harmless, but try using your NIV to prove to a cult like the Jehovah's Witnesses that Jesus is God..."

How is Romans 14:10 worded in the original text?

"And why judge your brothers? or why indeed do you despise your brother? For we shall all stand before the tribunal of God."

It must be noted that the word used in this verse is *theos* (which, quite literally means God), not *Iesous* (Jesus) or *Christos* (Christ). *Theos* was interpolated as *Christ* in the KJV. But, since Jesus, the Christ, is God, there is little difference in the ultimate meaning of this particular text. The tribunal is God's, the judge at the tribunal is Christ.

The letter continues:

"Read John 9:35 and see that they changed 'Son of God' in the A.V. 1611 to 'son of man' in the corrupt versions...Again, just one word changed, but a blatant attack on the Deity of Jesus."

And, again, referring to the Greek interlinear, John 9:35 reads:

"Heard Jesus that they cast him outside, and finding him, said: 'Do you believe in the Son of Man?'

Please note that the word for man as applied here is *anthropos* (meaning human being, or one with human frailties). The word for God is *theos*. In this verse, *anthropos,* not *theos,* is used.

He continues with John 6:47 by saying:

"The real Bible says 'Verily, verily, I say unto you, he that believeth on me hath everlasting life'. (This is Jesus speaking of Himself .) Your corrupt version says, 'I tell you the truth, he who believes has everlasting life!" Notice what they left out: two words, on me. Does this look like updating the language to you, or Bible tampering?"

The answer, again, is found in the interlinear. The text says:

"Truly, truly, I say unto you, the believer has life eternal."

There is definitely no Bible tampering, only an updating of the language. The writer of the letter continues by insisting, without furnishing any evidence, that

"...there are between 5,000 and 36,000 changes, depending upon which version you use...Like magic, 81 corrupt versions appear on the market today. Some of you ignorantly accept these imposters just because it says 'Bible' on the cover. Whoever said you can't judge a book by its cover could have been speaking of these so-called Bibles..."

The writer condemns harshly. But, he did raise a question which needed to be addressed by someone: is there a correct version of the Bible?

The language of the KJV is beautiful, and enjoys a special reverence all its own. The NIV, in my humble opinion, duplicates the meaning of the original text better than any other version, followed closely by both the NASB and the NKJV. The *Amplified Bible,* as its name implies, amplifies and expounds the meanings of key words and gives the reader a fuller understanding of what is being said, much like a thesaurus. *The Living Bible,* because of its simple text, currently outsells all other versions.

What is the best version? The one which best encourages the Christian to read the Word of God is the best version for that believer. There is only one Bible. Thirty-nine of its books were written in Hebrew, and twenty-six of them were written in Greek. One book, Luke, and a small portion of another, Daniel, were written in Aramaic. All translations and paraphrased versions came either from the original Bible, or were interpolated from one or more of the earlier versions.

Which quite naturally leads us to this question: what percentage of the most popular translation, the KJV, is dependent on previous translations rather than on the original text? In the Old Testament, 4% of the KJV text is the exact language of the *Wycliffe Bible;* 18% came directly from the *Tyndale Bible;* 13% came from the *Coverdale Bible;* 19% came from the *Geneva Bible;* 4% from the *Bishop's Bible;* and 3% came from other lesser known versions. Only 39% of the KJV text came from the original Hebrew text.

Approximately 85% of the New Testament was taken, word for word, from the *Tyndale Bible.* The remaining 15% came from the other versions in existence at the time. The original Greek text did not arrive in England until 1628, seventeen years after the *King James Version* was completed.

Was Mary, the mother of Jesus, a perpetual virgin?

Although the question appears to be clearly answered in Matthew 13:55 and Mark 6:3, it is a question which is much harder to answer than it appears on the surface. Centuries of Roman Catholic dogma has fostered the notion that Mary remained a virgin, and thereby sinless, throughout her life.

Adherents of this position maintain the brethren named in Matthew 13:55 and Mark 6:3 are not sons of Mary, but rather, are the sons of Joseph by a previous marriage. This argument falters when the word brethren is examined in the Greek text. Brethren, as used in Matthew 13:55, is *adelphos.* Used in this text, *adelphos* quite literally means *male children of the same mother.* Others adherents of the perpetual virgin status argue that brethren, as used in both verses, does not refer to blood relatives at all, but rather, speaks of the *brotherhood* of Jesus Christ. If that was indeed so, *adelphotes* rather than *adelphos* would more likely have been used, since *adelphotes* specifically means brotherhood.

The brethren referred to in Matthew 13:55 and Mark 6:3 (James, Joseph, Simon and Judas) were the half-brothers of Jesus, born after the birth of Christ to Mary and Joseph. James, after the ascension, became the leader of the Christian Church. James, who witnessed much of Christ's earthly ministry with skepticism, became a believer only upon the resurrection, when Jesus appeared before him (1 Cor. 15:7) in Galilee. From that moment he believed and became the recognized leader of the Church until he was stoned to death in 62 A.D.

Does the Bible forbid abortion?

The word of God impresses upon us that we are all living souls from the moment of conception. In Psalm 139:15-16, David wrote:

"My substance was not hidden from Thee when I was made in secret, and intricately wrought in the lowest parts of the earth. Thine eyes did see my substance yet being unformed; and in Thy book all my members were written, which in continuance were fashioned, when as yet there was none of them." (KJV)

God told Jeremiah,

> *"Before I formed thee in the womb, I knew thee, and before thou camest forth from the womb, I sanctified thee, and I ordained thee a prophet unto the nations."* (Jer. 1:5; KJV)

These two verses are so profound, I am almost at a loss for words when I contemplate their significance. Yet, I would venture that neither would sway anyone contemplating the sin of abortion. They are, after all, only words; and, not words of condemnation. To fully appreciate these words, you must look past them at the time when they were penned.

The world of science has provided us with an array of knowledge about our universe and about ourselves. With the aid of science we may now look inside the womb and see the life which grows from an unformed fetal state into a tiny human being that contains both arms and legs. Upon each arm, we expect to find a hand with five fingers; and upon each leg, a foot with five toes. Science has provided us with a wealth of information on how the fetus develops from the moment of conception. This was, however, knowledge unknown in David's day. David, without an anointing from God, would not know he was, at conception, unformed. He would have most likely thought he was initially a very tiny, perfectly formed human being. However, he could not possibly know his substance lacked human form without supernatural knowledge to pen those words.

The same is true of Jeremiah. He would have no knowledge that the body needed to be formed. He, like David, would logically believe, at conception, a perfectly formed body existed within the womb. In the case of Jeremiah, God acknowledged a personal relationship with the prophet from the moment of conception. Before his birth, God sanctified Jeremiah and ordained him as a prophet. God did this because, at the moment of conception, He recognized Jeremiah as a person—a human being. It goes without saying that God would not sanctify and ordain something which was not human. Therefore, God, the creator of all life, affirms the personhood of those within the womb.

For those who would dispute God's personal relationship with the fetal Jeremiah, we need look no farther than the Word of God. The word God used to describe his foreknowledge of Jeremiah in verse 5 is *yada. Yada* implies more than knowledge in an intellectual sense. *Yada* denotes a close, personal relationship such as that found between husband and wife, mother and daughter, or father and son.

In Luke 1:15 God shows Himself as having a personal relationship with yet another infant within the womb: John the Baptist. He declared in that instance that He would fill fetal John with the Holy Spirit. It goes without saying that if John was not a person in the eyes of God at that moment (during the sixth month of Elizabeth's pregnancy) (1:26, 36), the Holy Spirit could not have entered into him (1:40-44).

The medical community has never denied the infant who is being destroyed by the abortionist's instruments of murder, is, or more appropriately, was, a person. That has never been an issue. The issue has always been centered around viability: at what stage of development can the infant survive without the maternal lifeline. Yet, whenever it was a legal issue, the matter of viability became clouded.

In September, 1970, *The Journal of California Medicine* carried the following admonition: "The process of eroding the old ethic and substituting the new has already begun. It may be seen most clearly in changing attitudes toward human abortion. In defiance of the long held Western ethic of intrinsic and equal value for every human life regardless of its stage, condition or status, abortion is becoming accepted by society as moral, right and even necessary. It is worth noting that this shift in public attitude has affected the churches, the laws, and public policy rather than the reverse. Since the old ethic has not yet been fully displaced it has been necessary to separate the idea of abortion from the idea of killing, which continues to be socially abhorrent. The result has been an avoidance of scientific fact, which everyone knows, that human life begins at conception and is continuous whether intra- or extrauterine until death."

In other words, the medical community, while acknowledging that life begins at conception, suggested some two and a half years before the United States Supreme Court rendered its infamous *Roe v. Wade/Doe v. Bolton* decision, that public attitude would eventually overwhelm the thinking of the high court—providing a more palatable, politically correct name could be assigned to the act of murder. When the matter finally found itself before the Supreme Court, the issue was somehow no longer centered on life, but on the question of personal liberty.

The medical community, so vocal only two years earlier in their opinion of when life began, was suddenly mute on the subject. Seven old men, with no expertise in medicine, made a human life decision based on personal liberty—a point of law each understood. Their experience with human life had previously centered around legality: who can file, or defend, a legal action. Since the unborn required a surrogate, usually the mother or father, the unborn had, in their opinion, no legal standing. In their view, since an infant could not survive on its own until late in the third trimester, it could not be afforded legal rights until that time. Once that question of legal rights was settled in their mind, all that remained undecided was the issue of a woman's right to privacy—from her own unborn child!

On January 22, 1973, the United States Supreme Court decided an infant was not a defendable human being, and granted unrestricted first trimester abortion rights to the mother. States, according to the *Roe v. Wade* decision, as it has come to be known, could pass regulations governing second trimester abortions;

and they could prohibit third trimester abortions completely. The high court's initial legal opinion has since been modified. Abortion became such an unbelievable profit center for this new industry, a concerted effort was undertaken by some very expensive legal teams hired by abortion advocates like Planned Parenthood to contest every anti-abortion law in the land. Today lobbyists for the highly profitable abortion industry have successfully formulated a public stance that abortions are politically correct until the umbilical cord is cut. As a result of this lobbying effort, the Supreme Court curbed the rights of the States to either restrict or prohibit abortions at any time, up to and including birth! The Supreme Court has heard several challenges from abortion foes, but it has steadfastly defended its original position—a position which has already sanctioned the killing of more than 36,000,000 babies in the United States alone.

Although the high court has been reluctant to abrogate a woman's right to kill the life within her at any stage of development, up to and including the moment of birth, lower courts over the past 26 years have not hesitated to protect the rights of the unborn when petitions seeking that protection reach them. In many instances, pregnant women have successfully sued for paternity, with the courts quickly recognizing the rights of the unborn—at any stage of prenatal development! A fetus, according to federal law, can inherit an estate, or sue for injuries sustained within the womb. In federal court the fetus has every legal right of any other living person, except the uncontested right to life! It has been only in the state courts where the unwanted unborn has a chance to live, providing the baby has escaped a saline bath or the abortionist's scalpel for the first six months of life.

In an unprecedented landmark decision, the South Carolina Supreme Court ruled 3-2, on July 15, 1996, that a viable fetus is a person, and that a pregnant woman can be held criminally liable for endangering the health of that living person. The action before the court tested a 1984 law which allows South Carolina prosecutors to charge those involved with the injuring or killing of a woman's viable fetus—including both the physician who performs a third trimester abortion and the mother-to-be who permits it. In this particular instance, the petitioner before the court was a woman, Cornelia Whitner, who was arrested and tried for child abuse when her newborn son tested positive for cocaine. Whitner was found guilty and was sentenced to eight years in prison. Interestingly, when Whitner's case went to the state Supreme Court, the American Medical Association, the National Association for Families and Addiction Research and Education—and, as might be expected, the American College of Obstetricians and Gynecologists—filed briefs on Whitner's behalf. It is likely this case, with added support from the Center for Reproductive Law and Policy and Planned Parenthood, will eventually end up in the U.S. Supreme Court where the high court will be forced to address the issue from a perspective other than the personal liberty of the mother. Inasmuch as this law, if upheld by the highest appellate court in the land, could either reverse *Roe v. Wade* or greatly restrict the slaughter of America's future generations, it will be heatedly contested by abortion advocates and feminist groups.

It is obvious that a bizarre double standard exists. The medical community and the legal profession, when it suits their purpose, are quick to acknowledge, and, are even able to prove, that life begins at conception. Yet those who advocate a woman's right to an abortion are never challenged when they define life as beginning at the moment of live birth. Twenty years ago life was defined as beginning at the point when the infant could survive outside the womb. With all of our medical advances in the area of neonatal medicine, life is now defined as viable some four months earlier than it was when *Roe v. Wade* became the law of the land. Because of that, viability is no longer an acceptable yardstick by which the issue is measured. Today abortion is promoted as a personal liberty issue, with only the right of the mother to deny life to her child being considered.

To the justices of the high court who wrote their flawed decision into law, to the lawyers who argue a woman's right to kill her unborn, to the abortionist who murders a life which God granted, and to the woman who becomes a willing accomplice to that murder because she wanted a boy instead of a girl, or because she just wasn't ready to be tied down, God—the Ultimate Judge—defines life as that instant when body, soul and spirit come together within the womb. This union occurs at conception!

How does God, the Ultimate Judge of mankind, address the question of abortion? Quite simply, and in four single syllable words: *thou shalt not kill* (Ex. 20:13; Dt. 5:17; Mk. 10:9; Rom. 13:9; Jas. 2:11).

Does the Bible forbid cremation?

In the pre-church age the Jews were taught that cremation *(se'rephah,* the disposal of human corpses by fire) desecrated the handiwork of God. The practice of cremation was commonly observed in most parts of the world, dating back to the Stone Age. The Gentiles in the Middle East practiced cremation by burning *(se'raph)* the corpses of their loved ones on funeral pyres, much like the one upon which Indira Pryadarshiini Ghandi (1917-84), the assassinated Indian prime minister, was publicly cremated in a televised state funeral. The ashes of the deceased are collected, and either interred or scattered—depending, in many cases, on religious custom or dogma.

In the Hindu religion cremation is used almost exclusively. In Judaism it is strictly forbidden; and only recently was cremation approved by the Roman Catholic Church. As a mode of final disposal, cremation is practiced in most countries of the world, and is considered more acceptable in the Western world than in the East. However, in the United States, whose religious customs stem largely from Judaism, it is statistically rare. Most of those in America who desire to have their remains cremated are either atheists or agnostics. Rarely will a born-again Christian be cremated.

The Jewish *Mishnah* (the oral law), expressly forbids the practice of cremation, citing authority from Genesis 3:19 and Deuternomy 21:23. The ban against cremation is further strengthened in the eyes of the Jews by divine example. God buried Moses in a valley near Bath-Por in Moab (Dt. 34:5-6). Lying unburied symbolizes God's disapproval of the individual at the time of his or her death. When Abijah, the son of Jeroboam fell sick, Jeroboam sent his wife to Ahijah the prophet to see if Abijah would recover from his illness. Through Ahijah, God said,

> *"Dogs will eat those belonging to Jeroboam who die in the city, and the birds of the air will feed on those who die in the country. The Lord has spoken. As for you, go back home. When you set foot in your city, the boy will die. All Israel will mourn him and bury him. He is the only one belonging to Jeroboam who will be buried, because he is the only one in the house of Jeroboam in whom the Lord, the God of Israel, has found anything good."*
> (1 Ki. 14:11-13; NIV)

On one hand, God decreed that because Jeroboam, to whom He had entrusted the ten northern tribes of Israel, had led the Jews astray (1 Ki. 12:25-33) and caused them to sin, none of his household would be buried. Their flesh would be food for scavengers. It was a sign of God's utter contempt of Jeroboam. On the other hand, because Abijah, the son of Jeroboam, had personally found favor in the eyes of God, he would be accorded the right of burial (1 Ki. 14:14) under the law.

The early Church also forbade the practice of cremation. Early Church leaders believed that if the individual's body was utterly destroyed by fire, it could not be resurrected. It must be pointed out there is no scriptural basis for this belief. The Bible tells us when we die, our bodies will return to the dust from which it originated (Gen. 2:7, 3:19; Job 10:9, 30:19; Ps. 103:14, 104:29; Ecc. 3:20).

> *"All flesh shall perish together, and man shall turn again unto dust."*
> (Job. 34:15; KJV)
>
> *"Then shall the dust return to the earth as it was; and the spirit shall return unto God, who gave it."*
> (Ecc. 12:7; KJV)

We are made up of a natural body which is flesh, and a spiritual body, which is our soul (1 Cor. 15:44). When we become absent from the body, we will immediately be present before the Lord in our spiritual dwelling, which is our soul (1 Cor. 5:3). If you are away from your home, and it burns to the ground, you do not suffer death. The cremation of our physical bodies, our dwelling place, will not in any way affect our spirit body, which is, in reality, our life. Our soul is eternal; our human bodies are temporal.

Why then, does the Church frown on cremation? Because of its symbolic implications. While fire was used to burn incense *(qa'tar)* unto the Lord, and to utterly consume the burnt offering *(sa'raph),* fire is also the means by which God will destroy those who have unrequited sin (Dt. 7:7, 7:25, 12:3, 32:22; Josh. 7:15; 2 Sam. 23:7; 2 Ki. 23:20; 1 Ch. 14:12; Ps. 106:18, 140:10; Isa. 1:31, 9:18, 10:17, 32:12-14, 47:12-14; Jer. 4:4, 7:20, 21:10, 21:14, 32:29, 43:13; Ezek. 5:4, 20:47; Mic. 1:7; Mal. 4:1; Mt. 3:12, 13:30, 13:40; Lk. 3:17; Jn. 15:6; Heb. 6:8; 2 Pe. 3:10; Rev. 17:16, 18:8, 21:8). Symbolically, being spared from the fire is a sign of divine grace, as in Isaiah 43:2-3 and Amos 4:11.

Cremation is without a doubt pagan in origin. The one being cremated becomes a sacrifice to his or her god or gods. Manasseh (2 Ki. 21; 2 Ch. 33) reigned over Judah for 55 years and worshipped the pagan god Molech. Manasseh set up altars to Molech in both courts of the Temple as well as a place of sacrifice outside the East Gate of the city. Children were sacrificed to Molech from the East Gate by being thrown alive into the fire at the base of the altar. The bodies of those cremated were offered as an atonement for the sins of the idol worshippers. If the person's station in life was great enough, such as Indira Ghandi, the one cremated is offered as an atonement for the sins of his or her loyal followers. It is interesting how the counterfeiter mocks the sacrifice of Jesus Christ.

We are admonished in our Christian walk to present ourselves as living sacrifices, holy and acceptable to God, for reasonable service in His army. Our propitiation, our sacrifice, is not of ourselves or our loved ones. Our sacrifice is Jesus Christ. Our deaths will atone for nothing; not our sins, nor the sins of our families. Likewise, the method of our burial means nothing either. Whether we are buried, lie uninterred until wild animals and birds of prey strip the flesh from our bones, or we are cremated, means absolutely nothing. If we accepted Jesus Christ as our Lord and Savior, we will be with Him in Heaven. If we did not, our souls will burn in Hell. When everything is said and done, we will probably all agree that Job put it best:

> *"And though after my skin worms destroy this body, yet in my flesh shall I see God. Whom I shall see for myself, and mine eyes shall behold, and not another, though my heart be consumed within me."* (Job 19:26-27; KJV)

Does the Bible forbid divorce and remarriage?

How does the Bible address the question of divorce and remarriage? Does the Word of God expressly forbid divorce? Or, is divorce allowed, but remarriage not? Does the Word of God either allow or command the Church to excommunicate or disenfranchise believers who divorce and remarry?

It is not uncommon for churches in today's society to welcome paroled murderers, former drug dealers, and white collar thieves into their pulpits to testify what God has done to change their lives. The shelves of Christian bookstores are filled with bestselling titles bearing their names, their crimes, and their Christian witness. Yet to many in the church a divorce and subsequent remarriage is a crime worse than murder, and many Christians would more readily welcome the repentant murderer, a person whom they view as one whose sin is forgiven, than the remarried divorcee whose sin, they believe, is being renewed daily. The remarried man, in most congregations, is allowed to fellowship, but cannot assume any position of authority or leadership within the body.

The question of divorce and remarriage is not a new one. It was raised by the Pharisees to Jesus in Perea (on the Judean side of the Jordan River). Judea was governed by Herod Antipas who was involved in an incestuous marriage with Herodias, the legitimate wife of his half-brother, Phillip (Mt. 14:6; Mk. 6:17-18). It is likely that the Pharisees hoped Jesus, like John the Baptist before Him, would incur the wrath of Herod, be arrested and suffer a fate similar to that of the Baptist's (Mk. 7:17-18), solving their problem of how to deal with Christ's growing popularity among the people of Galilee.

At the very least, the Pharisees hoped to split the followers of Jesus over the issue. In the matter of divorce, half of the Galilean Jews ascribed to the view of Rabbi Hillel (who, like Jesus, was a direct descendent of David), and the balance to the more strict views of Rabbi Shammai. Hillel taught that a Jewish man could divorce his wife for almost any reason (*Mishnah, Gitten* 1.1-3, 4.7, 7.2, 9.10; *Sotah* 1.4-5) that suited him: if she was too slow, if she burned his meals, if she talked too much, or even if he suddenly fancied another woman. Shammai, on the other hand, insisted that a man could divorce his wife only if she did something immoral (*Mishnah, Eduyoth* 4.7-10).

In either school of thought, adultery was a crime punishable by death according to the Law (Lev. 20:10; Nbr. 5:11-31; Dt. 22:22-25). Adultery, only in the betrothal stage of marriage, was cause for divorce. Even then, the young woman risked stoning. If her espoused was greatly angered and jealously demanded vengeance, his espoused wife would then be stoned to death. Neither Hillel nor Shammai believed a woman had any legal right to sue her husband for divorce for any reason. Divorce was exclusively a man's prerogative.

When the Pharisees brought the adulterous woman to Jesus (Jn. 8:2), they did so believing they would successfully trap him (Jn. 8:6) once and for all. If Jesus took the more liberal view of Hillel, he would risk losing those followers who ascribed to views of Shammai. If He denied man's unqualified right to divorce on any ground, He would lose those followers who held Hillel's view. Also, if Christ failed to agree with the Pharisees that the woman should be stoned, they would have legal grounds to accuse Him of teaching a point of view contrary to the Scriptures. Had Jesus agreed with their verdict, it is likely they would have stoned the woman to death on the spot, and then reported Christ to the Romans as the person responsible for the incident. Roman law, and its penalty system, superseded all Jewish law in Israel as early as 30 B.C. Since the Romans were more liberal in their view of sex, their laws dealing with immorality were much more lenient. And while stoning was commonly practiced in the first century, A.D., it was illegal under Roman law if it was an independent action on the part of the Jews.

It should be noted that God recognizes marriage as a permanent union.

> *"So they are no longer two, but one. Therefore, what God has joined together, let man not separate."*
> (Mt. 19:6; NIV)
>
> *"You were united to your wife by the Lord. In God's wise plan, when the two of you were married, the two of you became one person in His sight...Keep faith with the wife of your covenant. For the Lord, the God of Israel, says He hates divorce and cruel men. Therefore, control your passions—let there be no divorcing of your wives."*
> (Mal. 2:15-16; LB)

Marriage has become a totally human establishment, governed not by the laws of God, but rather by the whims of man. In the United States today, 125 out of every 500 marriages in the population at risk (i.e., those currently living in a marital relationship) will end in divorce—and the divorce rate in America is on an upward spiral. As astounding as the figure is, published statistics indicate that 54% of the adult men and women in the United States have experienced at least one divorce.

The most publicized causes of divorce today are adultery and spousal abuse, although the courts generally recognize eight conditions which were grounds for divorce—the least of which is *no fault,* a vague term which simply means the marital partners just don't get along. The sacrament of marriage was intended to be a permanent, heterosexual (Mt. 19:4-5), lifetime union. The marriage covenant between a man and a woman typifies the covenant relationship between Jesus Christ and the church. In Ephesians 5:31 Paul cites Genesis 2:24 with this spiritual declaration:

> *"This is a great mystery...* (i.e., Mt. 13:11-12) *...but I speak concerning Christ and the church."*

Eve, bone of Adam's bones and flesh of his flesh, was also Adam's wife. In Adam, we see a *type* of Christ; and, in the woman, a *type* of the Church which came out of Christ's flesh (Hos. 2:2, 2:19-23; Jn. 3:29; 2 Cor. 11:12; Eph. 5:25-32; Rev. 19:6-9). In Matthew 19:4-5 Jesus affirms that God made man a man and woman a woman for the express purpose of marriage.

> *"For this cause...* (marriage) *...shall a man leave father and mother, and they two shall become one."*

We are God's creation. We came from Him. As the Church, we are returned to Him, a chaste virgin, in wedlock (2 Cor. 11:2):

> *"For we are members of His body, of His flesh, and of His bones."* (Eph. 5:30; KJV)

Two made into one flesh: Christ and the Church!

Because the marriage covenant typifies Christ and the Church, it must be viewed as a permanent union since God's covenant with the Church is permanent. The Church is the Bride of Christ. The dowry, His shed blood, was paid when Jesus went to the cross. The marriage will be consummated at the end of the age in Heaven, just prior to the Battle of Armageddon (Rev. 19:7-16). The covenant relationship between Christ and the Church is irrevocable. There is no divorce clause beyond the betrothal.

As we examine the spiritual nature of the marriage between Jesus and His bride, we can also see the attributes of the human marriage as well. They are precisely the same. In Matthew 19:9, Jesus said:

> *"Whosoever shall put away his wife except it be for fornication (porneia), and shall marry another committeth adultery (moichao); and whosoever marrieth her who is put away doth commit adultery."*

The *except* clause in verse nine is not a divine precept. Rather, it was inserted by Jesus due to the hardness of man's heart, and because of his unforgiving nature (Mt. 19:8; Mk. 10:5). Divorce is not, nor never was, part of God's grand plan for mankind.

When Jesus addressed the Pharisees at Perea concerning divorce, He spoke in terms of the marriage custom of the day. The first century Jew was, as I have already said, considered to be married from the moment of the signing of the marriage contract (i.e., the engagement). The betrothal was for an unspecified period of time, determined by the father of the groom. It was usually a period of at least twelve months. This was more than sufficient to determine if the bride was pregnant at the time of the betrothal. In the event the bride was found to be with child, she would be quietly put away, or stoned to death, and the matter ended.

It was during the betrothal period (Lk. 2:5) that Mary, the mother of Jesus, was found to be with child (Mt. 1:18-25; Lk. 1:26-35). Had he wanted to, Joseph could have legally put her away, or publicly accused her of adultery. If he had accused her before the court of the Sanhedrin, she would have been stoned to death (Dt. 22:12-20). If he divorced her without providing a writ of divorce (which, under those circumstances, he could not), she would have been disgraced for the balance of her life. No reputable Jew could have ever married her.

It is clear from the response of Christ's disciples in Matthew 19:10, "...if the case of man be so with his wife, it is not good to marry..." that they understood the divorce Jesus spoke of could take place only during the betrothal. Further, they realized Jesus was telling them that if the unfaithfulness of the wife was not discovered, or did not occur until after the marriage was consummated, the husband would be inseparably yoked to the unfaithful wife for life. Because of that, they concluded, it would be better not to marry.

> *"And unto the married: Let not the wife depart from her husband; but if she does, let her remain unmarried...and let not the husband put his wife away."* (1 Cor. 7:10-11; KJV)

Are there any circumstances under which God allows divorce and remarriage? There appears to be only two such sets of circumstances in the entire New Testament.

Paul addressed one issue with the Corinthians. Apparently many of the Christians living in Corinth were unequally yoked (2 Cor. 6:14) with unbelievers. Paul starts his narrative by affirming that a marriage between a Christian and a non-Christian was no different in the eyes of God than a marriage between two Christians. The Christian, Paul declared, could not leave the non-Christian (1 Cor. 7:13-14) because the non-Christian is sanctified by the believer. He continues by saying, in the event the believer, for any reason, does leave, he or she may not remarry. It is the responsibility of the Christian to make every attempt at reconciliation. It is only when we come to verse fifteen that we find an exemption that would allow a divorced Christian to remarry:

> *"If the unbeliever departs, let him depart...* (the spouse) *...is not under bondage...* (to the marriage vow) *...in such cases."*

Exactly what does that statement mean? It means that when an unbelieving partner breaks the marriage vow, the Christian is held blameless and may act as though the marriage had never taken place. In this instance the Christian is then free to remarry.

Scripture assumes that all men and women who make vows before God are knowledgeable of the Lord, are responsible to Him for their actions, and have determined to perform that which they promise Him. The unbeliever does not know God, and has no understanding of the nature of the vows made to Him (Nbr. 30:1-13; Ecc. 5:4-5; Mt. 13:10-17; Lk. 12:47-48; Jn. 9:41; 1 Tim. 1:12-13). The Word further tells us that God will still hold that person responsible for the vow which he made, but only to the extent of his understanding. We see from 1 Corinthians 7:15 that the innocent party is released from the pledge. The vow, which made God party to the promise, is dissolved, and the innocent party is free.

The institution of marriage in the United States is based on a combination of Judaism and both Roman and English law. The Jewish union was formalized with a legal ceremony. In first century Roman society, a man and woman formed a common law bond, without any legal formalities. Under Jewish law a woman could not file for divorce, but could remarry if her husband divorced her and provided her with a writ of divorce. Under Roman law either party could end the marriage simply by sending a letter of intent to the other party. Under English law grounds for divorce are established by the state through legislation.

The early Christian emperors of Rome brought marriage and divorce under the authority of civil law, and matters of divorce were settled in the courts. Justinian I, the sixth century lawgiver, attempted to restore the biblical concept of divorce, the view of the Roman Catholic Church, through the canon of Roman law, but was forced, because of public protest, to retreat from this position. The view of the Catholic Church, like that of Judaism, was that marriages were indissoluble based on Matthew 19:6: "What God has put together, let not man put asunder".

When Martin Luther broke away from the Catholic Church, he and other Protestants adopted a more liberal position, based largely on Luther's personal views. Luther believed that marriage, as a worldly commitment, was subject to secular, not religious, jurisdiction. Divorce, in most Protestant faiths, was allowed on the grounds of adultery, cruelty or desertion. It was over the issue of divorce which caused Henry the VIII to break from the Catholic Church and form the Church of England, naming himself its head in 1534. Thomas Cranmer, to secure the coveted position of Archbishop of Canterbury, agreed to nullify Henry's marriage to the first of his six wives. The Catholic Church excommunicated Henry in 1532, shortly after his marriage to Ann Boleyn. As the head of the Church of England, Henry VIII decreed that issues concerning divorce would be decided not in the civil courts of the land, but by Parliament. The House of Lords handled those matters until 1857.

Early settlers in America brought with them three views of divorce: the Catholic view that marriage was a godly sacrament from which there was no escape; the Protestant view that marriage was a secular institution, and that divorce was a matter for civil authorities; and the English view that divorce was a legislative matter that could be resolved through laws which established legal guidelines for the dissolution of marriage. The view that prevailed depended largely upon the colony in which the issued was raised. Virginia and Maryland, being predominantly Catholic, as well as most of the Southern colonies, did not recognize divorce. Massachusetts believed divorce was a legislative issue, and established seven grounds upon which divorce would be granted. These grounds became the basis of precedent for legal arguments in the courts of the various states as the fledgling colonies became a nation.

On several occasions over the past 100 years, lawmakers have attempted to enact federal legislation to establish uniform divorce laws. However since the Constitution clearly grants this right only to the states, those efforts have thus far failed. On at least two occasions, feminist efforts were launched to amend the Constitution to allow Congress to regulate divorce, an effort aimed primarily at the collection of alimony and child support payments. Those efforts failed as well. Recently, however, legislation was passed at the federal level which permits both state and federal governments to seize income tax refunds when state-initiated child support payments are in default. Most states now have reciprocal *deadbeat dad* laws which provide for the incarceration of those delinquent in either child support or alimony payments.

Attitudes about the institution of marriage and divorce have changed dramatically not only in this country, but in most Western nations as well. As society became more urban in character, it likewise became more secular in its perspective on life and the value system which contributes to the quality of that life. Beginning in the mid-sixties, humanism slowly supplanted Christianity as the religious foundation of law in America. Judicial opinions, which had previously been deeply rooted in family values, were suddenly more frequently based on the utopian principle of political correctness. The rights of the individual superseded the rights of society. However, the rights of society never seem to supersede the rights of the government. This new mindset, which has all but precluded God's tenets from consideration, now make it easier for couples to divorce without any stigma being attached to either the divorce or the remarriage. In fact, humanism has taken root so completely in our society that all of the sins of Sodom and Gomorrah, including homosexual marriages, have become, at least from a civil rights perspective, legally tolerated. Hawaii was expected to vote on legislation during the late summer or fall of 1996 which would legally sanction homosexual marriages, and afford those unions all of the legal rights accorded to traditional heterosexual marriages.

It is this attitude, combined with Big Brother's welfare system, which has led to the disintegration of the social structure of the United States. Although liberal statisticians vehemently deny it, the United States has the highest rate of divorce in the industrialized world—with at least 54% of the adult population having experienced divorce at least once.

Liberal statisticians prefer to make their comparison based on the population at risk, which ignores all elements of the population which are not currently married—simply because they are not currently married. The fact that they may be divorced does not enter into their consideration since they are only compiling data on those who are currently at risk of divorce. Looking at the population at risk, the divorce rate in the United States is 123 per 1,000 population. More accurately stated, the liberal's conservative estimate is that 123 out of every 500 new or existing marriages will ultimately end in divorce, a figure which suggests a divorce rate of 25%. However, a Harvard University Press study, published in 1989, projects a divorce rate of 67% in couples who married between 1980 and 1989.

The primary problem Christianity faces today with respect to divorce is the changing morality of a world society that has all but abrogated the role of God in the determination of right and wrong. The last society to do this was Sodom. God destroyed Sodom. Many of the issues which have become dilemmas for Christians are a direct result of this changing morality with liberal views concerning abortion, sexual promiscuity, homosexuality and divorce. However, although our politically correct liberal society has adjusted its ethics to make allowances for the new morality of humanism, the Word of God has not changed. That which was sin remains sin. That which was morally wrong remains morally wrong.

Marriage, under Mosaic law, was a covenant. While the Arab could divorce his wife with the spoken word, the Law of Moses required the husband to provide his wife with a writ of divorce (Dt. 24:1), in all cases except adultery, which spelled out the reasons for the divorce. This writ allowed the wife to remarry. Adultery was always punishable by death. The prophet Malachi condemned divorce, and severely rebuked those who practiced it (Mal. 2:14-16). Jesus eliminated all grounds for divorce under the Law with the single exception of adultery, which allowed remarriage only during the betrothal stage of the union, before the marriage was consummated. The Apostle Paul established only one criteria for the remarriage of the believer, and that was in the event the divorced spouse was a nonbeliever and the divorce was initiated by that person.

Does a remarried divorced person renew his or her sin each time the marriage is consummated? Many Christians view remarriage after divorce as a form of the unforgivable sin, which it is not. The unforgivable sin is a singular act, blasphemy of the Holy Spirit (attributing to Satan that which is accomplished by the Holy Spirit).

Although remarriage after divorce is not the unforgivable sin, it is a perpetual sin in the sense that each time the sexual act is committed by the marriage partners, they both commit adultery. If divorce could, in the eyes of God, dissolve the marriage, then, needless to say, sexual acts performed within the sanctity of that marriage would not be sin. However, since Christ proclaimed immorality, the marital unfaithfulness of one spouse, as the only legitimate grounds for divorce, we must assume that without such grounds, the first marriage must be construed as continually valid in the eyes of God. Additionally, according to Paul, if a couple is unequally yoked, and the nonbeliever breaks the marriage covenant for whatever reason, the marriage is deemed to have not occurred. Then and only then is the believer free to remarry.

Most pastors, even those holding the view that only unequalled yoked people can remarry under the circumstances put forth above, cite as evidence against remarriage, John 4:16-18. The conclusion is correct, the premise is not.

When Jesus told the Samaritan woman at the well

> *"You are right when you say you have no husband. The fact is, you have had five husbands, and the man you now have is not your husband. What you have just said is quite true."*
> (Jn. 4:18; NIV)

He was not suggesting that she was married, in a legal sense, to a sixth husband, and that marriage, like four of her other five, was not viewed as valid by God. The Samaritan woman was not married, in any sense, to the man with whom she was living. She was embarrassed by the fact that she was living in sin with a man to whom she was not married. Jewish law reasonably permitted that a divorced woman might remarry once or twice or, at the most, three times. Since the Samaritans were representative of those Jews not taken into the Assyrian captivity, it is likely that Samaritan customs would have been quite similar to the Jews. As such, it is logical to assume the Samaritan woman had stretched the limits of the law with respect to matrimony and, probably for that reason, she was not married to the man with whom she was living.

Christ's comment that she was not married to the sixth man was a statement of pure and simple fact. She wasn't. Had she been either ritualistically or legally married to the man with whom she was currently living, even under those circumstances, Christ's statement that she was not married would have been met with resistance. Instead, she concurred with Christ's assessment of her relationship with the man with whom she was living.

Jesus was not, in John 4:17-18, laying the ground rules for the presbyter to use in declaring remarriage after divorce nonexistent, although from other passages already cited we know that to be true. The purpose for His observations about the Samaritan woman was not to chide or condemn her for multiple marriages, but to reveal who He was, and to offer the Samaritans in Sychar the opportunity to receive eternal life.

Marriage, in the eyes of God, is a permanent union between a man and a woman. The vows spoken between each other constitute a vow made to God. We are cautioned in Scripture not to break vows made to God since they could have dire consequences. It is for this reason that common law marriage, marital commitments between two people with God as their only witness, are recognized as equally binding as those officiated by an ordained minister of God in many States. Marriage is a divine precept, with the rules established by God to propagate the human race. It does not matter if the marriage vows are spoken before a priest, a minister, a rabbi or a magistrate. The ritual is ceremonial, pretty much the way baptism is ceremonial of the *born-again* experience. The marriage vow, performed before man, is a permanent commitment before God. Even if we attempt to preclude any mention of God in the marriage vow by acknowledging the supremacy of the State alone to sanctify it, every marriage must be sanctified by God—if for no other reason than the fact that God alone possesses the tally sheet from which mankind will ultimately be judged.

EPILOGUE

IN CONCLUSION

Here we are, finally, at the end. The end of this book, the end of the age—*the times of the Gentiles*—and close to end of humanity as it is known by man. Before us lies the uncertainty of uncertain times. I have endeavored, with the assistance of the Holy Spirit, to provide you with much of the information you will require, and perhaps have even asked, to make informed decisions about your journey into that future and, at some as yet unknown time down the road, into eternity.

Humanism awaits the 21st century with utopian anticipation. It is, after all, the world humanism has carefully molded and shaped over the past eighty years. Early in the 20th century, the humanist judiciously planted the seeds of its secular ideology, knowing those seeds would slowly take root and grow, almost without notice, until the philosophical maze it created beneath the surface of civilization could spring forth and blossom, influencing every aspect of human thinking. Humanism, the philosophy of Sodom and Gomorrah now controls the thinking of man to such a degree that it cannot be eradicated from society without destroying society as well, which is precisely why an endtime judgment is promised to all the nations of the earth.

Man, with all his accumulated wisdom, has returned to the gates of the Garden, but he lacks the ability to enter since, having tasted the apple, mankind has chosen evil instead of good. Man believes the garden beyond the gate is Utopia, where mankind, deliberately blended into a singular nonracial society, will find harmony. However, just beyond the utopian oasis lies a desert. It is the desert of the Arabian peninsula where man's destiny will ultimately bring him to his final conflict.

Mankind can no longer alter its charted course. The die is cast. Those signs which Jesus told the believer to watch for have occurred, or are occurring as you read. The housecleaning of God, promised to begin in the church, has taken place. America, the last bastion of Christianity, whose job it was to evangelize the world—has entered a post-Christian era. Evangelists of the modern church now teach man about a blended God: a non-offensive composite deity which combines man and woman into a genderless, nonessential spirit being representative of all of the gods of Earth's contemporary societies.

It is, and has always been, the agenda of the United Nations and before it, the League of Nations, to create the perfect, utopian society. Utopia can be accomplished only if (1) all races are blended into one multiracial culture, (2) there is no economic diversity among mankind, (3) there is no political diversity among the peoples of the world, and (4) the population of the Earth does not exceed its ability to feed itself. The UN, like the League of Nations before it, was specifically chartered to obtain that objective: Utopia. A world without war. A world in which all men would live as brothers. A classless society in which all men would indeed be equal—their efforts notwithstanding.

The agenda of the UN has not evolved in secret. It has simply been ignored by a liberal press which largely agrees with it's utopian view. Those who track the published agenda of the UN, and compare it with the agendas of the various nations of the world, cannot help but notice similitudes of global political correctness, which is a phrase that was created to stifle opposition not only to global blending but to the other radical socialist programs of the UN which would otherwise not be acceptable to a conservative, family oriented population.

Since the mid-eighties, one of the primary concerns of the UN has been the blending of societies through interracial coupling. Interracial relationships are encouraged in the public schools of America, and those who feel uncomfortable with the concept of dating someone of another race are regarded, by definition of political correctness—as racist. Once mankind is sufficiently blended, racism will no longer exist. Racism is, inarguably, a virus which has affected the thinking of man for far too long. All mankind was created equal in the eyes of God, who has never judged man by the color of his skin, only the color of his heart. Skin pigmentation or the shape of the human eye has nothing to do with the measure of an individual; it deals specifically with geographic origins. Nothing more; nothing less. Since racism has been a contributing factor in countless conflicts between men, the elimination of racism was necessarily a priority of the UN.

In June, 1992, the United Nations began to focus, first, on the environment and, then, almost as an afterthought in that conference, population control. Viewing the world as grossly overpopulated, and not satisfied with the rate of abortions occurring in third world countries, the UN held its Conference on Environment & Development, called the Earth Summit, in Rio de Janerio, Brazil. The media largely ignored the abortion issue and instead, focused the world's attention on the rain forests of Brazil, which the liberal press declared were in danger of extinction by encroaching civilization. The agenda of the UN, however, was not simply to protect the rain forests of Brazil, but to establish a mandate by which it could serve as the administrator of worldwide environmental policy, creating and enforcing environmental regulations through the UN Environmental, Scientific and Cultural Organization. Americans praised their efforts to protect the rain forests of Brazil, largely because the UN's intrusion was focused on another country.

However, in September, 1995, members of the World Heritage Committee, a bureau of that same UN agency, visited Yellowstone National Park in Montana at the request of the Clinton Administration, to decide whether or not the New World Mine, a gold mine located outside of Yellowstone, should be reopened. The UN delegation, accompanied by Clinton's Interior Undersecretary George Frampton, determined reopening the New World mine which, as previously stated, is located outside of the park, would pose a threat to the ecology of Yellowstone. World Heritage committee president Adul Wichiencharoen of Thailand suggested the creation of a 18.2 million acre ecological barrier around the 2.3 million acre National Park to safeguard the habitat's perimeters from encroachment by man. Recreational and economic activities such as mining, logging and ranching, which already existed in the area since families have owned that land long before the park existed, would be forbidden anywhere within the protective perimeter. Even snow mobiling, a popular winter recreational sport in that region, would be banned. In fact, the suggested restrictions even excluded automobile traffic, effectively shutting down the National Park to any visitors except possibly hikers. Such restrictions would, needless to say, completely destroy the economy of that region.

The UN World Conference on Human Rights convened in Vienna, Austria on June 14, 1993 to discuss the concept of world citizenship in what was termed *Agenda 21*, a program establishing the framework of sustainable development, which the Conference concluded could occur only if, and when, the world begins to think of itself not as separate nations, but rather, as the human family. Prior to this conference, United States policy recognized political and civil rights as national in character, based on the laws of those particular nations.

Reversing long-standing U.S. policy, the Clinton Administration, obstensibly to avoid "...a sterile debate at Vienna...," agreed to officially recognize the economic, social and cultural rights of citizens within those third world countries in the name of human rights—the national politics of their respective governments notwithstanding. In doing so, the Clinton Administration altered the very nature of the UN, changing it from the voice of the industrialized nations to a forum for undeveloped third world countries; providing them with an international platform from which to demand international financial assistance so they, like the Western nations which until recently had economically dominated them, could develop their own economies and bring about a slow transfer of wealth from the industrialized nations to the languishing third world societies recently freed from the shackles of colonialism. The redistribution of world wealth is a core geopolitical issue within the UN.

In September, 1994, the UN International Conference on Population & Development was held in Cairo, Egypt. The agenda of the 1992 Earth Summit was expanded to include population control—abortion and a worldwide distribution of condoms. In conjunction with this UN effort, the 103rd Congress of the United States, the first Clinton Congress, enacted *The International Stabilization and Reproductive Health Act* (stemming from S.1096 and H.R. 2447), which amended the *Foreign Assistance Act of 1961,* and provided funds for a worldwide, UN sponsored abortion program, since according to the language of the legislation, there are currently "...three times as many people living on earth than what is sustainable..." In addition, this legislation also funded the Cairo Summit, whose primary theme was population control. (And we thought our only concern dealt with the distribution of condoms in our own public schools.)

The Social Summit, held in Copenhagen, Denmark in March, 1995, expanded on the themes of the three previous summits, adding global poverty, unemployment and social disintegration to their agenda. During this summit, the need for a worldwide tax was openly discussed, and approved, by the participants of the conference. Also, during this summit, the UN was unofficially empowered to create a new global civil society based on the equality of mankind. In this new global society the UN would become the military overseer of the world. Interestingly, it was almost a year earlier, in June 1994, that Clinton signed PDD25—the document considered so Top Secret by the Clinton Administration that it could not be viewed by members of Congress with oversight authority on matters of national security! PDD25, some members of Congress fear, has granted the United Nations limited control over the military forces of the United States.

Additionally, during the 1995 Social Summit, the world social order that was first advanced at the Commission on Global Governance in Stockholm, Sweden in April, 1991, and expanded upon in the UN Human Development Report of 1994, was proposed in the form of an international charter. The proposed charter, contained within the pages of the Human Development Report, reads somewhat like our own Declaration of Independence:

> *"WE THE PEOPLE of the world solemnly pledge to build a new global civil society, based on the principles of equality of opportunity, rule of law, global demographic governance and a new partnership among all nations and all people. We propose to build a society where the right to food is as sacrosanct as the right to vote, where the right to a basic education is as deeply enshrined as the right to a free press and where the right to development is considered one of the fundamental human rights.*
>
> *WE COLLECTIVELY PLEDGE to build new foundations of human security, which ensure the security of people through development, not arms; through cooperation, not confontation; through peace, not war. We believe that no provision in the Charter of the United Nations will ever ensure global security unless people have security in their homes, in their jobs, in their communities, and in their environment. We are fully convinced that diversity in our societies is our strength, not our weakness, and we intend to protect this diversity by ensuring nondiscrimination between all our people, irrespective of gender, race, religion or ethnic origin.*
>
> *WE COLLECTIVELY BELIEVE that our world cannot survive one-fourth rich and three-fourths poor, half democratic, half authoritarian, with oases of human development surrounded by deserts of human deprivation. We pledge to take all necessary actions, nationally and globally, to reverse the present trend of*

widening disparities within and between nations. We are convinced that it is possible to overcome the worst aspect of poverty in our lifetime through collective effort. We jointly affirm that our first step toward this goal will be to design a global compact that ensures that no child goes without an education, no human being is denied primary health care or safe drinking water and all willing couples are able to determine the size of their own families. We are conscious of our responsibility to present generations and to future generations, and we are determined to pass on to our children a rich, natural heritage and an environment sustained and whole.

WE INTEND to design a pattern of development cooperation based on open global markets, not protectionism on an equitable sharing of market opportunities, not charity, on an open policy dialogue between sovereign nations.

WE PLEDGE OUR DEEP COMMITMENT to a new social and economic philosophy that puts people at the center of our concerns, and creates unbreakable bonds of human solidarity.

WE STRONGLY BELIEVE that the United Nations must become the principle custodial of our global human security. Towards this end, we are determined to strengthen the development role of the United Nations and to give it wide-range decision-making powers in the socio-economic field..."

The world, in 1920, through the creation of the League of Nations, from which the UN was formed, created the framework through which Antichrist will gain control over the governments of the world (Rev. 13). Mankind has set into motion an irreversible course of action. Combine the current progression of the UN with the development of the European Economic Community (Rev. 18), and a demand from both that we establish a uniform global currency and a single global trading community, and it becomes all too obvious that the stage is set for the final theatrics of man, which will culminate with the final curtain call in the Valley of Megiddo.

Are our oil lamps full? Are we ready?

SUBJECT INDEX

B

C

D

H

I

J

K

L

M

N

O

P

Q

R

S

T

U

V

W

X

Y

Z